Representation and Democratic Theory

Edited by David Laycock

Representation and Democratic Theory

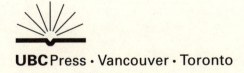

UBC Press · Vancouver · Toronto

© UBC Press 2004

All rights reserved. No part of this publication may be reproduced, stored in a retrieval system, or transmitted, in any form or by any means, without prior written permission of the publisher, or, in Canada, in the case of photocopying or other reprographic copying, a licence from Access Copyright (Canadian Copyright Licensing Agency), www.accesscopyright.ca.

14 13 12 11 10 09 08 07 06 05 04   5 4 3 2 1

Printed in Canada on acid-free paper

National Library of Canada Cataloguing in Publication

Representation and democratic theory / edited by David Laycock.

Includes bibliographical references and index.
ISBN 0-7748-1078-5 (bound); ISBN 0-7748-1079-3 (pbk.)

1. Representative government and representation. 2. Democracy.
I. Laycock, David H. (David Howard), 1954-

JF1051.R46 2004   321.8   C2004-900533-2

Canadä

UBC Press gratefully acknowledges the financial support for our publishing program of the Government of Canada through the Book Publishing Industry Development Program (BPIDP), and of the Canada Council for the Arts, and the British Columbia Arts Council.

UBC Press
The University of British Columbia
2029 West Mall
Vancouver, BC V6T 1Z2
604-822-5959 / Fax: 604-822-6083
www.ubcpress.ca

Contents

Acknowledgments / vii

Introduction / viii
David Laycock

Part 1: Representation in Response to Minority Rights, Multiculturalism, and Institutional Complexity

1 When (if Ever) Are Referendums on Minority Rights Fair? / 3
Avigail Eisenberg

2 Language, Representation, and Suprastate Democracy: Questions Facing the European Union / 23
Peter Ives

3 Getting to Yes: People, Practices, and the Paradox of Multicultural Democracy / 48
Catherine Frost

4 Feminist Engagement with Federal Institutions: Opportunities and Constraints for Women's Multilevel Citizenship / 65
Louise Chappell

Part 2: Reconceiving Representation through Citizenship and Community

5 Sharing the River: Aboriginal Representation in Canadian Political Institutions / 93
Melissa S. Williams

6 The Self-Government of Unbounded Communities: Emancipatory Minority Autonomy in China and Western Europe / 119
Susan J. Henders

7 What Do Citizens Need to Share? Citizenship as Reasonableness / 141
Jonathan Quong

Part 3: Pluralist, Deliberative, and Participatory Challenges to Representation

8 The New Constitutionalism and the Polarizing Performance of the Canadian Conversation / 161
Gerald Kernerman

9 Demanding Deliberative Democracy and Representation / 179
Greg Pyrcz

10 What Can Democratic Participation Mean Today? / 197
Mark E. Warren

11 Representing Pluralism: A Comment on Pyrcz, Warren, and Kernerman / 220
Simone Chambers

Conclusion / 234

References / 248

Notes on Contributors / 265

Index / 269

Acknowledgments

Two organizations played a key role in making this collection possible. First, the Canadian Political Science Association, through its 2002 program development funds, provided modest but crucial financial assistance for a full-day workshop entitled "Representation and Its Discontents," which took place at the CPSA meetings, 31 May 2002, at the University of Toronto. All but one of the chapters in this volume originated in this lively and productive workshop.

Once the manuscript had been submitted, SSHRC money became vital to publication with a scholarly press. I am pleased to acknowledge that this book has been published with the help of a grant from the Canadian Federation for the Humanities and Social Sciences, through the Aid to Scholarly Publications Programme, using funds provided by the Social Sciences and Humanities Research Council of Canada. I also gratefully acknowledge financial support for publication of this book by the Publications Committee at Simon Fraser University.

Finally, on behalf of all contributors to this volume, I would like to thank Emily Andrew and Darcy Cullen at UBC Press for their excellent work in the manuscript submission, evaluation, and editing stages of this publication process.

David Laycock
February 2004

Introduction
David Laycock

That representation is a highly problematic aspect of contemporary political life is beyond doubt. Contemporary challenges from both the political right and the political left to "politics as usual" are underpinned by profound doubts about the democratic legitimacy of the dominant forms of political representation. From the right, direct democracy is often presented as a partial remedy for failures of representational accountability and the purported power of "special interests." From the left, social movement activities, outside parties and legislatures, are seen as a response to party failures of inclusion and recognition, and to the power of corporate interests in public life. Both right and left claim that "ordinary people" are excluded from and disadvantaged by existing institutions and processes of representation. Virtually all media commentators and many incumbent politicians speak of a mounting "democratic deficit," and even superficial assessment of these claims uncovers at least some significant alleged shortcoming on the part of elected representatives or in the processes through which they act on the public's behalf. Academics and new social movement activists, on the other hand, speak of the failures of conventional democratic politics and institutions and of the need to engage nontraditional civil society actors in a re-energized and democratic public life, but seldom do they employ the language of representation to make their cases.

One could reasonably ask whether there is additional analytical or practical value in understanding the challenges and complaints of contemporary democratic politics with reference to the language and normative potential of representation. Directly or indirectly, contributors to this volume believe the answer is "yes." One of the key purposes of this collection is to show why we need to, and how we might, broaden the theoretical reach of representation by anchoring the political significance of popular and theoretical discourses of rights, citizenship, justice, equality, inclusion, and multiculturalism in understandings of representation and its discontents. Most chapters demonstrate the analytical necessity of relying far less on the link between representation and "institutional/legislative representative" than is typical of conventional liberal democratic theory and practice.

As a group, the chapters that follow show that, to productively engage a diverse landscape of intersecting identities, interests, associations, and institutional complexities, representation must be reconceived explicitly and carefully against a new social, political, institutional, and conceptual backdrop. This does not mean abandoning attempts to understand the procedural and normative aspects of legislative representation. Instead, the reconceptualization of representation in this volume seeks to connect the logic and purposes of this conventional representation to the representation of identities, social difference, cultural conflict, minority disadvantage, and discourses of social justice and to the searches for common citizenship that characterize the associational life of civil society outside legislatures, political parties, and competitive elections. It is not simply a random or coincidental fact that all of the contributors here have reached beyond the areas of legislative representation to indicate how contemporary democratic theory can make normative or even empirical sense of dynamic efforts to link citizens to political associations or policy determinations. They have reached into areas of public life where discontent with the processes and products of conventional representation is palpable and dramatically expressed. In their efforts to make theoretical sense of current attempts to address problems of contested citizenship, multiculturalism, social justice, and group recognition, the authors show how and why representation cannot realistically be understood in isolation from these attempts. The collection thus addresses important lacunae in academic political theory with respect to representation, while the contributions themselves typically return readers to broader issues related to citizenship, democracy, and civil society. Rather than simply accept that conventional representative institutions are not up to the job assigned to them by their nineteenth- and early-twentieth-century legitimizers, the authors believe that re-invigorating the civil society and participatory background conditions of representation and/or its up-front, policy-shaping processes is crucial to the validation and value of democratic politics.

In addressing contentious issues in the public life of modern Western societies, the contributors bring fresh approaches to theorizing the changing face of political representation and attempt to provoke further debate on the relation of representation to democratic citizenship. Some tackle the dynamics and problematic dimensions of representation head on, while others explore democratic participation, multicultural pluralism, contested citizenship, or other background conditions of contemporary representation. They relate majority and minority group rights, multiculturalism, justice, gender, citizen deliberation and democratic participation, the structuring power of language, and the dynamics of inter-regional conflict to current debates in democratic political theory. In this introduction, I broadly situate representation within the domain of contemporary democratic theory to set the stage for the more detailed analyses that follow.

Democratic Theory and the Problem of Representation
Understood in simple yet broad terms, political representation means "the arrangements by which some persons stand or act for others"[1] in public life. In one of the earliest and most poignant moments of modern democratic theory, Jean-Jacques Rousseau condemned such acting for others as a stake through the heart of popular sovereignty.[2] But since the latter part of the nineteenth century, most democratic theory has broadly supported representation as a necessary condition of whatever "rule by the people" can be made feasible within political systems that serve mass societies.[3]

In most democratic regimes since the mid-nineteenth century, representation has been widely accepted by rulers, citizens, and political theorists alike as the mainspring of governance involving elected legislatures. Yet prior to this, and notably at the founding of representative government in France, the United States, and the United Kingdom, representative government was seen as an alternative to democratic government. These early supporters of representative government believed that it could both retain the aristocratic principle of election and ensure that the voice of the people was safely mediated by the deliberations of their elected betters.[4]

The broad consensus on the inevitable importance of elected representatives in democratic institutions that exists in most Western polities can easily disguise profound disagreements over how particular "arrangements by which some persons stand or act for others" can advance the purposes of democratic self-government. These are not just normative disagreements over such purposes but also empirical disagreements about how or whether elections make representatives accountable to electors and how or to what degree citizen deliberations and expectations should shape representatives' decisions.[5] As Bernard Manin pithily expresses it, "we do not know either what makes representative government resemble democracy, or what distinguishes it therefrom."[6]

Deep disagreement also occurs over how instances or patterns of "representational failure" can be remedied by nonrepresentational yet still democratic action and decision making. Contemporary advocates of direct democracy often come close to accepting Madison's sharp distinction between representation and democracy, even though they line up for the latter and against the former, contrary to Madison's preference. Such advocates may also appear to endorse Rousseau's strictures against representative government on behalf of popular sovereignty, even if they reject the logic that Rousseau employed to support popular sovereignty against representation.⁷

Finally, we need to acknowledge dramatically diverse answers to the question of how (and whether) the agenda of representational practices should be set by our ranking and operational blending of basic normative goods such as liberty, equality, rights, justice, solidarity or community, citizenship, and pluralism. These normative mainstays of most variations on contemporary democratic theory may seem to contain the seeds of unambiguous support for democratic representation. But on closer inspection, there is a large variety of connections between the methods and especially the purposes of representation, on the one hand, and particular commitments to liberty, equality rights, and other foundational democratic values, on the other hand. There is nothing like a consensus around a "democratic theory of representation," either within modern political theory or among public groups with distinctive ideological commitments that they perceive as unambiguously democratic.

One way of thinking about the relationship of representation to these basic values is to think in terms of regimes of representation. A representational regime includes not just the participants in and structures of elections and legislative activities or decisions but also, obviously, the full range of executive decision making and whatever division of labour, or checks and balances, exists in the formal distribution of power and authority. Such a regime also includes, perhaps not so obviously, the activities of various organized interests in deliberations within various "policy communities" as well as the participation of various associations and organizations in public dialogue within the often "nested" spheres of civil society.⁸

Representational regimes are not merely institutional but also and unavoidably normative in character. They require but are not restricted to expressions of a general consensus about some aspects of basic political values and a consensus about means of facilitating peaceful resolution of disagreement over policy choices that reflect these values. Such realms of consensus typically include and condition public discussion about disputed elements among these values. Liberal democracies, for example, have a broad consensus on a minimum set of basic rights and liberties, share a minimum understanding of equality as formal rights for all citizens under the rule of law, agree that justice requires at least equal protection and civic rights under this rule of law, and make legal and institutional provision for pluralism within civil society and within some selection of state agencies. All of these values are reflected in a representational regime and contribute to its basic functioning.

But more precise expressions of beliefs about how basic normative values are to be politically instantiated and institutionally embedded also become a focus of debate within various decision-making institutions and political practices in any regime of representation. This is true of debates over such key political questions as liberty and its social preconditions, equality and its social scope, configurations of individual and group rights, the institutional architecture and programmatic reach of distributive justice, the nature of community and its interplay with social and political pluralism, and the character of citizenship. As the balance of public sentiments concerning these beliefs changes over time, successive governing parties and coalitions integrate provisional patterns of policy decisions related to these debates into the political order. Such changes are reflected in the design and operation of elements within the representational regime. This is seen in matters as obviously political as the extension of the franchise and other political rights. The political relevance of other expressions of institutional power – such as mandatory inclusion of workers in large firms' health and safety committees or the representational implications of campaign finance legislation – becomes clearer when seen from this angle. Even expectations about "normal" forms of communication by legislators and group spokespersons in various public policy forums take on significance within representational regimes, as Iris Marion Young shows indirectly in her analysis of the preconditions of inclusive democratic deliberation.[9]

It is now a truism that political legitimacy in modern politics relies on authoritative democratic decision making with at least some representative features, even if we are still much in the dark about how this legitimacy is linked to ideas and mechanisms of electoral mandates, government accountability, and citizens' expectations.[10] Thinking of "representational regimes" is a shortcut to acknowledging not just the practical centrality of representation to modern democratic decision making but also its centrality to the ways in which specific institutions and practices of representation crystallize provisional and practical meanings over a range of basic political values. In light of this truism and this intellectual shortcut, it is both surprising and instructive to reflect on how little direct attention representation has received in recent Anglo-American political theory.

A quick review of the Humanities and Social Sciences Index, and of the *Political Theory* journal since 1980, shows that representation has been a far more important theme in formal (rational choice), empirical, and comparative political science literature, and in contemporary literary criticism and theory, than it has been in normative political theory. Waves of democratization or at least decolonialization in the 1990s help to explain the recent political science boom in comparative empirical studies of political representation. And poststructuralism has certainly boosted, but is by no means the sole inspiration for, literary attention to representation. But why has representation been allotted relatively scant attention, and second-order conceptual status, in recent normative political theory? Here it is possible simply to broadly suggest how attention to several other themes has overshadowed and in some cases subsumed concern with representation by political theorists.

For those who have attempted to shed light on the role played by representation in political theory, Hanna Pitkin's 1967 *The Concept of Representation* is foundational. Her accounts of formalistic, descriptive, and symbolic representation, of the mandate-independence divide, and of the role played by interests in conceptualizations of representation set new and high standards for contemporary theorizing about representation. The problem, in retrospect, is that this study appeared to be almost too definitive at a time when momentum quickly shifted to questions of rights and distributive justice. With the publication of *A Theory of Justice*, John Rawls moved a whole host of institutionally anchored conceptual problems in political theory to the back seat. For over two decades, democratic theorists' hopes of helping to steer the vehicles of academic political theory were typically contingent on their using distributive justice-oriented maps and employing rights-based arguments as theoretical fuel.

Communitarian theorists' challenge to rights-based liberalism did not typically address issues of representation, in spite of their growing concern with citizenship. Indirectly, however, with their attention to group "recognition" as an antidote to community-disintegrating effects of individualism, communitarians such as Charles Taylor created theoretical space within which representation could have a more transparent, prominent, and practice-oriented home within democratic theory, even if this home was built largely by noncommunitarian theorists.[11]

Since the early 1990s, theorists of citizenship, justice, deliberation and associative democracy, equality, and the politics of difference have raised important questions about representation within democratic theory. Yet in acknowledging and exploring issues of representation in such contexts, political theorists have seldom awarded the problem of democratic representation a high theoretical profile or sought its normative footings, as they do for justice, citizenship, deliberation, difference, or equality.[12] Even when democratic theorists such as Ian Shapiro conscientiously and perceptively take power relations as a "central object of study" and offer a "focus on institutional redesign [that] takes institutions and practices as we find them,"[13] the issue of representation can easily slip through their theoretical nets.

When it comes to sidelining representation, the work on citizenship and deliberation is revealing and somewhat surprising. According to Kymlicka and Norman, citizenship theory blossomed as a way of finessing potentially conflicting concerns among political theorists about justice and community that had arisen in the 1970s and 1980s. Concern with citizenship arose in response to several broad phenomena: widespread alienation from "politics as usual" in both established Western democracies and Eastern Europe, concerns about supposed pathologies of the welfare state, and evidence that governability in democratic polities relies more on shared civic attitudes than theorists had tended to acknowledge since the 1960s.[14]

Yet neither Kymlicka and Norman's review of citizenship theory nor other contributions to the volume in which it appeared afforded substantial attention to representation as an expression or conduit of citizenship. Nor did these theorists of citizenship attend seriously to relationships between representation and other instruments of democratic participation. Will Kymlicka influentially addressed thorny problems of descriptive and substantive representation for Québécois and Aboriginal peoples in the context of his influential adaptation of liberal rights theory to the needs of multicultural citizenship.[15] But it seems to be significant that the second edition of his *Contemporary Political Philosophy*, which includes an updated account of citizenship theory, has no index entries under representation.

On the more radical shores of citizenship theory, Ernesto Laclau and Chantal Mouffe have tended to accept Michel Foucault's dismissal of anything resembling conventional representational politics. In their place, they endorse expressive politics by new social movement actors operating outside existing representative institutions and organizational vehicles.[16] Similarly, James Tully bids us to look beyond restrictive representative practices to discover the potential for "practices of freedom" that will constitute the "'democratic' side of practices of governance" in a period of globalization.[17]

Many contributions to citizenship theory over the past decade have adapted and appropriated it to show its relation to everything from postmodern extensions of feminist theory, to cosmopolitan democracy, to human rights promotion in international civil society, to neo-Gramscian formulations of radical democracy. On the empirical side, political scientists consider representation and "representational failure" through parties, corporatist institutions, new social movements, organized interests, policy networks, and even international regimes dealing with environmental or other regulatory issues. To such researchers, the disconnection between political theory and evolving political practices related to innovative representation and representational failures alike must reinforce the abstract character of political theory.

The same sense of disconnectedness has hovered over much of the literature on deliberative democracy. There are important exceptions. Iris Marion Young has recently attempted to address this by initiating a theoretical dialogue between deliberative and activist democrats, noting that such discussions are both difficult and necessary in societies with structural inequalities whose power relations are not amenable to change through deliberation alone.[18] James Fishkin and several colleagues have designed and implemented experiments in "national deliberative polls" in the United States, the United Kingdom, and Australia.[19] Mark Warren has offered a systematic theorization of the conditions and effects of associational life outside state institutional settings. In showing how complicated the associational foundations of deliberative politics are, he suggests many hypotheses concerning potential linkages between "second-order" representational practices by associations and the more conventional representational work of parties and legislatures.[20] And some political theorists have become involved in practical efforts to combine grassroots political organizing with empowerment through local-level deliberation.[21] But those most influential in delineating the philosophically distinctive foundations of its democratic potential – John Rawls and Jurgen Habermas – came close to ignoring how innovative representative practices and institutions might aid deliberative democracy.

One consequence of ignoring these synergies is that many cases for democratic deliberation are hard to penetrate in any but exceptionally abstract terms. We should acknowledge that several other foundational contributions to deliberative democratic theory, especially in the work of Joshua Cohen[22] and Jane Mansbridge,[23] have been less abstract. They have been concerned with demonstrating a fit between institutions and practices that facilitate deliberation, on the one hand, and its conceptualization as an expression of "public reason" and reflexive will formation, under conditions of social justice, on the other. Over the past several years, Mark Warren,[24] Iris Marion Young,[25] Robert Goodin,[26] Nadia Urbinati,[27] Michael Saward,[28] and Melissa Williams[29] have given substantial attention to the deliberation/representation interaction. But it remains true that most deliberative democratic theory has not explored how an unavoidably large range of the practices of public deliberation and representation would shape one another, were deliberation to play a more substantial role in contemporary democratic public life.[30]

Some of this inattention can be accounted for in terms of the perception and reality of widespread representational failures in Western polities, of the kind noted in the first section of Mark Warren's contribution to this volume. Clearly, these failures have motivated deliberative democratic theorizing by political liberals and radicals alike. Why return to the scene of democratic deficits if they are obviously bred by experience with faulty institutions? Shouldn't alternative approaches to democratic will formation be theorized independently of existing representative practices and in relation to distinctive first principles such as "public reason," or nondomination in deliberative interaction, before the inevitable accommodations with "actually existing representation" are theoretically negotiated? Perhaps the independence of representatives' decisions from the preferences of their electors is not the main reason for democratic deficits. But don't deliberative theorists still have good reasons to believe that public reason and thoughtful reconsideration of commitments will both be undermined by the clear distance between citizens and elected representatives in modern "polyarchies"?

These are understandable reasons for innovative democratic theory to maintain a healthy theoretical distance between deliberative democracy and the failure-strewn, legitimacy-deficient landscape of contemporary representational politics and institutions. It is hard not to be attracted by Rousseau's antirepresentational spirit when we reflect on the compromised institutions, and citizenship disempowering outcomes, of many conventional modes of representation in Western public life. Yet it is also unavoidable that in modern politics representative institutions will structure and provide many of the necessary, even if not by a long stretch wholly sufficient, conditions for vindicating deliberation and other dimensions of democratic participation. The citizenship and the broader democratic community that deliberation is meant to enhance will always develop in complex institutional settings.

Carole Pateman contended over thirty years ago that innovative participatory democrats had to understand their preferred and specific practices as supplements to, not replacements for, representative institutions and processes.[31] In a similar manner, deliberative democrats and citizenship theorists could creatively engage the real world of representation that frames deliberation and the goods of citizenship, public reason, and justice. While not the last word in democratic reform politics, representation can be made to serve these goods of citizenship, public reason, and justice far better than our current experiences suggest.

Taking such a stance need not entail accepting representative institutions, processes, and vehicles as they are. As will be evident in the remainder of this volume, there are many long-standing as well as reasonably recent reasons for discontent concerning "actually existing representation." But as recent work by Iris Marion Young, Anne Phillips,[32] Melissa Williams, Mark Warren, and others demonstrates, such discontent is no warrant for eschewing theoretical innovation in responding to the challenge of representation.

In tackling questions of representation head on, Young, Phillips, Williams, and Warren have shown that normative democratic theorizing is strengthened by considering concrete empirical cases of representational failure. Their studies have revealed how questions about particular regimes of representation can be intertwined with an interrogation of practical stances taken on issues of justice, rights, gender, and the normative and associational dimensions of meaningful citizenship and democratic will formation. In doing so, they acknowledge how this intertwining has developed within historically contingent but typically multicultural and otherwise pluralistic communities. An attractive additional consequence of their attention to actual cases has been construction of bridges between empirical political science and political philosophy in ways that assist others who wish to straddle this unproductive divide.

Over the past two decades, much of the most politically and theoretically innovative and influential bridging work of this type has been undertaken by feminist theorists. From our perspective, there are several striking things about this body of work. One is that the concerns with representation are intimately connected to concens with and conceptualizations of social justice, equality, and valorization of difference that have clear roots in women's movement experience over the past generation. In making these connections, feminists learned much from earlier civil rights struggles and discourses and theoretically prepared much of the ground worked by theorists of multiculturalism over the past decade.

Another notable aspect of feminist theory that directly engages the problem of representation is that its social movement roots are especially strongly reflected in the transition from second-wave emphases on the similarities of women's experiences under patriarchy to the emphasis on women's difference since the advent of third-wave feminism. Three prominent authors whose work illustrates the theoretical importance of this transition are Jane Mansbridge,[33] Iris Marion Young,[34] and Anne Phillips.[35] One sees in their work increasingly sophisticated accounts not just of women's need for group representation but also of the considerations that must shape something beyond essentialized, simple descriptive representation to do justice to the variety of women's experiences, interests, and perspectives. All three see the practical importance of a "politics of presence," through group representation in legislatures and other key decision-making institutions, to provide meaningful citizenship and social justice for women. Nonetheless, Young[36] emphasizes more than Phillips and Mansbridge the need for accommodations to the variety of ways that women (and other disadvantaged groups) communicate and thus find their voices and places in deliberative public life. In contending that such accommodations characterize not just formal, institutional politics but also informal political interactions in civil society, Young illustrates the potential normative and conceptual reach of a revised understanding of representation.

All three authors, joined now by the vast majority of feminist political theorists, insist on taking account of overlapping and sometimes conflicting identities when they inquire into how representational processes, institutions, forums, and communication must be improved to offer social justice and equal citizenship to women. In doing so, feminist theorists over the past twenty years have done much to reveal the complex conditions under which citizens develop and pursue interests, perspectives, and identities and the ways in which representation of these interests, perspectives, and identities becomes a cultural and associational as well as electoral/institutional matter.

Feminist theory continues to break theoretical ground in our appreciation of democratic politics, especially for theorists and activists involved with other disadvantaged groups. Melissa Williams, for example, has built on her widely regarded 1998 book *Voice, Trust, and Memory* to suggest, in this volume, how we might understand and institutionally remedy Canadian Aboriginal peoples' struggles for equal citizenship and effective representation. Like earlier feminist theorists, Williams sees such group-based remedies to women's and Aboriginal under-representation as a duty of justice. While many feminist theorists do not share her view that "descriptive representation with a difference" can generate just outcomes for oppressed minorities within a liberal philosophical or political framework,[37] they tend to share her view that few solutions will avoid enhancement of group-structured representation within legislatures and other policy-deliberating bodies. With their strong foundations in and connections to social movement activity, feminist contributions to theorizing representation are one of the best sources for reminding students of democratic theory that, with few exceptions until the rise of the "new right,"[38] the push for better representation has typically come from socially nondominant groups and has involved expanding the political realm in ways that harness rather than ignore the group associational differences that characterize modern societies.

Feminist theorists are not alone in seeing heightened roles for groups as crucial to the development of both more robust and more effective deliberative citizenship, on the one hand, and socially just policy, on the other. Just over one decade ago, Joshua Cohen and Joel Rogers initiated a normative and empirical exploration of the contributions that group-based "secondary associations" might make to "associative democracy" within an expanded framework of democratic governance that reaches well beyond legislatures into specific policy fields such as occupational health and safety and vocational training.[39] Paul Hirst has extended this case to fit a "changed conjuncture" in the political, social, and economic dimensions of contemporary welfare states, building on his exploration of early-twentieth-century British pluralism.[40] These associative democratic theorists make normative and policy-specific cases for applying the logic of Scandinavian-style "democratic corporatism" to Anglo-American policy development processes. Finally, Mark Warren's theoretical account of the democratic effects of associational structures and activities within contemporary civil society has opened up substantial space for both empirical investigation into these effects and normative consideration of the implications of such "democratic associational ecologies" for new representational structures in both civil society and the state.[41] It is easy to predict that feminist theorists and associative democratic theorists will soon find more common ground in their efforts to sketch innovative justifications of and designs for group associational and representative activity.

The unavoidable institutional "embeddedness" of representation may help to suggest why, with the kinds of exceptions noted above, it is typically considered a second-order theoretical problem, successful attention to which is simply instrumental to progress in tackling first-order normative problems such as justice, citizenship, equality, participation,[42] or individual autonomy. The explanation is not simply that particular problems of injustice, undemocratic or inegalitarian distributions of power, or tensions between majority and minority interests set the agenda for answers to questions about representation, giving these agenda-setting problems normative and conceptual priority. Beyond this, or perhaps because of this, it is notoriously difficult to generalize about solutions to problems of representation across regimes of representation.[41] This stands in contrast to what theorists have attempted when considering problems of justice, with universalizing devices such as original positions, ideal speech situations, or claims about natural and other rights.

Few citizens or political theorists would deny the logistical and functional advantages of representation, as opposed to participation by "all of the people," for governance of all but the simplest societies. At a normative level, however, one might argue that the problem of representation arises because of the inevitable plurality of answers in any large population to questions about the rank ordering of political goods and values. In this sense, representation is the minimum concession that democratic citizenship makes to this pluralism while acknowledging the impossibility of an overly demanding Rousseauian commitment to public life by all citizens in modern societies. That representation is not the only concession that democratic citizenship needs to make to social and political pluralism is, of course, amply demonstrated by much contemporary democratic theory, including most contributions to this volume.

Representational regimes take their logic and institutional shape from evolving patterns of social, economic, cultural, political, and technological dynamics and systems specific to particular societies. In this sense, democratic representation is a response to the factors of social differentiation and complexity that Mark Warren, in Chapter 10, contends do much to shape opportunities for democratic participation more generally. We can thus theoretically account for the character and implications of such structuring factors for challenges to representation but not necessarily move from this to a comprehensive single theory of representation that can answer all of these challenges.

While democratic theory unavoidably encounters a modesty-enforcing set of constraints when it confronts issues of representation,[42] a lot of important work nonetheless remains. Several broad and overlapping dimensions of this work can easily be identified. First, insofar as it provides a crucial point of contact between normative theory and the institutional environments within which this theory seeks to be relevant, representation is a crucial conceptual link between considerations of justice, rights, citizenship, pluralism, and community. This is the intuition that shapes the notion of "regimes of representation" presented earlier and is demonstrated in more or less concrete ways in most of the contributions to this volume. Second, the chapters here show that exploring the problems and contexts of representation illuminates the practical value of democratic theory to political science research and for the (re)design of democratic institutions and practices of citizenship. Such explorations inevitably must also take into account new forms of political action, new expressions of identity, and new sites of political conflict, such as those typical of new social movement organizations over the past generation. And third, in the service of these objectives, theoretical as well as theoretically driven empirical investigations into representation and its discontents can suggest ways of narrowing the gap between the historical promise and the current reality of democratic politics.

The chapters in this volume are organized into three sections, partly to aid an appreciation of the dialogues facilitated by their authors. Part 1 includes chapters by Avigail Eisenberg, Peter Ives, Catherine Frost, and Louise Chappell. They deal with the interaction between minority rights, multicultural social environments, multilevel sovereignty, and institutional responses to the tensions between majority and minority groups. Chapters by Melissa Williams, Susan Henders, and Jonathan Quong in Part 2 contribute to reconceiving the relationships between representation, citizenship, and community, in both national and international settings. Finally, in Part 3, Gerald Kernerman, Greg Pyrcz, Mark Warren, and Simone Chambers address pluralist, deliberative, and participatory dimensions of, and challenges to, representation, also in the context of increasingly multicultural national communities and politicized civil societies.

This grouping of papers is unavoidably somewhat arbitrary, since the authors' concerns and contributions frequently and fruitfully cross over these loose categorical boundaries. Taken as a whole, these chapters contribute many provocative questions and compelling analyses in support of a revitalized normative appreciation of the importance of representation to democratic theory and politics.

Notes
1. Pitkin (1987), 432.
2. Rousseau (1763), book III, ch. 15.
3. For the classic argument in this regard, see Mill (1861).
4. Manin (1997), ch. 4.
5. This theme unifies the contributions to Przeworski, Stokes, and Manin (1999).
6. Manin (1997), 6.
7. See Laycock (2000).
8. See Taylor (1995b).
9. See Young (2000).
10. See Przeworski, Stokes, and Manin (1999), Introduction and ch. 1, for an overview.
11. For an exception to this general pattern of communitarian inattention to the problem of representation, see Schwartz (1988).
12. See Kymlicka (1996); Young (1990, 2001); Shapiro (1999); and Dahl (1989).
13. Shapiro (1999), 232-33. Note that in *The State of Democratic Theory*, Shapiro (2003) also skirts the issue of representation almost entirely again.
14. Kymlicka and Norman (1995b).
15. Kymlicka (1995), ch. 7.
16. See Laclau and Mouffe (1985); Mouffe (1992); and Mouffe (2000).
17. Tully (2001b), 54.
18. Young (2001).
19. See Fishkin and Lufkin (2000) for an overview of these exercises.
20. Warren (2000).
21. See Fung and Wright (2003); and Sirianni and Friedland (2001). See also King (2003) for an exploration of deliberative decision making in international regimes.
22. See Cohen and Rogers (1995); and Cohen (1996).
23. Mansbridge (1992, 1995).
24. Warren (1996, 2001, 2002).
25. Young (2000).
26. See Goodin (2003), especially chs. 8-11.
27. Urbinati (2000).
28. Saward (2000 and 2003).
29. Williams (2000).
30. This is true of the most widely cited collections on deliberative democracy: Elster (1998); Bohman and Rehg (1997); and Benhabib (1996). Many books and articles on deliberative democracy have of course emerged since 1998, but even in this later literature studies that focus on the interplay between representative institutions and deliberative processes are relatively rare.
31. Pateman (1970).
32. Phillips (1995).
33. See, especially, Mansbridge (1993, 1999, 2000).
34. See, especially, Young (1990, 1997, 2000).
35. See, especially, Phillips (1991, 1995).
36. Young (2000).
37. Williams (1998, 238-43).
38. For an account of the new right critique of existing representative institutions, and its preference for "plebiscitarian" instruments of direct democracy as ways of circumventing such institutions, see Laycock (2001).
39. Cohen and Rogers (1995).
40. Hirst (1994); Hirst and Bader (2001); Hirst (1989). For another stimulating account of pluralist theory, which also seeks to retain some of its more innovative elements to address contemporary democratic challenges, see Eisenberg (1995).
41. Warren (2000).
42. Participation was the point of entry for C.B. Macpherson's brief but evocative attention to the problem of representation in Chapter 5 of his 1977 book *Life and Times of Liberal Democracy*. Few political theorists have read *Democracy in Alberta*, his earlier account

of the innovative approaches to representation taken by Canadian prairie farmers' movement activists and thinkers (Macpherson 1953), which provided his only extended and historically situated discussion of problems of representation in democratic theory. For whatever reason, Macpherson felt no urge to return to such problems in his later, more influential work.

43 This is one of the important implications for theorization of democratic representation emerging from Warren (2000).

44 For another perspective on the theoretical modesty forced on democratic theory by the problem of representation, which focuses more on the relationship between accountability and representation through the medium of elections, see Przeworski, Stokes, and Manin (1999).

Part 1
Representation in Response to Minority Rights, Multiculturalism, and Institutional Complexity

1
When (if Ever) Are Referendums on Minority Rights Fair?

Avigail Eisenberg

> Referendums are a bad way to make public policy, especially when it comes to protecting minorities.
>
> – *Vancouver Sun*, 28 October 1983 (in reference to the Manitoba referendums on French-language services)

When representative institutions lack the legitimacy to decisively resolve particularly important conflicts or debates, democratic communities have the option of holding a referendum. Today referendums are used "more frequently than ever before in liberal democracies."[1] Perhaps one reason for the surge in their attractiveness is that the electorate's political trust in leaders and legislators is steadily declining.[2] The less trust we have in our politicians, the more attractive democratic rule that relies on referendums will appear to be.

But some countries resist using referendums even when they experience conflicts that are particularly debilitating and even though the authority of political leaders to resolve such conflicts is especially questioned. In particular, multinational democracies rarely hold referendums. This is because, whereas referendums provide a means of implementing majority will, multinational democracies require governing strategies that depart from the majoritarian model.[3] Multinational democracies require methods of decision making that engender compromise and dialogue between different national groups. Referendums putatively provide little incentive to deliberate and don't encourage compromise. Belgium, Austria, and the Netherlands have rarely held a referendum. Israel has never enacted a referendum, a fact attributed to its ethnic and religious divisions. Canada is an obvious exception to this trend, as is the United States, where referendums are not only held but also often involve issues that have a direct impact on the interests and rights of national, linguistic, and ethnic minorities.

For instance, in the past twenty years, as Canadians have struggled through public policy and constitution making, to improve fragile relations between Quebec and Canada, and between Aboriginal and non-Aboriginal Canadians, numerous referendums have been held that have put to majority vote questions about the status and guiding principles that ought to govern the relations between Canada's national minorities and majorities. In 1983, thirty municipalities in Manitoba each held a referendum about a proposal by the provincial government to end its English-only policy and provide French-language services. This referendum was strongly criticized by church leaders and other elites as "deeply undemocratic" because it focused on minority rights. Even the most committed advocates of referendums considered it to have "probably constituted a setback for the cause of direct democracy."[4] Voter turnout was nearly double what it usually had been in municipal elections in Manitoba, and, by a margin of 3-1 and 4-1 (depending on the municipality), voters voted against the rights of the French-language minority. The matter ultimately found its way, through a reference case, to the Supreme Court of Canada, which ruled that laws in Manitoba had to be translated into French or else they would be invalid.[5]

In 1992, when the Charlottetown Accord was put to a national referendum, all Canadians were asked, among other things, whether Quebec should be recognized as a distinct society, whether Quebec should be guaranteed 25 percent of the seats in Parliament, and whether the inherent right to self-government for Aboriginal peoples should be included in the Constitution. Quebec held two referendums, in 1980 and 1995, that were both means whereby nationalist leaders sought to coalesce support for their sovereigntist causes. In both referendums, the status and interests of English and Aboriginal minorities within the province, as well as Quebec's relation to Canada, were at stake. These two referendums led to significant court cases as well. In 1996, the federal government asked the Supreme Court to rule on the terms by which Quebec could secede from Canada.[6] The court broadly set these terms and spelled out the general terms by which a referendum on secession ought to be conducted.[7]

In 2002, the BC referendum on the treaty negotiation process witnessed the same pattern of referendum and lawsuits interacting in the context of shaping fragile relations between a majority and a national minority, in this case Aboriginal people in British Columbia. The putative purpose of the BC referendum was to set out the principles by which treaties between Aboriginal and non-Aboriginal peoples in the province would be negotiated. The referendum contained eight questions that, if answered in the affirmative, would constitute guiding principles for provincial negotiators in the treaty negotiation process (see Appendix 1.1 on page 19). Two cases were launched against the referendum, both of which sought an injunction to stop the referendum in part by claiming that it would worsen relations between Aboriginal and non-Aboriginal people within the province.[8] The court cases failed, and the referendum was held. Thirty-six percent of the provincial electorate mailed in ballots; of the ballots that were not spoiled,[9] between 84.5 percent and 94.5 percent of the electorate endorsed the government's position on each of the eight questions.

Even though referendums may be useful means to resolve debilitating conflicts when all else fails, referendums on minority rights, especially the rights of national minorities, are more likely to deepen cleavages rather than mend them. This observation might not seem to be particularly controversial in the wake of the BC referendum.[10] But with surprisingly few exceptions,[11] research on the effects that referendums have on minority rights shows that minority interests fare no worse in referendums than they fare before legislatures.[12]

One aim here is to account for the discrepancy between evidence showing that referendums exacerbate cleavages and evidence showing that referendums have a benign impact on minority interests. One reason for this discrepancy is that most studies focus on comparing how a referendum question would be answered by the electorate and by the legislature rather than assessing the effects that the broader process of democratic mobilization that precedes and informs referendum politics might have on pre-existing cleavages in a society. A second reason, which forms the focus here, is that most studies fail to distinguish between referendums held on the distinctive status and rights of national minorities and those held on issues related to formal equality-seeking minorities. This distinction between national minorities (or any minority seeking rights or status different from those held by the majority) and formal equality-seeking minorities is crucial to understanding the effects of referendums on minority interests and more broadly on the political values of a community. If referendums are merely mirrors of public opinion, as some scholars believe them to be,[13] then they would not cause the sort of dissension that they do. Often referendums are attractive to elites and voters because they offer a unique platform, buttressed by specific democratic values, for advancing notions of political equality and community that are biased against recognizing special status or rights for any group within society, including protected minorities. Referendums are not always harmful to minorities. But they tend to be harmful to minorities that seek, or that are perceived to be seeking, rights and status distinct from those held by the majority. Referendums engage citizens in a democratic practice that highlights an understanding of political equality that is, in key respects, at odds with multinationalism. Therefore, referendums on issues related to national minority interests ought to be regulated in ways that counteract the biases that they exacerbate against the distinctive rights of national minorities.

Referendum Majorities and Minorities

Referendums privilege majorities against minorities in two ways. First, and most obviously, referendum outcomes are based on how the majority votes. If it wants, the majority can vote without even considering the interests of minorities, because referendums do not require that voters deliberate about their choices.[14] In this way, referendums are different from legislative processes because in legislatures debate and deliberation are supposed to precede voting. Not only can citizens refuse to deliberate before casting their votes in a referendum, but also referendums can provide little incentive for deliberation.[15] The majority will lack the incentive to engage in deliberation with a minority if it knows, in the context of a referendum, that, regardless of discussion or deliberation, its views will prevail at the ballot box. Conversely, when minorities know that their interests are not shared by the majority, they may view the referendum as hopeless and withdraw from participating in the process unless meaningful opportunities exist to deliberate and convince others of their position.[16] Indeed, many of the important innovations in referendums focus precisely on creating a deliberative context to precede the vote.[17] But few referendums are held in this manner, mainly because of the expense involved. With this noted exception, referendums are usually poor means to elicit compromises among the electorate.[18]

A second important way in which referendums privilege majorities more than legislatures do is that they often lack the sort of internal checks and filters that help to derail antiminority measures proposed in legislatures.[19] Some minorities have their interests secured through special legislative and constitutional protections that have arisen, historically, as a result of compromises between different national groups residing in the same state. Legislatures are often hesitant to revisit these protections, let alone to be responsible for rescinding them. However, the electorate may be less hesitant to put aside historical agreements if it is given a free hand to decide such matters within a democratic process, such as a referendum, that provides few incentives to compromise.

The reasons why majorities dominate minorities in referendums might appear to be obvious. Less obvious is why majorities don't dominate minorities in each and every referendum campaign. Many studies show that majorities often vote to protect minority rights. Frey and Goette show that, of the sixty-four Swiss referendums on civil rights that they surveyed, only nineteen (or 30 percent) had an antiminority result.[20] Donovan and Bowler survey gay and lesbian ballot initiatives in the United States and show that "well educated populations and large jurisdictions can lead to the adoption of direct legislation sympathetic to homosexuals."[21] Gamble's survey study, which provides the strongest argument against referendums on minority rights, nonetheless shows that sometimes – 22 percent of the time – majorities vote to protect minority rights. So under what circumstances are minority rights sometimes vindicated in a referendum campaign?

Many factors influence referendum outcomes, including where elite support lies, how campaigns are financed, whether referendums take place during times of economic hardship, and how ballot questions are worded.

With respect to referendums on minority issues, three factors have been cited to explain why majorities sometimes protect minority rights. First, the political culture of liberal democracies includes a general tolerance of and respect for minority rights, and voters carry these values with them to the ballot box. Second, if we accept that members of the majority vote in a self-interested manner, then majority endorsement of minority interests might signal that it is in the interest of members of the majority to vindicate minority rights.²² Third, community size seems to matter. In large communities, majorities tend to have greater respect for minority rights. For instance, according to Donovan and Bowler, smaller communities tend to vote against protections for gay and lesbian rights in the United States more often than do large communities.²³

An additional factor, or perhaps another way to read the factors cited above, is that members of the majority tend to support minority rights when minorities seek formal equality. A formal equality-seeking minority seeks benefits and protections similar to those enjoyed by other citizens. Formal equality requires, foremost, that individuals be protected against discrimination in public and private institutions and, more specifically, that they are not denied opportunities or benefits because of their religion, race, ethnicity, gender, or sexual orientation. In guaranteeing the formal equality of all citizens, the state's main concern is to protect the rights of citizenship that transcend group particularities and unite all individuals into a single state-based community.

In contrast, national minorities sometimes seek different status or rights than those of the majority. Members of national or insular minorities also require rights that protect them from being denied opportunities or benefits because of their religion, race, ethnicity, gender, or sexual orientation. But they may also require special rights or distinct status as additional means to protect them, their language, or their way of life from being dominated by the majority.²⁴ The rights or status that national minorities sometimes seek are special or distinctive in the sense that the benefits sought – such as the right to control the use of a particular piece of land or the right to be educated in one's own language – are available only to group members. Often the interests or goods that national minorities seek to protect through special rights are ones that the majority already enjoys. But the majority enjoys these goods without needing special rights or protections to continue enjoying them. In other words, the protections sought by national minorities are different from the protections enjoyed in the broader community, even though the interests or goods being protected through rights or status (e.g., language, self-government, education according to the specific cultural norms) are similar to those that the majority already enjoys by reason of its dominance as a majority.²⁵ In this sense, both types of minorities seek to enjoy similar goods. But the means to securing these goods are different for each minority. Formal equality-seeking minorities seek similar treatment and rights. National minorities seek distinct treatment or special rights compared with those of the majority.

Referendums and Equality for Minorities[26]

One might think that the only political ideal conveyed through a referendum campaign is that the majority rules. Some analysts go so far as to deny that referendums give voice to any particular values other than those to be calculated through the simple aggregation of private, individual preferences. Those who advance this position worry that referendums curtail the deliberative aspect of political decision making by sanctioning a procedure in which numbers rather than arguments count and in which voters may decide on an issue based on their private preferences without engaging in public and rational deliberation.[27] But the stance that votes in referendums are cast merely on the basis of private preferences formed in isolation from the community is importantly different from the stance that referendums cannot stimulate particular values or ideals in the minds of voters. Advocates of direct democracy often point out that referendums are a means of operationalizing an ideal of equality that, in giving the same weight to each individual's vote, requires that differences among people be ignored in the course of participating in a referendum. Participating in a referendum is a testament to one's membership as an equal in a community, and giving each person's vote equal weight in constitutive decision-making processes is a testament to a particular and compelling understanding of political equality, namely one which holds that all individuals have the same political status within that community.

The idea that referendums help to build undivided political community is not particularly controversial, especially in the context of democratic theory. For instance, Rousseau described the General Will as not merely the will of the majority, even though it was, in a sense, comprised of the will of most of the people; "what makes the will general," he argued, "is less the number of voters than the *common interest uniting them*."[28] Other theorists make a similar point: direct democracy does not seek to empower the formal will of a mathematical majority. Rather, its aim is to capture the "spirit which does justice to the whole of the community."[29] Benjamin Barber is emphatic on this point: "Majoritarianism," he argues, "is a tribute to the failure of democracy; to our inability to create a politics of *mutualism* that can overcome private interest."[30]

One of the key reasons why voters today are so attracted to referendums is that referendums advance a notion of political equality in which each participant has precisely the same political power. In particular, referendums appear to erase differences in status between citizens and elites.

Referendums have often been proposed as a way of undermining the power of political elites and wealthy interests, which are often the real targets of calls to give power to the people. Often the call for a referendum occurs when political distrust is high and related to a general distrust of all that divides and differentiates the people. Boyer, for instance, suggests that referendums are feared by political elites because they expose "the divisions and differences [that elites] prefer to pretend do not exist."[31] The 1992 Canadian referendum provides a particularly vivid illustration of the widespread desire to erase all differences among voters. According to Johnston et al.'s analysis, the politics surrounding the referendum "cut through coalition-of-minorities obfuscation" and advanced an ideal of voters applying "common sense without the encumbrances of special interests" and especially without the interference of elites whom the voters believed were "susceptible to lobbying by special interests."[32]

Despite the relation between the call for referendums and the distrust of political elites, elites are often just as enthusiastic as voters to employ referendums[33] and have demonstrated their keenness particularly in relation to issues that activate nationalist sentiments. In Yugoslavia, for instance, referendums became the key means by which voters gave voice to their distinct community memberships. Nearly twenty referendums were held in Yugoslavia between 1990 and 1993.[34] To facilitate expression of distinctive community sentiments, elites ensured that each referendum either was held in a distinct area of the country – such as Slovenia or Croatia – where a particular ethnic community was known to hold a majority or was open only to members of one ethnic group, such as Serbs in Croatia or Albanians in Macedonia. Only one attempt was made to hold a Yugoslavia-wide referendum, and it failed because elites could not agree on the question.[35]

In Quebec, referendums have also been used by elites to encourage the expression and development of a nationalist community. René Lévesque solidified support for his party by campaigning on the promise that, if elected, he would hold a referendum on Quebec's separation from Canada – which he held in 1980.[36] What was crucial about the 1980 referendum and the subsequent referendum held on secession in 1995 was that neither was accepted by elites in Quebec as a decisive vote against nationalist aspirations. Despite the fact that a majority in Quebec (though a slight majority[37]) voted against the sovereigntist option in both referendums, the prospect of holding another referendum continued to be attractive. The attraction remained, even in light of the likelihood of another defeat, because referendums coalesce communities and draw out communal values. As much as the referendums have alienated the allophone, anglophone, and Aboriginal minorities in the province, they offer Quebec nationalists yet another opportunity to focus the attention of francophones in Quebec on what they share – namely, their membership in a distinct national community centred on a shared language.

Because referendums activate communal values, they can present formal equality-seeking minorities with a good opportunity to find acceptance as equal members in the community on terms similar to those enjoyed by others in the community. Formal equality-seeking minorities may welcome a process, such as a referendum campaign, that focuses the voters' attention on what members of a community share and that emphasizes the common status of all members. Voters may be persuaded to endorse minority rights claims insofar as these claims validate and celebrate values important to the majority as well.

In this regard, Donovan and Bowler explain that, even though "a clear majority of Americans disapprove of homosexuality," the mass public is firmly committed to protecting the civil rights of homosexuals.[38] In this case, the protection of gay and lesbian minority rights might be explained in terms of majority self-interest; the majority will endorse minority claims if these claims help to reinforce values or rights from which the majority stands to benefit as well.[39] But, in most cases, endorsing the rights of formal equality-seeking minorities *is* the means by which majorities protect their self-interests, because the rights that formal equality-seeking minorities seek are precisely the same rights that the majority enjoys. By extending to others the same rights we enjoy, we protect and even enhance the values that we hold dear.

The protection of gay and lesbian rights has also been linked to community size; smaller communities tend to vote against protections for gay and lesbian rights.[40] But again the relevance of community size might be linked to the relevance of the type of minority claim at stake; because smaller communities tend to be more homogeneous, it might seem easier to identify the values shared by members of the community and to pinpoint, with some confidence, in the context of a referendum campaign, values – such as those related to sexual orientation or religious belief – that are not shared. Because larger communities often appear to be more diverse, members of these communities may not expect that any but the most fundamental values they hold will be shared widely.

The dynamics of referendums thus interact with majoritarian political culture in ways that militate against an understanding of political equality that recognizes the special status of any group in the community and are therefore more likely to threaten the rights of national minorities than those of formal equality-seeking minorities. Referendums activate a sense of community into which claims of special status fail to fit. This is not to argue that all referendums are inevitably hostile to the claims of groups seeking special status. But, unless special measures are taken to protect national minorities in referendum contests, they will convey and bolster an understanding of political equality that is in tension with claims to special status.

Some might argue that democracy in general is in tension with claims to special status for national or other disadvantaged minorities. This may be so. Clearly, much depends on the weight given to majority rule over other democratic values such as substantive equality and self-determination. Referendums stimulate the tension between democracy and multinationalism by giving much weight to majority rule and to undifferentiated equality. Moreover, in many jurisdictions, the results of referendums turn into public policy, and in this way referendums potentially have a great deal of power in political systems such as those of Canada and the United States to threaten the interests of groups holding or seeking special status.

How the Issues Are Framed

The argument so far, that formal equality-seeking groups fare better in referendum campaigns than do national minorities, might account for some of the disagreement in the literature about whether referendums threaten minority rights. If referendums on minority rights issues that focus on formal equality-seeking minorities were distinguished from those that focus on special status or national minorities, then it would be possible to compare the two types and determine whether one type of minority fared worse than the other in referendums. Unfortunately, distinguishing among referendums is complicated because it is difficult in many cases to tell which referendums are about national minorities or special rights and which are not. This is because, in the context of a referendum campaign, formal equality-seeking minorities can be made to appear as though they are seeking special status and treatment even when they are not. In addition, the interests of national minorities can be glossed over in the course of a referendum, through campaign appeals and advertising, by the wording of the question on the ballot, and through the manner in which the results are reported. Each of these factors can disguise relevant divisions in the population.

The fact that relevant divisions in the community can be obscured by the wording, campaign appeals and advertising, and the tabulation process of referendums provides the first hint that the division between formal equality-seeking and national minorities is crucial to understanding referendums in practice. To categorize a minority as either formal equality-seeking or national is often a matter of controversy and the subject of manipulation within referendum campaigns. Referendum issues that are about extending protections that all individuals enjoy to a minority group can be presented as though they are about treating one group of individuals differently from all the rest. For example, in 1992, Colorado voters were asked to approve an initiative, known as Amendment Two, to overturn local ordinances protecting against job discrimination on the basis of sexual orientation. Even though the issue at hand concerned whether gays and lesbians should be accorded the same protections as other people in the state, proponents of the initiative framed parts of their campaign in terms of "No Special Rights for Gays" as a means to attract voters to vote in favour of an amendment to overturn the ordinances. The wording of the amendment, especially its title "No *Protected Status* Based on Homosexual, Lesbian, or Bisexual Orientation," also falsely implied that, without the amendment, gays and lesbians would enjoy special status not possessed by other members of the community. This message was reiterated in the brief submitted to the US Supreme Court by the attorney general of Colorado, who defended the amendment by claiming that it "only eliminates laws and policies that gave gays and lesbians a 'special right' to be protected from discrimination."[41]

The distinctive treatment that groups are seeking can also be glossed over in the course of the campaign or by the way in which ballot questions are worded. This can be done by ignoring the issue of distinctive treatment and asking the electorate whether all individuals ought to be treated the same. For example, English-only referendums in the United States are usually run according to campaigns that highlight the common right to services in English and ignore – that is, fail to advertise the fact – that linguistic minorities might have distinctive interests at stake. Alaskans endorsed such a ballot measure in 1998. The first section of Ballot Measure No. 6 read, "The people of the State of Alaska find that English is the *common unifying language* of the State of Alaska and the United States of America, and declare a compelling interest in promoting, preserving and strengthening its use."[42] An Arizona initiative in 1988 contained similar wording. Both measures were approved by the voters (69 percent of Alaskans, 50.5 percent of Arizonans) even though in each state a substantial Aboriginal population struggles to protect its languages and in Arizona a significant Hispanic minority resides as well. In both cases, the wording of the question and the tabulation of results ignored relevant linguistic divisions in the population.[43] Referendum questions can be worded to further the referendum's effect of solidifying the majority's views of equal status and rights for all, contrary to the interests of linguistic minorities.

The point here is not merely that the interests of linguistic minorities do not prevail in such referendums. Rather, the problem is that referendums can easily obscure relevant divisions in the population by using the language of political equality in a misleading manner and thereby presenting to voters a false understanding of what is at stake for minorities. Providing services in a "common and unifying language" might not seem to be particularly "unifying" if voters are aware that indigenous peoples are strongly opposed to and disadvantaged by this measure. Similarly, voters might be less interested in denying rights to individuals based on sexual orientation if they view such a denial as singling out a particular group and withholding rights from that group that all other groups enjoy.

The BC referendum held in 2002 is a good example of how the reinforcement of formal equality-seeking values can be built into a referendum process in a way that disadvantages groups that already hold special status. The questions on the ballot (see Appendix 1.1) are designed to appeal to sentiments of formal equality as opposed to the protection or enhancement of the distinct rights or interests of the national minority.[44] The preamble provides the first and crucial cue concerning equality, which is then implicitly reintroduced in every question to follow. Most questions offer the voter a choice between endorsing formal equality for all British Columbians or rejecting formal equality in favour of an undefined alternative. Questions 3, 4, 5, and 8 specifically gloss over the distinctive values and interests of Aboriginal people and ask whether all British Columbians should enjoy similar rights in relation to hunting and fishing, access to parks and protected areas, subjection to standards for environmental protection, and payment of taxes. Question 6 also taps into formal equality by asking whether a form of government that all British Columbians enjoy, namely local government, ought to be a template for Aboriginal self-government. In each case, the alternative to endorsing formal equality is left entirely undefined. The choice of "no" indicates a rejection of the value of formal equality within British Columbia. Unsurprisingly, the results on the eight ballot questions were very similar: as mentioned above, questions were endorsed by between 84.5 percent and 94.5 percent of voters, depending on the question.

The BC referendum further obscured relevant community divisions through the process by which ballots were disseminated and collected. Ballots were mailed out to those registered as voters in British Columbia for the 2001 provincial election. Because voters were asked to mail in their completed ballots, results were not tabulated by polling stations, and thus the process could not reveal, even indirectly, how different communities voted. Moreover, because most Aboriginal people do not vote in provincial elections, few even received ballots.[45] By tabulating the ballots and reporting the results without acknowledging the different groups within the larger community, the referendum process portrays a community as though it lacks divisions relevant to the referendum questions.

Conversely, referendums can signal the importance of distinct status and interests within a population if a tabulation process is adopted that reports how different groups, such as different provinces, states, or national groups, vote in the referendum or by requiring double or compound majorities in order for the referendum to pass.[46] Double majorities are required of referendums held in many federal systems (e.g., Australia and Switzerland). Compound majorities have been suggested for national referendums in Canada with the additional proviso that a majority in Quebec must endorse any referendum that passes.⁴⁷

The BC referendum provides a particularly good illustration of how the wording of questions and tabulation process can be misused to obscure relevant divisions in the population. But it is not an isolated example. The tactic of obscuring or highlighting community divisions in order to ensure a particular outcome is used in many referendums, including the American examples mentioned above. In Canada, the United States, and Europe, the language of unity versus difference is employed frequently in referendum campaigns, especially those that deal with the interests of minorities, to evoke an anti-special rights ideal of political equality.

Further Evidence: Referendums in Divided Societies

The strongest evidence that referendums are biased against the distinctive interests of national minorities and that they exacerbate pre-existing cleavages in a community is indirect: most democratic states with strong national minorities do not hold referendums. According to Bogdanor, referendums are not suited to divided societies because the stability of such societies "requires strategies that depart from the majoritarian model."⁴⁸ As previously mentioned, countries such as Belgium, Austria, and the Netherlands rarely use referendums, and Israel has never used a referendum primarily because, according to Arieli-Horowitz, "striving toward direct democracy undermines the legitimacy of ... patterns of mediation and compromise" such as those that elites attempt to build through consociationalism.⁴⁹

Two putative exceptions to Bogdanor's rule only serve to reaffirm the destructive capacity that referendums potentially have in divided societies. The first exception includes referendums that are meant to be divisive. In Eastern Europe, referendums were used intentionally by political elites to coalesce nationalist communities and accentuate ethnic divisions. In many cases, the aim of elites was not to build bridges between distinctive groups within the community but to build fiefdoms. Although the disintegration of countries such as Yugoslavia was not directly caused by referendums, they were used to highlight divisions relevant within countries and important to their ethnic leaders. Referendums were an effective way to involve citizens in a form of "participatory ethnic posturing."

The second important exception is Switzerland. Over three-quarters of the referendums held worldwide are held in Switzerland, and, if for no other reason than this, the Swiss case is often used to counter the skepticism sometimes expressed about referendums. Switzerland appears to be a society in which referendum democracy works despite ethnic and linguistic divisions. But a closer look at "Swiss exceptionalism" leads to different conclusions. Most referendums held in Switzerland have nothing to do with issues that mobilize ethnic, linguistic, or religious cleavages in the country. Butler and Ranney, for instance, argue that a large proportion of referendums in Switzerland are incremental and technical in nature.[50] In defence of the Swiss experience, Frey and Goette argue that the civil rights of minorities do not fare poorly in Swiss referendums and report that only 30 percent of a total of sixty-four referendums included in their survey and held between 1970 and 1996 had antiminority results.[51] But again a closer look reveals that only twenty of the sixty-four referendums discussed by Frey and Goette were held federally and therefore across cantons. Forty-four of the sixty-four referendums (or 69 percent) surveyed were held either in the town or in the canton of Zurich. Zurich contains a significant French population in a German-dominated territory. Yet none of the referendums in Frey and Goette's survey were obviously connected to civil rights issues that engaged the ethnic divisions within these communities.[52]

In the United States, evidence suggests that referendums frequently exacerbate ethnic divisions specifically between the African-American and Hispanic communities on one side and the white community on the other side. In 1978, Derrick Bell Jr. called US referendums "democracy's barrier to racial equality."[53] A recent study of California referendums confirms Bell's pessimism in showing that racial and ethnic divisions are a distinguishing feature of the vote on referendums about minority rights.[54] In each of the "big three" referendums in California,[55] a white majority dominated Latino, black, and Asian minorities. In the case of Proposition 187, which sought to deny public education, health services, and social services to illegal aliens, the ballot measure was viewed as an "outright attack on the Latino community," 80 percent of whom voted against the proposition.[56]

More broadly, in a survey of seventy-four civil rights US initiatives on racial, ethnic, and linguistic minorities, gay men, lesbians, and individuals with AIDS, Barbara Gamble shows that, in an overwhelming 78 percent of cases, direct democracy leads to "majority tyranny."[57] Like Frey and Goette in their survey of Switzerland, Gamble does not distinguish between initiatives that involve national minorities and those that involve formal equality-seeking minorities. And it is difficult to know, without revisiting the details of each referendum campaign, which referendums might have involved campaigns, ballot questions, or tabulation processes that either obscured claims for special rights or status or presented groups as though they were seeking special status.[58] However, unlike Frey and Goette's survey, Gamble's survey includes some referendums that are indisputably relevant to national minorities: namely, English-only referendums. These referendums sought to declare English as the official language of a state or town and to deprive minority linguistic groups of services in any language other than English. Predictably, English-only referendums caused an uproar in many of the states in which they were held. For instance, in Alaska, opponents expressed the concern that the English-only measure might prevent Alaskan Natives from conducting meetings in their Native languages and might harm bilingual programs throughout the state.[59] Most prominent among the groups participating in the Alaska lawsuit was the Native American Rights Fund, whose lawyer argued that the ballot measure impairs "the rights of Alaska Native villages to freely choose, shape and control the forms of community self-governance that exist in their local communities." In Arizona, the Navajo also came out strongly against the Arizona initiative. Despite these concerns, 100 percent of the eight English-only referendums surveyed had antiminority outcomes.[60]

In Canada, as in the United States, the distinction between referendums on formal equality-seeking minorities and those on minorities seeking special status has eluded researchers primarily because, until 1992, few referendums focused on minority rights, let alone the rights of national minorities to special status.[61] But the exceptions again are instructive. In the 1980 and 1995 referendums on Quebec sovereignty association and secession, the government of Quebec provided no formal structures within the voting or tabulation processes that could aid in recognizing the relevant divisions between Aboriginal and non-Aboriginal and French and English groups. Although the votes of each community were not counted separately, some commentators translated vote totals into a rough reflection of how each national group voted. The failure to recognize officially the relevant divisions led the Inuit to hold a parallel referendum in 1980 in which 94 percent of Inuit voters voted against sovereignty association. In 1995, both the Cree and the Inuit held separate referendums that were parallel to the referendum on secession. Ninety-six percent of the Inuit and 96.3 percent of the Cree voted against secession. The Cree conducted an active campaign against the referendum and argued that, regardless of the outcome, the referendum could not alter Cree status and relations with the Canadian state.

The 1992 federal referendum on the Charlottetown Accord is instructive because it had many of the features required of referendums in divided societies. First, the language of the accord plainly stated that some groups, particularly Quebec, would receive distinctive treatment if the referendum passed, either through the distinct society clause or through the guarantee of 25 percent of the seats in Parliament. Second, the campaign conducted by the accord's proponents did not gloss over distinctive treatment. Rather, it attempted, for the most part, to explain to voters why distinctive treatment for some groups was fair. The referendum results, though not tabulated according to national group, were tabulated by province and were thereby able to highlight the potential division between Quebec and the rest of Canada. This division did not materialize because the accord was rejected both within and outside Quebec by similar margins.

According to some accounts of the 1992 referendum, the extensive campaign and the substantial participation that was encouraged leading up to the referendum might have contributed to the accord's defeat by generating political disaffection.[62] According to polling done during and after the campaign, the most controversial aspect of the Charlottetown Accord was the distinctive treatment that the accord offered to Quebec.[63] Opposition to the "distinct society" clause was ultimately responsible for defeating the accord in the referendum.[64] The clause was very difficult to sell in the rest of Canada because it asked Canadians living outside Quebec to recognize a status for Quebec that they could not claim for themselves or their own provinces. This fact was highlighted in former prime minister Pierre Trudeau's famous speech at Maison du Egg Roll, in which Trudeau accused the supporters of the accord of granting collective rights for some groups and not for others.[65]

Conclusion

The evidence presented here provides good reasons to be suspicious about referendums held on the status of national minorities. Confirming these suspicions would require a comprehensive re-assessment of recent referendums according to their apparent invocation of a rhetoric of distinctive rights and status or their attempts to obscure the distinctive rights and status that national minorities seek. Here the aim has been to provide some compelling reasons for why such a re-assessment ought to be undertaken. I have argued that referendums are attractive to elites and voters because they offer an important platform, buttressed by democratic values, from which to consult citizens about key issues of public policy. They are also a crucial means to promote specific political values related to equality and to a particular view of community. Referendums stimulate the endorsement of formal equality and, in doing so, conflict with recognizing distinct status or rights for any group. They also stimulate the endorsement of values we share and highlight the fact that, as citizens, we are essentially the same even though we might have different opinions about, for instance, whether bridges ought to be built or whether government ought to balance its budgets in all cases.

However, in the absence of special measures that aim at compensating for their biases, referendums are poorly equipped to recognize group differences in the constitutive values of a community and to convey in a sensitive manner how these play out in relation to specific policy issues. Because of these biases, referendums are not usually used in divided societies where successful compromises entail recognizing the different needs of distinct national communities. The exceptions to this, where referendums have been used to coalesce national minorities in divided societies, illustrate how effectively referendums can undermine unity in multinational states. Moreover, referendums are easily manipulated in societies where such divisions are intense or controversial.

The problem posed here might signal something more significant than the presence of a particular type of political manipulation during referendum campaigns. If referendums convey distinctive understandings of political equality and political community, as I have argued they do, and if these understandings threaten the distinctive status or rights of national minorities, then the impact of referendums on minorities may be felt beyond the referendum campaign. Moreover, if my argument is sound, then referendums held on the interests of national minorities, or groups that appear to be seeking special status, are more likely to result in the defeat of these distinctive interests than are referendums held on other minority issues. This is because referendums activate a set of democratic values that emphasize similar treatment and status for each member of the political community. In this sense, the medium, namely the referendum, is the message. According to referendum processes, legitimate democratic decision making requires first that each citizen have the same status, the same rights, and the same amount of political power and second that the majority's will is decisive.

Multinational democracies, though also built on the values of equality and equal rights, often require that some groups enjoy differentiated status and special rights as a means to secure substantive equality. Moreover, in most multinational democracies, democratic values such as self-determination, eliminating oppression, exploitation, and marginalization, and honouring treaties and other promises forged in the past to protect the distinctive interests or status of a group must be weighed along with formal equality and majority rule in constructing workable institutions and good public policy. If referendums are biased against minorities, if they work against the values of differentiated citizenship and special rights, and if they are more likely to further entrench divisions within a community based on questions about special rights, then it is reasonable to require legislation that compensates for the biases that referendums bring to questions that affect the constitutive values of a national minority.[66]

Referendums are often employed when representative institutions seem to be insufficiently accountable or lack legitimacy to resolve decisively important community conflicts. In this sense, referendums provide an important fail-safe for representative institutions. They allow communities to resolve debilitating conflicts in a decisive manner without relying on institutions whose authority over such matters is questioned by the electorate. Unsurprisingly, the sorts of conflict in which the accountability and legitimacy of representative institutions are likely to be questioned include the constitutive aspects of political communities, including the status of national minorities, questions of secession, and altering the fundamental rights of citizens. The project, then, is not to eliminate referendums but to regulate them in ways that counteract and compensate for their propensity to favour values, such as formal equality and majority rule, that bias proceedings against groups that seek or appear to be seeking distinctive status and rights.

Acknowledgments
My thanks to Catherine Frost and David Laycock for their helpful comments on this chapter and to the other participants at the CPSA workshop on Representation and Its Discontents, organized by David Laycock, Toronto, 31 May 2002. Thanks to Cara Macgregor and Conor Donaldson for their research assistance.

Appendix 1.1: BC Treaty Negotiations Referendum Questions
Whereas the Government of British Columbia is committed to negotiating workable, affordable treaty settlements that will provide certainty, finality and equality; do you agree that the Provincial Government should adopt the following principles to guide its participation in treaty negotiations?

1. Private property should not be expropriated for treaty settlements.
2. The terms and conditions of leases and licenses should be respected; fair compensation for unavoidable disruption of commercial interests should be ensured.
3. Hunting, fishing and recreational opportunities on Crown land should be ensured for all British Columbians.
4. Parks and protected areas should be maintained for the use and benefit of all British Columbians.
5. Province-wide standards of resource management and environmental protection should continue to apply.
6. Aboriginal self-government should have the characteristics of local government, with powers delegated from Canada and British Columbia.
7. Treaties should include mechanisms for harmonizing land use planning between Aboriginal governments and neighbouring local governments.
8. The existing tax exemptions for Aboriginal people should be phased out.

Notes
1. Mendelsohn and Parkin (2001b), 1.
2. See Johnston and Soroka (2001). Also see selections in Nye, Zelikov, and King (1997).
3. Bogdanor (1997), 88.
4. Boyer (1992), 156.
5. *Reference Re: Manitoba Language Rights* 1985 1 SCR 721.
6. *Reference Re: Secession of Quebec* [1998] 2 SCR 217.
7. In the context of this reference case, the Cree argued that Quebec secession could not take place without the consent of the Cree. Grand Council of the Crees (Eeyou Estchee). Factum of the Intervenor Grand Council of the Crees (Eeyou Estchee), *Reference Re: Secession of Quebec*, 1998 S.C.C.
8. See *Ke-kin-is-uks et al. v. British Columbia*, 28 March 2002, BCCA 238, docket CA029584, registry: Vancouver; and *Bob, Sam et al. v. British Columbia*, 15 May 2002, BCSC 733, docket L021077, registry: Vancouver. For an assessment of the constitutional dimensions of this referendum, see Mandell (2002).
9. Of the 790,182 votes received (36 percent of those mailed out), 26,702 were considered spoiled. Of the 763,480 eligible ballots considered for each question, an average of 8

percent of these votes were spoiled on individual questions. For a detailed report on the referendum, see Elections BC (2002).
10 Editorials and comment articles in the *Globe and Mail*, *Vancouver Sun*, and *Times-Colonist* before the referendum focused on the possibility of division and protest, while after the referendum editorials tended to detail the negative political consequences of holding the referendum. For before the referendum, see Ibbitson (2001); "Premier" (2001); and Zubyk (2001). For after the referendum, see "How" (2002); "B.C. Liberals" (2002); and "Treaty Referendum" (2002).
11 Notably, Gamble (1997).
12 See Boyer (1992), 250-52; Cronin (1989), 92; Donovan and Bowler (1998), 1023-24; Frey and Goette (1998), 1342-48; Magleby (1984), 196; and Zimmerman (1986), 95.
13 Boyer (1992), 251, maintains this latter position in arguing that "Plebiscites are like mirrors; they show us collectively, at the same time, the nature of our society."
14 See Chambers (2001).
15 See Jenkins and Mendelsohn (2001).
16 See Chambers (2001) and Laycock (2000).
17 In this respect, see Fishkin (1997).
18 As noted by Boyer (1992), 172, in relation to the infrequent use of referendums in Aboriginal communities.
19 Gamble (1997), 247.
20 Frey and Goette (1998), 1345.
21 Donovan and Bowler (1998), 1022.
22 Gamble (1997), 248.
23 Donovan and Bowler (1998), 1023.
24 Will Kymlicka offers the best-known defence of such rights. See his *Multicultural Citizenship* (1995).
25 For defences of group rights (including national, cultural, and linguistic minorities), see the essays in Kymlicka and Norman (1995a).
26 Some research discussed in this section is examined at greater length in Eisenberg (2001).
27 Chambers (2001); Elster (1986).
28 Rousseau (1913), book 1, ch. 4; emphasis added.
29 Barker (1942), 67-68.
30 Barber (1984), 198; emphasis added.
31 Boyer (1992), 251.
32 Johnston et al. (1996), 5, 12.
33 Mendelsohn and Parkin (2001a), 7.
34 Brady and Kaplan (1994), 207.
35 Brady and Kaplan (1994), 210.
36 In the 1980 referendum, the government of Quebec asked voters for "a mandate to negotiate sovereignty-association" with the rest of Canada.
37 In the 1980 Quebec referendum, 60 percent of the population voted "non." In 1995, 49.4 percent voted in favour of sovereignty, while 50.6 percent voted against it.
38 Donovan and Bowler (1997), 111.
39 Gamble (1997), 248.
40 Donovan and Bowler (1998), 1023.
41 Arguments of the Attorney General of Colorado in *Evans v. Romer*, 854 P. 2d 1270 (Colo. 1993), 1.
42 State of Alaska, Ballot Measure No. 6, 3 November 1998; emphasis added.
43 The Alaska measure was overturned in the state's superior court on 22 March 2002. See *Alakayak, et al. v. State of Alaska*. The Arizona measure was overturned by the Arizona Supreme Court in 1998. See *Ruiz et al. v. Hull et al.*, 191 Ariz. 441, 957 P.sd 984 (1998).
44 The presumption here is that Aboriginal people and the Québécois are national minorities. However, nothing in this analysis hangs on accepting this presumption since, in all the cases discussed in this chapter, a group can have distinctive interests and can advance its interests for special rights or status whether or not it is a national minority. The main point is that referendum politics often obscure the differentiated rights and status that

groups claim for themselves. This point is particularly well illustrated in campaigns in which national minorities are involved.
45 Thanks to Taiaiake Alfred for pointing this out to me.
46 This is not to say that identifying the results on a community-by-community basis is always a good idea. National minorities, and other groups, might have good reasons not to want their votes reported separately, perhaps because of fear of political reprisals from governments hostile to their interests.
47 Mendelsohn and Parkin (2001), 22.
48 Bogdanor (1994), 88.
49 Arieli-Horowitz (2002), 158.
50 Butler and Ranney (1994), 4, 25.
51 Frey and Goette (1998), 1345.
52 The referendum issues at the cantonal and municipal levels included public housing, youth and foreigners' rights, and drug policy. At the federal level, the referendum issues were policies toward foreigners, religious liberty, and what Frey and Goette label "miscellaneous."
53 Bell Jr. (1978), 1.
54 Hajnal and Louch (2001).
55 In addition to Proposition 187, the big three include Proposition 209, which ended affirmative action by state and other public offices, and Proposition 227, which would end the state's program of bilingual education and replace it with a one-year intensive English immersion program.
56 Hajnal and Louch (2001), 18.
57 Gamble (1997), 253.
58 Gamble includes in her survey at least two types of initiatives in which formal equality-seeking minorities are easily presented as though they are seeking special rights: namely, initiatives on gay and lesbian issues and those on affirmative action.
59 Elizabeth Manning, "Interpretation Differs on English-Only Bid," *Anchorage Daily News*, 4 November 1998.
60 In the context of Gamble's study, the average of 100 percent is significantly higher than the overall antiminority outcome of 78 percent for all cases.
61 Important exceptions include the Manitoba referendums held in 1983 (discussed above) and the plebiscite on conscription held in 1942. With respect to the 1942 plebiscite, Johnston et al. (1996), 256-57, write that, "Although a clear majority voted to relieve the Liberals of their anti-conscription pledge, the overall result masked one-sided opposition in Quebec." Despite the divisive effect of the plebiscite, the decision to hold it was probably, all things considered, the best way for the government to deal with the crisis.
62 Pal and Seidle (1993).
63 The accord also contained a clause that recognized the inherent right to self-government for Aboriginal people. Although Johnston et al. (1996), 89-90, found broad support for this clause, they noted that this support dissipated when voters were posed with more concrete policy questions that the general principle of self-government might entail, such as whether the right to self-government should allow for Aboriginal people to legislate different laws for themselves.
64 Johnston et al. (1996), 95, argue that supporting the Quebec element of the accord was critical as a determinant of whether a voter supported the whole accord or not.
65 The speech was published in Trudeau (1992).
66 Some areas of reform include regulations that guide the wording of ballot questions, the funding of campaigns, and the tabulation process. For instance, regulations could require that, before a referendum is held, legislators assess and report on the possible effects that the referendum might have on any national minorities living in the community. The questions on a referendum ballot could be subject to tests that ensure, for instance, that each referendum question deals only with a single issue, that no question contains double negatives, and that the question, or the legislation for which approval is sought, does not gloss over relevant divisions in the community. Campaign finance rules could be designed to ensure that groups are able to get their message out by, for instance, designating

some groups as official "intervenors" (akin to intervenor status granted to some groups in legal cases) and are eligible for special funding or advertising opportunities. For referendums that affect the rights or status of national minorities, the results of the referendum could be reported separately for each community, and a double or compound majority could be required for the referendum to pass. Referendums could also be designed around the idea of deliberative polling in which, after an initial ballot, citizens engage in deliberation and then a second official ballot is held. Each of these reforms requires further study and elaboration.

2
Language, Representation, and Suprastate Democracy: Questions Facing the European Union
Peter Ives

> Of course, democracy depends, in its turn, on the existence of a political culture shared by all citizens. But there is no call for defeatism, if one bears in mind that, in the 19th-Century European states, national consciousness and social solidarity were only gradually produced, with the help of national historiography, mass communications and universal conscription. If that artificial form of "solidarity among strangers" came about thanks to a historically momentous effort of abstraction from local dynastic consciousness to a consciousness that was national and democratic, then why should it be impossible to extend this learning process beyond national borders?
>
> – Jürgen Habermas (2000), 56-57

> The problems we have in Holland and most parts of the world are problems that have to do with security, immigration and people talking the language of the country they live in.
>
> – Marco Pastors, Dutch supporter of Pim Fortuyn (cited in Freeman [2002], A14)

> Every time the question of language surfaces, in one way or another, it means that a series of other problems are coming to the fore: the formation and enlargement of the managing class, the need to establish more intimate and secure relationships between the governing groups and the national-popular mass, in other words to reorganize the cultural hegemony.[1]
>
> – Antonio Gramsci (1975), 2346

The unprecedented enlargement of the European Union in 2004 raises to a new level many of the issues that have plagued this project of extending "democracy" beyond the nation-state. Of the immense number of questions to be worked out, from the makeup of bodies such as the European Commission to agricultural subsidies, taxation harmony, immigration, and security, the question of language policy may seem to be relatively minor. However, when considering the persistent problems that the European Union has faced in appearing overly bureaucratic and far removed from the majority of Europeans, concerns over a lack of democratic legitimacy, language and language policy are crucial. In 1993, Abram de Swaan described the process and debates on European integration like this: "There was much talk of milk pools and butter mountains, of a unitary currency, of liberalizing movements of EC citizens and restricting access for outsiders, but the language which these issues were dealt with remained itself a non-issue."[2] It took considerable time for the relationship between language and democratic practice to be seriously considered in public debate, in policy initiatives, and by scholars concerned with the "democracy deficit."[3]

As a political theorist, I am still concerned by the gap between the theoretical interest in language and empirical questions concerning the politics of language and language policy.[4] Twentieth-century political theory has been inundated by the topic of language, whether through structuralism and poststructuralism, psycho-analysis, the "linguistic turn" in philosophy, or "deliberative" theories of democracy. From Michel Foucault, Jacques Derrida, and Jürgen Habermas to Charles Taylor and Quentin Skinner, language issues have been at the forefront of political theory. The rich historical literature on nationalism and nation-state formation has shown that language "standardization" was of great importance to changes in nineteenth-century Europe.[5] Yet today, when it comes to the issue of how Europe can address the democracy deficit, most of the theoretical complexity of language is obscured.[6] Language is often mentioned to illustrate various points about multiculturalism, pragmatic problems, and different member states' histories but is seldom investigated with any of the insights from the various linguistically influenced perspectives.

For example, when advocating the construction of "supra-national political agencies" capable of democratic will formation through civil society and a European public sphere, Habermas almost parenthetically comments that, "Given the political will, there is no a priori reason why [Europe] cannot subsequently create the politically necessary communicative context as soon as it is constitutionally prepared to do so. Even the requirement of a common language – English as 'a second first language' – ought not be an insurmountable obstacle with the existing level of formal schooling."[7] That Habermas does not investigate whether there is or should be such a political will is symptomatic of the gap between political theory and the political practice of ordinary people.[8]

Habermas's entire theoretical framework is based on the idea of communication and heavily influenced by the philosophy of language. So it is surprising how seldom the issue of multilingualism is raised in his many discussions of democracy and multiculturalism in the European Union.⁹ When Habermas does address this issue in a few instances, he leaves it quite undertheorized. For example, after noting that there exist thirteen official recognized languages within the European Union, he states that "This constitutes at first glance an embarrassing obstacle to the formation of a shared polity for all. The official multilingualism of EU institutions is necessary for the mutual recognition of equal worth and integrity of all national cultures. However, under the veil of this legal guarantee it becomes all the easier to use English as a working language at the face-to-face level, wherever the parties lack another common idiom."¹⁰ Overcoming this "embarrassment" of multilingualism through a legal "veil" seems to be at odds with Habermas's more general project of encouraging multiculturalism and participation in an open European public sphere and civil society. As we shall see, Habermas is not alone in presuming that official multilingualism that recognizes cultural diversity is not at odds with the growing preponderance of English – a situation that I will argue may turn out to be an obstacle to the success of the European Union as a polity.

What are the implications of elected and/or delegated representatives operating in a language different from that of their constituents? Does it increase the distance between representatives and citizens? Is part of the purpose of political "representation" to translate citizens' desires into different languages? What if representatives are less competent or comfortable in the foreign language in which they have to operate? Are they at a competitive disadvantage compared with other politicians? Can there be fair, effective, and meaningful public and political deliberation across different languages? What if our deliberated agreements have slightly different connotations in the various languages used to reach them?

There is growing theoretical – and perhaps even public – acceptance of the idea that democracy is more than limited government with free and fair elections and the protection of civil rights. Many support the basic tenet of deliberative democracy, that for democracy to be legitimate requires, as Seyla Benhabib puts it, "free and unconstrained public deliberation of all about matters of common concern."¹¹ Clearly, which language or languages such public deliberation takes place in is an important common concern – a concern that no purely technical, pragmatic, or philosophical treatise can satisfy.

This raises a central question for all theories of deliberative and participatory democracy, the question of linguistic representation: How and in which language(s) do we deliberate about which language(s) we should be deliberating in? How do differing levels of linguistic competence and comfort (not to mention class, gender, and ethnic coding) relate to one's ability to participate in deliberation? Many have raised versions of such questions addressed to both Habermas in particular and theories of "deliberative democracy" in general. But they have done so at the theoretical level.[12] The European Union provides a specific and concrete context that poses questions of language, representation, and the future of democracy in our so-called "globalizing" world. If suprastate institutions such as the United Nations or the World Trade Organization are to play larger roles in our lives, the European Union may serve as an important test case for democratic representation in such institutions.

There is a small but growing literature that addresses language and European integration with the concerns of political theory (as opposed to the more policy-oriented and sociolinguistic perspectives of earlier literature).[13] Many argue, persuasively in my opinion, that the de jure position of institutional multilingualism of the EU institutions, which I will describe below, will be difficult to alter. The Treaty of Nice retains the provision that unanimous agreement by members of the Council of Ministers is required to alter the language policies of the EU institutions (Article 290).

However, English seems to be increasingly the de facto lingua franca in Europe. Many (including Habermas, as noted above) accept implicitly the argument that Eugène Loos makes explicitly, that there is no necessary conflict between these de jure and de facto situations. I will argue that there is, at the least, a tension between the two and that, as this tension grows especially with expansion of the European Union, it will exacerbate the democracy deficit. I will not base this argument on a theoretical exploration of language per se but show how this tension is observable within statements and policies of the European Union.

This chapter argues that de jure multilingualism and an increasing de facto use of English (at least among elites) can co-exist without conflict only if one accepts the basic vision of language articulated by John Locke: language is primarily an instrument of communication. From this perspective, de jure institutional multilingualism performs a symbolic function that, however important, is not at odds with the increasing spread of English and uses it for ease of communication among various political actors.

However, the European Union, especially the Committee of the Regions and the Parliament, but also the European Commission, has been strengthening its commitment to a vision of language from a philosophical tradition very different from the instrumentalist, Lockean approach to language. This is the tradition of German Romanticism, specifically as articulated by Johann Gottfried Herder and Wilhelm von Humboldt. From their perspectives, language is intimately related to collective culture and the entire framework through which one perceives the world.[14] From this cultural approach, there is an irresolvable tension between de jure multilingualism and de facto use of English. Because, from this perspective, language is not just a means of communication but also itself expresses a way of seeing the world, to use any one language, such as English, will have an impact on the content of any given conversation, including democratic debate. Accepting monolingualism, even in a lingua franca and de facto manner, means reducing cultural ways of interpreting the world to one common denominator.

This chapter will not pursue a theoretical analysis of these two approaches to language. I have engaged elsewhere in more extensive theoretical analyses of language and political theory.[15] Moreover, part of my concern is that political theorists such as Habermas and others (including myself) approach language in an overly abstract manner and do not take the actual practices of language, policy, and politics into account. So, in an attempt to help bridge the gap between theory and political practice, here I will focus on the empirical circumstances and policy documents and try to tease out the theoretical implications underlying them. I will not try to advance a theoretical argument about the coherence of these underlying Lockean or cultural visions of language. I should admit, however, to being more persuaded by the cultural approach for reasons that will become obvious.

I do not presume that these are the only two possible conceptions of language. Nor do I assume that some combination of these two is inherently impossible. Instead, I argue that the conceptualization of language is itself a political issue that cannot be decided conclusively by theoretical inquiry alone. This is based on the conviction that the relationship between democracy and language is ultimately one of political will: it should be up to the citizens of the democracies under consideration. If it is decided by default, as if it were beyond human control (or the control of citizens of a democratic jurisdiction), if the political choice of multilingualism is over-ridden, then the democracy deficit will increase. Such a situation may become the Achilles' heel of democracy within the European Union.

At present, it is unclear how the citizens of the European Union's member states could make adequate decisions about language policy or even deliberate on it. It also seems to be uncertain whether the current version of institutional multilingualism is a response, or suitable response, to concerns over democracy and whether linguistic rights can be accepted as a significant form of human rights.[16] For any or all of these issues to be addressed, the politics of language must be placed more clearly on the table for consideration.

Of course, this chapter can only begin to address a more limited number of issues. I am primarily concerned with illustrating that the European Union is increasingly adopting the cultural approach to language and that this move is often in explicit opposition to the discourse and assumptions of the Lockean approach.

After a brief discussion of some of the key theoretical questions about conceptualizing language and linguistic diversity, this chapter will describe the de jure institutional multilingualism of the European Union and then discuss how this amounts to at least a minimal general language policy. I will then turn to the de facto spread of English, followed by an analysis of some recent policies and statements that highlight the development of tensions among these different views of language.

Two Competing Visions of Language

According to the "instrumentalist" or "Lockean" view, language is a vehicle to transmit meaning, emotions, judgments, and information among individuals. John Locke articulated a detailed and influential version of this perspective in 1693. In *An Essay Concerning Human Understanding*, he argues that simple signs are combined to create mixed and complex ones. Ultimately, Locke's individualism dictates that signs or words are given their meanings by humans as individuals, not as collectives.[17] Locke is greatly concerned with misunderstandings and the "abuse of words" due to different people using a sign to signify different ideas. His corrective to such problems is always with reference to the object (sensible or insensible) for which the words ultimately stand.[18] Defending Locke against mischaracterizations that pit him too simplistically against Herder and other more cultural versions of language, even Bob Chase finally notes that, "As long as Locke clings to the notion that his 'simple ideas' are stubbornly uniform and are somehow present in the mind prior to language, and as long as he asserts that thought can consist solely in the mental manipulation of ideas, ... he blocks the way to a theory that would see language itself as the stuff of thought – or of any of the higher operations of human consciousness."[19] The philosophy of language may have proceeded well beyond Locke's theories, especially Anglo-analytic philosophy's shift in focus from words to prepositions.[20] Nevertheless, the general perspective that language is a vehicle through which individuals transfer ideas from one head to another is still common.[21] Michael Reddy has explored this basic approach in what he calls the "conduit metaphor," whereby language is seen as a container for sending the content of ideas or meanings. Thus, by speaking, we get "ideas across" to our listeners, it is difficult to "put ideas into words," and a student's ideas are "buried" in dense text.²² As we will see below, from this approach to language, linguistic diversity is a barrier to communication. It is an inefficient and poor vehicle for conveying ideas. Thus, linguistic diversity is an obstacle to European integration and democracy. If the purpose of language is to carry communication, then a language situation (monolingualism versus multilingualism) can be judged by its effectiveness in this regard.²³ The democratic imperative would be equality of competence among speakers, regardless of the language(s) used.

Various liberal theorists, such as Alan Patten, have tried to incorporate the importance of language for symbolic affirmation and individuals' identity promotion.²⁴ But as Denise Réaume argues, all attempts to locate the value of language recognition in purely instrumental, individual terms miss the "intrinsic value of each particular language – as a human accomplishment, an end in itself. Each language is itself a manifestation of human creativity which has value independent of its uses."²⁵ That is, there is something fundamental about language for which instrumentalist and individualist approaches to language cannot account. This collective, "intrinsic," and world-shaping aspect of language cannot be simply added on to fundamentally "instrumentalist" visions of language as a tool. As noted above, here I am not concerned with further supporting this theoretical argument. Rather, my point is that these "theoretical debates" have political implications, and many of the European Union's policies and statements contain explicit and implicit challenges to the Lockean view of language. A political theorist who supports the instrumentalist view may reply that the European Union is wrong to the extent that it adheres to noninstrumentalist views. One who rejects the instrumentalist view may attempt to describe its inconsistencies, inadequacies, and so forth. My project here is different. I want to show how theoretical questions of what language is play out on the political terrain of European integration and democratic legitimation.

There are a host of other traditions for thinking about language not as fundamentally a vehicle for communication but as central to culture, identity, how we perceive the world, and how we structure our lives. In the context of European philosophy, the names Johann Gottfried Herder and Wilhelm von Humboldt come to mind. Both men insisted that the particularities of different languages are integral to cultures and the lives of common people who created and spoke those languages.²⁶ Their ideas spawned differing schools of linguistics, from the relativism of Edward Sapir and Benjamin Lee Whorf to the "generative grammar" of Noam Chomsky.²⁷ This is not the place to discuss such developments or question the undemocratic aspects especially of Herder's thought.²⁸ Instead of engaging in such theoretical exegesis, I will add to such debates by focusing on how these theoretical ideas are in tension within contemporary EU policy discourse.

But before turning to this more empirical analysis, I need to drive home the implications of these two different approaches to language for thinking about linguistic diversity. Umberto Eco's fantastic study *The Search for the Perfect Language* draws attention to the history of linguistic diversity being understood as a curse. Eco relates it back to the biblical story of Babel as portrayed in Genesis 11, where, prior to God's punishment of human hubris, all humans spoke the same language. God confounded human language, introducing linguistic diversity as a curse, a punishment that would yield confusion and conflict. But Eco notes that this is not the only version of the story of Babel in the Old Testament. Genesis 10 actually speaks of linguistic diversity before the construction of Babel as the result of gradual migration of different families and nations across the globe. Eco argues that this underlying assumption that linguistic diversity is a curse is at the heart of a long European history of trying to reunite humanity by creating a single perfect language. Eco bases his study on a simple question: "If languages were differentiated not as a punishment but simply as a result of a natural process, why must the confusion of tongues constitute a curse at all?"[29] My argument is that Lockean, instrumental accounts of language find linguistic diversity to be a "curse" or, in nonbiblical language, a barrier impeding the purpose of language that must be overcome.

The cultural approach to language postulates linguistic diversity not as a curse to be overcome but as an inherent feature of cultural diversity. I do not want to imply that this cultural perspective on language is an endorsement of Herder's or Humboldt's specific assessment of cultural value or democratic practice. Antoine Berman, for example, argues that the German Romantics, including Herder and Humboldt, were most interested in foreign languages and cultures for purposes of co-optation and incorporation that would enrich German culture.[30] I do think, however, that the cultural approach to language is a necessary point of departure for insisting that translation between different cultures and languages is central to any collective and democratic process of deliberation.[31] The crucial point here is that the European Union has been strengthening its commitment to a cultural approach and in many important ways distancing itself from the instrumental discourse of language. One reason for this shift is the recognition that instrumentalist approaches to language devalue linguistic diversity as a negative obstacle. Such an approach to linguistic diversity is likely to be unsuccessful in fostering a more integrated Europe. Instead, as we shall see, the European Union has moved to a more positive celebration of linguistic diversity.

The European Union's Multilingualism

The Language Policies of EU Institutions

Although the European Union has been increasingly involved in social and cultural policy especially since the Maastricht Treaty, it still officially maintains that language policy is out of its jurisdiction. The European Union has no "active" language policy per se, and the whole issue has been carefully avoided.[32] Technically, language policy remains the domain of its member states even more than education and culture, which are specifically dealt with in Maastricht Articles 126 and 128. There is no parallel article dealing with language, nor is it mentioned as a part of culture (as is the practice in some specific policies). Before questioning whether such a stance is even tenable, I will lay out the EU policies pertaining to its own institutions' linguistic practices – what I will call institutional multilingualism. In this arena, the European Union maintains a uniquely high degree of multilingualism.

Since 1958, with Regulation 1, the Council of Ministers specified that Dutch, French, German, and Italian are all "official and working languages" of the European Community's institutions and that they all have equal status.[33] This set the precedent that the major official language of each member state is an official and working language of the institutions of the European Community. With each new member, a new official and working language was added, except in cases such as Austria, where German was already an EC language.[34] Moreover, with Article 217 of the Treaty of Rome, matters of language use of the Community's institutions must be determined by unanimous consent of the Council of Ministers. This illustrates the importance of language issues from the beginnings of the EEC (European Economic Community).

This provision was restated in the Treaty of Nice and applies to the countries to be admitted in 2004.[35] The current eleven "official and working languages" create 110 translation pairs that need to be accommodated by the EU translation bureau. With any new language, the number of new translation pairs increases exponentially (n^2-n). Thus, in 2004, assuming that Malta will follow the precedent of Luxembourg and not demand equal status for Maltese, there will be twenty-one "official and working languages," creating 420 translation pairs. The European Parliament is recruiting 200 new translators for the new MPs to be elected in June 2004.[36] About a third of the current staff of the European Union's institutions are involved in translation or interpretation.

Of course, this does not mean that all the proceedings of the institutions are translated into all the "official languages" – far from it. Some commentators use the distinction between "working" and "official" languages to describe how, in the halls of the Parliament and most bureaucratic exchanges, French and English are the languages used. The European Commission in general uses three "working languages": French, English, and German. Many of the important committees to draft proposals work in various combinations of a few working languages.³⁷

But what this official eleven- (soon to be twenty-one-) language policy does mean is that all the major treaties and binding laws are translated into each official language, plus Irish (as one might expect, considering that the laws are legally binding within each member state). Most committees choose one or a few languages in which their proceedings and correspondence take place, most often some permutation of English, French, German, Spanish, or Italian.

Below I will discuss how the designation of "official and working languages" affected EU policies, especially educational programs that before the mid-1990s were limited to such languages. The other major impact of this institutional multilingualism is that it shapes how individual citizens of member states interact with the EU institutions. Article 8d of the Treaty of Amsterdam explicitly states that any citizen can write to any institution in any of the working languages of the European Union and receive an answer in the same language. On 11 December 1990, the Parliament adopted for itself the principle of "complete multilingualism," a principle that it states is "consistent with the respect which is owed to the dignity of all languages which reflect and express the cultures of the different peoples who make up the European Community."³⁸ In this way, democratic representation is tied directly to being able to represent oneself in one's own language. Of course, this arrangement does not extend this ideal to those whose language is different from the official language of their country.

Nevertheless, such a commitment to multilingualism is a marked contrast to the United Nations, which has English and French as its working languages and English, French, Russian, Chinese, Spanish, and Arabic as its official languages. Given its 189 members, this is a small and particularly European-dominant language regime. Most other intergovernmental and international organizations have at most a few working languages. Thus, the European Union's institutional language policy is an ambitious project that holds potential for showing that linguistic diversity is not a curse to be minimized.

We can see this commitment to such a high, complex, and expensive degree of institutional multilingualism as the result of political will framed in the language of the Treaties of Maastricht and Amsterdam and many other high-minded statements about the importance of cultural diversity and linguistic sensitivity. Or, from a more pragmatic and political viewpoint, I should note that, because language is highly symbolic of power, prestige, and identity, any proposal to decrease the number of working languages even slightly will meet stiff resistance from any member state whose language is being demoted. This was evident when Malta insisted that Maltese be an official language of the European Union.

We must also recognize that, however ambitious the European Union's institutional multilingualism is, it supports a specific set of languages falling short of the general, if utopian, support for the worth and dignity of all languages. Thus, the treaties and major legislation are translated into Danish but not Turkish, even though the number of Turkish speakers in the European Union is greater than the number of Danish speakers.[39] This absence of even minimal representation is also true of many other non-autochthonous languages such as Hindi, Arabic, and so on. Thus, the European Union does not live up to the goal of respecting linguistic diversity and providing representation for its citizens in a corresponding manner.

Of the 370 million inhabitants of the European Union, speaking over thirty different languages, fifty million do not speak the major or official language of the country in which they live.[40] Thus, over 13 percent of Europeans' lives explicitly contradict the one-state language model. A more comprehensive language policy is envisioned by the fact that the interpretation service of the European Commission is equipped to deliver translation and interpretation in 121 languages.[41] The cost of maintaining such a vast number of official languages would, of course, be astronomical.[42] But the point is that the European Union's particular version of multilingualism is not complete multilingualism, or even complete European multilingualism, but assumes a monolingual state model. It favours eleven state languages, followed by Irish and Letzeburgesh.[43]

This situation becomes more significant given my next argument that the European Union's cultural and educational policies increasingly support an implicit language policy. The effects of such cultural and educational policies also promote a limited version of multilingualism that contains a hierarchy of languages. If we are asking questions about democracy at the European level, then these considerations must be factored into assessments of the "democracy deficit." This situation is further supported by Peter Kraus's argument that the role of language and language standardization differed considerably among nineteenth-century European nation-states. Kraus notes that France is the only member of the European Union whose Constitution refers to a single official language (the general model yielding the one-member-state, one-language formula).[44]

General Implicit Language Policy within Educational and Cultural Programs

I now turn to the argument that this language policy ostensibly covering only EU institutions in fact constitutes a general language policy – at least a minimal one. The institutional language regime may not have an obvious effect on language usage within the daily lives of all residents of EU member states. It may be tempting to isolate the linguistic policies and practices of the EU institutions from the much more complex questions of general language policy. This would effectively sever the questions of suprastate democracy from issues of language and democratic representation. It is also politically pragmatic for the European Union itself to distinguish its internal, institutional language usage from general language policy concerning citizens because linguistic politics is a mucky battlefield.

However, such a division obscures what is really at stake in the role of language policy for European integration and the democracy deficit. The question of language, as will be argued below, is one underdiscussed indicator of the much discussed *"demos," "no demos,"* or *"demoi"* theses in debates on the possibility of a European democracy.[45] With the Maastricht Treaty, the European Union embarked on a substantial increase in social and cultural initiatives. While ostensibly respecting the authority of member states and adopting the vague notion of subsidiarity, Maastricht includes articles specifically relating to educational and cultural policy (Articles 126 and 128). Article 126 gives the European Union the right to develop educational policies supporting and supplementing the member states' responsibilities. This most explicitly includes "developing the European dimension in education, particularly through the teaching and dissemination of the languages of Member States."[46]

Maastricht Article 128, "Culture," states that "The Community shall contribute to the flowering of the cultures of the Member States, while respecting their national and regional diversity and at the same time bringing the common cultural heritage to the fore." While this includes "artistic and literary creation, including in the audio-visual sector," it is notable that there is no mention of language or linguistic diversity. Nonetheless, with the impetus of Maastricht, the 1990s saw a great expansion of cultural and educational programs that involve language teaching and learning. These have a substantial impact on general language usage.[47]

The Lingua (launched 1989) and Erasmus (1987) programs foreshadowed this development and were greatly expanded after Maastricht by Socrates (1995 first phase, 2001 second phase) and Leonardo. The goal of Erasmus was to enable 10 percent of university students to spend time in another EU country.[48] Lingua is aimed at foreign-language teachers facilitating their training and travelling within the European Union. It covers the eleven official languages of the European Union plus Irish and Luxembourgish (or Letzeburgesh), with special attention to "the least widely used and taught languages *of the* Community."[49] But it does not include Catalan, Friulian, or Saami, let alone Turkish, Mandarin, or Arabic.

The Socrates program was launched in 1995 to "encourage cooperation between Member States" in the field of education to "support and supplement their action while fully respecting their responsibility for the content of teaching and organization of educational systems, and their cultural and linguistic diversity."[50]

These are just part of the general objective of the Council of Ministers that all pupils of the member states should "have the opportunity of learning two languages of the Union other than their mother tongue(s) for a minimum of two consecutive years during compulsory education."[51] This resolution provides quite specific pronouncements on how the languages of the Union are to be encouraged at all levels from early childhood to university and adult education, including measures for teachers' instruction, the use of new media technologies, and extensive language visits to other countries. In considering non-Union languages, the resolution makes a telling comment with no specific recommendations for how to achieve its goals: "the provision of teaching for languages which are less widely used or less frequently taught should be increased and diversified *as far as possible,* at the levels of teaching and throughout all types of curricula."[52] Given that these languages are excluded from all the previous provisions, this provision pales in comparison. Thus, the linguistic diversity that this policy seeks to foster is a specific diversity – the official EU languages – to the exclusion of other languages.

Joshua Fishman, one of the leading scholars in sociolinguistics, argues that such a specific or select diversity fostered by EU multilingualism is actually detrimental to what he labels "ethnolinguistic democracy." Because the ideal of equal respect for all languages is being applied only at the interstate level, it can create greater discrimination against minority languages at the subnational level. As he notes using a specific example, "The Netherlands is very certain that Nederlands is as good a language as English for the operation of the EC [European Community], but it is not sure that Frisian is as good a language as Nederlands for the operation of local public services in Friesland."[53] As a sociolinguist, Fishman is particularly concerned about the resources needed for and the commitment to corpus planning that actually make a language suitable for public administration and internationally intertranslatable with English as a global language. His assessment is related to my point above that a European multilingualism of eleven languages, however ambitious, is still a restricting language regime. It assumes that linguistic diversity exists at the national level and not below. Fishman goes further by suggesting that such an eleven-language multilingualism actually reinforces the power of official state languages over other nonofficial languages.

As with the policy governing language use in European institutions, the educational programs of the European Union foster not all linguistic diversity but a particular hierarchy of languages with the eleven official languages nearer the top. Increasingly, especially due to pressure from language activists, these programs include and emphasize minority and less-used languages (many of which are included in the eleven official languages). We shall see below that since the early 1990s there has been a trend to include and emphasize lesser-used European languages and those of future member countries and to pay greater lip service to all languages. But the structures and programs to promote linguistic diversity have so far predominantly favoured the eleven official languages.

As with many EU programs, the educational initiatives are designed to support and encourage the actions of the member states. In this sense, the Union does not formally tread on the toes of national sovereignty. But by the same token, such programs clearly have influence and are aimed at upholding the member states' official languages.[54] If we assume, as many linguists do, that languages compete with one another, such programs will be to the detriment of all nonofficial languages used in the European Union.[55] The Union highlights the notion that languages and linguistic diversity (at least within the eleven official languages)[56] are a wealth to be encouraged. In the field of education, language barriers are overcome through increased knowledge and learning of languages. And the diversity of eleven languages is deemed a rich resource to be exploited by the creation of multilingual citizens.

I contend that the particular combination of educational and cultural policies coupled with EU policies around its own institutional language practices constitutes a general language policy comparable to the language policies of Italy, France, and Germany in the nineteenth century. Numerous scholars have argued that European integration cannot be equated with the nineteenth-century unification of European nation-states.[57] Both Kraus and Loos support this assessment with specific reference to language policy.[58] But if we look at what actually constitutes "national language policy," we find that legislation such as Quebec's Bill 101, which attempts to censor specific linguistic usage, tends to be anomalous. Language policy is more often constituted by educational policy that fosters specific language usage and the subsidizing of grammar books, dictionaries, and the like.

This is not the place to engage in a detailed historical comparison between the nineteenth-century language policies of Italy or France and EU educational and cultural initiatives. But as Charles Tilly notes in describing the consolidation of European nation-states, "Through schools, museums, literature, and rules of public administration [European states] began imposing national languages selected or adapted from dialects that had previously abounded in their territories."[59] Tilly's description of the language policies clearly includes the realm of activities over which the

European Union is increasingly taking jurisdiction. While the Union is using its educational, cultural, and information technology initiatives to foster not one but eleven languages, it is still promoting certain language usage over others – the essential method of national language policies. Of course, it is significant that the EU educational initiatives do not constitute a policy in terms of an educational system or an over-ruling of member state autonomy with regard to education and the like. Nevertheless, to the extent that the various EU programs and initiatives on education, culture, and information technology are effective, they constitute a de facto language policy.

Indeed, as we shall see below, in the discussions around the European Year of Languages 2001, eEurope, and other initiatives, the European Commission, the Council of Ministers, the Parliament, and the Committee of the Regions all make this strong connection between education, culture, and language. Given these conditions, it seems to be increasingly untenable to maintain a sharp distinction between policies that govern the EU institutions and a more general European language policy for all citizens of Europe. As with education, culture, and other areas, the European Union is very careful to attempt to work with, encourage, and complement the actions of its members. It tries hard not to over-rule them and often invokes the notion of subsidiarity. But unless these encouragements are ineffective, they do constitute the promotion of specific language usages that inherently deters other language practices. Thus, the European Union is following an ambitious policy of multilingualism that I argue extends well beyond the borders of its own institutions. This constitutes its de jure multilingualism with de facto effects.

The Implications of de Jure Multilingualism and de Facto Increase in English

Using Pierre Bourdieu's concepts of "linguistic capital" and "symbolic power," Eugène Loos argues persuasively that it will be almost impossible to decrease the number of working languages or change the precedent that one official language of each member state becomes an "official and working" language of the EU institutions. However, he suggests that this de jure multilingualism does not rule out a de facto use of English as a lingua franca, creating a possible "balance between a workable communicative situation and the respect for a multilinguistic EU democracy."[60] In this way, Loos argues that there is no necessary conflict between de jure multilingualism and de facto operations in English.

The de facto spread of English is certainly beyond doubt. The recent *Eurobarometer* survey on language confirms the growing spread and use of English. Forty-one percent of the non-British Europeans surveyed said that they "know" English as a foreign language.[61] The *Economist* interpreted these results to mean that "English *is* the EU's lingua franca ... the European Union's tongue."[62] The *Guardian* responded similarly, adding that, since Romano Prodi, president of the commission, used English instead of Italian in his address at the Helsinki Summit in 1999, English is also the "working political language."[63] If we are concerned with democracy, then we should question such a hasty conclusion, given that it leaves out the 59 percent of the respondents who do not "know" English and underestimates the effects of different competency and comfort levels. However, the status and spread of English are clear.

While more complex in diagnosis and prescription, Peter Kraus's analysis of this situation is not altogether different than that of Loos. Kraus explicitly discusses the complexity of language politics as tied to the democracy deficit, the historical unification of European nation-states, and the symbolism of European integration. But he too sees the growing dominance of English as a de facto trend "at least at the level of economic, cultural and political elites." Like Loos, he argues that this de facto trend cannot be translated into a de jure reality because "any attempt to concede English an openly privileged position in the all-European communication network provokes decidedly negative responses by those EU members fearing the political devaluation of their state language."[64] And he connects this double bind with the problems of any attempt to create a European public sphere "from above" since it is likely to create an anti-European backlash.[65] But, like Loos, Kraus argues that this seeming "stalemate" is solvable. He proposes that various different "solutions" can be attained at different levels of government within the European Union, its member states, and their subnational and regional units. This involves importing the ambiguous concept of subsidiarity into the "language question" and combining it with ideas of passive bilingualism. Thus, the most local level of governance would make the important decisions about its own language policy. But this could be quite a different "solution" from the linguistic arrangements at higher and larger levels of government. Such arrangements could involve varying levels of distinction between competently speaking a language and passively understanding it. Kraus applauds such an approach since, among other reasons, it turns language issues into public concerns, matters of public debate and discussion. He suggests that this would add to the democratic legitimacy of Europe.

In many ways, I concur with Kraus except to the extent that the ambiguity of his approach results in the increasing gap between de jure and de facto language situations.[66] Where Kraus argues that language problems should be split up and approached in a plural fashion, I think that doing so may further add to the very nondemocratic split – to which Kraus himself calls attention – between the well-educated business and political elite (who may use English) and average European citizens (who may be much less comfortable in the language used to decide how they should be governed). Kraus's position may be productive in going beyond a dogmatic insistence that citizens cannot be represented in a language or languages different from those that they actually speak. His vision entails differing levels of multilingualism among citizens and insists that language use and language policy should be a topic about which representative democracy makes decisions. Ultimately, however, as I will argue below, Kraus's framework refuses to decide between two fundamentally different and conflicting notions of what language is. These two different conceptions of language also correspond to different political ideals that specifically involve incompatible notions of the role of language within democratic representation.

EU Policies Involving Language

Both the instrumental and the cultural perspectives on language are evident in EU policy documents. Moreover, they are competing with one another, and, in the past few years at least, the latter seems to be taking the upper hand. It would be overly simplistic to attribute this trend solely to a concern with the democracy deficit and an attempt to redress the perception that the European Union is overly bureaucratic and out of touch with most Europeans, but it certainly takes place within this context. Of course, it is possible that an expensive and complex multilingual arrangement may be perceived as the result of petty national pride and "out of touch" with the global trend toward English. This remains an open debate, but it is already well under way within EU policy documents.

It is not uncommon to find linguistic diversity being discussed as a problem, obstacle, or impediment to integration in various policies, especially those on commerce, media, and technology from the early 1990s. The Telematics program is one example of this. As a chief component of the Directorate General XIII on the Information Society, from 1994 to 1998 its budget was 898 million ECUs. The Telematics program terminology of "language engineering" promoted the "harnessing" of maximum information transfer.[67] Computer translation was to remove the barriers of linguistic diversity. As Brian Blunden told the audience of a conference on European Telematics sponsored by the European Commission, "Ultimately speech input and automatic machine translation will also make linguistic barriers irrelevant."[68] Thus, linguistic diversity is "protected" only through making it irrelevant and invisible, not because it is valued as a rich aspect of life.

Even in its decision on a program to promote linguistic diversity in the "information society" (i.e., the Internet), the Council of Ministers describes such diversity as a barrier: "Whereas industry and all other players concerned must work out specific and adequate solutions to overcome the *linguistic barriers* if they are to benefit fully from the advantages of the internal market and remain competitive on world markets ..."[69] In its response to the council's decision to fund such programs, the Committee of the Regions (COR) pinpoints the exact philosophical tension in which I am interested. It is worth quoting a long section to make this clear:

> Computerized systems are an excellent tool for systematization, generalization and dissemination of terms, vocabularies, dictionaries and other standardized information ... Languages and linguistic expression, *on the other hand*, are a cultural phenomenon, intimately tied in with the cultural sphere where they are used. While computerized systems are designed with a view to simplification, language systems are based on a wealth of nuances and expressions. The COR therefore stresses that the programme presented has not paid sufficient attention to *these two aspects* and suggests that the Commission communication should be supplemented by a discussion that highlights this *contradiction* between the two objectives of the programme.[70]

COR is making explicit the trend toward promoting linguistic diversity because it is integral to culture and how people perceive and engage in the world that has become increasingly strong in numerous policies since the mid-1990s. In contrast to the very vocabulary of the Telematics program that ended in 1998, the eEurope program launched in 1999 to co-ordinate information technology initiatives contains a Multilingual Information Society Program dedicated to promoting linguistic diversity, industries related to language and translation, and accessibility of the Internet in various languages.[71]

On 19 January 1995, the Parliament unanimously adopted a resolution exhibiting this point.[72] It reaffirmed the equal status of all eleven European languages and noted that appointing separate "working languages" would downgrade a considerable proportion of EU inhabitants to "second class citizens."[73] It stated that all citizens must be able to address each and every EU institution in their own language, regardless of technical and financial costs. Of course, parliamentary resolutions are not binding, and without the Council of Ministers the Parliament remains ineffective.

However, the council has been adopting similar positions. In education, there has been some movement toward accepting the notion that all languages, not just official or state languages, are important for European integration. So, where Socrates I excluded all languages besides the eleven European languages,[74] Socrates II is open to non-EU countries, including Iceland, Norway, Central and Eastern European countries, Malta, Cyprus, and Turkey. Socrates II includes not only the majority languages of these countries but also minority languages.

Moreover, 2001 was declared the EU Year of Languages. In their decision, the Parliament and the Council of Ministers argued that the ability to use foreign languages is essential to Article 18 of the treaty: "to move and reside freely within the territory of Member States." They also explicitly included language within Article 151 on contributing to cultural diversity and repeated their earlier sentiment that "All the European languages, in their spoken and written forms, are equal in value and dignity from the cultural point of view and form an integral part of European cultures and civilisation." They thus connect linguistic diversity to the "concept of European citizenship." Especially compared with the earlier language of the council quoted above, it is striking that linguistic diversity is nowhere here presented as a barrier, obstacle, or impediment to integration. Quite the contrary, linguistic diversity is an asset to be celebrated.

Obviously, the politics and rhetoric involved in such policy documents are the result of complex negotiations, compromises, and jostling for power. The policies may not have simple or straightforward effects when implemented. There remains great ambiguity as to whether by "European languages" this decision excludes Arabic, Hindi, Chinese, and so on and implies that they are unequal to "European languages." But if we look at this and other documents, it seems that the EU institutions have rejected Locke's view of language as primarily an instrument of communication, Genesis 11's view of linguistic diversity as a curse, and the argument that the "language problem" will soon be solved by the de facto spread of English or through computer translation. While neither the Parliament nor the Council of Ministers states it explicitly, they have come much closer to the position expressed by a participant at a conference on language and the European Union organized in part by the European Parliament: "if a language policy that favours multilingualism is going to cost money, then let it cost money, because it is vital for the democratization of our societies."[75]

This analysis does not indicate that the cultural vision of language has totally triumphed over ideas about language rooted in an instrumentalist or Lockean vein. The political and technical problems associated with communication in a supranational framework are complex, and the current round of unprecedented enlargement promises dramatic changes of various kinds. However, the cultural vision of language is clearly gaining prominence, as I have shown: educational programs are adding nonofficial EU languages to their purview; language issues are gaining a higher profile within the EU institutions, including declarations such as the 2001 Year of Languages; and even in the realm of telematics and language "engineering" there is an avoidance of "demonizing" linguistic diversity, since it is now recognized as being associated with "cultural diversity." It is difficult to know the extent to which some of this is superficial, and, as the technology for computer translation becomes better, perhaps the European Union will decrease its commitment to teaching and fostering multilingual citizens.

I am not contending that the European Union has found a solution to the challenges that language poses for democracy. For example, Juan Delgado-Moreira's analysis of the use of "culture" in EU policies applies also to language. Delgado-Moreira argues that the commission, on the one hand, justifies spending on cultural projects as an aspect of its resource redistribution policy aimed at fostering social cohesion within the European Union necessary for stability required for economic prosperity. On the other hand, such cultural projects are supposed to foster European civic identity or a transnational notion of citizenship. Delgado-Moreira argues that, because the former takes place on the local and regional levels where nationalism is embedded, it is necessarily at odds with the idea of European civic identity that is, in effect, an attempt to counteract such nationalism.[76] Multilingual policies seem to contain similar contradictions, often trying to shore up national languages (especially against the threat of English) in the name of linguistic diversity but dampening linguistic diversity at the local level through the hegemonic status of the national language.

Nevertheless, paying closer attention to the changing assumptions about what language is and how linguistic diversity is depicted has serious implications for understanding democratic representation. When the dominance of English is viewed as inevitable (beyond democratic control) or multilingualism is relegated to a de jure ideal, the possibilities of democratic representation are severely handicapped, and the de facto, daily lives of Europeans are affected.

Conclusion

Extending democracy beyond the borders of the nation-state is one of the most pressing goals of our so-called globalizing world. Suprastate, international, and transnational organizations seem to have a growing impact on our daily lives, yet they are out of the realm of significant democratic control or accountability. For democracy to be anything but a hollow ideal, average people must be able to have an impact on these institutions and how they operate. I do not think that it is just coincidence that such circumstances have come to the fore as many political theorists have raised theories of "deliberative" and "participatory" democracy, insisting on the importance of civil society and public spheres for debate and discussion.

The language situation in the European Union provides an ideal intersection where these issues of globalization and democracy meet theories of deliberative and participatory democracy, public spheres, and civil society. Precisely because it has taken on more powers and responsibilities associated with sovereignty than other supranational organizations such as the United Nations, the World Trade Organization, nongovernmental organizations or transnational corporations, the European Union is a crucial site of investigation. For the same reasons that the term "democracy deficit" became common as a criticism of the European Union before its more general application to these other organizations, the Union is more than just one case study among others of the future of democracy.

I have argued that, within the policies and documents of the institutions of the European Union, there are different and competing notions of what language is and how it is related to democratic representation. These documents and policies seem to challenge the assumptions of Habermas, Loos, and others that a de jure multilingual arrangement can proceed in harmony with the de facto increase of English as a working language of the Union, its institutions, and its communications with citizens. To side with Habermas and Loos because they have a more accurate theoretical picture of language (not that I think they do, but even if they did) would be to reject the notion that language is fundamentally a human institution and that our use of it is under our control. The European Union itself seems to be strengthening its commitment to a more cultural approach to language at odds with the presumptions of a Lockean vision of language in which linguistic diversity is a barrier to communication. While we should not jump to the conclusion that this more cultural approach to language is the direct result of concerns over democratic legitimacy, or that it will address such concerns, this acceptance does demonstrate a degree of what Habermas calls political will formation at the (perhaps elite) level of the institutions involved. So far, I do not see any development of a political will in favour of "English as a second language." This option seems to be driven by a sense of inevitability or pragmatic concern over the cost of multilingualism.

Of course, there is continuing contradiction and tension within the European Union's various policies and positions, especially among the different institutions. And much more detailed research is required to assess the forces and politics involved that yield the documents and policies like the ones that I have discussed. Nevertheless, to assume that the continued spread of English as a "lingua franca" for the European Union – not due to some conscious public political debate but as a default – is not in tension with the vision of a multilingual, multicultural, democratic political entity is deeply flawed. Such an assumption has repercussions for any theory of deliberative democracy and the democratic potential of suprastate organizations.

Acknowledgments

I would like to thank Heather Beattie, my research assistant for this project, and the Social Sciences and Humanities Research Council of Canada for its financial support. I would also like to thank UBC Press's anonymous reviewers for valuable suggestions for revision.

Notes

1 Author's translation. For a slightly different translation, see Gramsci (1985), 183-84.
2 De Swaan (1993), 244. De Swaan (1999), 13-24, repeated this assessment when a significant amount of scholarly work was being published on the topic.
3 See Loos (2000), 37-53; and Kraus (2000), 138-63. Before this work, the field in English was characterized by a focus on policy issues, planning, and human rights to the neglect of questions of democratic theory: see Coulmas (1991); and Skutnabb-Kangas and Phillipson (1994). The non-scholarly press has become increasingly interested in this issue: for examples, see "English" (2001); and Black (2002).
4 Patten (2001) makes a similar argument about the general dearth of attention to language policy from what he calls "the normative point of view," meaning liberal theories of citizenship, rights, multiculturalism, and the like.
5 For example, Anderson (1991); Bourdieu (1991); Bell (1995); and Weber (1976).
6 Walzer (1998), 10-11, has summarized the democracy deficit as when "democratic politics in the ordinary sense, the open competition of parties and leaders, will remain national in character while Euro-wide decision making will continue to take place largely out of public view." Habermas (1997) describes it more specifically as the result of binding law made at the EU level that is not made through a state with a democratic constitution, legitimate monopoly on violence, and internationally recognized sovereignty. This volume is one example of the neglect of language within debates over democratic legitimacy and the future of the European Union.
7 Habermas (1997), 264. He has also admitted that the language problem is one of the potential pitfalls in his "third way," besides Euro-skepticism and Euro-mercantilism. See Petrucciani (1998) for an account of his lecture at the Goethe Institute in Rome on 10 June 1998.
8 Habermas discusses the importance of language to German unification and relates that process to the current EU development but omits any actual discussion of a common EU language. See "What Is a People?" in Habermas (2001b), 1-25. I discuss similar omissions in the work of Umberto Eco and Jacques Derrida in previous papers: see Ives (1998, 1999).
9 See, for example, Habermas (1998, 2001b).
10 Habermas (2001a), 19.
11 Benhabib (1996), 68.
12 The many feminist critiques of Habermas that led him to re-articulate his theory of communication and public sphere in *Between Facts and Norms* are one example, including those of Nancy Fraser, Iris Marion Young, and the collection *Feminists Read Habermas*; see Meehan (1995). I also have in mind the type of argument that Melissa Williams makes in Williams (2000) and Denise Réaume's argument in Réaume (2000) that Kymlicka's framework is insufficient to account for the non-individual nature of language.
13 See Phillipson (2003). While Phillipson is most concerned with policy and is not a political theorist, he provides a thorough overview and insightful analysis of many of the political and theoretical issues at stake. In the past few years alone, there have been a large number of works on language and the European Union; see, for example, Julios (2002); and Carson (2003).
14 The complex reasons for their increasing acceptance of strong connections between language and culture are beyond the scope of this chapter. I commend the attempts of the European Union to accommodate multilingualism (which Catherine Frost discusses in the next chapter), although, as will become obvious below, they often do not go far enough, and some measures may strengthen some national languages but be detrimental to other languages. Of course, such strategies may not necessarily be responses to pressures against the European Union's lack of democratic legitimacy. They may have more to do with the symbolic importance of language to national politics and could, as Cris

Shore (1997) suggests, represent more conservative and static attempts to manipulate culture for political purposes.
15 Ives (2003), especially on Habermas, 158-75. See also Ives (1997).
16 See the contributions to Skutnabb-Kangas and Phillipson (1994).
17 Locke (1995), 321-423.
18 Locke (1995), 384-424.
19 Chase (1997), 79. I have explored this issue at greater length in Ives (1997).
20 Moreover, other philosophies distinct from that of Locke share with him the presumption that linguistic diversity is a problem to be overcome. As Anthony La Vopa (1995), 16, testifies, "In the philosophical tradition in which Kant (and the young Habermas) stood, linguistic diversity was something of an inconvenience, a drag on philosophers' aspirations to commune above everyday speech and across national boundaries, a realm of universal abstractions."
21 Searle (1975).
22 See Lakoff and Johnson (1980), 11-13; and Reddy (1979).
23 An underlying assumption here is that society is constituted by isolated individuals prior to language and that language is one thing that enables them to be connected.
24 Patten (2001). See also Kymlicka (1995, 2001).
25 Réaume (2001), 249-51.
26 For an argument highlighting their commonalities, see Helfer (1990).
27 While Chomsky often attributes his fundamental insights to Humboldt, the influence is quite one-sided. I have discussed this in part in Ives (2001).
28 The classic defence of Herder's thought vis-à-vis democracy is Bernard (1965). For a recent balanced summary, see La Vopa (1995), especially 17-20. The other classic essays include Berlin (1976); and Taylor (1995).
29 Eco (1995), 6-10.
30 Berman (1992).
31 I address this in greater detail in Ives (2000) and in Chapter 3 of Ives (2003). The importance of translation to my argument here is thanks to the participants of the Representation and Its Discontents Workshop at the Annual Meeting of the Canadian Political Science Association, 31 May 2002.
32 Loos (2000), 146; De Swaan (1999).
33 Only the Court of Justice is exempt from the requirement that all languages be accorded equal status.
34 Luxembourgish (or Letzeburgesh) was exempted even though it is the mother tongue of most Luxembourgers presumably because German and French are also widely spoken and official languages of Luxembourg and because French is historically the language of administration and professional usage. Irish is another special case since, although it is an official language of Ireland, only about 30,000 Irish speak it as a mother tongue. So it has official recognition but not equal status (see Catherine Frost's chapter in this volume for further discussion). Only the treaties and major legislation are translated into Irish. German accounts for both Germany and Austria, and Belgium is accounted for by French and Nederlands (Dutch).
35 Negotiations with potential members do not follow this multilingualism, and Robert Phillipson notes several cases in which English was granted precedence over Polish and Czech at times, including that the English version of agreements was the only "authentic" one. As Phillipson (2003), 123-24, points out, "in theory" this should change as candidates become members.
36 Black (2002).
37 Phillipson (2003), 117-20, notes that the distinction between "official" and "working" languages derives from the League of Nations as adapted by the United Nations and that in the EU context any such distinction is misleading. The increasing use of English has given rise to concerns particularly about barriers to democratic equality. See notes by Truchot, Skinner, and Tanzilli (1999), 89-92; and Phillipson (2003), 110-38.
38 See Fishman (1994). Fishman notes the irony that this resolution was adopted because of pressure from Catalan activists trying to gain some official recognition for their language, which it has not attained.

39 For a discussion, see Barbour (1996). Ironically, the membership of Cyprus will make Turkish an "official and working" EU language, even though the number of its Turkish speakers is far fewer than Germany's Turkish speakers.
40 Fisk (1996), 177.
41 Truchot, Skinner, and Tanzilli (1999), 90.
42 In 1994, the Parliament spent a third of its budget on translating and interpreting. But, as Bister-Broosen and Willenmyns (1999) point out, compared with the entire EU budget, translation and related services constitute only 2 percent, less than the commuting costs for Parliamentarians between Brussels, Strasbourg, and Luxembourg.
43 As we'll see below, various regional languages have been added to Lingua, Socrates, and other programs even with an emphasis over the major languages.
44 Kraus (2000), 146.
45 For example, the debate in Gowan and Anderson (1997) among Grimm, Habermas, and Weiler. See also Smith in the same volume, 318-42.
46 Treaty Establishing the European Union, Article 126.2.
47 As we shall see, this connection between education, culture, and language, while implicit in EU policy in the early 1990s, became increasingly explicit especially with the European Year of Languages 2001.
48 Gubbins (1996) discusses the outcomes of these programs, noting that, in 1993-94, 118,000 students took part in Lingua and Erasmus, representing only 1.5 percent of the European university student body, at the cost of 73.98 ECUs. Moreover, the students chose disproportionately to go to the countries where the European Union's most prominent languages are spoken, 33 percent to the United Kingdom, 22 percent to France, 10 percent to Germany, and 8 percent to Italy, thus not supporting the diversity of all the EU languages equally.
49 Document 598PC0329. Decision No. 819/95/EC, *Official Journal of the European Communities* L087 (20 April 1995): 10. Hereafter cited as *OJ*.
50 *OJ* L087 (20 April 1995): 10.
51 This resolution notes immediately following that it is still for each member state to determine language skills necessary for competence and certification. "Council Resolution of 31 March 1995 on Improving and Diversifying Language Learning and Teaching within the Education Systems of the European Union," *OJ* C207 (12 July 1995): 1-5.
52 *OJ* C207: 4; emphasis added.
53 Fishman (1994), 55.
54 The actual effectiveness of these programs needs to be examined. But here it is significant that, even if ineffective, these policies define the more general advocacy of the protection of cultural and linguistic diversity.
55 For one explicit example of this approach by a political scientist, see Laponce (1987). Réaume (2000), 251, takes a similar position. For an opposing perspective, see Barbour (1996).
56 Irish and Luxembourgish were added to the proposals for the second phase of Socrates, 1 January 2000-31 December 2004; see Document No. 598PC0329.
57 The European Commission itself made this argument as early as 1975 in its submission to the Tindemans Report; see Bainbridge (1998), 466.
58 Kraus (2000), 138-41; Loos (2000), 45. Virginie Mamadouh (1999), 120, sees greater parallels between the current phase of EU integration and the European "nation building" processes of the nineteenth century.
59 Tilly (1992), 707.
60 Loos (2000), 48.
61 "Executive Summary" (2001), 1. French was next, with 19 percent. Fifty-three percent of all Europeans surveyed said they can speak at least one European (i.e., official) language in addition to their own mother tongue. We should also keep in mind that the level of competency might not translate into the ability to follow political discussions without significant use of time and energy, let alone an equal ability to participate in politics with fluent or native English speakers.
62 "English" (2001), 50; emphasis added. Adding in British citizens and presuming that English is their mother tongue, the *Economist* suggests that well over half of EU citizens

speak English and that this growing trend means soon there will be no de facto language problem. Obviously, the European Union is not a superstate, but from a democratic perspective we might argue that it is not good enough that over half of the citizens of France speak the only official language of the country. By neglecting the large numbers of people who do not speak any English, this perspective severely handicaps overcoming any democracy deficit, let alone the point that those who speak English may not speak it well or comfortably or want their political participation to be in English.

63 Black (2002b), 15.
64 Kraus (2000), 159.
65 Kraus's solution is different from that of Loos in that Kraus explicitly condones linking language questions with ongoing public debates about Europe's political future, presumably exposing the incompatibility between the de facto and de jure language situations. He terms his proposal the replacement of "official officialism" with "plural pluralism" by making political and linguistic compromises at different levels of institutions. Thus, the European Union should not attempt to adopt any universal language policies or resolve the questions at all levels but allow for various language regimes for local, regional, national, and Union-wide levels. Given the recent electoral success of Le Pen and other indications of extreme right-wing resurgence, such backlashes pose a significant danger.
66 The distinction between de jure and de facto (used by Loos and Kraus) is not that between ideal and actual but that between the multilingualism that is "according to the law" – that accords with the legal framework of the European Union contained in its treaties and legislation – and the actual linguistic practices that occur both inside the EU institutions and between those institutions and citizens.
67 See <http://www.cordis.lu/telematics/home.html>.
68 Blunden (1998).
69 "Council Decision" (1996), 40; emphasis added.
70 *OJ* C337: 50; emphasis added.
71 See <http://europa.eu.int/information_society/eeurope/index_en.htm>.
72 As cited and discussed by Bister-Broosen and Willemyns (1999), 718-19.
73 The irony here with the language of "inhabitants" as opposed to citizens is that those who have a nonofficial language for a mother tongue are relegated to "second class citizens" by this decision's logic.
74 For example, a 1996 project funded by Lingua A that included Catalan specifically noted that the funds for that component were derived from elsewhere. See <http://europa.eu.int/comm/education/socrates/lingua/comp/act-a.html>.
75 Reported by Truchot, Skinner, and Tanzilli (1999), 96.
76 Delgado-Moreira (2000).

3 Getting to Yes: People, Practices, and the Paradox of Multicultural Democracy
Catherine Frost

This chapter starts out as an attempt to make sense of two very different accounts of the relationship between democratic practices and multicultural realities. It ends by arguing that what makes these accounts so different is also the key to reconciling democratic and multicultural principles when they pull in different directions.

The two accounts appear in this volume. One is offered by Peter Ives and the other by Avigail Eisenberg. The setting of each is quite different. One is concerned with the European Union, while the other draws heavily on Canadian examples. Yet there are important similarities between them. Both are concerned with how democratic institutions or practices may help or hinder us when it comes to multicultural recognition. Specifically, each asks whether particular institutions – language policy in Ives's case and referendums in Eisenberg's – help us to achieve group-based accommodation. Yet the two accounts reach very different conclusions. Ives ends on a harmonious note, suggesting that democratic institutions are catching up with multicultural realities, while Eisenberg ends on a note of caution and advises us that some kinds of democratic practice may work against such accommodation.

In the discussion that follows, I raise a number of concerns regarding the approaches adopted in these accounts. In the case of Ives's account, I argue that the role of language cannot be neatly sorted into either intrinsic or instrumental value categories because people may favour one language for instrumental reasons and another for intrinsic reasons. These different choices mean that any conclusions about the relationship of language and democracy based on this distinction are tenuous.

In response to Eisenberg's account, I suggest that we may be facing a bigger challenge than Eisenberg acknowledges. Even given the problems inherent in certain democratic practices, we cannot get away from the need to ratify the legitimacy of multicultural measures. But what if the obstacles to multicultural justice lie not just with the principles we find in particular practices or institutions but also with those we find in people? If this is the case – if people's democratically expressed preferences arise in understandings of justice that can make multicultural accommodation harder to achieve – then we face a daunting task. We need to find ways to transform these understandings without doing violence to either the democratic or the multicultural features of our communities.

We might call this the "paradox of multicultural democracy," naming it after another multiculturalism paradox coined by Ayelet Shachar.[1] Shachar's "paradox of multicultural vulnerability" points out that in accommodating certain minority cultures we may unwittingly be putting at risk the rights of some vulnerable group members. Yet if we do not find ways to accommodate those cultures, then we risk hollowing out our multicultural commitments. The "paradox of multicultural democracy" involves a similar catch-22 situation. If we submit multicultural measures to democratic review, then we run the risk that the measures will be rejected. If we do not, then we risk hollowing out our democratic life.

How can we resolve this paradox? To reconcile rights protection and multiculturalism, Shachar develops a jurisdictional solution based on power-sharing practices and institutional innovation. Perhaps institutions and practices are where we should begin as well, this time with a view to reconciling democratic and multicultural priorities. If, as Eisenberg argues, referendums handicap efforts at multicultural accommodation because of a built-in predisposition toward formal equality, then perhaps there are other democratic practices that engage a different understanding of equality. One such practice, I suggest, is deliberative democracy, because it aims at reaching a more nuanced understanding of justice, one that draws on deep intuitions about what seems to be fair.

In fact, Greg Pyrcz in this volume tries to apply the deliberative democracy solution to the problem of achieving a just community. But what Pyrcz leaves out of his account is, I suggest, exactly what has the greatest potential for achieving the transformation we need. That is, he leaves out popular participation. Instead of delegating democratic deliberation to a representative, as Pyrcz recommends, or curtailing the wayward use of referendums as Eisenberg suggests, I argue that we need to harness the transformative potential of democratic participation, whether that is through deliberative practices, the judicious use of referendums, or any other means that seem fitting. Only in this way can multiculturalism become grounded in people's preferences and not just in public institutions.

Multilingualism under the European Union

Let me begin with Ives's account of multilingualism in the European Union. Ives takes us on something of an emotional roller coaster through this account because at one moment it seems that we should be ready to denounce the Union's insensitive policies and at the next that we should congratulate the Union for its insightful stance on language. Yet at the end of the day, there is a distinct feeling that, whatever stumbles it may make, the European Union is at least headed in the right direction. It has come down on the right side of the diversity conundrum. Let me recap how this account unfolds.

Ives begins with an important question. What is the relationship between democracy and language? He does not answer this question himself, but he does give us two perspectives on the issue. The first is a Lockean view, which sees language as something instrumental and suggests that linguistic diversity can be an inconvenience or a barrier to communication. The second is a Herderian view, whereby language is intrinsically valuable and the maintenance of linguistic diversity is key to other goods (e.g., authenticity).

Ives then sketches three possible responses to the language situation in the European Union. The first is what we might call "full multilingualism" under which no language is disadvantaged by the institutionalization of the Union. The second, which we might call "broad multilingualism," pretty much reflects the existing EU policy and amounts, as Ives suggests, to a hierarchy of languages (eleven working languages plus two special-case languages – Irish and Luxembourgish – into which treaties and major legislation are translated). And the third is what amounts to "the triumph of English," which involves the de facto pre-eminence of English so that linguistic diversity is no longer a particular challenge. As we can see, the three options line up nicely with the two views of language outlined earlier. For instance, option 1 ("full multilingualism") lines up with Herder, option 3 ("triumph of English") lines up with Locke, and option 2 ("broad multilingualism") is a compromise position that can go either way. Insofar as it operates to narrow language options, it leans toward Locke; insofar as it operates to broaden language opportunities, it leans toward Herder.

We learn from Ives that EU policy has leaned in both directions over time, but there is reason to hope that it's going with Herder in the long run because it refuses – at least in its rhetoric – to see linguistic diversity as an obstacle. There are efforts to encourage Europeans to learn a range of languages, for instance, and there is at least a principled recognition of the significance of all languages spoken by the peoples of the Union. Ives cautions that some problems remain. Some languages are still not getting a fair deal, and more needs to be done. But he does suggest that, insofar as the underlying drive is toward the expansion of language opportunities, and reflects "the notion that all languages, not just official or state languages, are important for European integration,"[2] we can draw inspiration from the EU example. This definitely constitutes an uplifting concluding note in Ives's account.

But to draw inspiration from this example, we first need to share with Ives the belief that the Herderian view of language is to be preferred, since in his chapter he opts to argue from example rather than engage with the theory behind these complex alternatives.[3] There is also a possibility that these developments in EU language policy are the result of pragmatic adaptation and therefore may not entail any great conclusion concerning a principled view of language. It is not clear how this possibility affects the endorsement of multilingual values that Ives detects in EU policies.

But I want to focus on a puzzle that lurks in the background of this entire account. This is the puzzle surrounding the "plus two" languages. These languages – Irish and Luxembourgish – are official languages of EU member states that operate their public lives in another language. Irish public life takes place largely in English, while the public life of Luxembourg occurs in French. Recognition of these languages is clearly important to these populations, but not being established as working languages does not seem to present a barrier to their democratic participation in the Union. What does this tell us about the intrinsic versus the instrumental view of language? It certainly looks as though the Irish and the Luxembourgish have adopted an instrumental approach when it comes to their own public lives. This does not mean that the significance to the group of the indigenous language has diminished, however, although the basis of that significance may well have shifted. Even when it is not the language of everyday life – including everyday politics – the intrinsic value of the language may still remain high. It may be seen as connecting the people to their heritage, serving as the "vehicle of three thousand years of history," for instance, as Eamon de Valera once described the Irish language.[4] De Valera was *taoiseach* (prime minister) of Ireland for most of the period from 1932 to 1959 and made this comment as part of an appeal for the recovery of Irish as a working language. Yet though his sense of attachment to the language was popularly endorsed, initiatives aimed at re-establishing it did not meet with the success that he had hoped for, and many were eventually abandoned.[5]

The Irish example is worth thinking about here because it presents a perplexing combination of high support for a language as a cultural object and low support for day-to-day bilingualism. It therefore illustrates how a disjuncture can develop between language attachment and language use. The Irish language was in steady decline throughout the twentieth century, and estimates are that today only 2 percent of the population in the Republic of Ireland could be classified as Irish speaking, and even these communities contain sizable minorities that hardly if ever use Irish in their daily lives.[6] Yet support for Irish in ceremonial or symbolic use – such as in legislative debate, public signage, and public broadcasting – has not suffered from this decline. Instead, it has increased. Likewise, the government's decision to back away from compulsory Irish education measures coincided with a small renaissance in Irish immersion schooling, driven largely by parents' groups.[7] So, while voluntary attachment to the language remains strong, this attachment does not require that the Irish language be front and centre even in Ireland's public institutions. This situation led the country's leading language-planning committee to speculate that, in spite of its high cultural valuation, the Irish language "is not an issue of great significance to most people in their everyday perceptions of politics and political goals."[8] The implication is that, even when a language has clear intrinsic value, this may not be an obstacle to a population acting as if language is an instrumental choice.

It should be acknowledged, of course, that in the Irish case the changeover to English owes a great deal to a history of discrimination and disadvantage. Luxembourg also had a taste of colonialism. So the decline of the indigenous language in favour of a foreign one has a troubled history in each case. And there are valid questions to be raised concerning translation and authenticity. Can aspirations and priorities arising in one language setting ever be fully represented in another? Perhaps this is part of the reason why these "plus two" languages are supported by their populations: because there is something represented in and through them that is not available through English or French.[9] Whether that "something" is essential to the democratic process, however, is not self-evident given their examples. When we look at cases such as the Irish one, we see that language use does not lend itself to neat categories of intrinsic or instrumental value, categories that could clearly indicate its role in democracy. Instead, some populations adopt positions that combine instrumental and intrinsic value positions. Reflecting these valuations in our democratic institutions, then, will likely call for solutions that do not fit neatly into the instrumental and intrinsic categories either. This insight might help to explain the European Union's invention of a somewhat untidy "plus two" category of language status, but it also adds a new layer of complexity to Ives's democracy-language dynamic.

Whatever the relationship of language to democracy, however, Ives's chapter challenges us to account for the generous way in which language issues are approached in the European Union. How is it that the Europeans, when it comes to minority issues, prove so generous that they accommodate an expanding range of languages, while in Canada the real and pressing needs of national minority groups often get short shrift? Let me now turn to the second account – Avigail Eisenberg's account of direct democracy and group-differentiated minority rights – to see what we can learn from it.

Group Rights in Referendums

In her account of multiculturalism and democratic practice, Eisenberg warns us of the dangers seeded at the heart of referendum democracy. The problem is that referendums tend to stack the deck against the accommodation of certain kinds of minority rights. She cites one referendum on Aboriginal negotiations in British Columbia as a case in point, and the example illustrates how the process can be used to undermine multicultural policies.

Yet I want to start by formulating from Eisenberg's account a more general – and more provocative – question than Eisenberg develops, and I want to consider this question from the point of view of a democratic representative. If the population you are engaged in representing will not, when you ask the people for their preferences, return to you a decision that captures their real interests or long-term goals (including the pursuit of a just society defined in multicultural terms), then what are you to do? This dilemma should sound familiar to us since it amounts to the "paradox of multicultural democracy" in the introduction to this chapter.

Now one possibility is that what we are faced with amounts to a framing problem. And there is plenty of evidence in Eisenberg's work to suggest that we need to pay close attention to this possibility. In other words, the way in which the referendum question and process are framed may make it appear as if the majority has little to gain and a lot to lose by supporting the rights of a minority group. If this is the case, then what we need are rules to control the framing process. While there will be inevitable debates over how best to enact these rules, we can at least agree that the goal of such measures is to achieve better democracy, not less of it.

But Eisenberg suggests that the problem runs deeper than this. She suggests that referendums model a certain ideal of equality – equality as undifferentiated treatment. This modelling effect makes it much harder to advance claims for special rights or accommodations based on differentiated treatment and means that referendums are especially bad ways of dealing with national minority issues. Yet, to achieve just co-existence in populations that have multicultural, multinational, or otherwise complex group politics, we may be obliged to provide special rights or special status to particular groups. There can be many justifications for such measures. Will Kymlicka, for instance, bases his defence of minority rights largely on the requirements for liberal autonomy, saying that we need secure cultural and social settings within which to exercise our capacity for choice.[10] Iris Marion Young, meanwhile, relies on a remedial approach to group rights, saying that patterns of domination and oppression make special rights necessary to balance things out.[11] And Eisenberg's own work notes how minority rights can serve to level the playing field by providing for minority cultures the kinds of opportunity and support that can be taken for granted when one is a member of the dominant culture.[12] What theories like these have in common, however, is the belief that, although they involve special or differentiated treatment, such rights or status can sometimes amount to a kind of equality too. Let us call it "complex equality."

Eisenberg tells us that referendums create an additional hurdle to advancing ideals of complex equality because they create a powerful demonstration effect. Referendums on group-differentiated rights are telling people that undifferentiated equality is the ultimate political standard while asking them to endorse a system of differentiated equality as a means to fuller justice. It certainly seems that there are mixed messages here, and Eisenberg is right to raise a red flag over the issue. This being the case, we do not just need better rules on holding referendums; we also need better ways of ratifying rights and accommodations. In fact, we have to ask, should referendums ever be used to validate such arrangements, or is this unwise and unfair? Maybe what we need are new ways of confirming group-differentiated measures as part of our political landscape that avoid the mixed messages of referendums and that won't unconsciously pervert the outcome in the same way that manipulative framing can consciously pervert it.

But there is a third possible explanation for the poor record of group-differentiated rights under referendums. And this third explanation is the most troubling and the most challenging of all. What if these referendums are tapping into a *genuine* preference for undifferentiated equality or community rather than engendering it through manipulative framing or even through the demonstration effect of the referendum itself? What if we face a majority population that puts undifferentiated equality and community first, together with a minority population that needs group-differentiated rights and distinct communities to be treated fairly? If this is the case, then referendums will not get us to justice, plain and simple. Surely the upshot, then, is to curtail or highly circumscribe their use.[13]

But right away we run up against a legitimacy issue. Referendums have legitimacy in spades – which is the problem. They provide a tremendous endorsement of a certain ideal of community and equality – the one based on undifferentiated treatment and status. We have to ask, then, what do we have to put up against that in defence of those compromises necessary in a multinational state?

Focusing on reforming referendum use is certainly better than nothing, given this scenario, but it is still a negative strategy aimed at controlling or circumscribing the *expression* of those preferences that fall short of full (multicultural or diversity-based) justice. And it may prove to be a limited strategy for three reasons. First, it may backfire (people may say,

"Now we can't have real democracy because of those special interests"). Second, it may be a null outcome since it may only displace the preferences to legislatures (since governing parties may develop platforms or agendas to express indirectly the same sentiments that we encounter in referendums). And third, it is ultimately not transformative of those preferences.

Eisenberg's account of referendum democracy leaves us a lot less hopeful for the future of multicultural politics than does Ives's. The kind of democracy we encounter in her account hasn't yielded an expanded understanding of justice, and it doesn't look as if it will any time soon, even with reformed referendum laws. But before the picture becomes too dark, I want to take a question that I raised in passing in this section and see whether, by re-examining it, we can restore some hope for the fate of group-differentiated rights in those democracies that need to employ them.

Grounding the Legitimacy of Complex Equality

The question that I want to consider is concerned with the legitimacy issue. What do we have to defend the "compromises" (Eisenberg's term) necessary in multicultural democracies? Referendums can legitimize outcomes because they nicely align with ideals of formal equality. So what serves to legitimate efforts at more complex equality? Note that I say legitimate, not justify. As theorists, we may be convinced of the justice of group-differentiated rights (assuming that we're all multiculturalists now), but if we face a population that isn't we have a problem. Answering this question is important because it tells us what weighs in on the other side of the scales when seeking public ratification of group-specific rights or other multicultural measures. But it is also important because it may help us to identify other means of ratification – a challenge that I suggest is raised by Eisenberg's work.

So what do we have to defend complex equality? I can think of three candidates that might weigh in on the multiculturalist side: history, law and institutions, and our sense of fairness. In the first case, history may have left us with certain obligations that underpin the provision of group rights.[14] Histories that feature treaty agreements, colonization, discrimination, and so on all yield special circumstances that make formal equality a seemingly inadequate response. If we believe in honouring our obligations, and if group-differentiated rights are a matter of historical responsibility, then this can and should be used to reinforce their legitimacy.[15] The difficulty is that we are leaning on an arbitrary principle when we rely on the role of historical responsibility. Not all histories yield the kinds of responsibility, or the sense of responsibility, that can lend legitimacy to group-differentiated rights.[16]

Alternatively, we could try appealing to existing laws and institutions, those that endorse a more complex idea of justice. Some have argued, for instance, that as an institution Canadian federalism "rests on a complex form of fraternity," one that sounds like the complex equality that multiculturalists have in mind.[17] Citizens who believe that their own standing owes something to the protections made possible by these laws and institutions may be more ready to recognize the legitimacy of other claims grounded in the same legal order.[18] The problem, of course, is that the legal approach cuts both ways. Documents such as the Canadian Charter of Rights and Freedoms are seen by some as threatening the spirit of group accommodation that was traditionally part of Canadian federalism by privileging individual rights over this sense of complex fraternity.[19]

Yet whichever side of the debate they favour, laws and institutions still form only one part of the legitimacy equation, as David Beetham tells us. According to Beetham, public legitimacy actually has three parts. The first concerns the laws and rules of a community, the second concerns shared beliefs, and the third concerns consent to authority.[20] Even if sound laws stand behind a given measure, a legitimacy deficit can still develop if public sentiment is not in accord. Therefore, we need something to firmly ground legitimacy in at least the considered judgments, if not the spontaneous preferences, of the contemporary population.

So we turn to a third approach, one rooted in our basic sense of fairness. I want to explore this option in more detail since it gets at the idea of deeply held preferences – those of people as well as those in institutions. Joe Carens has argued that, while abstract ideals of justice have strong appeal, we are also equipped with a more elementary and more nuanced sense of fairness in the form of our moral intuitions. This intuitive sense of fairness appreciates the many different forms that justice can take in different situations because it facilitates a more complex view of matters. In a Burkean twist on the multicultural argument, Carens suggests that we can find evidence of this subtle moral compass at work when we look at long-standing practices that accommodate complex ideas of justice. In other words, he suggests that in some cases important moral insights may already be "embedded" in our practices, insights sometimes missed when we consider justice in its idealized or theoretical form.[21]

To tap into this moral resource, Carens recommends an approach characterized by what he calls "justice as evenhandedness," and he says that it already accounts for a range of modifications that we often make to strict liberal equality. If he is right, then the "evenhandedness" inherent in existing efforts to accommodate minority groups suggests that we may already have a source for the legitimacy we need. What we should be doing, therefore, is finding ways to better tap into the intuitive sense of justice that these efforts and practices reflect and use these intuitions to extend the reach of complex equality.

How does one tap into these intuitions? Carens recommends a process that he calls "reflective disequilibrium," which involves using both principle and experience to mutually modify one another.[22] But we still need to identify a method that captures this process – something that involves going back and forth between intuitions or ideals and the real-world experience of living with others. One method that might work involves a deliberative democracy approach. Deliberative democracy aims to provide a public airing of arguments and ideas and then to challenge those arguments in light of different people's experiences and perspectives. Rather than arrive at a judgment through deductive reasoning, deliberative democracy, as one writer puts it, aims at capitalizing on "collective knowledge."[23] Mutual adjustments in earlier positions allow participants to reach an understanding that, while it may not reflect an elegant or formal view of justice, may better capture it through adaptation and complexity.[24]

But the problem is that this process rests heavily on our existing intuitions about justice. This is certainly a key part of legitimacy – as noted earlier – but it also lands us back in the original conundrum: that an attachment to formal equality and community may be deeply rooted among populations faced with claims to group-differentiated rights. In the end, appeals to intuitions about justice will only be as good as the intuitions themselves. If, as Carens suggests, some sense of evenhandedness is already hardwired into our thinking on justice, then we should stand a good chance of achieving complex equality. But this ideal still needs to be activated – needs to be brought to the fore within societies where formal equality has monopolized the political imagination.

When we take stock of the legitimacy assets that count in favour of group-differentiated rights, we find that we have some promising resources at hand. History, law, and our sense of fairness can all lend weight to the cause and should be employed along with or as a counterbalance to referendum-style democracy. But fighting individual legitimacy battles over the ratification of rights in the face of preferences for formal equality (referendum-inspired or otherwise) is still a short-term strategy. The representative who chooses this course will be a busy figure indeed. In fact, this figure has already been sketched in some regards by another contributor to this volume, who, like Ives, provides an upbeat account of multicultural democracy. I want to take a closer look at this account because I think what makes for a happy outcome in it reveals a great deal about where the real rewards of multiculturalism are to be found.

Transformation in Democracies

In Chapter 9 of this volume, Greg Pyrcz offers an account of an ideal representative in a nonideal world. His work advances a Rousseauian model of representation, when Rousseau did not believe in representation, and marries it with a deliberative democracy ideal of preference formation in which "thick" public deliberation is "not strictly required."[25] Instead, Pyrcz tells us that a representative should ask him- or herself which preferences citizens would arrive at through deliberation under ideal conditions. With this insight – and ever vigilant to his or her own weaknesses, which might colour these conclusions – the representative then seeks to guide a population toward this position, especially where its existing preferences fall short of the speculated outcome. Wary of the potential for abuse, Pyrcz cautions that in the final analysis, if they persist in their prior preferences, the people are ultimately to be heeded.

The Rousseauian flavour of this account is unmistakable, except that here we are guided toward justice instead of forced toward freedom. Still, at first blush, it looks as if Pyrcz's approach might hold some promise for the dilemmas that we face in multicultural democracies.[26] Can it provide an answer? Can we look to our representatives to lead us out of this quagmire by knowing us better than we know ourselves and acting on the preferences which we would will if we had the chance? Unfortunately, I do not think that Pyrcz can make this happy ending work, and it is not just because he has attempted an unusual mating of theories in his account.

At one level, the model is excessively idealistic – when would this paragon of virtue ever get elected in the first place, let alone remain both tuned in to the (ideal deliberative) General Will as well as alert to his or her own weaknesses? But Pyrcz is aware of this problem, and he counters that all models of representation are idealistic at some level. Fair enough; let us set that objection aside. What I am going to suggest is that the model is in fact not ideal enough. It has left out of the equation something that made the original two theories – from which this model is hybridized – work. That is, both involve a process that has a transformative effect on the participant population.

Pyrcz recognizes the need for transformation, but he goes about it in a different way from either Rousseau or deliberative democracy. Both democratic deliberation and Rousseau's direct participation in the General Will have this effect *from within* because of the virtues and commitments that the process calls upon in the participants. Pyrcz's model supposes that it can be guided from *without*. His representative is meant to steer the population toward its real interests, and, because this figure serves as a kind of deliberator by proxy, Pyrcz believes that we can leave out the requirement for "thick" participation. But without a deep involvement in the process, the people being represented are unlikely to have a deep commitment to the result, an outcome that both Rousseau's and the deliberative democracy model have built into them.[27] Indeed, what these two models tell us is that for democracy to be a transformative process – indeed for it to be truly democratic – it is not sufficient to be handed the results, even by the most enlightened representative. As leading deliberative democracy theorists Gutmann and Thompson put it, there should be no division of labour in the deliberative process. While representation is a necessary part of modern democracy, they stipulate that deliberation should never be delegated upward in such a way that "representatives give reasons while citizens merely receive them."[28]

Pyrcz's model, I am afraid, comes dangerously close to this arrangement. Pyrcz may have been inspired by the image of Rousseau's Legislator, the source of the initial and most crucial transformation that prepares the population for democracy.[29] But two things should be noted about the Legislator. First, he is nearly godlike in his insights – he "understands the passions of men without feeling any of them." This is unlike the fallible figure that Pyrcz has in mind as his representative. Second, the Legislator completes his critical task and retires his position. His office is "neither that of the government or that of the sovereign"; he must not "have command over men" because he has had command over laws.[30] The Legislator, therefore, is not a figure whom we should draw on lightly when thinking about contemporary democracy. Moreover, what we are concerned with here is a more modest goal than that of Rousseau's Legislator. We aim at the transformation of democratically expressed preferences, not at the transformation of the human character. My point is that in the two models that Pyrcz draws upon, transformation is a *function* of participation – either through silent voting in the case of Rousseau's General Will or through a very public process of deliberation.[31] To establish new understandings of what just politics requires, then, we need to look to our systems of participation rather than to our representatives, however divine.

This conclusion leads us back to our original problem. If we do not seek "thick" means of public participation, then we will not be particularly democratic, and we will stand less chance of harnessing the transformative power of democratic procedures. But if we do, then we may get policies that are not particularly multicultural and may not reflect an adequate standard of justice.

Although it looks as though the challenge of multicultural justice opens uncharted and potentially hazardous territory for democratic theory, the participation quandary that it raises is not actually a new one. For instance, Dennis Thompson takes from John Stuart Mill's writings on representation the idea that participation and what Mill calls "competence" are mutually limiting. On this account, participation rights are modified by the need to ensure that citizens have developed an adequate appreciation of the challenges of right government. But Mill also believed that competence and participation are mutually *reinforcing*. In other words, participation provides the education – the transformative power – that allows people to develop competence in justice and collective self-rule.[32] This emphasis on participation as a means of transformation, even when there are concerns about the popular understanding of justice, suggests that we should see democratic participation not only as an opportunity to extend ideals of formal equality but also as a means to contest them.

Mill did not assign priority between the principles of participation and competence, but we would not want, I think, to adopt his idea that we are better off when some people are granted more political influence than others on the ground of their supposedly superior insight. We can, however, take from his work the idea that the appropriate level or kind of democratic participation is not a straightforward given. Democracies are responsible for ensuring not just that participation takes place but also that the way in which it takes place is appropriate to achieving the goal of a just society. In other words, how we participate may not be a uniform equation for all issues; instead, participation should be organized in relation to how deeply an understanding of the requirements of justice is rooted in our societies. If a population is particularly enamoured of one concept of equality, then we should engage participation for reasons of both legitimacy and transformation, but we should engage it in a way that avoids reinforcing a limited view of what justice looks like.

So what is a representative to do? Ironically, the answer may be less, at least less representation. Instead, representatives would be wise to focus on means of public participation and ratification that build toward the transformation of preferences. Looking at the question of principles in people, it turns out, brings us back to those that we find in institutions and practices. Only now what interests us is their transformative potential – their capacity to help align democratically expressed collective preferences with the requirements of justice, as we understand them. The legitimacy question must be addressed, however, even for multicultural measures of a pressing nature, because without it the outcome may yield alienation rather than transformation. If referendums have that legitimacy, then we should be ready to use them under careful conditions, along the lines that Eisenberg has stipulated. Her discussion of the vices and virtues of referendums is a helpful reminder that part of the work of democratic representation involves choosing the right tools for the job. Reforming referendum practices so that they do not present an obstacle to multicultural justice is a critical task. But so is identifying other, perhaps better, tools that engage the public while enriching its understanding of what justice requires.[33] When faced with claims to multicultural accommodation, our ultimate aim should be not just to achieve a particular "yes" outcome but also to achieve a community for whom that "yes" feels right.

Conclusion

In the final analysis, democratic justice, including democratic justice in multicultural societies, is the outcome of at least three interrelated elements. First, it is shaped by the principles enshrined in public institutions and practices – institutions such as representative government, multicultural or multinational commitments, and group and individual rights. Second, it relies on the intentions of the population itself, which must be prepared to engage in personal or interpersonal interrogation of convictions about justice and the good. This second element cannot be represented (as Rousseau tells us) or delegated through a division of labour (as Gutmann and Thompson indicated). This requirement – to will justice and the good – is the reason that market-based analogies are insufficient when thinking about political participation. It remains the cornerstone of democratic life as well as its greatest resource for transformation. And third – and this is where most of the attention has focused in this discussion because it covers the realm of participation – it involves the expression, in the form of democratic preferences, of the revisable understandings that people hold about how particular policies or measures relate to justice. This third element can give rise to the kinds of tension that we have been considering, when a population, even one that wills justice, holds convictions that can obstruct its realization. Participation creates this problem, but I have argued that it may also be our best way out of it.

Note, however, that nothing in this account of the participation issue promises that the tension between participation and justice will ever be fully resolved. Each time we consult a population, we take a chance that the returned preferences will be poorly aligned with what justice requires. If the result is badly out of alignment, then we need to find ways to address this problem. But this tension also has an important function within a democratic system. Not only does it indicate where work needs to be done to advance popular understandings of justice, but it also reminds representatives and theorists alike that we too must be ready to question our understandings and convictions. A society that does not involve some tension between the preferences of the population and those of its political or intellectual elite is, most likely, a society in which something has gone badly wrong. Rather than seek to eliminate or avoid this tension, we should regard it as an indispensable guide.

Getting back to our first two accounts of multiculturalism, we can now speculate on what made one happy and the other less so. Eisenberg's account of referendum democracy's failure to serve more complex ideals of equality and community makes sense because the process does little to transform preferences in the direction in which we believe justice to lie. In Ives's case, the prospect looks more promising because the European

Union as an institution already has a built-in appreciation for the role of complex equality – it is a basic premise of a system that came together through state-based groups and that organizes its representation along these lines. This institutional structure exists because European member populations understand the significance of group accommodation to the legitimacy of their common political project. In short, for complex equality, multicultural justice, or group-differentiated rights to have legitimacy, we need laws and institutions that entrench these principles, but we also need a community that intuitively recognizes the justice of these measures.

This second element, I would argue, is precisely what is missing in many attempts to establish group rights or accommodations within multicultural democracies. What we need, therefore, is a process that can do the transformative work envisioned by Rousseau or deliberative democracy, and we need it at a mass level in substantially diverse societies. At this stage, the reader may well decide that we would be better off taking our chances finding Pyrcz's paragon. But some process for transforming the preferences of a population from within is both a crucial task for many multicultural democracies and, it seems, an inevitable part of the pursuit of justice.

The two accounts by Ives and Eisenberg that prompted this exploration capture the two sides of the multicultural project. In one account, we begin with steadfast multinationalism and work toward greater democracy; in the other, we begin with a very direct form of democracy and work toward greater multinationalism. Given the difficult questions posed by these accounts, it is hard to avoid the conclusion that these two goals or principles – extensive democracy and extensive multinationalism or multiculturalism – are in tension, if not at odds. Which leaves us with a difficult bind, the only solution to which seems to involve transformation to a society that values its multinationalism as much as its democracy – however utopian that goal may seem.

Of the two authors, Ives takes the more optimistic route and suggests that some transformation of civil society is inevitable in the European Union and that there is reason to hope that it will yield both more multiculturalism and better democracy. Eisenberg, on the other hand, takes a darker view of things and, by suggesting reforms to referendum use, offers us a solution that does not make multiculturalism rest on the success of social transformation. In the end, I can't really say which is the wiser assessment, but I do wonder whether, when it comes down to the business of transformation, it is easier to get to democracy from multiculturalism than it is to get to multiculturalism through democracy.

Acknowledgments

I thank Avigail Eisenberg, David Laycock, and the anonymous reviewers of this volume for helpful comments on this chapter.

Notes

1 Shachar (2001).
2 See page 40 in this volume.
3 Ives does cite the work of theorist Denise Réaume, who argues in favour of the intrinsic view of language, but then says that he prefers to contribute to this debate by illustrating how institutions are adopting this perspective. See page 29 in this volume.
4 Monynihan (1980), 467-68.
5 Early measures to re-establish Irish included the 1922 requirement that candidates for civil service employment be competent in Irish and the 1933 measure that made Irish a requirement of high school completion. Both were repealed in 1973. The 1920s also saw a short-lived attempt to make Irish the primary language of instruction in all schools, although this plan proved unworkable. For more on the language policies of the early Irish state, see Fanning (1983); Foster (1988); and Lee (1989).
6 Ó Raigáin (1997), 166.
7 For an excellent discussion of Irish language use and attitudes toward language, see Ó Raigáin (1997), especially Chapters 5 and 6.
8 Advisory Planning Committee of Board na Gaeilge, cited in Ó Raigáin (1997), 191.
9 For an argument that the Irish language reflects a unique cultural and social perspective, see Tovey, Hannan, and Abramson (1989). Note that this apologia on the continued significance of the Irish language is published in English.
10 Kymlicka (1995).
11 Young (1989).
12 See page 7 in this volume, Chapter 1 generally; and Eisenberg (2001), 151.
13 I should note that Eisenberg stops short of this conclusion and does not suggest that we abandon referendums as democratic instruments, merely that we recognize them as inherently biased.
14 For instance, history is a major element in the approach that Will Kymlicka takes when he distinguishes national minorities from immigrant or polyethnic groups and awards the former a more extensive set of rights than the latter. Strictly, Kymlicka differentiates the groups based on what he calls "societal institutions." However, it turns out that groups with particular kinds of historical experience – colonization, mass expulsion, or collective settlement, for instance – are the ones that have these institutions and a valid claim to maintain them. Immigrant groups, on the other hand, have made a choice to "uproot themselves" and therefore do not have a claim to the same kinds of accommodation. So, in effect, it is something that took place in their *past* that distinguishes these groups. See Kymlicka (1995), 95-101.
15 The means of public ratification that arise from history might involve the recognition and retelling of the relevant history. One example of this idea at work would be truth commissions. Unlike referendums that assume all should have an equal say, truth commissions are premised on the idea that, because of their experiences, some have more to say and that we should pay special attention to them in forming our understanding of the requirements of justice in our communities.
16 Kymlicka (1995), 116-20, recognizes this problem with the historical argument, although history plays a significant part in his own accommodation model.
17 LaSelva (1996), xiii.
18 One means of public ratification based on this approach might be to develop a process for confirming that the group-differentiated rights in question are appropriate under the terms already articulated as acceptable or even desirable under the laws or institutions of a state. In other words, we might employ something that amounts to a kind of "good housekeeping seal of approval" that could be given before any matter goes forward to the public.
19 Yet even the Charter may contain group rights and accommodations that can lend credence to the legitimacy of multicultural measures. Consider, for example, the language rights for English and French speakers that are protected under the Charter. As Pierre Coulombe (2000), 284, explains, establishing official bilingualism may have played an important role in the eventual introduction of official multiculturalism, partly for instrumental

reasons (as part of Trudeau's effort to dilute the bicultural model of Canada) but also partly for fairness reasons. "Having provided historical justice to two of the founding peoples," Coulombe speculates, "a spirit of fairness" then led the state to extend some form of recognition to other cultures as well.
20 Beetham (1991), 15-20.
21 Carens (2000), ch. 1.
22 Carens (2000), 4.
23 Valadez (2001), 32.
24 Deliberative democracy does not inherently recommend a particular understanding of justice or equality. So, while an assumption of reasonable pluralism may, as Joshua Cohen argues, be one of the background assumptions of deliberative democracy, there is no automatic guarantee that the outcome of using this approach would be a system of special rights or status aimed at achieving complex equality. However, following Eisenberg's example, we might argue that deliberative democracy *models* an ideal of equality in the way that it heeds and respects different perspectives. Likewise, good arguments are what carry weight in a deliberative process rather than head counts, again modelling a different understanding of equality. For more on how the requirements of deliberative democracy engage a system of relationships that respect pluralism and difference, see Cohen (1996); and Gutmann and Thompson (1996), especially chs. 1 and 2.
25 Pointing out these contrasts amounts to a glib kind of commentary. I therefore want to acknowledge that I do think it is possible to employ Rousseauian ideals to help us think about representative politics regardless of where Rousseau himself stood on the issue.
26 This seems like an appropriate place to acknowledge that the system of government outlined in *The Social Contract* was not, according to Rousseau, a democracy since democracy was a system so demanding that it was fit only for the gods; see Rousseau (1968), book 3, ch. 4. However, it does conform to what we would generally call a democratic system.
27 Carole Pateman (1970), ch. 2, for instance, stresses the role of participation in Rousseau's system because she argues that it served both to educate the population for government and to reconcile it to collective decisions.
28 Gutmann and Thompson (1996), 358.
29 See pages 184-91 and 196n16 in this volume.
30 Rousseau (1968), book 2, ch. 7.
31 I should also note that the General Will – the outcome of the transformative experience that Rousseau outlines – both calls for and inculcates a political status and self-understanding of the undifferentiated kind. But while this outcome is central to Rousseau's theory, it is achieved through a closely specified voting practice, and it is not clear that the transformative effect of democratic participation must always lead in this direction, especially when other kinds of democratic practices are involved.
32 Thompson (1976).
33 The reader might well ask how this approach differs from Pyrcz's stance, since in both cases the representative seeks a transformation in popular preferences to better align them with justice. The difference is that in Pyrcz's account this transformation is the work of a personality, whereas I am arguing that such transformation can be a by-product of popular participation.

4
Feminist Engagement with Federal Institutions: Opportunities and Constraints for Women's Multilevel Citizenship

Louise Chappell

Historically, Western political institutions have failed to secure the equal representation of men and women. Women in general have found it more difficult than men have to achieve equal nominal or substantive representation through traditional representative institutions such as electoral systems, political parties, and legislatures. Moreover, women from minority groups have found it difficult to achieve even the low levels of representation reached by women from majoritarian backgrounds. The disparity in representation between men and women is due in part to the influence of the political cultures and ideologies that underpin institutions. It is also a result of endogenous institutional factors. Although political institutions appear on the surface to be neutral, benign entities, they are, as feminists have pointed out, imbued with gender (and race and class) characteristics at both structural and normative levels.

Identifying the gender features of political institutions has been an important first step in understanding and challenging women's underrepresentation. Armed with this knowledge, women's activists have extended the push for equality by working as agitators within and outside institutions. It has been their aim to unsettle the "taken for grantedness" of underlying gender assumptions and thus make institutions more "women friendly." Feminists have not only worked in traditional representative institutions such as political parties and parliaments but also developed innovative strategies to engage with bureaucratic, judicial, and federal institutions. These activists can claim some success for their efforts across this range of institutions. Advances include an improvement in the number of women standing for, and being elected to, legislatures; the creation of women's policy agencies and women-sensitive policies; the appointment of progressive judges who have developed a feminist jurisprudence; and women's increased involvement in federal and intergovernmental structures.

The institutional inroads made by feminists may not have secured complete gender parity, nor is there any guarantee that the changes will be enduring. As women's activists throughout the Western world have discovered, the election of a conservative government can easily close a window of political opportunity and set up a series of constraints for working toward gender equality within the institutions of the state. Nevertheless, feminist praxis has shown that the gendered nature of institutions is not fixed or permanent; underlying gender norms and structures within political institutions can sometimes be "dislodged" so as to open up new spaces for the representation of women and their interests.

The focus of this chapter is on the engagement of feminist activists in Australia and Canada with federal structures. It examines the gender aspects of federalism and the extent to which feminists have been able to challenge these aspects in order to enhance the supraregional interests of women. The study demonstrates the value of feminists looking beyond traditional representative institutions and of developing innovative strategies across the institutional spectrum. It also raises new questions about whether the existence of tiered government structures strengthens women's opportunities to experience dual citizenship or divides their energies and efforts.

As a key feature of the political landscape in both Australia and Canada, federalism is gradually beginning to receive attention from feminist scholars. In Australia, Gwen Gray mentions federalism as a positive factor influencing the development of the women's health sector, while Helen Irving considers the significance of federal design features at the time of federation. In Canada, Jill Vickers and Alexandra Dobrowolsky give federalism some attention, but both suggest that it is an area that needs further exploration.[1] In an important article, Canadian feminist political scientists L. Pauline Rankin and Jill Vickers have undertaken to compare three Canadian provinces – Alberta, Ontario, and Newfoundland – to illustrate the importance of federalism for feminist activists. Their work focuses on the importance of space for feminist activism and demonstrates "the way patterns of political activism differ significantly from place to place."[2] Recently, Vickers and Sawer have also contributed a comparative study of constitutional politics in Australia and Canada, which includes a discussion of federal relations.[3]

Although not addressing the particularities of Australia and Canada, one other significant comparative study that considers how federal structures shape the choices of feminist activists is Banaszak's research into the suffrage movements in the United States and Switzerland.[4] Banaszak is particularly interested in how federalism has influenced the political opportunity structure (POS) for those struggling to gain the women's vote. An important point to emerge from her account is that differences in feminists' engagement with federal institutions can affect their strategic choices. She notes how the US suffrage movement was influenced by existing federal arrangements when creating its own structures and how it "took full advantage of its own federal structure to spread the knowledge and information about tactics to local areas."⁵ By contrast, Swiss activists were less inclined to work with federal structures or to organize themselves along federal lines and thus missed an important opportunity to garner support for their cause.⁶

Although Banaszak's work can be seen to be groundbreaking in the feminist literature, it fits within a more general and extensive literature on the engagement of social actors with federalism.⁷ Moreover, her argument that federalism can create opportunities for "trailblazers" (in this case, US suffragettes) who can use federalism to their advantage also has a long heritage. Pro-federalists have long advocated this form of political system on the grounds that it promotes innovation and can lead to flow-on reforms across jurisdictions.⁸

Other arguments in favour of federalism are also relevant here. Many of its defenders begin from a liberal democratic position, advocating federalism because of the way that it disperses political power, limits government, and breaks up majority rule.⁹ As well as stimulating innovation, it is seen to protect against central tyranny, reconcile unity and diversity, and increase citizen participation in the political process.¹⁰ Most relevant from a social activist point of view are those arguments that suggest that federalism enhances participation in political decision making. Proponents argue that this multi-tier system of government "establishes a system of dual citizenship or double democracy."¹¹

These arguments have not been accepted unquestioningly. Critics of federalism respond by arguing that it creates waste and duplication, replaces a tyranny of the majority with a tyranny of the minority, and leads to conservatism and parochialism.¹² The latter is seen as a particular problem for those promoting "progressive interests." Adopting a pro- or anti-federalist stance is perhaps too simplistic. As Paul Pierson notes, it is important not to make generalizations about the consequences of federalism for social policy because of the "substantial variation among federal systems in crucial features of institutional design."¹³ The same can be said for making assumptions about the effect of federalism on social actors, including feminists. In Pierson's view, there are three important design features that influence the operation of federal states: (1) the distribution of powers between the constituent units, (2) the representation of these units at the national level, and (3) the extent of commitment to fiscal equalization across units. As this chapter demonstrates, the federations of Australia and Canada are different from each other in each of these crucial design features and, as a result, offer feminist activists different opportunities and constraints.

Table 4.1

Federalism and political opportunity structures

	Australia	Canada
Division of political and fiscal authority	*Structures* **Positive** High federal political and fiscal capacity combined with moderate state political capacity	*Structures* **Negative** Moderate federal political and fiscal capacity combined with high provincial political and fiscal capacity
Intergovernmental mechanisms	*Structures* **Negative** Nominally male **Positive** Creation of effective national women's policy machinery	*Structures* **Negative** Nominally male **Moderate** Creation of women's policy machinery *Norms* **Negative** Perceived to be undemocratic and elitist
Salience of territoriality	*Norms* **Moderate** Ameliorated by political and fiscal division of powers and party system	*Norms* **Negative** Territoriality strong at expense of gender interests **Positive** Ameliorated by politicization of non-territorial identities through the Charter of Rights and Freedoms
Intervening institutions	*Structures* **Positive** Symmetrical, class-based party system reduces salience of regional interests *Norms* **Positive** ALP representation Protection of gender interests	*Structures* **Negative** Asymmetrical party system reinforces importance of regional concerns at the expense of nonterritorial ones.

This chapter considers the features of the Australian and Canadian federal systems and asks two key questions. First, have feminists found, as Banaszak notes in relation to suffragettes in the United States, that a two-tier system has enhanced their ability to achieve their aims? Second, can feminists in either country or both countries take advantage of a system of "double-democracy" or "dual citizenship," as Galligan suggests?

Engaging with Federalism: Australian and Canadian Feminist Experiences

Australian and Anglo-Canadian feminists have had different experiences with their federal governments. Whereas Canadian feminists outside Quebec have faced a mostly positive POS in relation to the central government, their relationship with, and attitude toward, federalism has ranged from outright hostility to ambivalence. By contrast, Australian feminists have generally reflected a favourable attitude toward federal arrangements and have taken advantage of the political leverage offered by the multi-level system by shifting their attention between the federal and state levels as opportunities have arisen.

Australian Feminists and Federalism: Playing the Two-Level Game

Federalism has not been an issue central to Australian feminist discourse. To the extent that they have focused on it, feminists have tended to adopt a relatively sanguine attitude toward the institution. On the one hand, they have supported the arrogation of power to the central government in areas such as welfare, child care, and family law.[14] On the other hand, they have tended to espouse the view that federalism offers them multiple opportunities for pursuing their objectives. Longtime feminist activist Eva Cox concurs with this positive assessment, arguing that, under federalism, "feminists and other lobbyists [can] play off the different levels of government to gain advantages for the less powerful." Cox goes on to defend the federal status quo: "There are claims in Australia that we are over-governed and that we have too much reliance on government. There are those who want to abolish the states and those who are always suspicious of the Commonwealth. However, as an activist over the past two decades, I am happy to see what we have remain and even stay a little confused and overlapping. The demonising of state and public power ignores the possibilities of using these powers to mediate and control the powerful."[15]

Carmel Flask and Betty Hounslow, feminists active in the women's services sector, echo Cox's sentiments: "The Australian federal system, with its different tiers of governments, not only creates complexity, it also allows further opportunity for manoeuvring. Times can be instanced when some battles have been won (and lost) because of the complexity of state and federal funding systems and the negotiations that occur between bureaucrats across departments."[16] As Sawer notes in relation to the femocrat strategy (in which feminists enter the bureaucracy to develop women's policy), having a federal system has meant that, "when progress has been blocked at one level of government, it has been possible for them to continue at another."[17]

As has been seen, some feminists espouse the idea that federalism allows them to exploit openings at different levels of government – an idea that has been largely borne out in practice. This has been made most obvious in relation to the femocrat strategy. Femocrats began their work at the federal level in 1974 under the Whitlam Australian Labor Party (ALP) government, but the network spread quickly as opportunities arose to enter state bureaucracies. During the 1970s and early 1980s, when the Fraser Liberal coalition government was paring back women's policy machinery at the federal level, state Labor governments were opening up opportunities for femocrats to enter the bureaucracy. This occurred in South Australia (1976), Tasmania (1976), New South Wales (1977), and Western Australia (1983). Women's advisory positions were also established under conservative governments in Victoria (1976) and the Northern Territory (1982). These developments can in some ways be seen as analogous to the case of US women's suffrage campaigns mentioned earlier. Once women's policy machinery had been entrenched federally, it set an example for other governments to follow. Femocrats at the federal level had been the initial trailblazers. When key states such as New South Wales and Victoria came on board by creating openings for this strategy, they set an example that other states (with the exception of Queensland)[18] were willing to follow.

Feminist lobbyists have also been able to take advantage of Australian federalism by shifting their focus between different levels of government, depending on where they perceive they can make the greatest inroads. For the most part, this is where ALP governments have been in office. Lobbying around the issue of women's refuges provides an excellent example of how feminists have made the most of having a two-tiered government system. The refuge movement is a good case to consider when examining the effects of federalism because it shares a number of features with other women's groups: it aims to provide services to women, based on feminist principles; it is dispersed throughout the country; and it must relate to both levels of government.

During the early 1970s, much of the feminist effort around women's refuges was directed toward the central government. Feminist activists needed financial support and realized that, with the reformist Whitlam government in office, they were most likely to find it at the Commonwealth level.[19] After securing in 1974 funding from the federal government for "Elsie," the first Australian women's refuge (located in Sydney), femocrats within the federal bureaucracy worked with feminists on the outside to lobby the Whitlam government to provide a national program. In June 1975, Canberra responded, providing over $200,000 in direct funding to eleven refuges throughout the country.[20] Once the national program was in place, femocrats put pressure on the refuge movement to become a national organization, thus enabling it to deal more effectively with the federal government. It refused, arguing that such a move would threaten its autonomy and grassroots strategy.[21]

As it happened, the refuge movement's decision not to focus on Canberra was a prescient one, since in 1976 the incoming conservative Fraser coalition government devolved primary responsibility for administering refuges to the state level. From this time on, feminists divided their attention between the Commonwealth government, which continued to provide the bulk of the funds for the refuges, and the state governments, which oversaw the administration of these funds. On those occasions when Canberra made changes in its policy on refuges, feminists targeted the federal government. For instance, in 1977, when the federal cabinet stalled on its commitment to refuge funding, femocrats and external women's activists alerted the media and convinced the Australian Broadcasting Commission (ABC) to produce a Four Corners documentary program on the issue.[22] In 1981, when responsibility for refuges was further devolved to the states, members of the women's movement staged a protest in Parliament House in Canberra.[23]

However, not all the attention has focused on the Commonwealth government. Because of the states' role in administering refuges, feminist refuge groups have also been active at this level. For instance, throughout the 1970s and 1980s, activists lobbied intransigent governments in Western Australia and Queensland to change their policies.[24] Within state bureaucracies, femocrats have attempted to influence the development of policies in this area. A case in point relates to the NSW femocrat Carmel Niland, who encouraged external women's organizations to pressure the Wran Labor government not only to pick up the Commonwealth shortfall for refuges but also to fund its own.[25] In Victoria too, under the Cain Labor government, femocrats were able to make some headway in securing state funding for refuges. By the mid-1980s, Melbourne's most prominent feminist refuge, Halfway House, believed that state funding was secure enough to discourage it from "join[ing] in with other refuges in a campaign to restore federal control over refuge funding."[26]

The experiences of the refuge movement provide a good example of how federalism has shaped the strategies of Australian feminists. Similar stories can be found in relation to child care and the women's health care movement.[27] Rather than focus on one level of government, feminist activists have shifted their efforts between the two, according to when and where new opportunities or constraints arise. Their capacity to keep their issues on the agenda by exploiting the openings at federal and state levels suggests that Australian federalism has, at various times, afforded them a system of "double democracy" or multiple citizenship. It cannot be assumed, however, that all federal systems provide the same positive POS. As the experiences of Anglo-Canadian feminists attest, federalism can also function to frustrate feminist objectives.

Anglo-Canadian Feminists and Federal Structures

Since the late 1970s, feminists, along with the rest of Canada, have been heavily engaged in constitutional debates, which have included issues related to federalism. As a result, Anglo-Canadian feminists have articulated their attitudes toward federalism much more fully and frequently than have their Australian counterparts. Nevertheless, feminists are far from having reached a consensus within this institutional arena. As noted below, Quebec feminists tend to take a pro-provincial stance, while Aboriginal women tend to take a stance in line with their own nation-building objectives. Within the Anglo-Canadian feminist community itself, there is a variety of positions. As the work of Rankin and Vickers shows,[28] women activists in Alberta, Ontario, and Newfoundland all respond differently to the question of engaging with national/subnational political spaces, depending upon the opportunities, history, and culture of each province. Despite this diversity, the position most strongly articulated from within the mainstream Anglo-Canadian movement, especially through the National Action Committee on the Status of Women (NAC), has been a strong preference for strengthening Ottawa's power vis-à-vis the provinces.

Anglo-Canadian feminist attitudes toward federalism were highlighted most clearly in the late 1980s and early 1990s during the debates surrounding the Meech Lake and Charlottetown constitutional accords.[29] Most Anglo-Canadian feminists adopted a "no" stance toward both accords. The reasons for their position are enlightening. First, they objected to the processes by which the accords were devised and how they were to be ratified. After being so directly involved in influencing the provisions of the Charter in the early 1980s, members of the Anglo-Canadian women's movement were outraged when the Meech Lake Accord was drawn up in secret and presented to the community as a fait accompli.[30] They were also critical of the fact that it was to be ratified by provincial legislatures rather than by the people.

Second, many Anglo-Canadian feminists feared that the adoption of the Meech or Charlottetown Accord might threaten women's rights in Canada by creating a hierarchy of rights – with Aboriginal people and multicultural groups gaining protection at the expense of women.[31] Third, and most pertinent, Anglo-Canadian feminists did not want any further devolution of spending powers to the provinces. Feminist organizations, including NAC and LEAF (the Legal Education and Action Fund), presented submissions to the parliamentary committee on the Meech Lake Accord, arguing that women were especially dependent upon the provision of social services, such as health care, provided through federal grants and cost-sharing programs.[32] In their view, as Judy Rebick argued in the *Globe and Mail* on 25 August 1992, enabling provinces to "opt out" of federal programs would create "a checkerboard of social programs across Canada, leaving women in small provinces without access to programs available in larger provinces."[33] Many Anglo-Canadian feminists were also conscious that universal projects, such as a national child care program (on the agenda since the 1970 report of the Royal Commission on the Status of Women), would be in jeopardy if greater decentralization occurred. In a speech on the Charlottetown Accord, NAC president Judy Rebick voiced a common concern: "Let us say that we were successful in electing a national government committed to publicly funded child care ... They would be unable to implement such a reform under this agreement because as a national government they would be unable to set the standard for public child care. The government would have to go to the first ministers and try to negotiate it. Even if it were negotiated, Alberta or Ontario could opt out with compensations and say that its program was compatible with national objectives."[34]

A further problem for Anglo-Canadian feminists during the Meech Lake debates related to granting greater autonomy to Quebec. Some feared that any future retrograde decisions made in that province on issues such as family law and abortion might set precedents that could be upheld by the Supreme Court of Canada and, therefore, have flow-on effects for women's rights across the country.[35] In other words, they feared the consequences of successful conservative trailblazers in Quebec.

Underlying feminist claims were long-standing anti-provincial sentiments driven by the belief that the second tier of government was intolerant of women's issues.[36] As one feminist put it, "As a woman from B.C., a province which has suffered government by car dealer for all but four of the past forty years, ... I fear ... powers being devolved to my province."[37] Vickers summarizes the position of these women: "Relatively few Canadian women outside of Quebec would accept the proposition that provincial governments, as they have been constituted to this point, have been particularly responsive to the attitudes and aspirations of their women citizens."[38] However, as Rankin and Vickers also point out, there are some exceptions to this rule.[39] For example, in Newfoundland feminists have been active at the provincial level and have found it to be supportive of some of their aims, especially under the Peckford PC government.

The differences between feminists inside and outside Quebec with regard to the issue of federalism and decentralization could not have been more marked. As Busque explained during the Meech Lake debates, "While Quebec women had (and still have) a tendency to distrust federal intrusion in areas that are exclusively provincial jurisdictions, and are favourable to the possibility of opting out with financial compensation, women in other provinces feared negative use of power to opt out." In her view, this was because Anglo-Canadian feminists "were concerned that federal standards would not be applied and even feared that the money recovered would be used improperly. This attitude on the part of (Anglo) women appears to us to stem from having higher expectations of the federal government than of provincial governments."[40]

For a number of reasons, Quebec feminist support for provincial funding arrangements was not surprising. First, francophone feminists in that province have always hitched their cause to that of Quebec nationalism. The slogan "No Women's Liberation without Quebec Liberation, No Quebec Liberation without Women's Liberation," which became the catch-cry of Québécois feminists during the early 1970s, indicates the strength of this link.[41] Unlike the goals of feminists in the rest of Canada, the goals of feminists in Quebec are not at odds with territorial claims but wedded to them. Rankin and Vickers note that "successive Quebec governments have been eager to draw women's movements into the nationalist cause and have often responded positively to women's advocacy as an element of the nationalist struggle."[42]

Second, Quebec feminists face entirely different institutional and political arrangements than do their sisters in other parts of the country. This difference has resulted in Quebec feminists achieving some of their key goals at the provincial level. As noted in relation to the bureaucracy, the Quebec provincial government has provided ongoing funding for the Conseil du statut de la femme, which is well supported by the feminist community.[43] It has introduced a legislatively based bill of rights and has introduced reforms in key "women's policy" areas, such as equal pay and child care.[44] The position of Quebec feminists reflected the view that federalism can provide feminists with a multilayered opportunity structure, providing that their goals are compatible with those of the provincial government. As Sawer and Vickers note, within the Franco-Quebec women's movement, "decentralization [and] diversity" have been favoured over centralization as a way to achieve feminist goals.[45] The significance of these points was not lost on Anglo-Canadian activists who, during the constitutional debates, were forced to rethink their position on federalism so as to incorporate the views being expressed by their Quebec and Aboriginal sisters. They responded with their own asymmetrical "three nations constitutional vision." This "vision" recognized the right of Quebec and

Aboriginal women to a separate constitutional identity while at the same time acknowledging that Anglo-Canadian women perceived the federal government as a better protector of their rights than the provinces. NAC presented this vision in the following terms: "NAC's policy has been support for the right of Aboriginal peoples to self-government, support for the right of the people of Quebec to self-determination in defining their relationship with the rest of Canada, and support for strong, central government in the rest of Canada."[46]

Much to the dismay of many Anglo-Canadian feminists, the failure of the Meech Lake and Charlottetown Accords has not stopped the trend toward greater decentralization within Canada. NAC, and Anglo-Canadian feminists more generally, have continued to oppose this trend. In a 1995 press release, NAC criticized the Chrétien government's reduction in social program transfers to the provinces, the minimization of national standards on transfer payments to the provinces, and the shift toward block funding: "The politicians are implementing ... the Charlottetown Accord through the back door despite the 'NO' vote to the constitutional referendum. Our social safety net will collapse as provinces compete to run the cheapest programs."[47]

The anti-provincial views expressed by Anglo-Canadian feminists have been reflected in their practice. In the main, they have attempted to circumvent the effects of living in a decentralized federal system by maintaining a focus on Ottawa, using the Charter, and being "centrist" in their demands.[48] At the same time, feminists have, on occasion, been heavily engaged in lobbying at the provincial level. One notable example occurred during the Charter debates when Anglo-Canadian feminists successfully mobilized to pressure provincial premiers to protect the proposed sex equality guarantees. Feminist success in this endeavour demonstrated that the federal system could provide "some leverage for women."[49] However, feminists feared provincial interference in sex equality issues and were lobbying to have the premiers agree to leave this area of rights outside provincial jurisdiction. In other words, through these efforts Anglo-Canadian feminists were seeking a way to counter, rather than harness, the centrifugal dynamic within Canadian federalism.

The centralist stance of the Anglo feminist community has not stopped its members from engaging with subnational governments. However, this engagement is less uniform in Canada than it is in Australia. The willingness of feminists to become involved in provincial-level activism has varied markedly between the provinces, and within the provinces it has varied markedly between institutions. As Rankin and Vickers illustrate, in Alberta feminists made some early strides in entering the parliamentary arena but have since become disengaged from mainstream politics; in Newfoundland, as femocrats, they found opportunities within the bureaucratic realm; and in Ontario they have tended to shun provincial institutions in favour of federal ones.[50] In British Columbia, under the NDP government, feminists also made some headway by working within bureaucratic institutions.[51]

Signs are that, in the future, there will be a stronger imperative for feminists to engage with provincial institutions. Even with the counterweight of the Charter, the reality is that in Canada provincial governments are becoming increasingly powerful. Consequently, to remain effective, feminist organizations must turn their attention to this level of government. As Arscott, Rankin, and Vickers argue, "As the effects of decentralization are felt more acutely, provincial and territorial governments inevitably will loom larger as important sites for women's struggles for equality."[52] There is some evidence that NAC is responding to this reality by re-assessing its stance toward provincial politics. In 1995, incoming NAC president Sunera Thobani made it clear that, to deal with the shift of power to the provinces, efforts were being made to have the organization adopt a more provincial focus and to structure itself along regional lines.

There are obvious differences between how Australian feminists and Anglo-Canadian feminists approach federalism. In neither country is there a unified position with regard to which level of government is the most conducive to feminist aims. The feminist community in Australia has tended to be more optimistic about the opportunities afforded by federalism than has the feminist community in Canada. Regardless of where feminists reside, they have attempted to make use of the political leverage afforded by multilayered government, switching their focus between state and federal arenas as opportunities arise. In Canada, while there is diversity of opinion within the Anglo strand of the movement with regard to where best to concentrate feminist efforts, the major focus has been on the federal government, with a great deal of skepticism toward the opportunities available at the provincial level. These responses suggest that federal institutions do not offer the same opportunities for political activists, that the specific features of a given federal system make a difference with regard to the available POSs.

Political Opportunities and Constraints in Australian and Canadian Federalism

Differences between the Australian and Canadian federal systems are evident at both a structural level and a normative level. Important structural differences include the division of political and fiscal powers between the levels of government as well as intergovernmental mechanisms. Normative differences, especially the degree of emphasis on territorial claims, are also obvious. These attitudinal differences have been largely influenced by feminists' experiences with federal institutions.

Division of Political and Fiscal Authority in Australia

The foundations of Australian federalism are quite different from those of Canadian federalism. The Australian federal compact was neither an attempt to unite disparate ethnic groups nor an attempt to protect distinct regional identities. The driving force behind Australian federalism was a political imperative: it was a compromise struck between pre-existing political entities to advance their common economic and defence interests. The objective of the initial compact was to constrain the power at the centre and to leave most of the authority with the states. The Australian Constitution enumerated a limited range of powers for the federal government, including customs and excise, provided for concurrent powers between the federal and the six state governments, and left the residual powers with the states.

Canberra's revenue-raising capacity has been at the heart of its control. In essence, it has been able to secure "a monopoly over the lion's share of revenue sources," while the states and local government have been left with separate tax bases, which are "grossly insufficient for their expenditure needs."[53] High fiscal capacity has enabled the federal government to intervene in state policy areas that are technically outside its constitutional jurisdiction. Since the 1970s, it has done this primarily through Section 96 of the Constitution, which provides the Commonwealth with the power to make Specific Purpose Payments (SPP) to the states. These payments specify the policy terms and conditions under which the grants can be used.[54]

One effect of Canberra's fiscal dominance was to bring about a high level of equalization between the states. Through the auspices of the Grants Commission, the Commonwealth government has allocated SPPs and unconditional grants to the states. The philosophy underlying the formulae used to allocate grants is, according to Painter, "one of a 'fair go': the right of all citizens to an equal opportunity of being provided with an equivalent range of public services."[55] To a large extent, equalization has been achieved through the subsidization of the smaller states by the larger ones – much to the chagrin of the latter. The equalization principles pursued in Australia go much further than do those of other federations, including Canada and the United States. In these other federations, states are compensated for disabilities to their revenue-raising capacity but not for the differential in costs related to the provision of services. In Australia, equalization funding takes both factors into account. According to Self, these measures have had a profound influence on the nature of Australian federalism. In his view, they "reduce the incentive and the need for states to pursue different policies." Moreover, he suggests, Australia's "equalisation policy can be seen as one way of seeking to approximate federalism to the conditions of a unitary state."[56]

Self's argument, however, is somewhat overstated. Although centralization and equalization are key characteristics of Australian federalism, it would be incorrect to assume that the states operate merely as the agents of the Commonwealth. Despite their weak fiscal capacity, they do exercise a level of political capacity. An important characteristic of Australian federalism is that there exist "active, vigilant, rival governments" who have "the capacity and the will to assert their autonomy and their difference."[57] It may be the case that the Commonwealth has the ability to set policy guidelines and has control over finance; nevertheless, "the key to implementation of a policy is frequently in the detail. This is more likely to remain in state hands."[58] The states thereby retain an independent role within Australian federalism.

In line with my central argument regarding the importance of gender norms, it is interesting to note here what Australian feminist and political scientist Helen Irving has to say about Australian federalism. According to her, there is a gender division at the very heart of the Constitution: "When we look closely at the ... 1901 Constitution ... a pattern emerges where the public and external become identified as national and thereby as appropriate to the Commonwealth jurisdiction. For the most part, the domestic and familial – the sphere which constituted the greatest sources of interest to women activists – is left to state jurisdiction, often meaning in this period, to the private sphere. The nation, it might seem, is public and male, and the state the sphere of the female."[59]

The division of powers in Australia may have gendered foundations, but they have, to a large extent, been eroded. Over time, the intent of the constitutional founders has been reversed. Through High Court decisions and the Commonwealth's creative use of existing powers (especially in areas related to arbitration and conciliation, defence, tax, and external affairs), the federal government has come to be the dominant partner in the federation.[60] Since the 1940s, the arrogation to the federal government of powers that were previously the exclusive responsibility of the states – especially in the welfare field – has also helped to tip the balance in the Commonwealth's favour. While the states still have some responsibility for "the domestic and familial," many of these responsibilities are now shared with the Commonwealth.

The political and fiscal features of Australian federalism can be seen to have contributed to feminist strategy about how and where to agitate for reform. For a start, it has been logical for them to target the federal arena. The Commonwealth has responded to pressure from feminist activists to intervene in women's policy areas within its own jurisdiction as well as in areas that would otherwise be the responsibility of the states. Canberra has used its external affairs powers to develop sexual discrimination legislation, and it has used its conciliation and arbitration powers to develop equal pay legislation.⁶¹ It has legislated for the maternity allowance, child endowment payments, widow and sole parent pensions, and federal public service equal opportunity policies. The federal government has also relied upon its fiscal clout to act unilaterally, or jointly with the states, to gain a foothold in policy areas that are not enumerated under the Constitution. Such areas include women's refuges and domestic violence, women's health, and child care.⁶²

The degree of equalization inherent in Australian federalism has also shaped the strategic focus of Australian feminists. Through fiscal and legislative means, Canberra has sometimes been able to respond to feminist lobbying and so bypass recalcitrant state governments. For instance, through its enactment of the Sex Discrimination Act, the federal government was able to ensure that women in Queensland and Tasmania – two states that had refused to develop their own anti-discrimination legislation – had some degree of protection with regard to sex discrimination.⁶³ When these two states also failed to create their own women's policy agencies, the Commonwealth stepped in and funded women's information services in both through the federal Office of the Status of Women.⁶⁴

In Australia, the degree to which the Commonwealth has been able to become involved to create national women's policy issues, either through its constitutional authority or through its financial capacity, has meant that Australian women are less likely to be treated differently because they live in one state rather than another. In contrast to their Canadian counterparts, they have therefore had less reason to fear the development of a checkerboard of policies across the country. But it would be wrong to assume that it is only central control and uniformity – two "anti-federal" tendencies – that have shaped feminist responses. Another important influence, one that arguably offers them the opportunity to enjoy a system of "double democracy," has been the states' political capacity and willingness (on occasion) to "go it alone" in a range of policy areas, including abortion, equal employment opportunity, domestic violence, sexual assault, and child care. For instance, during the Fraser coalition government period, when the Commonwealth "dilly-dallied" on sex discrimination legislation, most of the states took action to introduce it.⁶⁵ State governments have also been prepared to take the initiative in providing support for some women's services when they have been stalled at the national level. This occurred in the late 1970s in New South Wales when the Wran ALP government started funding women's health services after the federal Liberal government withdrew Commonwealth funding for these programs.⁶⁶ Again, during the 1980s, when conservatives held power in Canberra, the South Australian government agreed to provide 100 percent of the funding for women's health centres.⁶⁷

Division of Political and Fiscal Authority in Canada

The Canadian federation is markedly different from the Australian federation. It is asymmetrical, built on an underlying multi-ethnic and multilingual foundation, with francophone Quebec existing alongside predominantly anglophone provinces. It is also based on strong economic and geographical regional cleavages, with the Maritimes, the Prairies, and the West Coast defining themselves against the centre: that is, Ontario and Quebec. The ethnoregional nature of the Canadian federation has meant that it has developed as a relatively decentralized system, which can be seen to run counter to the intentions of its constitutional founders. It was their aim to create a federal system with a strong central government, vesting Ottawa with innumerable powers and the ability to override conflicting provincial laws. However, over time, the balance of power within the Canadian federation has shifted toward the provinces. This shift has occurred in part through judicial interpretation that "gave broad reading to provincial jurisdiction over property and civil rights and a narrower interpretation than originally intended to federal powers."[68] Quebec's claims to sovereignty have also contributed to greater decentralization and paved the way for other provinces to make their own claims for increased autonomy.[69] In recent years, the provinces have come to reject any notion that the national government is a superior level of government, instead claiming that Canada has eleven equal governments (ten provincial and one federal).[70]

The strength of the Canadian provinces has been enhanced by two factors: their constitutional authority and their fiscal capacity. Provinces have jurisdiction over many policy areas, including local government, primary and secondary education, and most areas of noncriminal law. They also control key social policy areas, including health care, social welfare, and tertiary education. Since the 1950s, the growing cost of these programs has led the provinces to depend increasingly on federal co-ordination and financial support.[71] Through the use of federal spending power, Ottawa was able to assert some control over provincial policy fields such as health and social welfare. However, in recent years, the role of the federal government in provincial affairs has been challenged. Interference by the federal government through tied funding has been highly contentious, with many provinces asserting their claim to autonomy.[72] Political pressure from Quebec and other provinces has led to the federal government's gradual withdrawal from shared-funding programs in areas such as health, social services, unemployment insurance, training, and the labour market. In their place, provinces have been granted unconditional block funding.[73] While Ottawa continues to have some hold over the purse strings, it has gradually lost control over directing how provinces spend their money.

Subnational autonomy has been further enhanced as a result of the provinces' extensive fiscal capacity. Unlike the Australian states, the Canadian provinces can operate in every tax field except customs, excise, and domestic property.[74] The move by the provinces to re-enter the field of income taxation after the Second World War, and to collect rents from their own resource bases, has significantly contributed to their vitality.[75] Cullen summarizes the position of provinces as having "considerable scope to develop (and protect) their own economies (and identities). Although not entirely fiscally independent, the provinces also enjoy significant, provincially based, revenue raising capacity."[76] Not all provinces enjoy the same degree of fiscal autonomy. Indeed, significant discrepancies exist between the provinces in terms of their revenue-raising capacity. For instance, oil-rich Alberta is able to raise much more revenue than are the less prosperous Maritime provinces. Efforts have been made to minimize these differences through federal government transfers.[77] Because these efforts have focused only on adjusting for differences in the revenue-raising capacity of the provinces (and not on the cost of expenditure), the effect of federal transfers has been nowhere near as dramatic as it has been in Australia.[78] As a result, greater regional variations have developed in Canada compared with Australia.

Centrifugal pressure has undoubtedly been the strongest dynamic in Canadian federalism. However, countervailing tendencies also exist within the federation. Just as in Australia, where federal strength has been checked by state autonomy, so too in Canada centralizing forces have countered provincial autonomy. The most obvious and powerful of these has been the Charter of Rights and Freedoms.[79] The main political purpose underlying the Charter was Trudeau's pan-Canadian nationalizing vision. Trudeau made his intentions clear in 1967 in a speech on constitutional reform: "The adoption of a constitutional Bill of Rights is intimately related to the whole question of constitutional reform. Essentially we will be testing – and, hopefully, establishing – the unity of Canada."[80] It was introduced in an attempt by Ottawa to bypass provincial governments and to speak directly with the citizenry.[81] To some extent, it can be argued that the Charter has been successful since it has helped to foster the development of a national rights community. As discussed below, feminists, along with Aboriginal groups, have certainly taken advantage of this opening. In other ways, though, the Charter and Trudeau's constitutional vision have failed. Because the Charter did not deal successfully with either the duality issue with regard to Quebec or address regional concerns (especially in the west), constitutional reform has contributed to the tension between Ottawa and the provinces.[82] Rather than stem centrifugal forces, constitutional reform has arguably served to encourage them.

In Canada, federal political and fiscal arrangements have influenced Anglo-Canadian feminist strategies, albeit in a negative way. Despite the presence of strong centrifugal and regional pressures, these feminists have been reluctant to look toward the provincial level. As noted earlier, there has been some engagement with provincial institutions (e.g., in British Columbia and Newfoundland and, in earlier periods, Alberta). However, many Anglo-Canadian feminists and the key feminist organization, NAC, have preferred to maintain their focus on Ottawa. The federal government, especially during the Trudeau era, has helped to encourage this effort in two ways: through Women's Program funding and the Charter of Rights and Freedoms.

Since the 1940s, the Canadian federal government has been involved in providing financial support for the creation of interest groups. The purpose of this funding has been twofold: to be able to communicate easily with the public that it serves, and to strengthen the allegiance of certain interest groups with the central government rather than with the provinces. The Trudeau government, which came to office in 1968, can be seen to have overtly focused on the latter task. Governing at a time when centrifugal forces were at their peak, it saw funding interest groups as a way to advance its own vision for Canadian unity and explicitly linked this to notions of "participatory democracy," national unity, and citizenship.[83] The Women's Program, established in 1974 by the Department of Secretary of State, was part of this effort.[84]

The program was established to support the development of groups involved in promoting understanding and action on Status of Women issues. The program has funded not only national groups but also provincial and municipal groups.[85] The program has established offices in all major regional centres to administer funding applications and to make recommendations to head office with regard to grant allocations. Although the program cannot provide money for women's services, since this is a provincial responsibility, it has provided funds to enable organizations to lobby the provincial governments on matters that relate to legislation or funding for these services. According to a senior Women's Program officer, "the regional nature of the program has created an interesting situation where in some cases the program is funding groups to protest against provincial policies. An example of this occurred when the program funded women's groups to lobby the Alberta government to stop its changes to the health system."[86]

The Women's Program has been crucial in encouraging Anglo-Canadian feminists to look toward Ottawa. As Vickers argues, the program's funding made it logical for women's groups to "construct themselves as part of the federal government's community of clients," even if their main activity related to the provinces.[87] Its influence as a centralizing force for feminists was weakened under Mulroney when he cut funding levels and provided financial support to the anti-feminist REAL women's organization – a trend that continued under the Chrétien Liberal government.[88] Nevertheless, the program's legacy is still obvious. In Phillips's view, "the expectation has been created that the funder of minority interests will also be their protector."[89]

The Charter, introduced in an attempt to counter decentralizing forces, has also influenced the strategies of Anglo-Canadian feminists. Not only has it provided them with the ability to engage in a litigation strategy,[90] but it has also helped them to avoid the "patchwork" effect that they so fear will result from greater devolution of services. According to McLellan, many Anglo-Canadian feminists have come to perceive the Charter as an instrument that they can use to ensure "a comparability of benefits, legal conditions and support programs wherever they might end up living."[91] As noted earlier, they have been able to use the Charter to good effect, winning important cases pertaining to equality, reproductive, and employment rights – rights that affect women regardless of where they live. In short, the Charter has given Anglo-Canadian feminists an instrument with which to counteract increasing forces of decentralization and, even at a time when provinces are increasingly important, a reason to maintain a national focus.

Intergovernmental Mechanisms
Over the course of the past two decades in Australia and Canada, federalism has increasingly taken on an executive form. In both countries, a vast array of formal and informal intergovernmental mechanisms has been created to facilitate communication and joint action between elected and nonelected officials at the national and subnational levels of government. Canada's federal-provincial forums, which include conferences between first ministers as well as meetings between ministers and bureaucrats responsible for particular policy areas, are mirrored in Australia by the Special Premiers' Conference, the Council of Australian Governments (COAG), and ministerial councils.[92] Although the Canadian intergovernmental system is vast, according to Watts's comparative survey of federations, the system in Australia is more formalized.[93]

Intergovernmental mechanisms have, at least in a nominal sense, been highly gendered. In both countries, women have been poorly represented in most of the machinery of executive federalism.[94] The uneven gender balance may be less a function of federalism per se than a reflection of the under-representation of women in political leadership positions, in cabinet, and in the upper echelons of the public service. Nevertheless, it has meant that women have been mostly absent from the leadership positions in these increasingly important institutions. On a more positive note, executive federalism has also opened up some opportunities for the advancement of women's policy. In Australia and Canada, intergovernmental women's policy machinery has been created, including meetings between national- and provincial-/state-level Status of Women's ministers and bureaucrats. This machinery has been especially important in the Australian case. During the late 1980s and 1990s, femocrats in state jurisdictions co-operated with those at the federal level to fashion national policies concerning child care, domestic violence, women's health, and other areas that required joint government action. Most recently, the Howard Liberal government has joined with the states to implement the national Partnerships against Domestic Violence Program, which provides funding for research on domestic violence at the Commonwealth level as well as in each state.[95]

In line with their general attitude toward federalism, Anglo-Canadian feminists have tended to be more wary of these intergovernmental institutions than have Australian feminists. They have joined with others in criticizing these institutions as undemocratic and elitist.[96] Their opposition to these structures was most obvious during the debates around the Meech Lake Accord. They were highly critical of the elitist process used to devise the accord. NAC's anti–Meech Lake slogan – "Don't let eleven men threaten the legal rights of over half the population" – summed up the mood in the Anglo-Canadian feminist community with regard to the workings of executive federalism.[97]

It may also be the case that the link between feminists and executive federalist institutions has been weaker in Canada than in Australia because of its less institutionalized "femocracy." Without comprehensive or entrenched women's policy machinery, Canadian feminists have found it difficult to utilize the executive federal structures at their disposal. Rankin and Vickers support this view, at least in relation to anti-domestic violence policy making. Their research found that the links between Canadian femocrats at all levels of government working in this policy area were very weak and that federal arrangements were so complex that it was difficult for those working either inside or outside the state to develop a co-ordinated approach to the issue of domestic violence.[98]

Federal Norms
As with other institutions, not only structures but also underlying norms have played a role in shaping the POS open to feminists within federalism. The very term "federalism" is, as Watts notes, "basically not a descriptive but a normative term." It is, as he points out, "based on the presumed value and validity of combining unity and diversity and of accommodating, preserving and promoting distinct entities within a larger political union."[99] However, it is important to note that federalism

seeks to accommodate and to preserve a distinct form of diversity – one based on territory. In Whitaker's view, "The essential organising principle of federalism is territoriality ... Federalism as a system of representation ... is predicated along the axis of space and its political organization."[100] Gagnon agrees, arguing that "central to any view of federalism is the respect for diversity, which implies the maintenance of territorially based communities with specific identities."[101]

The strength of territorial representation as an underlying norm of federalism has some profound consequences. While it empowers certain ethnoregional groups, it does so at the expense of other "nonterritorial" groups. As White argues, "the most marginalised will be as marginal in a federal system as they are anywhere else; neither the theory nor the practice of federalism is about equalising democratic weight beyond the perimeters of its recognised territorial structures."[102] The significance of this point has not been lost on the Canadian Aboriginal community, which has pushed strongly for a vision of federalism that is not based on territorial boundaries but able to embrace group identity as a form of representation.[103] Feminists have also been alert to the significance and limitations of privileging territorial concerns. For Vickers, "the territorial organization of politics suppresses interests and needs which are not territorially contained."[104] She notes that federal arrangements might suit certain groups of women, such as francophone feminists living in Quebec, who have been able to use their unique ethnoregional position to further gender-based interests. However, outside these exceptional cases, women (and, more specifically, sex/gender interests) are not politically relevant. The problem for feminist activists in federal systems is that "political institutions are structured to represent geographically organized political interests, while women are geographically dispersed."[105]

How has federalism's emphasis on territoriality influenced the political opportunity structure open to Australian and Canadian feminists? In Canada, because the provinces have enjoyed more political and fiscal autonomy than have the Australian states, and because of the ethnoregional character of Canadian federalism, the politics of territory has been particularly salient. The consequences have been that gender (and other identity) interests have been downplayed, if not ignored, within federal debates. The emphasis on territorial issues has no doubt contributed to women's activists' disinclination to engage in provincial politics.[106] However, as noted, a parallel force is at work in Canada – the centralizing dynamic of the Charter of Rights and Freedoms. To some extent, it can be argued that the entrenchment of the Charter has provided space for representation of cleavages that are nationwide and nonterritorial, such as those based on race and gender identities.[107] The Charter not only offers the women's movement opportunities to engage in a litigation strategy to advance its interests in the face of legislative barriers but also provides women with an instrument (albeit a limited one) with which to challenge the politics of territory that inhibits the representation of gender concerns.

Territorial interests are also important in Australia. Turf wars between the federal and state governments are a feature of the political landscape and at times dominate the political debate. In Australia, though, these interests are ameliorated to some extent by the fact that regional cleavages are less obvious than they are in Canada and the fact that there is no imperative to embrace a second majoritarian culture. Furthermore, the nature of the party system and the presence of a progressive political party, which has traditionally been focused on class issues, have acted as counterweights to territorial concerns. As has been noted earlier, feminists in Australia have made gains at both the state and the federal levels when there has been an ALP government in office. It would be incorrect to assume that these mediating factors have meant that gender interests are central in Australian political debates. Nevertheless, exploiting the opportunities provided by a progressive party at both levels of government, Australian feminists have, at certain times, taken advantage of federalism's multiple access points in order to influence policy and services for women.

The experience of Australian and Canadian feminists with regard to federalism provides some support for the arguments of Banaszak and Galligan: that is, it can open new spaces for political activists and provide a system of "dual citizenship."[108] The Australian case demonstrates that, where feminists face a system within which both levels of government have some political and/or fiscal authority, and within which territorial concerns are ameliorated by equalization concerns and the presence of a progressive political party, opportunities for dual citizenship can emerge. However, as Pierson makes clear, different federal systems can produce different results. This is obvious from the comparison presented here. Anglo-Canadian feminists confront a highly decentralized system, with the norm of territoriality being strong and with mediating party structures being weak. Operating within these conditions, Canadian feminists have not always found that federalism offers them a system of double democracy; rather, they have found that it is better to direct their efforts toward the national government and to use the Charter to advance their nonterritorial claims. There are signs that centrifugal forces will lead to greater decentralization in Canada. These forces, along with evidence that certain provincial governments (e.g., the former NDP governments in British Columbia and Ontario) can be supportive of feminist demands, might lead Anglo-Canadian feminists to look more closely at the experience of their Quebec counterparts and find new ways to engage with federal institutions.

Notes

1 See Gray (1998); Irving (1994); Vickers (1990, 1993, 1994); and Dobrowolsky (2000).
2 Rankin and Vickers (1998), 342.
3 Sawer and Vickers (2001).
4 Banaszak (1996).
5 Banaszak (1996), 217.
6 Banaszak (1996), 67.
7 See Coleman (1987); and Bakvis and Chandler (1987).
8 See Nathan (1992); and Gagnon (1995).
9 See Galligan (1995), 35-53.
10 For a summary, see Nathan (1992), 97.
11 Galligan (1995), 51.
12 See Maddox (1996); and Riker (1964).
13 Pierson (1995), 450-51.
14 Sawer and Vickers (2001).
15 Cox (1995), 48, 49.
16 Flask and Hounslow (n.d.).
17 Sawer (1990), 140.
18 Queensland did not create a women's unit until after the election of the Goss ALP government in the early 1990s.
19 Dowse (1984), 145.
20 Townsend (1994), 3.
21 McFerren (1990), 194.
22 Dowse (1984), 152.
23 Healy (1991), 193.
24 See McFerren (1990).
25 See Sawer (1990), 155. Niland has also been credited with achieving a similar outcome in the women's health field; see Smith (1984).
26 Dowse (1984), 156.
27 See Brennan (1994); and Gray (1998).
28 Rankin and Vickers (1998).
29 The 1987 Meech Lake Accord was devised by the federal and provincial governments with the intention of bringing Quebec into the "constitutional fold." Although supported by Quebec, it failed to be ratified by provincial legislatures and eventually foundered. The Charlottetown Accord represented another try at incorporating Quebec as well as a response to Aboriginal demands for constitutional recognition. It also failed when it was rejected in a national referendum in 1992.
30 See *Action Now* 2, 7 (1987).
31 See *Feminist Action* 3, 2 (1988); and McLellan (1991).
32 See *Feminist Action* 3, 3 (1988).
33 See also Dobrowolsky (2000), 86. Anglo-Canadian feminists' fear of women having uneven rights across the country was not new. They had made this point in their campaign in 1978 against the transfer of divorce to subnational governments; see Burt (1988), 76.
34 Cited in McRoberts and Monahan (1993), 105.
35 McLellan (1991), 19.
36 McLellan (1991), 26.
37 Day, cited in Vickers (1993), 269.
38 Vickers (1990), 22.
39 Rankin and Vickers (1998).
40 Busque (1991), 160.
41 Dumont (1992), 76.
42 Rankin and Vickers (2001), 17.
43 Rankin and Vickers (2001), 17.
44 For a discussion of the role of feminists in Quebec politics, see Tremblay (1997).
45 Sawer and Vickers (2001), 19.
46 NAC (1995), n.p.

47 NAC (1995), n.p.
48 Dobrowolsky (2000), 25.
49 Dobrowolsky (2000), 65.
50 Rankin and Vickers (1998), 348.
51 Teghtsoonian (2000).
52 Arscott, Rankin, and Vickers (n.d.), 41.
53 Galligan (1990), 25. The states collect between 15 and 20 percent of their revenue, while being responsible for approximately 40 percent of total government outlays. Federal government transfers cover the rest.
54 The use of SPPs increased dramatically under the Whitlam government. Between 1972-73 and 1975-76, SPP assistance to the states increased from 26 percent of total funding to the states to 48 percent. In 1995-96, SPPs accounted for 53 percent of total payments to the states; see Joint Committee of Public Accounts (1995).
55 Painter (1997b), 203.
56 Self (1989), 80.
57 Painter (1996), 86.
58 Gillespie (1995), 168.
59 Irving (1994), 196.
60 Gray (1991), 18.
61 See s. 51 (xxix) and s. 51 (xxxv) of the Australian Constitution. In this case, the federal government was able to invoke the UN Convention on Elimination of All Forms of Discrimination against Women, to which it was a signatory, to intervene in an area of state jurisdiction.
62 In the late 1980s, under the Hawke government, the Commonwealth was able to enter the women's health field despite many of the services being the responsibility of the states. It did this through the development of the National Women's Health Program, a joint Commonwealth-state program in which the Commonwealth was the dominant financial partner. In the first four years of the program, the Commonwealth provided 50 percent of the total $36 million budget, and in the second four-year phase of the program it committed itself to $30 million of the $60 million budget. Canberra has also been able to play the dominant role in the development of child care policy even though it holds the responsibility for this area jointly with the states. In 1994-95, of the $1 billion spent on child care services, the Commonwealth contributed 90 percent, with the balance provided by the states; see OSW (1994), n.p.; and Council of Australian Governments Child Care Working Group (1995), 10.
63 Simms and Stone (1990), 289.
64 OSW (1989).
65 Simms and Stone (1990), 289.
66 Smith (1984), 4.
67 Sawer (1990), 13.
68 Hurley (1997), 115.
69 Corbett (1990), 301.
70 Simeon (1988), S14.
71 McIver (1995), 220.
72 Watts (1996), 41.
73 Maslove (1992), 170.
74 McIver (1995), 226.
75 In 1994-95, provinces received on average only 18.7 percent of their income through federal government transfers. The rest was made up of a combination of income tax, consumption taxes, licence fees, and government levies. According to Watts's (1996), 71, survey of federations, Canada is second only to Switzerland with regard to the extent of provincial autonomous revenue-raising capacity.
76 Cullen (1989), 129.
77 In 1994-95, the four wealthiest provinces received between 11 percent and 20 percent of their total revenue from federal transfers, whereas the four Atlantic provinces received between 36 percent and 43 percent; see White (1997), 169.
78 Watts (1996), 47.

79 The Charter, however, contains a major compromise for the provinces. Section 33 allows provincial governments to introduce legislation "notwithstanding" most Charter provisions.
80 Trudeau (1967), 54.
81 Cairns (1995b), 200.
82 McIver (1995), 236.
83 Phillips (1991), 190.
84 Pal (1993), 14.
85 In 1985-86, the Women's Program provided $10.8 million in funding for 650 groups across Canada: 37 percent of the funds were allocated to national groups, while 63 percent went to local, regional, or provincial groups; see House of Commons Standing Committee on the Secretary of State (1987), 7, 12. In 1990-91, only 39 of the 457 women's groups funded by the Women's Program were nationally based. The remainder were provincially based. Interestingly, Quebec had the most groups – 117 – funded by the program. The most populated province, Ontario, followed with a total of seventy-six groups; see Phillips (1991), 200.
86 Interview with the author (1995).
87 Vickers (1990), 22.
88 See Phillips (1991), 201. The Women's Program suffered a further cut of 5 percent when it was merged with Status of Women Canada in 1995; see *Action Now* 5, 2 (1995).
89 Phillips (1991), 205.
90 See Dobrowolsky (2000); and Chappell (2002).
91 Cited in Vickers (1993), 271.
92 For a discussion of intergovernmental machinery in Canada, see Hurley (1997); in Australia, see Painter (1997b), 204-207.
93 Watts (1996), 52.
94 In Australia, there have been only two female ALP state premiers, Carmen Lawrence (Western Australia) and Joan Kirner (Victoria), both of whom were appointed to office for brief periods of time. A similar pattern has emerged in Canada. In June 1993, Kim Campbell was appointed prime minister. She lost office at the December 1996 election. In April 1991, the Social Credit Party in British Columbia appointed Rita Johnson as premier, a position that she lost in the election of October 1991. Canada's second female premier, Catherine Callbeck, headed the Prince Edward Island government for three years, beginning in 1993.
95 Chappell (2001).
96 A widespread critique of the move toward executive federalism focuses on its undemocratic nature. Opponents argue that intergovernmental institutions are elitist and bypass democratically elected parliaments; see Painter (1998); and Watts (1996).
97 *Action Now* 2, 7 (1987): n.p.
98 Rankin and Vickers (2001), 57.
99 Watts (1996), 6.
100 Cited in Gagnon (1995), 193.
101 Gagnon (1995), 28.
102 White (1997), 18.
103 Rocher and Smith (1995), 56.
104 Vickers (1994), 14.
105 Vickers (1990), 20.
106 Vickers (1990), 22.
107 Rocher and Smith (1995), 63.
108 See Banaszak (1996); and Galligan (1995).

Part 2
Reconceiving Representation through Citizenship and Community

5
Sharing the River: Aboriginal Representation in Canadian Political Institutions
Melissa S. Williams

> The public mind sees a logical contradiction that no complicated legal theory can overcome: how can you be a member of a "First Nation" and then turn around and say that you are part of another nation – Canada? You can't – not as a citizen of a liberal democracy based on the principles of equal representation and majority rule.
>
> – Taiaiake Alfred (2000), n.p.

> We are all part of one another, although not always harmoniously so. The future of Aboriginal peoples, whether or not they have a land base that is a requisite for effective self-government, is within Canada. If that "withinness" means that Canada is to be more than a container, or a mini-international system, we need bonds of empathy so that our togetherness is moral as well as geographical. The obvious moral bond is a shared citizenship.
>
> – Alan Cairns (2000), 211

Aboriginal people in Canada are starkly under-represented in Canadian legislative institutions, and such has always been the case.[1] Until the 1960 amendments to the federal Indian Act, status Indians were legally excluded from the electoral franchise. Since Confederation, only fourteen Aboriginal people have been elected to the federal Parliament. In 2000, three Aboriginal people were elected to the House of Commons; if Aboriginal people were represented in proportion to their share of the Canadian population, they would hold eleven seats.[2]

Yet enhanced representation in mainstream legislative institutions has not, by and large, been a goal of Aboriginal leaders or scholars in Canada, primarily because it appears to stand at odds with the more important goal of Aboriginal self-government.[3] To seek enhanced representation in the institutions of Canadian democracy appears to be tantamount to embracing shared citizenship with non-Aboriginal Canadians. How can it be possible to insist upon an inherent right of Aboriginal self-government, grounded in a "nation-to-nation" relationship with the Canadian government, while also laying claim to full participation in that government's legislative institutions? These appear to be mutually exclusive political goals: egalitarian inclusion through shared representative institutions, or political autonomy through separate institutions of self-government. Opposing proposals for reserved Aboriginal seats in the New Brunswick provincial assembly, the executive director of the Union of New Brunswick Indians argued, "What it boils down to is [that] we are a nation and, by becoming part of someone else's system, we are going to give that up."[4]

Aboriginal people have good reason to be suspicious of the language of shared citizenship. Extension of the franchise to status Indians in 1960 was, as noted above, through amendment of the Indian Act. But since its first passage in 1876, the Indian Act was the legal instrument through which the federal government pursued policies of forcible relocation, cultural annihilation (e.g., through making traditional practices illegal), and aggressive (and often intensely cruel) assimilation (especially through residential schooling). Given that enfranchisement was understood by the federal government as another – albeit kinder – tool for assimilation, it is no wonder that many Aboriginal people viewed it with skepticism. Similarly, the federal Liberal government's 1969 White Paper, which proposed the abolition of the Indian Act and the elimination of all legal distinctions between Aboriginal and non-Aboriginal people in Canada, promoted assimilation in the name of equal citizenship. However benevolent the motives underlying the White Paper, it clearly construed equal citizenship in terms of an undifferentiated legal and social status for Aboriginal and non-Aboriginal people alike.[5] This history makes it easy to understand why Aboriginal people keen to preserve and protect Aboriginal cultural identities and practices might reject the language of shared Canadian citizenship. Taiaiake Alfred expresses the objection to this language in characteristically pithy style: "Has the citizenship legally forced on our people a generation ago helped get our land back, gain compassion for past injustices, or made our communities healthier? Of course it hasn't (we should also remember that citizenship was rejected by the Elders in most communities). Forty years of citizenship and we're more assimilated now than ever before, and we're losing our languages and traditions at a heartbreaking rate. What citizenship has done over the years is undermine in people's minds the idea that we have a separate existence and distinct collective rights."[6]

It is not my purpose in this chapter to review the normative arguments that support the claim to a right to Aboriginal self-government. Others have done that work very well.[7] There are undoubtedly further theoretical and institutional puzzles to solve in conceptualizing the right to self-government, including the nettlesome question whether the right is an "inherent" or natural right of self-determination of peoples, grounded in common law, established in constitutional law, grounded in extralegal moral arguments from the idea of individual autonomy, or justified as the sole pragmatic solution to the cruel legacies of colonialism. Whatever the normative and legal foundation of the right to self-government, for the purposes of this inquiry I take the right itself as settled from a moral point of view.[8] On a practical level, I take the essence of a right of self-government to be that Aboriginal communities should have the power to make authoritative and binding decisions on matters that affect themselves alone, according to their own internal standards of political legitimacy, without the oversight or sanction of non-Aboriginal institutions.[9]

Is it truly the case that the goal of self-government is incompatible with the goal of enhanced representation in shared institutions within Canada? Are Aboriginal critics of the latter goal correct in their belief that there is an inescapable logical contradiction between these two forms of political empowerment? These are the questions that I wish to explore in this chapter, if only in a preliminary way. My inquiry proceeds in four stages. First, I examine three key proposals for enhanced Aboriginal representation in federal legislative institutions: those of the Royal Commission on Electoral Reform and Party Financing (hereafter RCERPF), the Charlottetown Accord that was rejected in the 1992 federal referendum, and the Royal Commission on Aboriginal Peoples (hereafter RCAP). In this section, I will explore the strengths and limitations of each of these proposals as efforts to reconcile the goals of Aboriginal self-government and Aboriginal empowerment within shared institutions.

Two unresolved theoretical issues render these proposals inadequate as answers to the question whether self-government and enhanced representation conflict: the meaning of citizenship, and the requirements of political legitimacy. In the second section, I contrast two understandings of citizenship, one grounded in a notion of shared identity and the other based on what I call "shared fate." The latter, I argue, provides a more promising way of conceptualizing the relationship between Aboriginal peoples and Canadian citizenship in a future world where the right to self-government has been established in practice. Here, following the lead of many Aboriginal (and some non-Aboriginal) thinkers, I explore the idea of the "two-row wampum" as a model for the relationship between Aboriginal peoples and the Canadian state. As John Borrows has argued, the two-row wampum is helpful in enabling us to imagine a citizenship grounded not in a shared civic identity but in the shared fate of Aboriginal and non-Aboriginal people living on Turtle Island, in the territory that most of us now call Canada.[10]

The third section of the paper addresses concerns of political legitimacy by examining arguments that there must be a trade-off between self-government as a right *against* the state and group representation as a right *within* the state. Would a dual structure of self-government and enhanced representation constitute an illegitimate expansion of political powers for Aboriginal peoples, enabling them to pass legislation from which self-government rights would exempt them? Although this is a valid worry on the theoretical plane, I argue, it can be resolved through careful institutional design.

In the final section of the chapter, I offer a brief sketch of institutional reforms that could reconcile Aboriginal peoples' interest in self-government with their interest in enhanced representation in shared Canadian institutions and address some possible objections.

Proposals for Aboriginal Representation in Shared Canadian Institutions

The Royal Commission on Electoral Reform and Party Financing

In its 1991 final report, RCERPF recommended the establishment of Aboriginal constituencies within the existing constitutional framework for elections to the federal House of Commons. An important constraint of existing electoral law is that seats in Parliament are apportioned to provinces on the basis of provincial populations. Without constitutional amendment, enhancing Aboriginal representation would have to be based on establishing Aboriginal constituencies within provincial boundaries. Within this constraint, however, the commission's recommendations were quite creative. Because Aboriginal populations are geographically dispersed within provinces, the use of geographically defined electoral districts for parliamentary elections could not yield a sufficient number of Aboriginal-majority constituencies to secure anything close to proportionality in Aboriginal representation. Thus, the practice of "majority-minority" districting, used with considerable success to enhance African-American representation in the United States,[11] would not be an effective tool for significantly enhancing Aboriginal representation in the House of Commons. Instead, the commission recommended that a portion of each province's share of legislative seats be designated as special Aboriginal constituencies, which would fall within provincial boundaries but need not be geographical constituencies.

The number of Aboriginal constituencies allocated to each province would be based on the total number of Aboriginal voters within the province. Acknowledging that Canadian law permits deviations in the size of electoral districts in order to facilitate the representation of distinct "communities of interest," the commission recommended as generous an allocation of seats as possible for Aboriginal constituencies. Existing law permits a deviation of 15 percent from the electoral quotient.¹² Thus, the commission recommended that the number of Aboriginal constituencies per province be "equal to such integer as is obtained by dividing the number of [Aboriginal voters] by a number equal to 85 percent of the electoral quotient for the province."¹³ In other words, the commission's formula would secure somewhat more than a proportionate share of legislative seats for Aboriginal voters. The commission calculated that, according to this formula, up to eight Aboriginal constituencies could be created across the provinces.¹⁴ Assuming that these constituencies would return Aboriginal representatives, this method could secure close to a threefold increase over any past level of Aboriginal representation in the House of Commons.

The commission was also sensitive to the concern that individual members of Aboriginal communities should not have a political identity imposed upon them by the Canadian state but should have a choice as to whether to be represented in Aboriginal or in general constituencies. Accordingly, it recommended that, at the time of electoral enumeration, Aboriginal citizens would specify whether they wished to vote in a special Aboriginal constituency or whether they wished to be counted in the general voter rolls. The total number of Aboriginal constituencies per province would be based on the number of individuals who chose to be counted on the Aboriginal rolls. The commission further recommended that enumeration as an Aboriginal voter be based on self-identification but that an adjudication procedure be established for cases in which an individual's claim to Aboriginal identity was in dispute.¹⁵

In proposing special Aboriginal constituencies, the RCERPF report explicitly denied that there is any necessary contradiction "between the goal of Aboriginal self-government and the objective of a more effective say for Aboriginal peoples in Canada's central political institution." "On the contrary," commissioners argued, "a cogent and persuasive case can be made that both processes are complementary and mutually reinforcing." Furthermore, they maintained that the creation of special Aboriginal constituencies would secure a political voice for Aboriginal people who were not tied to the sort of land base commonly presupposed in treaty negotiations and in designing institutions for Aboriginal self-government. "Finally," they argued, "the creation of Aboriginal constituencies would not abrogate or derogate from any Aboriginal treaty or other rights and freedoms that pertain to Aboriginal peoples. However, the establishment of a process whereby Aboriginal constituencies could be created would require the explicit and substantial support of Aboriginal people."¹⁶ Despite these assurances, the commission did not proceed to spell out the "cogent and persuasive case" for the mutual reinforcement of enhanced representation and Aboriginal self-government. In short, it did not advance a theory of the relationship between the idea of Aboriginal peoples' nationhood and Aboriginal inclusion in shared political institutions.

The Charlottetown Accord

Canada's most recent round of constitutional negotiations, in which four Aboriginal representatives sat at the table with first ministers, produced a sweeping array of proposals for constitutional change. The resulting Charlottetown Accord, defeated in a Canada-wide referendum in 1992, would have radically transformed the constitutional status of Aboriginal peoples in Canada.[17] Had it succeeded, the accord would have secured both a constitutional recognition of an inherent right of Aboriginal self-government and a dramatic enhancement of Aboriginal representation in both the House of Commons and a reformed "triple-E" ("equal, elected, and effective") Senate. It would also have entrenched a role for Aboriginal peoples in the appointment of justices to the Supreme Court and empowered an Aboriginal Council of Elders to provide guidance to the Supreme Court on cases concerning Aboriginal issues.

The accord left many institutional details to be hammered out in future negotiations. It would have directed Parliament to pursue the question of Aboriginal representation in the House of Commons "in consultation with representatives of the Aboriginal peoples of Canada" after receiving the report of the House of Commons committee that reviewed the recommendations of the RCERPF report.[18] The reformed Senate was to comprise sixty-four members, with six senators elected from each of the provinces and two from each of the territories. The accord provided that "Aboriginal representation in the Senate should be guaranteed in the Constitution" and that Aboriginal seats in the Senate would be "additional to provincial and territorial seats, rather than drawn from any province or territory's allocation of Senate seats." In addition to assigning Aboriginal senators the regular role and powers of other senators, the accord proffered the possibility that on issues of Aboriginal concern a double majority would be required to pass legislation.[19] However, the accord did not specify the number of seats to be held by Aboriginal senators.

Article 41 of the accord stated categorically that "The Constitution should be amended to recognize that the Aboriginal peoples of Canada have an inherent right of self-government within Canada." It would have entrenched a "third order" of Aboriginal government within Canada, joining the federal and provincial governments in the very foundation of the constitutional order. The accord was clear that, in the areas of its application, Aboriginal jurisdiction would be independent of both federal and provincial jurisdiction. The proposed language for constitutional amendment on the meaning of self-government was as follows:

The exercise of the right of self-government includes authority of the duly elected legislative bodies of the Aboriginal peoples, each within its own jurisdiction:
  a to safeguard and develop their languages, cultures, economies, identities, institutions and traditions; and,
  b to develop, maintain and strengthen their relationship with their lands, waters and environment so as to determine and control their developments as peoples according to their own values and priorities and ensure the integrity of their societies.[20]

As Alan Cairns notes, "One of the implicit paradoxes of the Accord was the tension between its proposals to reduce the federal Parliament's jurisdiction over Aboriginal peoples by implementing self-government while simultaneously advocating an enhanced and explicit Aboriginal representation in both houses of Parliament."[21] Like the RCERPF report, the Charlottetown Accord clearly presupposes that there is no necessary contradiction between the claims of self-government and those of enhanced political representation in shared institutions, but it does not set out a theoretical argument to persuade us of this. Like the RCERPF report, the accord leaves us without sufficient resources to answer Taiaiake Alfred's challenge.

The Royal Commission on Aboriginal Peoples

RCAP's *Final Report,* issued in 1996, acknowledged the proposals of the RCERPF report and the Charlottetown Accord for enhancing Aboriginal representation in parliamentary institutions. Yet the RCAP commissioners were not satisfied that these proposals successfully resolved the tensions between representation and self-government. Echoing Aboriginal leaders' reluctance to embrace enhanced representation as a political goal, the commissioners expressed concern "that efforts to reform the Senate and the House of Commons may not be compatible with the foundations for a renewed relationship built upon the inherent right of Aboriginal self-government and nation-to-nation governmental relations. Three orders of government imply the existence of representative institutions that provide for some degree of majority control, not minority or supplementary status."[22] Beyond this, however, the report offered little critical analysis of the specific proposals for increased Aboriginal influence in the two Houses of Parliament. Rather, the commissioners simply noted that "Canadian political institutions often lack legitimacy in the eyes of Aboriginal people. Many have noted that Aboriginal peoples were not involved in designing the Canadian state or in fashioning its institutions and processes. Second, there are good reasons to question the capacity of Canadian political institutions to represent Aboriginal people. Until recently, Aboriginal people were systematically denied participation in the Canadian political process, and only a handful of Aboriginal people have sat in Parliament since Confederation."²³

RCAP's response to justifiable Aboriginal distrust of existing parliamentary institutions was not to seek reform within those institutions but to create an altogether new institution that would stand alongside them in the legislative process. Ultimately, RCAP advised, Aboriginal peoples' interest in representation at the federal level could be reconciled with the goal of genuine self-government through the creation of a third chamber of Parliament to go with the third order of government: a House of First Peoples. This third chamber would be comprised of between 75 and 100 Aboriginal representatives. Elsewhere in the report, the commission proposed that Aboriginal self-government should eventually be structured through the consolidation of between sixty and eighty autonomous Aboriginal nations, and these nations would be the units from which Aboriginal representatives would be elected to the House of First Peoples. RCAP suggested that, while every nation would have at least one representative, more populous nations and confederacies might have more than one.

The report proposed that a House of First Peoples "should have real power": "By this, we mean the power to initiate legislation and to require a majority vote on matters crucial to the lives of Aboriginal peoples. This legislation would be referred to the House of Commons for mandatory debate and voting."²⁴ For models for the role of the new third chamber, RCAP turned to the examples of Saami parliaments in Scandinavian countries. While praising these institutions for their recognition of the distinctiveness of Saami culture, the report acknowledged that in their current forms the Saami parliaments "lack clout." Yet the report failed to make clear how the proposed House of First Peoples would overcome the limitations of the Saami parliaments. Given that the report did not specify any institutional linkage between a vote in the third chamber and the vote in the House of Commons, it is not clear what recourse Aboriginal peoples would have – beyond an appeal to public opinion – were their proposals systematically to be outvoted after being referred to the House of Commons. This seems to be a considerably weaker security for Aboriginal interests than the double majority requirement proposed by the Charlottetown Accord.

Since the creation of a House of First Peoples would require constitutional amendment, RCAP proposed an interim measure to create an Aboriginal parliament through federal legislation. This parliament would have a consultative function in relation to both the House of Commons and the Senate. Since there are many Aboriginal communities that have not yet developed strong institutions of self-government, RCAP proposed that the federal government should adapt the RCERPF report's formulas for Aboriginal electoral districts as the basis for elections to the Aboriginal parliament. But again the report offered no argument as to why representation in an Aboriginal parliament with no power over federal legislation is preferable to the RCERPF report's proposals for Aboriginal representation, and full voting powers for representatives, *within* the House of Commons. The answer to this puzzle, once again, lies in RCAP's apparent supposition that seeking real political clout within shared parliamentary institutions would compromise Aboriginal claims to the right of self-government. Although the report stressed the importance of "more than symbolic representation" for Aboriginal peoples within Canadian federalism,[25] RCAP's own proposals appear to support institutions that symbolically represent the distinctiveness and autonomy of Aboriginal nations at the cost of legislative powers within parliamentary institutions.

Unresolved Tensions between Self-Government and Enhanced Representation

As we have seen, the RCERPF report, the Charlottetown Accord, and the RCAP report all ultimately avoid the question whether there is an inescapable contradiction between self-government and self-representation within shared institutions. The first two offer proposals for enhanced representation while giving assurances that it does not conflict with self-government without offering an argument as to why worries about incompatibility arise and why they are not warranted. The third abandons representation in shared institutions for two reasons: the historical lack of legitimacy of those institutions in the eyes of Aboriginal people, and the concern that a "nation-to-nation" relationship between Aboriginal peoples and Canada would be compromised by the sharing of political institutions. But RCAP fails to articulate the reasons why we should believe that the two forms of Aboriginal empowerment conflict. The first two proposals deny the conflict, and the last affirms it, but they all fail to offer reasons for their judgments.

In fact, I believe that there are two distinct sets of reasons why people believe that self-government and representation conflict. The first stems from an understanding of citizenship as grounded in a shared national or civic identity. This understanding of citizenship informs the judgment of Taiaiake Alfred that it is impossible simultaneously to be a citizen of a First Nation and a citizen of the "Canadian nation." Citizenship as shared identity seems to presuppose an ordering principle that subordinates group or cultural identity to the identity of shared citizenship in cases in which the two conflict. If accepting Canadian citizenship entails putting aside Aboriginal identity in such cases, then many Aboriginal thinkers want nothing to do with it. Since political representation in shared institutions implies shared citizenship, they would prefer to forgo it in favour of self-government.

The second source of potential conflict between representation and self-government is grounded in an account of political legitimacy. Here the core idea is that, to the extent that Aboriginal communities lie beyond the authority of federal and provincial institutions, their members should not exercise political power within those institutions. As Will Kymlicka expresses this point, "in so far as self-government reduces the jurisdiction of the federal government over a national minority, self-government seems to entail that the group should have *reduced* influence (at least on certain issues) at the federal level ... For example, it would seem unfair for Quebec MPs to decide federal legislation on immigration if the legislation does not apply to Quebec. The same would apply to Aboriginal MPs elected by specially created Aboriginal districts voting on legislation from which Aboriginals would be exempt."[26] Kymlicka's argument goes to the heart of conceptions of democratic legitimacy. The concept of legitimacy rests on the notion that political decisions that affect the lives of individuals should be justifiable to those individuals through reasons that they can accept as valid. From this standpoint, the opportunity to participate in an exchange of reasons concerning matters of joint concern is an indispensable element of democratic legitimacy and supports the idea of the self-representation of affected groups in political decision making. But the right of Aboriginal self-government entails that Aboriginal communities should be exempt from the obligations of general legislation where those obligations conflict with community autonomy. Where such exemptions are in place, Aboriginal participation in the formulation of general legislation would appear to give Aboriginal representatives too much power in the political process, since it would mean that they would be able to impose requirements on others to which they themselves are not subject. Since one of the safeguards of legitimate government is that lawmakers are bound by the laws that they impose on the rest of the community,[27] there is indeed a contradiction between Aboriginal self-government and Aboriginal representation in shared institutions.

None of the foregoing proposals for Aboriginal representation directly confronts these two sides of the tension between Aboriginal representation in shared institutions and the aspiration to Aboriginal self-government. Does this mean that the conflict is unavoidable and that we face a radical choice between these two paths? To the contrary, I believe that the goal of a legitimate, postcolonial relationship between Aboriginal peoples and non-Aboriginal Canadians would be served by pursuing both goals simultaneously. To defend this position, however, will require two separate arguments, one addressed to the challenge from the concept of citizenship and the other to the challenge from the concept of political legitimacy.

Citizenship as Identity versus Citizenship as Shared Fate[28]

At the core of much contemporary democratic theory lies the supposition that meaningful democratic citizenship requires that citizens share a subjective sense of membership in a single political community defined by a commitment to core democratic values. This sense of shared membership, theorists argue, constitutes a distinctive *identity:* that is, it partially constitutes individuals' understandings of who they are.[29] Political membership is internalized as an *affective bond* to the political community and its other members. Joseph Carens calls this the psychological dimension of citizenship: "[One] way to belong to a political community is to *feel* that one belongs, to be connected to it through one's sense of emotional attachment, identification, and loyalty."[30]

This sense of shared belonging, many argue, is a crucial underpinning of two central goods of democratic governance: distributive justice and social stability. On the first point, the argument is that individuals will not be willing to make the sacrifices necessary to sustain redistributive programs (whether in the form of universal health care, public education, or social welfare payments) unless they feel some sense of affective attachment to those who stand to benefit from social redistribution. On the second point, theorists argue that social order is threatened if individuals and groups develop too strong a propensity to view the state, and each other, in wholly instrumental terms. A sense of loyalty to a shared political community functions to temper political self-interest for the sake of preserving the stability of political institutions.

It is precisely this conception of citizenship that, I believe, makes many Aboriginal thinkers nervous about the idea of Aboriginal citizenship within Canada. This is the worry that Taiaiake Alfred expresses in the opening quotation: if citizenship is a form of individual identity, then how is it possible to embrace an identity as a Canadian citizen without giving up something of Aboriginal identity? And, indeed, I believe that contemporary democratic theorists give some warrant to this concern. While many have striven to reconcile the concept of democratic citizenship with a robust account of cultural and social diversity in contemporary democratic societies, there is a notable tendency to suppose that, when the obligations of citizenship conflict with those of cultural membership, citizenship must prevail. Shared citizenship thus requires "a commitment to a common authority that can *override local interests, local decisions, and local ways of knowing.*"[31] As Stephen Macedo argues, "A liberal polity does not rest on diversity, but on *shared political commitments weighty enough to override competing values.*"[32]

I have argued elsewhere that the conception of citizenship as shared identity is inescapably tied to the history of nationalism and nation building characteristic of the modern nation-state that emerged in the nineteenth century.³³ That history is rife with examples of how the project of nation building developed at the expense of cultural, ethnic, and religious minorities. Although contemporary democratic theorists are keen to distance themselves from this past, I believe that a conception of citizenship grounded in a notion of shared identity cannot entirely remove the threat of cultural marginalization for minorities, even when theorists construe identity in terms of shared values rather than shared national or racial identity. Although I cannot develop the argument fully here, I think that Aboriginal critics of the goal of shared citizenship are right to be wary of the concept insofar as it is offered in the language of identity.³⁴

Nonetheless, I depart from critics such as Alfred who reject the goal of shared citizenship altogether. The challenge is rather to develop a conception of citizenship that avoids the risk of cultural marginalization and resists the temptation to ground citizenship exclusively in the concept of the modern nation-state and its corollary theory of sovereignty. The concept of citizenship expresses the idea that human freedom requires some agency over the political structures that shape our lives³⁵ and that we can exercise that agency only as participants in a collective project.

As a collective project, however, meaningful citizenship does require that we define the boundaries of political community. If shared identity is unsatisfactory as the source of those boundaries, what is the alternative? I want to suggest that an alternative lies in what we might call "citizenship as shared fate." The core of this idea is that we find ourselves in webs of relationship with other human beings that profoundly shape our lives, whether or not we consciously choose or voluntarily assent to be enmeshed in these webs. What connects us in a community of shared fate is that our actions have an impact on other identifiable human beings, and other human beings' actions have an impact on us.

A community of shared fate is *not* an ethical community as such. That is, its members are bound to each other not by shared values or moral commitments but by relations of interdependence that may or may not be positively valued by its members. Our futures are bound to each other, whether we like it or not.³⁶ There is no plausible alternative to living together. In this way, a community of shared fate is a descriptive rather than a normative category. White slaveholders and black slaves formed a community of shared fate. The future of one was inextricably tied to the future of the other. Black and white South Africans formed a community of shared fate before constitutional reform as much as they share it afterward. In North America, Native peoples' fate was tied to that of non-Natives the moment European explorers landed on their shores. We have been thrown together by the circumstances of history, often without choosing to be thrown together.

But communities of shared fate may be more or less legitimate. They constitute moral communities the moment their members undertake to treat one another justly.[37] Indeed, the basic account of legitimacy proffered by most contemporary democratic theorists suggests a conceptual connection between the idea of a community of shared fate and the idea of legitimacy: legitimacy consists of the ability to justify actions to those who are affected by them according to reasons that they can accept.[38] We can use John Rawls's language to distinguish better from worse communities of shared fate: for Rawls, a well-ordered society is one in which individuals *agree* to share one another's fate.[39] Since communities of shared fate entail relations of *reciprocal* interdependence and interconnection, the standard of legitimacy also entails a requirement of *reciprocal justification*.

The idea of citizenship as shared fate is implicit in many recent accounts of citizenship in multicultural societies. Like national identity, a conception of citizenship as shared fate requires that individuals be able to *imagine themselves* in a network of relationships with other human beings, some of whom they may never meet face to face. But in contrast to national identity, there is nothing in the idea of shared fate to require that it is a shared *cultural* identity or heritage that links human beings in bonds of interdependence and mutual accountability. Although shared cultural identity may be *one* source of a subjective sense of shared fate, it is not the only source. *Institutional linkages*, particularly those that have hitherto secured the functions of democratic self-rule and self-protection, are another important source of shared fate. Whether or not I see myself as culturally connected to Newfoundlanders, it remains the case that the institutions of representative government that link my political representation to theirs in the Canadian Parliament also link my future to theirs. This is not irreversibly the case, but, since these institutions are one of the strongest forms of political accountability we have going, I would do well to see my fate as tied to theirs until some equally or more effective institutional alternative is in place. *Material* linkages are also important sources of shared fate, whether in the form of economic interdependence, environmental impact, or natural resource access and use.

In conceiving of citizenship as shared fate, there is no reason *in principle* to privilege one set of linkages over others. But it is true that to be active and effective citizens – to exercise the agency to *reshape* those connections through shared political judgment and action – requires one to understand oneself as situated within networks that have some connection to one's lived experience. These networks of interdependence have a history, and we judge their legitimacy or illegitimacy well only by understanding how they have come to take the shape they have and what possibilities we may imagine for the future. So the idea of shared fate does rest on powers of imagination but not on an imagined *identity* as such. Nonetheless, historical imagination is clearly an important part of a capacity for citizenship within a community of shared fate. We can see from this that the creation of subjective consciousness of a community of shared fate is itself a political achievement, for it involves choosing among different histories that may privilege some structures of interconnection or interdependence and suppress others.

Thus, citizenship as shared fate means seeing our own lived experiences of social practices and institutions – and therefore our narratives about those experiences – as entwined with the experiences and narratives of others. Sharing citizenship, then, means sharing a narrative of some sort with others. This idea of citizenship as shared and interconnected narratives has been gaining currency in recent Canadian political theory. Jeremy Webber, for example, has emphasized the importance of conceiving the bonds of social unity in Canada in terms of an ongoing "Canadian conversation" that structures continuing debates about principles, political players, and issues. The conversation itself has a history that is contested, and by participating in it individuals contribute to shaping its future.[40] But sharing membership in one community of shared fate by participating in its narrative is by no means an exclusive proposition. Every community is constituted by a multiplicity of narratives that intersect at some points and not at others. This holds for local communities and cultures as well as for political community at the level of the constitutional state. As James Tully has argued in his book *Strange Multiplicity*, contemporary constitutionalism is marked by its dialogic and pluralistic character: "There is not one national narrative that gives the partnership its unity, but a diversity of criss-crossing and contested narratives through which citizens participate in and identify with their association. Constitutions are not fixed and unchangeable agreements reached at some foundational moment, but chains of continual intercultural negotiations and agreements."[41]

How does an idea of citizenship as shared fate lead us to conceptualize the relationship between Aboriginal peoples and non-Aboriginal Canadians? It is helpful here to turn to the image of the *Kaswentha* or two-row wampum treaty, the historical form of agreement between the Iroquois confederacy and the British crown since the seventeenth century.[42] Indeed, many Aboriginal and some non-Aboriginal thinkers have invoked the two-row wampum as a model for the relationship.[43] The symbolism of the two-row wampum belt has been eloquently summarized by Native scholar Robert A. Williams, Jr.:

> There is a bed of white wampum which symbolizes the purity of the agreement. There are two rows of purple, and those two rows have the spirit of your ancestors and mine. There are three beads of wampum separating the two rows, and they symbolize peace, friendship and respect. These two rows will symbolize two paths or two vessels, travelling down the

same river together. One, a birch bark canoe, will be for the Indian people, their laws, their customs and their ways. The other, a ship, will be for the white people and their laws, their customs, and their ways. We shall each travel the river together, side by side, but in our own boat. Neither of us will try to steer the other's vessel.[44]

For the purposes of imagining a just relationship between Aboriginal peoples and non-Aboriginal Canadians in the present and the future, some commentators on the *Kaswentha* stress two of its features: the distinctness and separateness of the two purple rows, and the relationship of peace, friendship, and respect symbolized by the rows of beads that lie between them. The separateness of the two rows represents, in particular, the right of self-government of Aboriginal peoples as a right against external intervention in their communities' affairs. "In this respectful (co-equal) friendship and alliance," Alfred notes, "any interference with the other partner's autonomy, freedom, or powers was expressly forbidden."[45]

Less frequently discussed, however, is the background of white beads that represents the river on which both vessels journey. The three rows of white beads between the two vessels' paths separate Aboriginal and non-Aboriginal people from one another, but they also relate them by specifying the norms that they should follow in dealing with one another: peace, friendship, and respect. These, together with the rows of white beads that lie on either side of the vessels' paths, between each vessel and the river's banks, offer the strongest metaphor for what I am calling citizenship as shared fate. Ovide Mercredi and Mary Ellen Turpel mention the significance of the river when they state that "The two-row wampum captures the original values that governed our relationship – equality, respect, dignity *and a sharing of the river we travel on.*"[46] However distinct the lives and pursuits of Aboriginal peoples and non-Aboriginal Canadians, they are joined to each other by virtue of the single space within which both exist. This space, this river, is the domain of a citizenship that they share. Borrows offers a powerful interpretation of the *Kaswentha* along these lines:

> The three rows of white beads represent a counterbalancing message that signifies the importance of sharing and interdependence ... The ecology of contemporary politics teaches us that the rivers on which we sail our ships of state share the same waters. There is no river or boat that is not linked in a fundamental way to the others; that is, there is no land or government in the world today that is not connected to and influenced by others. This is one reason for developing a narrative of Aboriginal citizenship that speaks more strongly to relationships that exist beyond "Aboriginal affairs."[47]

To put this conception in less metaphorical terms, we might think of the three elements of the *Kaswentha* – the two vessels and the river – as constituting three analytically distinct normative and legal spaces:

1. In keeping with the goal of Aboriginal self-government, there must be a normative-legal space governed *exclusively* by the norms and commitments affirmed by Aboriginal peoples themselves. These norms may be traditional Aboriginal norms (some of which have still to be recovered from the ashes of cultural destruction wrought by colonialism), or they may be adaptations of the norms of democratic constitutionalism that Aboriginal peoples have come to view as beneficial for their communities, or they may be a hybrid of traditional and modern norms. It is important to note that the content of these norms will inevitably vary between Aboriginal communities as a consequence of their diversity. The distinguishing feature of this normative space, however, is that its content will be based upon the choices and judgments of Aboriginal members of the community in question, without interference from the Canadian state.
2. The second normative-legal space should be governed by the norms expressed within Canadian institutions and practices of constitutional democracy, in all their pluralism and complexity. This space may (and does) certainly include borrowings from diverse normative traditions, perhaps including Aboriginal ones. The distinguishing feature of this space is that, ideally, its content derives from the choices and judgments of Canadian citizens within democratic institutions.
3. The third normative-legal space is that occupied by both Aboriginal peoples and non-Aboriginal Canadians. This is the terrain of shared jurisdictions and shared political, economic, and ethical concerns. The need to give content to this third normative space arises from the fact that living together is a seemingly inescapable feature of our future. In order to avoid relations of domination, the terms of living together must be agreed to by both parties on a basis of equality. This is certainly not the whole of normative space, but it is one that needs attending to. Among other things, the boundary drawing that delineates the scope and jurisdictions of the other two spaces must occur here.

The rejection of citizenship as identity, then, should not lead us to abandon the idea of shared citizenship altogether. To the contrary, defining the terms of a just relationship between Aboriginal people and non-Aboriginal Canadians seems to presuppose that we constitute a shared political community at some level. The fact that we belong simultaneously to a multiplicity of political communities need not entail that we assert a hierarchy among them. But to move from an abstract conceptualization of a just relationship to its implications for concrete practice requires a focus on questions of institutional design, to which I now turn.

Political Legitimacy and the Risk of Over-Representation

Will Kymlicka's argument concerning the conflict between self-government and enhanced representation, discussed above, is the most careful and nuanced treatment I have yet encountered on this subject. Let me begin, then, by examining his argument in closer detail. As I have noted, his starting point is to reject arguments, such as those made by the RCERPF report and implicit in the Charlottetown Accord, that representation in shared institutions and self-government are mutually supportive. Although Kymlicka acknowledges that self-governing communities should have a voice in institutions responsible for delineating the boundaries between the jurisdictions of the federal government and those of Aboriginal governments, as well as institutions that have decision-making power in areas of shared or conflicting jurisdiction, he argues that there is a direct trade-off between having a voice in these institutions and enjoying enhanced representation in federal legislative institutions. "If anything," he argues, "the logical consequence of self-government is reduced representation, not increased representation. The right to self-government is a right against the authority of the federal government, not a right to share in the exercise of that authority." Kymlicka draws the conclusion that "self-government for a national minority seems to entail guaranteed representation on *intergovernmental* bodies, which negotiate, interpret, and modify the division of powers, but reduced representation on *federal* bodies which legislate in areas of purely federal jurisdiction from which they are exempted."[48]

As Kymlicka acknowledges, however, it is an oversimplification to claim that there is an either/or choice between representation and self-government. What are the complexities of Aboriginal circumstances within Canada that would temper this judgment? The first is that the federal government in Canada has a special fiduciary relationship with Aboriginal people, recognized by law in the British North America Act as well as in treaties. Many policy areas that, for non-Aboriginal Canadians, fall within provincial jurisdiction, are federal responsibilities with respect to Aboriginal people.[49] These include the critically important areas of housing, education, and health care provision. Until these responsibilities are wholly transferred from the federal government to Aboriginal jurisdictions, Aboriginal people have a strong interest in ensuring adequate representation in the House of Commons. Although the RCERPF report did not spell out the relationship between this point and self-government claims, it emphasized this point in its arguments for Aboriginal representation in the House of Commons.

This first rationale for enhanced Aboriginal representation in federal legislative institutions will presumably fade as the institutions of Aboriginal self-government develop. To the extent that the goal of self-government is realized, more and more of the functions currently within the domain of federal jurisdiction will be transferred to Aboriginal institutions. Ideally, this expansion of Aboriginal jurisdiction will apply to an ever-increasing number of Aboriginal communities until all of the communities that seek to govern themselves possess powers (in relation, e.g., to housing, education, health care, and criminal justice) that currently belong to federal institutions. Yet a rising proportion of Aboriginal people within Canada spend some or all of their lives outside the territorially based reserves that are the current basis for Aboriginal self-government. Although the right and powers of self-government do have implications for Aboriginal people living off-reserve, it is difficult if not impossible to imagine a regime in which such individuals' lives could be wholly covered by Aboriginal jurisdiction. This is particularly true for Aboriginal people living within large and diverse urban areas. True, the application of federal and provincial law to these individuals can be moderated through Aboriginal institutions, as is already the case in some aspects of the criminal justice system and in the provision of some social services. But the fundamental reality is that it is federal and provincial law, rather than Aboriginal law, that regulates Aboriginal people's lives when they are living in mainstream Canadian society. For this rapidly growing segment of the Aboriginal population, political representation in shared institutions at both the federal and the provincial levels is crucial for the protection of distinctive Aboriginal interests and concerns. Unless the demographic trends change, this is a feature of Aboriginal life in Canada that is here to stay, which no degree of territorially based Aboriginal self-government can alter.[50]

Another factor complicating the relationship between representation and self-government is that many policy areas appropriate for federal and provincial jurisdiction will impinge on territorially based Aboriginal communities even when the full range of powers associated with self-government has been secured to them. This is clearest in domains such as environmental regulation, energy policy, and wildlife management policy, where the decisions of federal and provincial legislatures will affect the circumstances facing Aboriginal communities surrounded by lands that fall within the jurisdiction of these levels of government. Since neither pollutants nor wildlife respect political boundaries, what can self-governing Aboriginal communities do to protect their natural resources if federal and provincial legislatures fail to protect the resources that lie within their territorial jurisdictions? Given the current weakness of international and transnational regulatory regimes, securing an Aboriginal voice appears to rest heavily on Aboriginal representation within the legislative bodies that currently govern these policy areas. And like the interests in representation that stem from the significant number of Aboriginal people living off-reserve, this interest is not likely to fade in time.

The Institutions of Aboriginal Representation

As Kymlicka notes, "A comprehensive theory of group representation ... may need to be both institution-specific and issue-specific."[51] Of course, the complexities of institutional design, combined with the necessity of negotiations over such design with Aboriginal peoples, make it impossible to specify with finality or total concreteness what a system combining self-government and self-representation would look like. But the proposals formulated by RCERPF, in the Charlottetown Accord, and by RCAP offer a good place to start. In fact, I think it quite plausible that some combination of all three sets of institutional proposals provides a helpful model. Each of the proposals offers something valuable, and neither considerations of shared citizenship (read as "shared fate") nor those of political legitimacy preclude adopting all three: an Aboriginal parliament as a consultative body to federal institutions, plus separate Aboriginal representation in a reformed Senate, plus enhanced representation within the House of Commons.

The first institution, a House of First Peoples, could be established more or less along the lines proposed by RCAP. Since this body would not have direct powers of legislation, but would refer matters to the federal Parliament for debate and vote, it would not entail a duplication of functions or a greater share of decision-making power for Aboriginal people within Canadian institutions than non-Aboriginal Canadians enjoy. As RCAP contemplated, representatives within this body could be selected from the separate Aboriginal nations or peoples that possess or seek the powers of self-government. It might also make sense to designate some of the seats within this body for Aboriginal persons living off-reserve, especially those in large urban areas, to ensure that this population has a voice within the broader community of Aboriginal peoples. It is conceivable that this body could be developed from the bases established by already existing representative bodies such as the Assembly of First Nations, the Inuit Tapiriit Kanatami, the Congress of Aboriginal Peoples, the Métis National Council, and the Native Women's Association of Canada. Symbolically, this institution would represent the distinctiveness and autonomy of the diverse Aboriginal peoples living within the territory that we call Canada.

The second institution for Aboriginal representation would be the Senate. Although the Charlottetown Accord did not specify the number of Aboriginal representatives in the reformed Senate, it seems sensible to suppose that it would be at the same level as the provinces. Following the

Charlottetown proposal, then, there would be six Aboriginal senators. Placing the number of Aboriginal senators on a par with that of provincial senators is unobjectionable insofar as the Aboriginal population in Canada exceeds that of the smaller provinces. The Charlottetown Accord was again not specific as to the electoral mechanism by which senators would be selected, but it makes a great deal of sense to use some device of proportional representation (PR) for these elections, both within provinces and for the Aboriginal seats. Empirical study of electoral systems makes it clear that PR enhances the electoral prospects of both women and minorities,[52] and I can think of no reason to suppose that this is a less desirable tendency of democracy for Aboriginal people than for others. For purposes of Senate elections, a Canada-wide Aboriginal electoral roll could be created based on the decision of individual Aboriginal voters to be enumerated for these seats rather than for provincial Senate seats. Symbolically, separate representation for Aboriginal peoples within the Senate would represent Aboriginal peoples as a distinct partner in Canadian confederation and as a "third order" of government within Canadian federalism.

Finally, Aboriginal representation within the House of Commons could roughly follow the suggestions of the RCERPF report. This presupposes that elections to the House of Commons would continue to be based on a system of single-member districts and that special Aboriginal constituencies could be established as part of each province's share of legislative seats.[53] To avoid the challenge to legitimacy that would arise from Aboriginal legislative power over matters from which self-governing Aboriginal communities are exempt, as discussed above, Aboriginal legislators would recuse themselves from voting on legislation from which their constituents obtained the exemptions that enable Aboriginal self-government. Undoubtedly, this issue-specific recusal would sometimes be a source of disagreement, but in principle it should be possible to set up an adjudication process to determine when an Aboriginal representative in the House of Commons should recuse him- or herself from an issue-specific vote. Symbolically, measures to enhance Aboriginal representation in the House of Commons signify the agreement between Aboriginal persons and non-Aboriginal persons to share resources, on terms of equality, within the territory that we call Canada.

Some Objections

Although I hope to have established that there is no necessary logical or ethical contradiction between the two routes to Aboriginal empowerment, it is reasonable to raise a number of skeptical challenges to the project of enhanced Aboriginal representation in shared institutions. One set of challenges concerns the difficulty of designing representative institutions in a way that adequately recognizes and responds to the stunning diversity of Aboriginal peoples living in Canadian territory. Not only are there vast cultural differences across Aboriginal peoples, but there are also great differences in terms of population, territory, economic resources, treaty relationships, and jurisdictional capacities. Aboriginal peoples clearly do not constitute a unitary group, and there is some risk that a generalized and abstract discussion of Aboriginal representation inevitably skirts the question of how to incorporate different communities' diverse interests into a shared system of political representation.[54]

This is a more complex problem than I can address fully in this chapter, but let me respond to it in a preliminary way. It is certainly true that all three institutional proposals would require aggregating a number of Aboriginal communities for purposes of selecting a single representative. Thus, each Aboriginal representative would represent a constituency that is itself very diverse internally. But this is true for other representatives as well; every riding contains a diversity of interests, and every representative confronts the dilemma whether to attempt to define and speak on behalf of the common interests of her constituency or to speak on behalf of the narrower majority that elected her. Aboriginal members representing internally diverse Aboriginal constituencies would also have to confront this dilemma. But this challenge can be rendered less problematic from the standpoint of democratic principles the more carefully the representative works at developing structures of consultation *within* a diverse constituency. There is no reason that prevents – and there are many reasons to encourage – the formation of constituency-wide consultative bodies that might themselves be based on the representation of the distinct Aboriginal communities within a single constituency. Political representation is intrinsically a "two-level game" in which the representative performs a dual role of communication and negotiation: within the broader representative institution to which she has been elected, and within the constituency from which she has been elected.[55] The activity of representation involves moving constantly back and forth between these two sites of deliberation and negotiation. Thus, while it is true that the inevitable diversity of Aboriginal constituencies poses a challenge to Aboriginal representatives, this is a challenge endemic to political representation as such and one to which theories of representation have already spoken.

A different skeptical challenge addresses the strategic incentives that Aboriginal leaders have to eschew enhanced representation as a political goal. Dominique Leydet suggests an intriguing parallel between the political risks that confront Aboriginal leaders and those that confront Quebec sovereigntists.[56] Both sets of leaders believe that a greater degree of political autonomy for their communities is the most promising route toward the flourishing of those communities. The more persuasively these leaders can argue that central Canadian institutions are illegitimate because they fail to treat their communities justly, the more politically saleable are their claims for greater political autonomy. These leaders therefore face a dilemma: if they support reforms in central institutions that render those institutions more legitimate, then they may undermine their own political case for greater autonomy. I believe that this is a shrewd analysis and that it may go a long way toward explaining why Aboriginal leaders have been so reluctant to embrace enhanced representation (though it would require close empirical study to confirm that this strategic reasoning is the predominant factor at play in Aboriginal leaders' thinking). But it describes a risky political strategy, one that closes off the possibility that the two forms of Aboriginal empowerment could be mutually reinforcing. There is no way to know a priori whether it is possible to develop a winning political rhetoric that conveys the need to pursue both self-government and enhanced representation simultaneously. It is clear that neither the RCERPF report nor the Charlottetown Accord discovered such a rhetoric, despite their support for a dual strategy of Aboriginal empowerment. In any case, it is certainly not my role to recommend or prescribe political strategies; again, my purpose here has simply been to show that there are no necessary ethical or logical impediments to the pursuit of both empowerment goals.

This chapter has examined the relationship between two paths toward a postcolonial relationship between Aboriginal and non-Aboriginal persons within the territory called Canada: enhanced representation in shared Canadian political institutions on the one hand and Aboriginal self-government on the other. I have argued against two positions. The first is that there is an inescapable contradiction between these two goals, and the second is that there is no contradiction between them at all. It is true that a concept of citizenship as identification with and loyalty to a shared nation makes it impossible to conceive of an Aboriginal citizenship that does not give priority either to Aboriginal identity or to Canadian identity. But this is not the only conception of citizenship available to us, nor is it a conception of citizenship that can be viable in our fast-changing world of globalization and multiple memberships. A new conception of citizenship, one that recognizes our obligation to strive toward justifiable relationships with all those affected by our decisions, can release us from this dilemma. It is also true that the ideal of political legitimacy directs us to deny decision-making power to those exempt from the force of joint decisions, and this does generate a tension between the two forms of Aboriginal empowerment. But this tension can be resolved through the careful and creative redesign of political institutions. We need not choose either sanguinity or resignation as a response to the tension between these goals. Here, as in most human affairs, our best bet is political creativity guided by a will to achieve justice.

Acknowledgments
I gratefully acknowledge invaluable feedback on this chapter from Frances Abele, Cathy Bell, Alan Cairns, Paul Chartrand, David Laycock, Dominique Leydet, Jonathan Quong, Peter Russell, Richard Simeon, and two anonymous reviewers. While I have endeavoured to meet the important challenges that they raised, I am under no illusion that I have wholly succeeded. By no means should they be held accountable for my arguments here.

Notes
1. In the Canadian context, the term "Aboriginal" denotes several distinct social and legal categories of persons. The federal Indian Act distinguishes between Indians, Métis, and Inuit. "Indians" include people who have descended from the diverse indigenous communities of the eastern shores and woodlands, the prairies and mountain regions, and the western coastal regions. Under the Indian Act, there are "status Indians" or "registered Indians" whom the federal government recognizes as belonging to a particular band or reserve. There is also a category of "nonstatus Indians" who are clearly of Aboriginal descent but who do not enjoy the same special rights as status Indians. "Indians" are also often (and increasingly) referred to as "First Nations," reflecting both the distinctness of their cultures from one another and their presence on Canadian soil prior to the arrival of European settlers (i.e., the English and French "nations" of Canada). Inuit are Aboriginal peoples who occupy the far northern regions of Canada, are culturally similar to one another, and are culturally distinct from the First Nations of the south. Métis people descended from the union of French fur trappers with indigenous women. The term "Metis" (without the accent) is sometimes used to refer to the descendants of unions between indigenous women and non-French European men. These unions produced communities of people who developed their own distinctive culture. For a more detailed description of legal and cultural distinctions among Aboriginal people in Canada, see Chartrand (1995, 2002); Giokas and Groves (2002); and Frideres and Gadazc (2001, ch. 2). For a comprehensive ethnographical and historical overview, see McMillan (1995).
2. Aboriginal People's Commission (2000).
3. An important exception is legal scholar John Borrows, who argues in favour of Aboriginal representation in shared institutions in his important new book. See Borrows (2002), especially ch. 6.
4. Cited in Knight (2001), 1093.
5. For a much more thorough and nuanced account of this history, see Carens (2000), 185-88.
6. Alfred (2000), n.p.
7. See, especially, Macklem (1995, 2001); Kymlicka (1995), especially chs. 5 and 6; Borrows (1992, 2002); and Johnston (1989). Note that theorists offer a variety of normative arguments for a right of self-government: as an inherent right of self-determination, as grounded in common law, as secured by treaties, as embedded in constitutional law, and as grounded in the individual's interest in autonomy and equality.
8. For a sympathetic critique of this position, which questions the value of such broad rights for Native peoples in different settings, see Tom Pocklington's discussion in Carmichael, Pocklington, and Pyrcz (2000), ch. 6. Don Carmichael strenuously defends such a general right in his reply to Pocklington in the same chapter.
9. Thus, I am also begging the question whether, in the Canadian context, the Charter of Rights and Freedoms should be binding on Aboriginal governments. I am, however, sympathetic to the treatment of this issue by the Royal Commission on Aboriginal Peoples in its *Final Report* (1996), vol. 2, Part 1, 226-34.
10. Borrows (2002), ch. 6.

11 See Williams (1998), especially 205-207.
12 The electoral quotient is the total number of voters divided by the total number of legislative seats.
13 RCERPF (1991), 189.
14 RCERPF (1991), 186.
15 RCERPF (1991), 190.
16 RCERPF (1991), 185.
17 Section 35 of the 1982 Constitution Act of Canada did recognize "existing aboriginal and treaty rights" but did not explicitly identify self-government as among such rights. In 1995, however, Jean Chrétien's Liberal government did recognize a general Aboriginal right of self-government as protected by Section 35. For an overview of federal government policy concerning Aboriginal rights, see Chartrand (2002).
18 Charlottetown Accord (1991), Article 22.
19 Charlottetown Accord (1991), Article 9. The double majority requirement would entail that, on legislation concerning Aboriginal peoples, both a majority of Aboriginal senators and a majority of the entire Senate would be necessary. For a discussion of the institutional device of double or "concurrent" majorities, and their derivation from the thought of the antebellum South Carolina senator John C. Calhoun, see Williams (1998), 43-45.
20 Charlottetown Accord (1991), Article 41. Note that the phrase "duly elected" may be highly controversial among Aboriginal leaders and thinkers, some of whom argue that conditioning self-government on elections is incompatible with traditional understandings of political authority and legitimacy. See, for example, Alfred (1999), 24-30, 107-108. I am far too ignorant of indigenous understandings of political legitimacy to be able to comment on this critique, though clearly it raises a profoundly important and difficult question for both theory and practice. There is the further nettlesome question of the appropriate role for non-Aboriginal theorists in analyzing internal standards of legitimacy for Aboriginal governance structures. This is yet another issue on which my own views remain unsettled.
21 Cairns (2000), 83.
22 RCAP (1996), vol. 2, 377.
23 RCAP (1996), vol. 2, 375.
24 RCAP (1996), vol. 2, 375.
25 RCAP (1996), vol. 2, 382.
26 Kymlicka (1995), 143.
27 For further discussion on this topic, see Williams (1998), 166.
28 Much of the following section is a highly condensed version of arguments developed in Williams (2003).
29 "Citizenship is not just a certain status, defined by a set of rights and responsibilities. It is also an identity, an expression of one's membership in a political community"; Kymlicka (1995), 301.
30 Carens (2000), 166; emphasis added. Carens goes on to emphasize, contra many conventional understandings of citizenship, that this psychological dimension of citizenship need not go hand in hand with the legal rights of citizenship: one can have a subjective sense of membership without the legal rights, and one can have the legal rights without the felt sense of membership.
31 Feinberg (1998), 49; emphasis added.
32 Macedo (2000), 146; emphasis added.
33 Williams (2003).
34 Moreover, if it is the case that citizenship as identity is intrinsically linked to the idea of the nation-state, then we must question whether it is a viable understanding of democratic agency in the era of globalization and the diminishing relevance of the concept of state sovereignty. See Williams (2003) for further discussion.
35 Elsewhere I have articulated two dimensions of this agency in terms of the *functions* of citizenship: self-rule and self-protection. The function of self-rule has its origins in classical republican understandings of citizenship (which realize what Isaiah Berlin, following

Benjamin Constant, called "the liberties of the ancients"), whereas the function of self-protection is expressed in modern liberal theory ("the liberties of the moderns"). See Williams (2003).

36 In some ways, then, my aspirations for shared citizenship are more minimalist than those of Carens, for whom ties of "regrettable necessity" are something that we should wish to move beyond. Although I agree that sharing citizenship is easier and more inspiring when it involves a more positive psychological stance than regrettable necessity, I believe that achieving a sense of shared membership that was perceived as *legitimate*, even if a regrettable necessity, would be a remarkable moral accomplishment. For the time being, I am happy to set my sights there.

37 One might object – as indeed Alan Cairns and Jonathan Quong have objected – that this undertaking is synonymous with a sense of shared civic identity and that therefore the distinction between citizenship as identity and citizenship as shared fate collapses. This challenge raises very difficult questions in moral psychology. What gives rise to the sense of justice and the will to legitimacy? What motivates the powerful to acknowledge the justice claims of the weaker? What is the source of solidarity? Defenders of citizenship as identity often suggest that shared identity plays a causal role in the motivation to treat others justly and that therefore if we seek justice we must promote a sense of shared identity among those whom we would join in just relationships. I find this argument dubious on both empirical and normative grounds and would argue that efforts to promote shared political identity usually do more harm than good. Instead, I suggest, we should view the causality as pointing in the opposite direction: if you treat others in accordance with principles of legitimacy, then they will come to identify their good with yours. Perhaps sharing citizenship on a basis of this type of democratic legitimacy would ultimately produce a sense of shared identity among most citizens. But this shared identity is best understood as a by-product of just relationships, not as a political end in itself.

38 Contemporary theorists, including Habermas (1996), 103-104; Rawls (1993), 136-37; Scanlon (1982, 1998), ch. 5; Gutmann and Thompson (1996), ch. 2; and Cohen (1989), all agree on this fundamental notion of legitimacy.

39 Rawls (1971), 102.

40 Webber (1994), ch. 9; see also Kymlicka (1998), 173-77.

41 Tully (1995), 183-84.

42 Tully notes that the *Kaswentha* was used at least as recently as 1990, in the settlement reached between the governments and the Haudenosaunee confederacy at Kahnesetake following the Oka crisis; see Tully (1995), 127.

43 See, for example, Borrows (1997); Mercredi and Turpel (1993), 35; Alfred (1999), 52; and Tully (1995), 127-28.

44 Cited in Borrows (1997), 164.

45 Alfred (1999), 52.

46 Mercredi and Turpel (1993), 35.

47 Borrows (2002), 149.

48 Kymlicka (1995), 143.

49 See Kymlicka (1995), 227-28, note 17.

50 This is a strong point of emphasis in Alan Cairns's recent book *Citizens Plus*, in which Cairns argues that the ever-increasing urban Aboriginal populations do not meet RCAP's conditions for national self-government. See Cairns (2000), especially 123-26, 128-32.

51 Kymlicka (1995), 228, note 17.

52 For more detailed discussion of these advantages of PR, see Williams (1998), 215-21.

53 Proposals to adopt proportional representation for elections to the House of Commons persist, and I am supportive of them. If PR were adopted, then Aboriginal representation in the House of Commons could be secured through a number of devices. Maori representation in New Zealand's recently adopted PR system would, in that case, provide a useful model that could be adapted for Aboriginal representation in the Canadian context.

54 I am grateful to Frances Abele, Cathy Bell, and Alan Cairns for pressing me to think further about these issues.

55 Hanna Pitkin identifies this bidirectional dimension of the representative's communicative duties as the source of the inadequacy of either a pure "delegate" or a pure "trustee" model of political representation; see Pitkin (1967), 218-25. Anne Phillips makes a similar point in her discussion of the role of political representatives within institutions that contain moments both of deliberation (with other representatives) and of accountability (to electorates); see Phillips (1995), especially 159-60. The notion of "two-level games" as features of international negotiations was developed in Putnam (1998). For a similar conceptualization of federal-provincial diplomacy, see Simeon (1972), 237.
56 Personal communication, 10 January 2003.

6
The Self-Government of Unbounded Communities: Emancipatory Minority Autonomy in China and Western Europe

Susan J. Henders

This chapter considers the possibility of emancipatory self-government for minority communities. It asks how we might escape the tendency of minority territorial autonomy arrangements to reproduce the individualistic, exclusionary identities that make the "nation-state" model dysfunctional and oppressive and that give rise to the demands for minority self-government in the first place. By individualistic identities, I mean identities assumed to be fixed, discrete, internally homogeneous, and ontologically prior to relations with other "selves."[1] Minority territorial self-government arrangements are conventionally understood as ways of escaping the failure of representative institutions and other dimensions of the "nation-state" model of citizenship to recognize internal diversity, particularly the identities of ethnically distinct regionalized communities.[2] However, these self-government mechanisms tend to (re)produce the very individualistic conceptualizations of the collective "self" and autonomy that make the "nation-state" model ethically problematic. This chapter asserts that this paradox is not inevitable and is being challenged by members of some minority communities who advocate forms of self-government that recognize the fluid, overlapping, internally diverse, and contested nature of the collective "self." That is, they assert a "self" that is relational and unbounded. Such conceptualizations do not sit well with the "nation-state" model's presumptions that polity and community are both bounded and neatly coincide.

Specifically, this chapter explores contemporary struggles over minority autonomy in China (in Tibet and Hong Kong) and Western Europe (in Corsica and Catalonia) to identify these challenges and the possibilities for more emancipatory self-government within them. For Hong Kong and Catalonia, the chapter identifies emergent postnational norms and practices of "multi-realmed citizenship" potentially creating alternative political spaces, norms, and forms of representation that challenge individualistic understandings of these communities. This reformulated citizenship could contribute to more inclusive and just processes of self-government for those in Hong Kong and Catalonia shut out of and oppressed by the prevailing autonomy arrangements. For Corsica and Tibet, the chapter identifies norms and practices of nonviolence that, informed by feminist and Buddhist ideas, potentially transcend the exclusionary identities and the cycles of insecurity that bring so many ethnonationalist struggles to profoundly unethical impasses. The chapter argues that the norms and practices of multi-realmed citizenship and nonviolence offer possibilities for realizing an unbounded minority "self" as the foundation of a more emancipatory self-government. By unbounded, I mean a collective minority "self" recognized as deeply connected to rather than separate from the "other" and as internally heterogeneous and negotiated rather than internally coherent and fixed. For an unbounded "self," autonomy is achieved, paradoxically, not through *separation from* but through recognition of *a shared origin and destiny with* the "other" both within and without. Its realization is inhibited partly because vulnerable groups strategically employ individualistic conceptualizations of their identities to counter more powerful, individualistically conceived majority and "nation-state" identities, reflected in and reinforced by individualistic human rights and other political norms at multiple levels.

The Tensions in Minority Self-Government

Minority territorial autonomy arrangements aim to ameliorate the failure of the majoritarian, egalitarian, and individualistic representational and other citizenship and constitutional norms and practices to recognize and protect regionalized substate communities with distinct identities. Minority territorial autonomy arrangements create asymmetrical distributions of territorial political authority and "differentiated citizenship"[3] that violate "nation-state" preferences for homogeneity and equality. They do so by establishing political institutions whose legitimacy is derived from their claim to be more representative of minority values and preferences. These institutions of self-government typically have authority in those functional areas and realms of governance thought necessary to preserve the minority's distinct and cherished values from the preferences of the majority, in the territory deemed to demarcate the minority community's boundaries. For its part, the central or federal government retains authority over functional areas and realms of governance necessary to preserve the state as a whole and protect values shared by the minority and wider state community. In this sense, minority territorial autonomy arrangements are compromises between the ideal of independent statehood for the minority and of boundary maintenance and a symmetrical distribution of territorial political authority and equal citizenship rights for the state. They adjust the "nation-state" to the realities of regionalized cultural differences without giving up the "nation-state" model altogether.

A number of contestable assumptions about culture and identity underlie this view of minority autonomy arrangements. It assumes that collective identities – whether of the state, majority, or minority community – are individualistic. Culture is assumed to be descriptive, static, and bounded rather than a political process characterized by ever-contested and negotiated identities and boundaries. This individualistic conceptualization of minority self-government sees all members of the minority community as having the same identity and preferences. Therefore, each is equally better represented through regionalized autonomous functional and governmental domains affecting areas of life most closely connected to the community's distinct identity. In individualistic conceptions of minority self-government, political contestation is assumed to occur mainly between the central and autonomous regional governments or between the minority and the state-wide majority.

However, this conceptualization of minority autonomy comes into question once the collective minority "self" is reformulated as relational rather than individualistic. We cannot assume that the representational and other citizenship gains from autonomy flow evenly to everyone in the autonomous territory if the minority "self" is fluid, overlapping, and internally contested rather than fixed, discrete, and internally coherent – and if culture is a set of political and normative claims rather than a descriptive attribute. Once the "self" is reconceptualized as relational, much of the political contestation associated with autonomy arrangements can be seen to occur *within* the minority region, focusing on differing understandings of the identity and boundaries of the community and the values to be advanced through institutions of self-rule. This is why Kymlicka[4] objects to minority self-government to the extent that it involves policing the identities of the people of the minority region, thereby undermining their individual freedom in the name of community solidarity or purity, with particularly oppressive effects for women and immigrants and others whose identities challenge dominant understandings of the minority "self." Moreover, if, as relational conceptualizations of the "self" contend, identities are intersubjectively (re)produced rather than atomistic givens ontologically prior to social relations, then minority autonomy arrangements will not necessarily reduce insecurity for either the minority or the majority community. If they are based on individualistic understandings of cultural difference that reproduce an exclusionary understanding of the "self" and the "other" – the minority and the majority – then minority self-government will undermine the scope for compromise, understanding, and tolerance. For these reasons, writers sometimes dismiss minority autonomy as a short-sighted instrumentality on the part of state elites or a power grab on the part of minority elites. By institutionalizing cultural differences, minority self-government is said to foster instability and, to the extent that they reinforce exclusionary cultural differences, take the state down the slippery slope to secession.[5]

These dangers are not inconsequential, but they are contingent. They assume that minority autonomy arrangements necessarily cast the "self" in individualistic terms, violating the human experience of identity as fluid, overlapping, internally contested, and socially (re)produced. They assume that, despite the changeable, multilayered, contested nature of lived culture, minority autonomy arrangements must institutionalize and fix for all time *one* understanding of the minority "self," thereby (re)producing oppressive power relations *within* the minority community and mutually antagonistic and irreconcilable differences *between* it and the rest of the state. This negative prognosis ignores the possibility of more emancipatory forms of minority autonomy potentially emergent in contemporary struggles over territorial self-government in culturally regionalized states. By emancipatory self-government, I mean forms of autonomy and related representational and other citizenship practices that make possible the (re)production of valued collective minority identities without oppressing the most vulnerable people within the autonomous territory and without (re)producing the exclusionary minority and majority identities that create insecurities in and between both communities.

I extrapolate this understanding of emancipatory self-government from Mackenzie and Stoljar's feminist-inspired notion of personal relational autonomy and from Tully's[6] identification of the dialectical nature of the politics of recognition. Tully says elsewhere that most analyses of the politics of recognition assume that "under some considerations of justice and stability members will reach agreement on a definitive form of recognition for all affected." Using this criterion, most minority autonomy arrangements fail because they never permanently satisfy all the participants. However, a different picture emerges if we instead understand that "the experience of cultural difference is *internal* to a culture," rather than solely associated with an external "other," as most liberal, communitarian, and nationalist approaches assume. Because cultural difference is "aspectival," "cultural horizons change as one moves about." The "other" is not only without but also *within*. As Tully points out, it is this very "interculturality" that makes possible creative forms of accommodating cultural difference that do not institutionalize fixed and exclusionary "self"-"other" dyads.[7]

Drawing from Tully,[8] I believe that all institutions and practices of self-government are inherently unjust in that they always fail to recognize and represent some members. Nevertheless, minority autonomy arrangements can be made more emancipatory if they allow for open-ended, dialectical constitutional processes involving unbounded "intercultural" "selves" rather than assuming stable, uncontested, individualistic identities. In this complex dynamic, both the imposition of and the resistance to homogenizing, exclusionary identities within the politics of minority self-government arrangements occur continuously on multiple planes. As Tully points out, the goal is not to find the "solution" to cultural difference but to ask "what form of democracy enables the politics of recognition to be played freely from generation to generation, with as little domination as possible." Freedom, not recognition, is the aim, "the freedom of the members of an open society to change the constitutional rules of mutual recognition and association from time to time as their identities change."[9] Additionally, to make this process emancipatory, the least powerful members of society need substantive freedom, including but not limited to the economic means to participate in and meaningfully affect political decision making whether directly or through representative mechanisms. In this way, self-government built on a recognition of "interculturality" constitutes the "self" as unbounded and autonomy as an open-ended process centred on substantive rather than merely formal inclusionary recognition and participation. It involves both recognition and distributive justice.[10]

To summarize, minority autonomy arrangements typically arise out of the representational and other shortcomings of the individualistic "nation-state" and its model of citizenship. They typically reproduce the same problems. Yet in the cases examined below, contestation over the meaning of self-government reveals the potential for forms of regional autonomy that protect minorities but at the same time recognize internal diversity and do not institutionalize insecurities. These possibilities will seem idealistic to some readers, who may share my awareness of the seemingly insurmountable power differentials that stand in the way and the understandable tendency of threatened minorities to take refuge in individualistic understandings of their collective identity. Nevertheless, to stress only the barriers to relational, unbounded self-government, ignoring its emergent potential in contemporary political struggles, has the political effect of reifying and naturalizing the status quo as stable, inevitable, and beyond human modification. By identifying the alternative paths being charted in Tibet, Hong Kong, Corsica, and Catalonia, this chapter instead reveals that status quo as unstable, tension-ridden, contingent, and malleable. It uncovers the fragility of its roots in the very contestedness of individualistic conceptualizations of the "self," the "other," and autonomy itself.

Emergent Possibilities for a Self-Government of Unbounded Community

Like the vision of self-government and a citizenship of "shared fate" embodied in the two-row wampum belt discussed by Melissa Williams in the previous chapter, the following pages identify potential routes out of the representational crisis of the "nation-state" model, those associated with an emergent multi-realmed citizenship and with the norms and practices of nonviolence.

Emancipatory Self-Government through a Citizenship of Multiple Realms

In both contemporary Western Europe and China, post-Westphalian institutions and contemporary capitalism create the possibility for a self-government of unbounded community, achieved through a reconceptualized citizenship.[11] Referred to here as multi-realmed citizenship, these norms and practices have the potential to break the state monopoly on citizenship and "nation-state" mechanisms of representation without reproducing individualistic conceptions of "differentiated citizenship" of autonomous community. A citizenship of multiple realms gives individuals and communities rights and recognition in multiple jurisdictions simultaneously, such that each realm prevents the other from permanently entrenching hierarchical and exclusionary identities. Continuous tension and contestation among the realms (re)constitute the minority and majority "selves" as unbounded. The following paragraphs explore the potential of multi-realmed citizenship in Catalonia, an autonomous community in Spain, and in Hong Kong, a Special Administrative Region in the People's Republic of China (PRC).[12]

Catalonia

Andrew Linklater has identified several of the features of the multi-realmed citizenship immanent in Western Europe.[13] These include strong substate regional sentiments in most if not all states; the establishment under the Maastricht Treaty of the Committee of the Regions, which gives regional and local authorities an advisory role in European Union policy making; the EU principle of subsidiarity whereby policy decisions are to be made at the lowest possible level of government; the institutionalization of an EU citizenship with limited rights, duties, and participatory institutions and processes; the signing of the European Charter of Regional or Minority Languages; and scope for citizens to appeal the decisions of national courts to the European Court of Human Rights. Importantly in the search for checks on the potential tyranny of minority autonomy regimes, some states allow the citizens of autonomous regions to appeal the legislation of regional parliaments directly to the European Court of

Justice and the European Court of Human Rights rather than to statewide courts. This is the case for Scotland and Wales.[14]

Although far from fully formed or uncontested, Western Europe's immanent multi-realmed citizenship reflects postnational understandings of transnational and supranational community and citizenship as means of addressing concerns about democratic legitimacy and representation deficits in all realms. In this reformulation of citizenship, the transnational, suprastate, state, and substate realms co-exist in an ongoing, fluid, and indeterminate relationship, sometimes competing, sometimes co-operating, in a series of shifting hierarchies, each checking the potential excesses of the other. In this way, multi-realmed citizenship defends "the normative ideal of forms of political community which release society potentials for achieving levels of universality and difference."[15]

The Catalan Generalitat, the government of the Catalan autonomous community, has actively promoted the building of multiple realms of governance in Europe. Along with its extensive efforts to construct its own autonomous political institutions within Spain, the Generalitat under Catalan nationalist Convèrgencia i Unió (CiU) president Jordi Pujol has aggressively lobbied for direct representation for regional governments in EU institutions. Constructing a "Europe of the Regions" has been a pillar of the Generalitat's extensive international activities.[16] However, these efforts have done relatively little to establish a "thick" notion of multiple and overlapping citizenship, to borrow Linklater's term.[17] Rather, the Generalitat's promotion of a role for regional governments in EU policy making has aimed mainly to expand Catalan economic competitiveness, promote the flowering of Catalan language and culture, and increase Catalan political autonomy vis-à-vis the Spanish central government.[18] Nevertheless, immanent within the Generalitat's engagement in multi-realmed *governance* is the possibility of a multi-realmed *citizenship,* with some potential to make Catalan self-government more inclusive of its ever more culturally and socially diverse population, one of its greatest challenges.

Catalonia is home to one of Spain's culturally distinct historic regions. The great majority of residents speak Catalan,[19] a Romance language related to the Castilian spoken in much of Spain. Catalonia's history as a separate, commercially important polity in premodern Europe and its nineteenth-century leadership in Spanish industrialization are sources of pride and identity for many Catalans. However, as a consequence of Catalonia's long-standing importance to the Spanish economy, large numbers of Castilian-speaking immigrants have come to Catalonia seeking work. They and their descendants currently make up about 50 percent of the region's residents. The similarity between the Castilian and Catalan languages has aided efforts by immigrants to learn Catalan as part of the attempts of regional authorities to revitalize the use of this language in education and other public spheres. However, in the past decade or so, the region has seen the arrival of growing numbers of non-Castilian-speaking immigrants, especially from Morocco and elsewhere in North Africa but also from China and Pakistan. Catalonia now has Spain's largest concentration of economic immigrants – about 28.6 percent of the Spanish total.[20] Current estimates suggest that fewer than 20 percent of new immigrants to Catalonia speak Castilian, let alone Catalan.[21]

To the extent that Catalan self-government focuses only on representing a linguistically and ethnically defined Catalan "nation" and its Catalan-speaking elites, it will undermine the ability of immigrants, particularly non-Castilian-speaking recent arrivals, to enjoy full citizenship. Catalan self-government will become an instrument of an exclusionary bourgeois and cultural nationalism that constitutes the immigrant as a worker and cultural outsider rather than a citizen with representation and other social and political rights. The danger is real. Amnesty International has raised concerns about racist attacks on immigrants, whom some regional residents blame for unemployment and crime.[22] A discourse of civic Catalan nationalism has long competed with a more exclusionary ethnic nationalism.[23] In recent years, however, ethnic nationalist discourses have sometimes taken on an anti-immigrant tone, particularly near elections, though there have also been anti-racist reactions. Even Pujol has expressed concern that the new immigration could threaten the recovery of the Catalan language, while in 2001 Heribert Barrera, a former Catalan Parliament president, declared that the region was being swamped by non-Catalan-speaking immigrants.[24]

Do the emergent multi-realmed citizenship norms and practices associated with European integration offer, as Linklater implies, political spaces and resources that can be used to contest exclusionary outcomes for immigrants in regions such as Catalonia that claim to be culturally distinct?[25] In other words, can multi-realmed citizenship foster an *inclusionary* Europe of the Regions, supportive of a form of self-government that both protects Catalonia as a distinct society and incorporates immigrants as full citizens, both socially and politically? A preliminary review suggests that there is only limited evidence of progress in this direction.

EU citizenship developed partly to address the democratic and representational deficit in Europe, but it remains derivative. That is, it is restricted to the nationals of EU member states, excluding other EU residents (so-called third country nationals or TCNs), including many immigrant workers and their European-born children. Particularly from the early 1990s on, the EU Commission began promoting the expansion of the political and social rights of TCNs in Europe and its own jurisdiction in related areas. For instance, the 1997 commission-proposed Convention on the Rules for Admission of TCNs to the Member States of the European

Union allowed for member state discretion but proposed to give TCNs full mobility rights for employment and equal treatment with EU nationals in matters such as work and training, trade union and association rights, and access to housing and schooling.[26] Meanwhile, due to the lack of a coherent, centralized group representing immigrant stakeholders across the EU, the commission also fostered and funded the establishment of pro-immigrant, European-wide nongovernmental organizations. These were supposed to be a source of information and legitimacy for the commission efforts to push its electorally unpopular pro-immigrant agenda and to expand its jurisdiction in immigration and immigrant inclusion policy.[27] While not grassroots initiatives, these pro-immigrant groups did have links to national, regional, and local associations, including some pro-immigrant groups in Catalonia, which had been some of the earliest to organize in Spain.[28] The efforts of EU-level pro-immigrant groups to gain full EU citizenship for long-term, legally resident TCNs have converged with the commission's efforts to promote a Europeanized "denizenship." However, these efforts have been largely unsuccessful. The Amsterdam Treaty did extend anti-discrimination rules in the European Union to include the grounds of race and ethnic origin. Nevertheless, the focus of the Council of Ministers in recent years has been less on immigrant inclusion than on security and border control issues related to immigration, such as the harmonization of member state policies on access to immigration and asylum.[29] Recent policies of the Spanish government, which has formal jurisdiction in such matters, have similarly securitized immigration.

There are a number of other reasons for caution about the prospects for an immigrant-inclusive European "denizenship" or citizenship simultaneously to expand the citizenship of immigrants within Spain and Catalonia. For one, the bundle of rights provided by European citizenship is limited and a supplement to rather than a replacement for nationality in a member state. National, regional, and local authorities still control access to most social and political entitlements, and the European Union has little jurisdiction and few resources beyond an increasingly well-developed discourse of immigrant inclusion and citizenship.[30] The commission's aims may also prove to be more instrumental than progressive. Geddes suggests that the commission tends to promote inclusion to the extent that it expands its own authority and influence, and stresses "economic citizenship" and market-driven civil rights rather than social and political rights.[31] In order to expand its influence, it might also give in to the securitization of immigration policy stressed by member state governments.

In Catalonia specifically, there is limited evidence of the feedback of EU-realm, pro-immigrant efforts to the region. Catalan-based immigrant and immigrant advocacy associations as well as local authorities did participate in commission initiatives aimed at immigrant inclusion in the 1990s, such as the Cities against Racism program, which brought together NGOs and local authorities from European towns and cities. The Local Integration Partnership Action project, which promoted the development of local anti-racism action plans, also saw participation from Catalonia. The latter project resulted in Barcelona City Council establishing, with commission backing, an advisory Municipal Council for Immigrants. In the absence of electoral rights for immigrants in Spain, the Municipal Council for Immigrants aimed to find other ways to enhance immigrant political participation and representation in municipal decision making. The goal was to improve municipal policies relevant to immigrants, and to make Barcelona a "plural city" that recognizes its increasingly diverse cultures and combats racism, xenophobia, and discrimination.[32] The Catalan Parliament does not have a regional equivalent to the municipal council for immigrants, though the Generalitat now has an immigration department. In 1993, the Parliament, at the urging of NGOs, passed a resolution asking the Spanish government to sign and ratify the International Convention on the Protection of the Rights of All Migrant Workers and Members of Their Families "to complete the legal regulatory framework on foreigners' stay[ing] in Catalonia."[33]

While there remain significant contradictions between Catalan self-government goals in the area of culture and the inclusion of immigrants at the regional level, there is some convergence between the political aims of the Generalitat and pro-immigrant groups at the EU level. Extending European citizenship to TCNs would require a dismantling of the state's formal monopoly on citizenship rights, while erecting a direct role for regional governments in EU policy making would similarly require a further severing of the state monopoly on representation and policy making, beyond what is being accomplished with the gradual enhancement of the role of the European Parliament and the Committee of the Regions. It remains to be seen whether the Catalans' reported sense of themselves as the most European of Spaniards[34] will encourage them to support a form of multi-realmed citizenship inclusive of both immigrants and culturally distinct territorial communities, particularly since an expanded EU role in immigrant social and political inclusion policies could mean less scope for expanding regional authority in this area, as well as expanding the use of Catalan in public spheres.

Hong Kong

Across the world in the Hong Kong Special Administrative Region (SAR), the emergence of a post-Westphalian, multi-realmed citizenship is at an even more embryonic stage, yet the possibility exists. This potential is emergent in the political struggle, occurring in multiple political realms, over the nature of Hong Kong identity and the values to be promoted by Hong Kong's institutions of self-government. The dominant institutions and discourses of autonomy in the SAR constitute Hong Kong as a patriotic Chinese, hypercapitalist society committed to a free-market economy, small government, a low-tax regime, minimal social entitlements, and creating equal opportunities for its people to work hard and make money.[35] Liberal rights and freedoms and the rule of law are valued mainly because they enhance Hong Kong's competitive advantage and should be overridden when they threaten more important values, particularly patriotism, understood as loyalty to the PRC government.[36] The Basic Law provides for the possibility of democratizing Hong Kong political institutions. However, the big business and pro-China representatives who currently dominate the executive-led political system assert that democratic representation would lead to an expensive welfare state and confrontational politics that would sap Hong Kong's economic vitality, political stability, and good relations with the PRC government.[37] The identities and needs of the poor, many women, Tanka boat people, environmentalists, workers, pro-democracy and human rights advocates, and foreign workers, among others, are not represented in the institutions of self-rule or the dominant discourse of Hong Kongers as patriotic *homo economicus*.

On 1 July 2003, Hong Kong people showed their unwillingness to accept this understanding of their community and its values when they participated in a massive public demonstration to protest the illiberal anti-subversion law proposed by the HKSAR government, backed by the PRC government.[38] The inability of Hong Kong's representative institutions – the nondemocratically chosen chief executive and the only partly democratic Legislative Council – to allow for accountable government and meaningful, inclusive, and open-ended contestation over values pushed nearly 500,000 people into the streets. Combined with discontent over government handling of continuing high unemployment and the SARS outbreak, widespread public rejection of the anti-subversion bill and demands for democratization proved the dominant portrayal of Hong Kong as a community of apolitical hypercapitalists to be illusory. The government at least temporarily backed down on the anti-subversive law. Given continued political, social, and economic constraints on political deliberation, however, other realms of citizenship offer potentially important political spaces for articulating alternative conceptions of Hong Kong identity and values by those excluded by the institutions and discourses of self-government. This possibility of a multi-realmed citizenship of Hong Kong people exists within the external dimension of Hong Kong's autonomy and within the "flexible citizenship" practices of its transnational elites.

External Autonomy Hong Kong first achieved an exceptional level of external autonomy in economic and cultural affairs under the British colonial government. Its high degree of international legal personality now rests on the Sino-British Joint Declaration and the Basic Law, the constitutional foundations of Hong Kong's self-rule since it returned to Chinese rule in 1997. As befits one of the world's most important trading economies and regional financial centres, the HKSAR government participates in its own right in some forty-four interstate organizations and adheres to dozens of international agreements directly or through Chinese government accession.[39] Most of the agreements are economic in nature. However, among them are fifteen international human rights instruments, including the International Covenant on Civil and Political Rights (ICCPR) and the International Covenant on Economic, Social, and Cultural Rights (ICESCR), as well as a number of specialized human rights conventions.[40] The significance of these human rights treaties for multi-realmed citizenship lies in their potential to detach rights, participation, and identity from the territorial state and autonomous region. Of particular interest in this regard are the reporting mechanisms required of treaty signatories – the PRC government on behalf of the HKSAR – and the scope for nongovernmental organization participation in the international monitoring of treaty compliance.

By signing the ICCPR and ICESCR on behalf of the HKSAR, for example, the PRC government has committed itself to make regular reports regarding compliance with its treaty obligations to the appropriate UN supervisory committees. The PRC government permits the HKSAR government to draw up the reports independently and defend them in the relevant UN forums, apparently without PRC interference. On the one hand, the risks to the PRC and SAR governments are minimal: the UN treaty bodies may criticize the HKSAR and PRC governments' human rights records in Hong Kong but have no authority to sanction in case of a breach.[41] Moreover, individual Hong Kong citizens have no right to make direct claims that the HKSAR and PRC governments have violated their internationally protected rights before the relevant UN treaty bodies.[42] On the other hand, Hong Kong citizens, acting through nongovernmental organizations (NGOs), have limited scope to provide UN bodies with alternative assessments of the human rights situation in the territory. They have made great efforts to exploit this opportunity. Hong Kong NGOs were some of the first nongovernmental actors to use the scope for NGO involvement in the ICCPR reporting process through the UN Human Rights Committee.[43] They began their work in 1978, only two years after the ICCPR came into effect and was first extended to Hong Kong by the British authorities.[44] Hong Kong human rights organizations remain one of the most active groups of NGOs in the UN Human Rights

Committee and are internationally noted for their large numbers at the committee's Geneva meetings.[45]

In many ways, these UN forums do little directly to challenge exclusionary identity discourses and autonomy in Hong Kong and do not replace the need of the territory's people for democracy, redistributive justice and other elements of open-ended, emancipatory, and inclusive autonomy. Nevertheless, the activism of Hong Kong human rights NGOs has the potential to create postnational political spaces and citizenship where Hong Kong people are recognized and can participate and claim rights currently under- or unprotected in regional and state realms. If only through NGO "proxies," they can articulate alternative understandings of their community's identity and values to supplement still uncertain efforts to create inclusive democratic spaces in Hong Kong itself.

"Flexible Citizenship" Multi-realmed citizenship is also immanent in Hong Kong in the ways in which members of its technical, professional, and managerial classes select different spaces for investment, work, and family relocation. Typically, Hong Kong's mobile managers work and/or invest in China while simultaneously seeking formal citizenship, education for children, and opportunities to diversify economic risk in (mainly democratic) states such as Canada and the United States. At the same time, they maintain a family and business presence in and a strong attachment to Hong Kong.[46] Aiwah Ong calls these practices "flexible citizenship." They are a potential basis for a form of multi-realmed citizenship that simultaneously vests citizenship in multiple states and substates rather than in the emergent postnational realm.

Are the "flexible citizenship" practices of Hong Kong transnational elites potentially emancipatory? Could they move Hong Kong toward a more inclusive form of self-government for the territory by creating new channels for securing rights, recognition, and participation for those currently excluded by the discourses of patriotic *homo economicus*? Given the highly instrumental nature of "flexible citizenship," and the fact that it mostly involves privileged members of Hong Kong's middle class, there is a danger that these practices will serve only to entrench the status quo. By establishing formal citizenship in democratic states, Hong Kong transnational elites gain access to political, civil, and social rights, including representation. With liberal citizenship thus secured for the next generation, they may be uninterested in struggling for emancipatory autonomy in Hong Kong itself.

Nonetheless, the possibility of a more emancipatory outcome remains. The very mobility of Hong Kong managers and their capital and skills means that they have some leverage with which to pressure Hong Kong policy makers to adopt more inclusive norms and practices. Even if their decisions originated in instrumental concerns,[47] the fact that members of Hong Kong's transnational middle class have sought passports and education for their children mainly in democratic states suggests a belief that democracy brings benefits. The appreciation and growing experience of democracy could generate over time more widespread demands for an open, democratic Hong Kong much in the way that some other diasporas in democratic states have become active proponents of democracy and human rights in their "homelands."[48] The transformative potential of "flexible citizenship" perhaps also comes from its destabilizing of the "nation-state" model of citizenship and its individualistic, exclusionary identities. For "flexible citizenship" challenges the dominant "standardizing cultural narrative" of modern Chineseness, on which PRC and, increasingly, Hong Kong authorities have relied for their legitimacy,[49] breaking its claim that state and ethnic nation neatly coincide and monopolize citizen identity, loyalty, and interests. In this way, "flexible citizenship" practices undermine individualistic understandings of the Hong Kong and China "selves," a step toward a more emancipatory self-government.

Self-Government through Nonviolence
The two examples to which I turn next – contestation over minority autonomy in Tibet and Corsica – suggest another route to an unbound minority "self" and emancipatory self-government, the path of nonviolence. Although of different philosophical inspiration – Buddhist in the case of Tibet and feminist in the case of Corsica – these visions of nonviolence as a path to emancipatory autonomy both emerged from ethnonationalist struggles associated with especially high levels of physical and other violence.[50] They both suggest that the minority "self" cannot be autonomous in an emancipatory sense without rejecting violence and the individualistic identities and related cycles of insecurity that it (re)produces.

Tibet
When the Dalai Lama received the Nobel Peace Prize in 1989, it was partly in recognition of his radical proposals for achieving Tibetan self-government made public in 1987 and elaborated upon in his 1988 Strasbourg Proposal and subsequent public statements. Both the authorities in Beijing and some Tibetan nationalists have rejected the plan, for it defies the bounded individualistic identities and "nation-state" model on which both sides rely. The Five-Point Peace Plan, as the Dalai Lama's proposal was known, envisioned bringing peace to the Tibetan plateau and self-government to Tibetans through recognition of the ways in which Tibet and China are unbounded "selves" deeply connected with one another.

The Five-Point Peace Plan was explicitly rooted in the Buddhist teachings of nonviolence, or *ahimsa,* and compassion. The latter term refers to a universal responsibility for and identification with the "other" and with all creation. The teachings of *ahimsa* and compassion, as interpreted by the Dalai Lama, tell us that neither the suffering of Tibetans nor the Chinese state's security fears in Tibet can be alleviated through the actualization of the collective "self" against the "other." Rather, Tibetans and Chinese will become free through cultivating universal responsibility and generating love and compassion for others – even those considered enemies and culturally foreign. Freedom does not come from separating the "self" from the "other" in order to achieve the former's actualization, as assumed by individualistic autonomy. Instead, it comes through transcending the "self" by realizing a profound empathy and connectedness with all forms of life.[51]

Joanna Macy links the individualistic "self" with philosophical traditions based on linear understandings of causality, including dominant strands of Western thought.[52] Linear causality assumes a one-way relationship between a cause and its effect. It assumes an understanding of power as "power over." By contrast, Macy notes that early Buddhist teachings on *pataicca samuppāda,* or "dependent co-arising," see causality as reciprocal. Cause is influenced by effect even while also creating it, an understanding akin to the deep interdependence of all things. Underlying linear causality is a notion of "separate selfhood." However, under "dependent co-arising" there is no separate "self" because, "Mutually conditioned, everything subsists in relationship and knows no independent self-existence." Echoing some of the imagery of the two-row wampum, Macy writes that "The individual 'self,' neither isolable or fixed, is seen as a flowing stream, a stream of being, a stream of consciousness."[53] The Dalai Lama's vision of self-government reveals the extent to which our understandings of self-rule and autonomy are based on linear causality and the assumption that separate collective "selves" exist and can separately self-actualize. In a world of reciprocal causality, questions of the autonomy and survival of the "self," as well as relationships, understood as links between separate entities, are misplaced as normally understood: the self of a "dependent co-arising" phenomenal world does not exist apart from that which acts on it and on which it also acts. Mutual causality constitutes the "self" as unbounded and a process rather than as a separate, fixed being.

To achieve an autonomy of connectedness, the Five-Point Peace Plan was to demilitarize and make nuclear free the Tibetan plateau, including the present Tibet Autonomous Region (TAR) and the eastern provinces of Kham and Amdo currently outside the TAR. This Zone of *Ahimsa* would be "a sanctuary of peace and non-violence where human beings and nature can live in peace and harmony."[54] The Chinese government could retain overall responsibility for Tibetan foreign relations but would withdraw its troops and military installations from the zone, enabling Indian and Nepali authorities to withdraw theirs from the Himalayan border regions and allowing Tibetans to enjoy self-rule. The plateau would be declared the world's largest natural park and governed according to sustainable development policies. Regional and international organizations promoting human rights would be encouraged to establish bases in the zone.[55]

The Zone of *Ahimsa* would create the conditions in which Tibetans could govern themselves and protect their culture, religion, and "national" identity in ways currently not possible in the TAR and other Tibetan areas in the PRC.[56] This is because, according to the Dalai Lama, self-government is impossible unless Tibetans and Chinese realize that their communities are deeply interconnected with and influenced by one another as well as their neighbours. They are unbounded. By establishing a demilitarized and nuclear-free space with an economy based on sustainable development, Tibet would be a site for overcoming "fragmented consciousness and a self-centered spirit."[57] This would alleviate the security concerns of Indian and Chinese authorities, as well as those of Tibetans themselves, all of which form a fundamental barrier to Tibetan self-government. Paradoxically, from the perspective of individualistic notions of autonomy, self-government is realized not through violent nationalist struggle and the cultivation of separateness but through nonviolence and a recognition of connectedness. Under the Dalai Lama's proposal, Tibet would be "associated" with China,[58] neither entirely separate nor a part of the state as understood in "nation-state" terms, a hybrid status more akin to pre-Westphalian polities in Central Asia.[59]

The Dalai Lama's proposal calls for Tibetan self-rule through democratic political institutions.[60] He does not elaborate upon the representational mechanisms that would be consistent with his vision of relational self-government. Nor does he explicitly address the difficulties, also evident in the HKSAR, of establishing a meaningful democracy in part of an authoritarian state. The Dalai Lama's 1988 Strasbourg Proposal stated that, in its relationship of "association" with China, the Tibetan government should have "a democratic system of government entrusted with the task of ensuring economic equality, social justice and protection of the environment. This means that the government of Tibet will have the right to decide on all affairs relating to Tibet and the Tibetans."[61] The proposal does not specify mechanisms for ensuring that vulnerable groups and individuals within Tibet are protected, though such mechanisms would presumably be needed to make Tibetan democracy consistent with the principles of compassion and the dependent co-arising "self." Elsewhere the Dalai Lama has written that democracy is consistent with Buddhist teachings.[62]

In summary, the Five-Point Peace Plan reminds us of relational alternatives to individualistic autonomy and the connectedness, and therefore the unboundedness, of all things. Yet it also affirms the enduring appeal for beleaguered minority nationalists of the false security provided by the individualistic nation-state model of minority self-government.

Corsica
A feminist movement against violence in Corsica called Manifeste pour la vie, or Manifesto for Life, similarly draws attention to the impossibility of achieving emancipatory self-government through violent means. However, unlike the Dalai Lama, Manifeste argues that exclusionary and hierarchical gender identities sustain political, including nationalist, violence.[63] Although Manifeste does not present a coherent, fully developed relational alternative to individualistic autonomy, such a vision is inherent in the assertion that transforming gender relations, and ending the oppression of women, would help to end violence at all levels, making a more emancipatory self-government and a more inclusive, open-ended understanding of Corsican identity possible.

Manifeste pour la vie grew out of the seemingly chronic problem of physical violence in Corsica. Historically, the island has had a reputation for violent vendettas linked with clan politics and clan-state clientelism. With the rise of Corsican nationalism in the 1960s came nationalist violence, leading to a surge of violent attacks in the late 1970s. These events partly precipitated the French government decision to grant a special statute to Corsica, giving it limited autonomy in 1982.[64] The special status was also part of wider central government efforts to create a layer of regional representative institutions that would improve democratic accountability and economic planning across France. However, the concessions did not end nationalist or other violence on the island. Nationalist attacks continued as the implementation of the special statute hit the brick walls created by the French constitutional norm of equality and, in Corsica, differences of opinion about the island's identity, boundaries, priorities, and future relationship with the rest of France. By the mid-1990s, nationalist violence had again intensified and was increasingly hard to distinguish from ordinary criminality and clan vendettas.

Then, in the few days between Christmas 1994 and New Year's Day, there were four deaths from terrorism in the city of Bastia. A group of Corsican women decided that they had had enough of the violence and of the local code of silence and state inaction that created a climate of impunity and lawlessness on the island. "It was four [assassinations] too many," Marie-Thé Mariani, a founder of Manifeste pour la vie, recalled later. "At first there were some thirty of us, of diverse backgrounds. However, all of us wanted to act against the violence, the terrorism, the death, the law of silence."⁶⁵ The movement gained support from people with a wide range of opinions about the island's future status in France. This may explain why its spokeswomen seem not to have addressed the status question directly in their writings. What united the 5,000 people who signed the original manifesto was a desire to halt violence and the local and state norms and practices that sustained it. Manifeste held regular protests. The demonstration that it organized after the unprecedented February 1998 assassination of the French prefect in Corsica, Claude Erignac, drew some 60,000 people into the streets of Bastia and Ajaccio.⁶⁶

Mariani wrote that the emancipation of Corsicans from oppressive constructions of their identity would require a transformation of gender relations. She claimed that Corsica is not naturally violent and lawless. Rather, it became so because of specific constructions of gender rooted in dominant interpretations of Corsican culture. To Mariani, the violence of some Corsican nationalism is deeply rooted in a machoistic ideology that has created an "overarmed island where, from adolescence, all adult males regard the carrying of arms as a matter of virile pride" and where "the formulation 'Me, woman, mother, sister, wife of Corsica' ... tends to reduce women to their belonging to a man or to an ethnic group and makes them bringers/bearers of exclusion."⁶⁷ To be Corsican is to remain silent about violence out of loyalty to family, clan, and nation. Mariani claimed that the island media reflect these norms, regularly reporting violence with an acknowledged nationalist political purpose while maintaining the social taboo against discussing supposedly nonpolitical, ordinary violence such as muggings and sexual assaults.⁶⁸

The organizers of Manifeste pour la vie called neither for autonomy nor for the removal of special status, but for a "prosperous, open and democratic Corsican society." They said that this could be achieved only through an end to the violence, lawlessness, and traditional gender identities that (re)produced exclusion, oppression, and insecurity, perpetuating violence in both the public and the private realms. They criticized Corsican men and women for succumbing to oppressive gendered appeals to Corsican identity and for caving in to the fear that maintained the code of silence. They condemned Corsica's traditional politicians (those associated with mainstream state-wide rather than Corsican nationalist political parties) for failing to take an explicit stance against nationalist and other violence. From the French state, they demanded that the law be enforced equally in both public and private domains, that justice be exercised dispassionately, that negotiations between the state and "armed men" end, and that public policy making and management be conducted with transparency.⁶⁹ Notably, however, this was not to be a straightforward attempt to use the constitutional norm of equality to block "differentiated citizenship" but a demand that the power of the law be used equally to end violence and insecurity. For the organizers of Manifeste, these steps would permit the building of more open, less exclusionary and oppressive understandings of the Corsican "self." Their lobbying during the so-called Matignon Process of negotiations on Corsican status after 1999 reflected their ongoing concern that, without an end to violence, insecurity, and the oppressive gender identities that they sustained, the expanded autonomy promised under the Matignon Law would only perpetuate oppression and exclusion.

Manifeste pour la vie participants have mainly taken political action through street protests, petitions, and the lobbying of politicians and state officials. Some have also supported the campaign for gender parity in elected political assemblies across France, targeting the Corsican Assembly in particular. Some Manifeste participants were candidates in the two all-women electoral lists that contested the 1998 Corsican Assembly elections.[70] Pauline Sallembien-Vittori, a candidate and Manifeste participant, has written that the transformation of the island requires the public involvement of women committed to equality and justice.[71] Although the July 2003 referendum on extending Corsican self-government and introducing gender parity in the Corsican Assembly was narrowly defeated, the French government went ahead with legislative changes to introduce parity.[72]

Thus, for Manifeste pour la vie, challenging the masculine nature of nationalist politics and representative institutions is part of wider efforts to challenge what it is to be a Corsican man or woman and to be self-governing as a collectivity. Their critique points to a way to transcend individualistic conceptions of "nation" so that issues of internal exclusion, injustice, and insecurity can be addressed, particularly but not exclusively as they affect women. Emergent in the Manifeste movement is the possibility of rethinking the Corsican "self" and the nature of self-government, beginning with an end to the violence perpetuated by Corsicans, the state, and contemporary gender relations.

Minority self-government premised on individualistic conceptions of collective identity replicates the representational and other shortcomings of the "nation-state" model of political community and citizenship. It too often creates oppression for vulnerable groups and individuals within minority communities and insecurity for both state and minority, ironically, in the name of overcoming it. However, despite these shortcomings, the quest of minority territorial communities for forms of political community that provide them with recognition, control, and choice is often legitimate. The challenge is to create forms of territorial autonomy that overcome the shortcomings of individualistic autonomy but still recognize the legitimate desire of vulnerable minorities to enjoy forms of citizenship, including representation, that protect their distinctive values.

The possibilities for such an emancipatory self-government identified in the politics of nonviolence and of multi-realmed citizenship are in some ways incommensurable, drawn as they are from distinctive philosophical starting points and political practices. The barriers to their realization are substantial. Among them are powerful state and regional elites for whom self-government is a means to preserve the economic and political status quo and to deny class, ideological, gender, and other internal diversity, as in Hong Kong. Exclusionary understandings of the ethnic minority "nation" perpetuate unequal and oppressive gender relations and contribute to general societal insecurity, as in Corsica, and which inhibit the full citizenship of new immigrants, as in Catalonia. Moreover, powerful states and nationalist movements deny the intersubjectivity of collective identities and, therefore, undermine security by failing to recognize interconnectedness, as in Tibet. Human rights and other state system norms premised on individualistic understandings of the "self," and on the state as the highest form of political community, create additional incentives for insecure minorities to portray themselves as unified and discrete, an issue that I have discussed elsewhere.[73] Yet, despite these and other difficulties, the contemporary politics of self-government contains immanent possibilities for alternative forms of self-government, based on multi-realmed citizenship and nonviolence, which recognize the internal diversity and external connectedness through which the "self" is deeply entwined with the "other," both without and within.

Acknowledgments

I would like to thank David Laycock and two anonymous reviewers for their thoughtful and helpful comments on earlier versions of this chapter. I remain solely responsible for any weaknesses or errors that remain.

Notes

1 My formulation of the individualistic "self" is drawn from Mackenzie and Stoljar's (2000) feminist critique of individualistic personal autonomy.
2 In the present analysis, citizenship implies more than legal status with related rights and duties. It also includes the recognition of identity and meaningful participation in political community, civil society, and public spheres, including but not limited to representation; see Wong (2002), especially 64-65. Thus, citizenship is not synonymous with nationality and is not conferred only by the state through its laws and regulations. Substate public authorities, including those of autonomous regions, also play important roles in determining who enjoys citizenship in all its dimensions, as do civil society and economic actors.
3 Kymlicka (1995).
4 Kymlicka (1995).
5 See Friedlander (1991); Frye (1992); Heisler (1990); and Safran (2000).
6 Tully (2001a).
7 Tully (1995), 13-14, 56.
8 Tully (2001a).
9 Tully (2001a), 4-5.
10 See Rankin and Goonewardena (2003).

11 On the post-Westphalian transformation, see Zacher (1992).
12 For background on these autonomy arrangements, see Henders (1997).
13 Linklater (1998). I prefer the term "multi-realmed citizenship" to his "multi-leveled citizenship" since the latter implies a vertical relationship among the loci of citizenship, whereas the former encompasses both vertical and horizontal possibilities, such as the "flexible citizenship" practices discussed below; see Ong (1999). The term "multi-*realmed*" also moves away from the presumption that identities are necessarily hierarchical.
14 Keating (1999).
15 Linklater (1998), 181.
16 Garcia (2001).
17 Linklater (1998), 200-201.
18 McRoberts (2001); Garcia (2001).
19 The 1996 census found that 95 percent of Catalan residents understand Catalan and that approximately 79 percent speak the language (see Sharrock [2003]). Catalan is also spoken in the Balearic Islands, Valencia, and part of Aragon.
20 Madrid follows closely behind with 27.2 percent, followed by Andalusia at 11.3 percent, Valencia at 6.4 percent, and the Canary Islands at 5 percent; see Gómez and Tornos (2000), 7. Approximately one million foreign nationals live in Spain.
21 Burgen (2003).
22 Fraerman (2003); Amnesty International (2001); European Monitoring Centre on Racism and Xenophobia (2001).
23 McRoberts (2001), 111, 162.
24 Sharrock (2003).
25 On the debate over whether relatively weak pro-immigrant advocacy groups within states can increase their resources through the political spaces and resources provided by interstate organizations, see Kastoryano (2002); Soysal (1994); Keck and Sikkink (1998); and Geddes (2000).
26 Geddes (2000).
27 On the contributions of one of these organizations, the EU Migrants' Forum, see Mukherjee (1996). For a proposal on third-country national EU citizenship, see European Union Migrants' Forum (1995).
28 See Bolin et al. (2002), 11-12; and Gómez and Tornos (2000).
29 Geddes (2000); see also Føllesdal (1998).
30 Føllesdal (1998).
31 Geddes (2000).
32 Fundació CEREM (1998).
33 December 18 (2003).
34 McRoberts (2001).
35 See, for example, Hong Kong chief executive's policy speeches in Tung (2003), especially paragraphs 27-29; and Tung (2000), Part 4.
36 See Jones (1999); and speeches by HKSAR chief executive, Tung Chee Hwa, in Tung (2003), especially paragraphs 27-29; and Tung (1997), paragraphs 11 and 24.
37 Under the Basic Law, Hong Kong's legislature currently has thirty directly elected members, twenty-four chosen by functional constituencies mainly representing business and professional sectors, and six chosen by a nondemocratic, 800-member Electoral Committee dominated by pro-China business and professional interests. The Electoral Committee also selects the chief executive, who is then appointed by the PRC central government. Not only is the political system strongly executive-led and dominated by pro-China and pro-business representatives, but also, in practice, no one is chosen to be chief executive without PRC approval. Moreover, the nondemocratic Standing Committee of China's National People's Congress can overturn SAR laws that it rules do not comply with Basic Law provisions on "affairs within the responsibility of the Central Authorities or regarding the relationship between the Central Authorities and the Region" (Basic Law Article 17). Thus, Hong Kong people can participate in and contest elections for half the legislative seats, but their representatives have no final decision-making authority. Additionally, the directly elected representatives in the legislature do not represent the range of political opinion in the territory since the electoral system

disproportionately awards seats to minority parties (voters cast a single, nontransferable ballot for a party list in five geographical constituencies). In recent elections, minority parties have been conservative pro-business and pro-China in orientation; see White (2001), 25-29.
38 Cheung and Lee (2003).
39 Henders (2000). The Portuguese and Chinese governments also applied the Hong Kong model of external autonomy to Macau; see Henders (2001).
40 For a complete list, see HKSAR (2003).
41 Farer (1993).
42 The PRC government, like the British government before it, has not accepted the ICCPR First Optional Protocol for Hong Kong.
43 For Hong Kong NGO submissions to the various UN human rights treaty-monitoring committees, see the website of the Hong Kong Human Rights Monitor at <http://www.hkhrm.org.hk>, viewed 21 November 2003; for submissions with respect to CEDAW, see the Faculty of Law, Centre for Comparative and Public Law, University of Hong Kong website at <http://www.hku.hk/ccpl/cedawweb/ngo.htm>, viewed 20 June 2000.
44 Interview with Paul Harris, Human Rights Monitor, 21 May 2002.
45 Loh (1999), 71-72. For details of NGO criticisms of the HKSAR human rights record, see US Department of State (2000) and subsequent annual State Department reports on human rights in Hong Kong.
46 Ong (1999), 12, 123-24; Chan (1997); Wong (2002).
47 Wong (2002), 79.
48 See Shain (1999).
49 Siu (1994); Lau (2001), 68.
50 On the history of the Tibetan struggle for self-government, see Smith (1996). On Corsican nationalism, see Lefevre (2000).
51 On Asian concepts of freedom and their differences from those Western notions of freedom rooted in the experience of slavery, see Kelly and Reid (1998).
52 Macy (1992). A major exception in the Western tradition is general systems theory. For a comparative discussion of early Buddhism and general systems theory, see Macy (1992). My thanks to Martin Morris for this reference. Some feminist theory offers other exceptions within the "West"; see Mackenzie and Stoljar (2000).
53 Macy (1992), 110.
54 Dalai Lama (1989a).
55 Dalai Lama (1989a, 1989b, 1991, 1997); see also Smith (1996), 600-601.
56 Dalai Lama (1989a, 1989b, 1991, 1997).
57 Dalai Lama (1997).
58 Smith (1996), 608-16.
59 Henders (forthcoming).
60 See Dalai Lama (1992a).
61 Dalai Lama (1988).
62 See, for example, Dalai Lama (1999).
63 On nationalism and gender more generally, see Kandiyoti (1996); and Anthias and Yuval-Davis (1989). On the ways in which violence performatively constitutes identities, see Campbell (1998), especially ch. 2.
64 See Lefevre (2000).
65 Mariani (1996).
66 See *Le Figaro* 8 February 1999.
67 Mariani (1996, 2001).
68 Mariani (2001).
69 Manifeste pour la vie (1996).
70 Lefevre (2000); Sallembien-Vittori (1999).
71 Sallembien-Vittori (1999).
72 Guiral and Hassoux (2003).
73 Henders (forthcoming).

7
What Do Citizens Need to Share? Citizenship as Reasonableness
Jonathan Quong

Any robust conception of political representation must ultimately be grounded in a broader theory of citizenship and justice. Bringing these "background" theories or assumptions into the light is, I think, useful when assessing some of the thornier questions surrounding political representation raised in this volume. This chapter therefore does not address the question of political representation directly but looks at whether there is a defensible conception of citizenship, considered at a more general level, on which we might base our theories of political representation.

One question that has occupied much of the literature in contemporary political theory, and occupies several of the chapters in this volume, has to do with the *substantive content* of a liberal democratic conception of citizenship. Which attributes, beliefs, ideals, or other characteristics do citizens need to have in common for a liberal democratic regime to be fair, functional, and reasonably stable? This question is particularly troubling in light of what Rawls has called "the fact of reasonable pluralism."[1] The mere fact of cultural, religious, and philosophical diversity would not necessarily be problematic. The fact of *reasonable* pluralism poses a challenge for any conception of citizenship for the following reason. Given what Rawls calls the "burdens of judgement" (e.g., complex evidence, disagreements over the weighting of values, vagueness of moral concepts, etc.),[2] we should expect different people living under conditions of freedom to arrive at different conclusions about how best to live life, even if they are all rational. This means that it is reasonable to expect widespread disagreement about the good life, even if the "right" answers about ethics and the good life seem to be perfectly obvious. This type of pluralism is meant to be permanent – it will not disappear over time, and thus any workable conception of democracy must be compatible with this reality. Like scarce resources, it is one of the unalterable circumstances of justice. Given this level of reasonable diversity, how can citizens be expected to share anything at all, let alone be required to give priority to their civic obligations over their conceptions of the good?

Any conception of citizenship is therefore caught between two seemingly contradictory conditions, which can be formulated as follows. First, a conception of citizenship must be demanding. It must require citizens, at least some of the time or in some domain of action, to prioritize their civic obligations over their other commitments. What exactly ought to be prioritized, of course, will vary depending on the conception, but the principle of civic priority is significant. Citizens need to prioritize those civic commitments that engender or facilitate a liberal democratic regime that is fair, functional, and reasonably stable.[3] We can call this *the civic priority condition*. Any workable model of citizenship needs to meet this condition. Second, a conception of citizenship needs to be compatible with the fact of reasonable pluralism. That is, an account of citizenship cannot require citizens to have more in common than the fact of reasonable pluralism will allow. This is the *reasonable pluralism condition*. These two conditions seem to pull in opposite directions. One condition requires that citizens share at least one thing that over-rides their other commitments, whereas the other raises doubts about whether citizens can share anything at all. Finding a way to resolve this apparent dilemma has been one of the major projects in contemporary political theory. This chapter looks at several recent conceptions of citizenship in order to see if any of them can meet the two conditions set out above and thereby solve our dilemma.[4]

First, there is the model of *citizenship as nationality*. David Miller, for example, has recently argued that, in order to achieve the kind of social justice that ought to be one of a liberal democratic state's highest priorities, citizens need to share in a common sense of national identity. Second, there is the conception of *citizenship as liberal virtues*. On this account, advanced by William Galston, among others, citizens need a shared commitment to certain liberal virtues in order to sustain a liberal democratic state. Third, there is the conception of *citizenship as shared fate*. The claim here, made (in this volume) by Melissa Williams, is that citizens needn't share anything other than simple interdependence. I argue that all three models of citizenship are unsuccessful because each one fails to meet one of the two required conditions. In the final part of the chapter, I therefore offer an alternative conception of *citizenship as reasonableness*. I argue that the only thing citizens need to share is a commitment to public justification along the lines offered by Rawls in his recent work. This common commitment to reasonableness meets both the civic priority condition and the reasonable pluralism condition and thus is the best available answer to the question "What do citizens need to share?"

Citizenship as Nationality

One of the oldest and most widespread beliefs about citizenship is that it ought to coincide with national identity. States, it is often assumed, ought to be nations, or nations ought to have their own states. Either way, citizens ought to share a common national identity. Whether nations should have the "right" to statehood is, of course, separate from the issue of whether citizens ought to be co-nationals, even if an affirmative answer to each produces the same result. In this section, I am interested only in the latter question. Why exactly is it important that citizens share a common national bond?

One of the most persuasive recent accounts of why citizens should share a national identity is offered by David Miller.[5] Miller actually makes a wider argument in favour of recognizing the political salience of national identity, but I restrict this section to an examination of his claims that political authorities "are likely to function most effectively when they embrace just a single national community."[6] Miller offers two general reasons why we should favour a view of citizenship that requires a common national identity. First, the smooth functioning of political society requires the existence of a certain degree of trust or solidarity between its members. This is especially true, he argues, if we believe that one of the state's legitimate functions is to redistribute resources "to those not able to provide for their needs through market transactions."[7] Because national communities, according to Miller's definition, are moral communities with corresponding duties and obligations to co-nationals, "social justice will always be easier to achieve in states with strong national identities and without internal communal divisions."[8] Second, Miller argues that the proper functioning of a democracy (deliberative democracy being his preferred conception), demands that citizens, at least some of the time, focus on the common good rather than on their own narrow interests. A common national identity, according to Miller, is a prerequisite to achieving this kind of civic commitment from citizens: "to the extent that we aspire to a form of democracy in which all citizens are at some level involved in the discussion of public issues, we must look to the conditions under which citizens can respect one another's good faith in searching for grounds of agreement. Among large aggregates of people, *only a common nationality can provide the sense of solidarity that makes this possible.*"[9]

This argument presents shared nationality as an indispensable means to achieve important civic ends such as economic redistribution and deliberative democracy. The case for understanding citizenship to require a shared national identity in this way fails for several reasons: empirical, normative, and conceptual.[10] On the empirical side, it is easy to cast doubt on the strong assertion that redistributive justice is always easier to achieve in nationally homogeneous communities. As Miller is aware, countries that appear to be multinational, such as Canada, Switzerland, and Belgium, all have relatively generous redistributive systems compared to a mononational country such as the United States. Although these examples apparently undermine Miller's thesis, he argues that the *content* of a national culture must be considered relevant in facilitating redistributive justice, not just its *existence*. In other words, although the existence of a shared national culture is a necessary condition for achieving social justice, it's not a sufficient condition. The content of the national culture must also involve a commitment to redistributive policies. This apparently explains the American case. Furthermore, Miller argues that Canada, Switzerland, and Belgium have succeeded in institutionalizing redistributive policies "partly because they are *not* simply multinational, but have cultivated common national identities alongside communal ones."[11]

Unfortunately, this response to empirical objections poses even deeper conceptual and normative problems. At the conceptual level, Miller's argument begins to look dangerously circular. If a commitment to redistribution needs to be part of the national culture, then the argument about the presence of nationality becomes more or less irrelevant to the argument, which is reduced to the tautological claim that a commitment to redistributive policies is required to get a commitment to redistributive policies.

At this stage, the definition of nationality also becomes problematic. Nationality is, for Miller, defined by five key characteristics: (1) shared belief, (2) common history, (3) active participation, (4) territorial claims, and (5) a distinct public culture.[12] Defining nationality in this way is significant because it appears to permit real diversity within a single nation. Nationality, Miller is keen to argue, does not require political, cultural, or social homogeneity; it only requires a shared public culture that will "leave room for many private cultures to flourish within the borders of the nation."[13] Shared nationality thus appears to meet the reasonable pluralism condition set out earlier. For instance, "sharing a national identity does not ... mean holding similar political views,"[14] something that obviously would violate the reasonable pluralism condition. The problem is, for Miller's conception of nationality to do the instrumental work that he claims it can regarding distributive justice, co-nationals do in fact need to hold the same political views, namely those about redistribution. Miller cannot have it both ways. Either the shared national public culture is "thin" enough to permit a diversity of political views, in which case it cannot generate the civic obligations that he claims it can, or the national public culture does contain "thick" norms and beliefs (including political views), but then it runs afoul of the fact of reasonable pluralism.

Miller's conception of citizenship as nationality can thus either meet the reasonable pluralism condition, but only at the price of failing to deliver on its civic priorities, or it can meet the civic priority condition, but only by sacrificing its compatibility with the fact of reasonable pluralism. This is the normative critique that ultimately makes any version of the citizenship as nationality argument (not just Miller's) unacceptable. The content of a national culture (for the definition of nationality to make any sense) will inevitably contain norms, principles, or attitudes that conflict with the norms, principles, or attitudes of other reasonable people. Requiring citizens to share a common national identity is wrong because it will always require either the exclusion or the assimilation of different, but equally reasonable, identities.

Citizenship as Liberal Virtues
Another approach to citizenship that has much intuitive appeal has to do with civic virtues. To sustain a healthy liberal democratic regime, surely all (or more plausibly most) citizens must possess certain character traits or virtues necessary to maintain the system. For elections to have some degree of legitimacy, we need to have enough citizens willing to go out and vote. If the rule of law is to be upheld, then citizens must respect the decisions of the courts. If anything, then, citizens need to share the virtues that make liberal democracy possible. Which virtues need to be shared will depend, of course, upon one's conception of liberal democracy. The focus in this section will be on the approach proposed by William Galston, which I've dubbed *citizenship as liberal virtues*.[15] Galston argues that liberalism represents a particular, although widely inclusive, vision of the good life and social justice. Given its particular conception of social co-ordination, liberal democracies have obviously developed specific institutions and practices that underpin that liberal conception. Citizens, according to Galston, need to possess distinctively liberal virtues in order to sustain the liberal goods provided by the institutions of a liberal democracy.[16]

Galston believes that many different sorts of virtues are necessary to sustain a liberal democratic society as a whole: social virtues, economic virtues, as well as political virtues of citizenship and leadership. The specific virtues that pertain to citizenship in Galston's theory include a respect for the rights of others, the ability to evaluate candidates for political office, and the capacity to be moderate and exercise self-restraint in making demands on the resources of the state.[17] There are also general political virtues (those that both citizens and elected officials must share) that are (1) a commitment to resolve political disputes through open public dialogue and (2) a sincere commitment to avoid hypocrisy – that is, a belief that you ought to practise the principles that you advocate in public.¹⁸ This list seems to be relatively uncontroversial, and Galston is surely right in thinking that citizens must possess these virtues in order to sustain a liberal democratic regime. His list also has the advantage of appearing fairly minimal and thus more likely to be compatible with the fact of reasonable pluralism than the conception of citizenship as nationality. Indeed, Galston's approach seems to be able to meet both the civic priority and the reasonable pluralism conditions. So far, so good.

The problem, however, is that Galston's account of civic virtues doesn't stand alone. That is, Galston doesn't believe that the *only* virtues citizens need to share are those listed above. Those are simply the virtues that citizens need to exercise qua citizens. Individuals have many other social roles in his conception of liberal democracy, and these roles come with corresponding liberal virtues. There are, for instance, the general virtues of a liberal society, which aim at sustaining two key features of liberalism: individualism and diversity. To sustain the individualism of a liberal society, Galston argues, individuals must possess the virtues of independence, fidelity, and familial solidarity (strong families are necessary to foster independence in children). To maintain the diversity of a liberal society, individuals need to exercise the virtue of tolerance.¹⁹ Liberal economies also require the abundance of certain virtues in order to survive: work ethic, adaptability, and a moderate willingness to prioritize savings over immediate consumption.²⁰

This list of liberal values that Galston believes are necessary to sustain a healthy liberal democratic society as a whole is far more demanding than the "bare bones" list of civic virtues that initially seemed to meet our two conditions. If citizens must also possess these other virtues, such as familial solidarity or economic adaptability, then Galston's conception no longer seems to be compatible with the fact of reasonable pluralism. There are many reasonable conceptions of the good life that simply don't value the sorts of general virtues required by Galston's scheme. We surely don't want to label certain citizens as unreasonable (and thus outside the domain of political justification) simply because they don't value familial solidarity or because their conception of the good eschews the modern capitalist work ethic in favour of a more spiritual or "simple" lifestyle.

There are two ways of defending Galston's conception of citizenship from this critique. First, one could respond that it is unfair to consider anything beyond those virtues specifically listed as political virtues when deciding if his theory meets our two necessary conditions of citizenship. The initial question was, after all, what do *citizens* need to share, not consumers or family members. This response fails for the following reason. Galston is careful to differentiate his theory of liberalism from that of Rawls and other so-called political liberals. According to Galston, "liberalism cannot do without, and presupposes, a non-neutral account of the human good."[21] Galston is therefore deeply critical of Rawls's attempt to draw a line between politics and more general questions about the good life and how individuals can achieve it.[22] Unlike the vision of liberalism offered by Rawls, the virtues of citizenship for Galston are merely part of what goes into sustaining liberalism more generally – they certainly cannot be held apart and considered independently of the fact that they are meant to sustain a uniquely liberal (for Galston, this means individualistic and diverse) conception of the good. In sum, one cannot coherently claim that his civic virtues meet the reasonable pluralism condition by asserting that they are somehow independent of the other liberal virtues that he espouses.

This conclusion, however, suggests a second and more fundamental way of defending Galston's theory of citizenship as liberal virtues. If Galston rejects the core political liberal distinction between politics and the good life, then surely it's unfair (or at least uninteresting) to use an assumption from political liberalism as the criterion by which his theory is to be judged. This second response in Galston's defence also fails to be convincing. It confuses the condition set at the chapter's outset – namely, that a conception of citizenship ought to be compatible with the fact of reasonable pluralism, with the political liberal distinction between politics and the good life. In other words, Galston's conception of citizenship shouldn't be rejected on the ground that it fails to observe a distinction between politics and the good life: this would clearly be a bizarre method of evaluating a theory explicitly opposed to such a distinction. Rather, Galston's model of citizenship is inadequate because it cannot properly accommodate the fact of reasonable pluralism. It may be unable to do so *because* Galston refuses to accept the distinction between politics and the good life as valid, but it's important to see that this is not *why* his version of citizenship as liberal virtues fails to meet our conditions. Furthermore, Galston accepts the idea that a theory of politics and citizenship ought to be compatible with the pluralism and diversity of modern societies – indeed, it is one of the primary themes of his most recent book, *Liberal Pluralism*. It is therefore perfectly reasonable to judge his theory on the basis of whether it meets this condition.

In summary, because Galston's list of civic virtues cannot be uncoupled from his wider theory of the good life and other more contentious liberal virtues, it seems to be fair to conclude that his conception of citizenship is not compatible with the fact of reasonable pluralism.

Citizenship as Shared Fate

Melissa Williams provides yet another answer to the question "What do citizens need to share?" Her chapter in this volume addresses a key question surrounding the issues of Aboriginal representation and self-government:

is there a contradiction between the notion of Aboriginal self-government and a belief that Aboriginals also ought to have special group representation within Canadian legislative bodies? Her answer is interesting and original. Williams argues that there is a contradiction only if citizenship is defined as a "shared identity," but there needn't be a contradiction if we define citizenship as a "shared fate." While I agree that there isn't an inherent contradiction in the political goals of self-government and special group representation for Aboriginals, I'm not sure that I agree with all the reasons that Williams provides to support this conclusion.

My concern has to do with the chapter's core distinction: citizenship as shared identity versus citizenship as shared fate. Williams makes the strong claim that "a conception of citizenship grounded in a notion of shared identity cannot entirely remove the threat of cultural marginalization for minorities, even when theorists construe identity in terms of shared values rather than shared national or racial identity."[23] This claim raises several troubling questions. What does it mean to be unable to "entirely remove the threat of cultural marginalization"? Surely the aim of constructing a civic identity is always fraught with risk – we simply do our best to mitigate against bias. More importantly, though, can democratic or political values never be free from cultural bias?

In the imagery of the two-row wampum belt, as described by Williams, the Aboriginal and Canadian communities are represented as two separate boats, each travelling down the same river, hence the idea of a shared fate without a shared identity. What supposedly unites the Aboriginal and Canadian communities are three beads or values that connect the two boats: peace, friendship, and respect. The clear implication is that these are three values on which both communities agree. In Rawls's terms, they would be the political values that form the basis of an overlapping consensus. What makes a consensus *overlapping* for Rawls is the fact that different citizens endorse these basic political values for different moral reasons. The different reasons arise due to the plurality of reasonable comprehensive doctrines that we can expect to find in any modern, free society. In other words, we agree to the overlapping consensus because, from within our own comprehensive doctrines, we can see good moral reasons for supporting it.[24]

Since the two communities have a shared fate, they will, for the reasons outlined by Williams, often need to reach joint political decisions. If such political decisions are to be legitimate, then they must, according to her own definition of legitimacy, be subject to reciprocal justification. Peace, friendship, and respect are presumably the values from which any such reciprocal justification will have to be derived. My point is that the three values mentioned in the "shared fate" conception of citizenship have been given the status of *political* values in the Rawlsian sense: they are presumed to be mutually acceptable to the two communities. If political values overlap between the two communities in this way (and surely some do), then why can't these values serve as the basis for a conception of citizenship as shared civic identity? Such a model of citizenship would "remove the threat of cultural marginalization" since it would be based on mutually acceptable political values. On closer inspection, then, the distinction between the two conceptions of citizenship presented by Williams doesn't hold up very well. If, even under the "shared fate" model, there are neutral political values tying the two communities together, then it seems as if the distinction, as drawn in her chapter, actually collapses. What is unique to the shared fate model if it too relies on the idea of shared political values?

If a conception of citizenship as shared identity can be neutral in this way, are there compelling reasons to prefer it to the shared fate conception? As noted in the chapter by Williams, the shared fate conception is "a descriptive rather than a normative" model of citizenship.[25] I think that there are legitimate reasons to be worried that a shared fate model will lack the normative stability needed to make our civic bonds *moral* rather than just instrumental. Shared political values (as well as civic allegiance to those values) are needed to move beyond what Rawls calls a mere modus vivendi. A legitimate state should be more than just compatible with all reasonable comprehensive doctrines: it should be morally compelling to adherents reasoning from within such doctrines. This, according to Rawls, is what it means to achieve stability for the right reasons – to generate the normative allegiance of actual citizens over time. Citizens, Rawls argues, must be able to recognize the constitution and other major institutions of the state as worthy of their continued support. This seems to be the concern raised at the outset of Williams's chapter in the quotation from Alan Cairns, in which he argues that, if Canada is to be more than an empty container, then there needs to be a moral bond of citizenship.[26]

Because citizenship in practice requires what I refer to above as normative stability, and because this stability must in turn be anchored in core political values, there will always be a need to fashion agreement on certain core political values to make any conception of citizenship hold together. If this is true, then shared fate alone can never be a sufficient basis for a conception of citizenship because the mere fact of co-existence doesn't tell us how we ought to regulate that co-existence. That is, it fails to meet the civic priority condition explicated at the beginning of this chapter. The shared fate conception, in its eagerness to accommodate the fact of reasonable pluralism (and to rule out relations of domination between groups), doesn't require citizens to share anything at all. Any workable conception of citizenship, however, needs both elements: shared fate and shared values. I agree with Williams regarding the desirability of the two-row wampum belt vision of Aboriginal/Canadian citizenship, but it seems to me that the imagery presents a vision of two communities with a shared fate and shared civic values. Given that Aboriginals and other Canadians share a common fate and certain political values, it doesn't seem to be implausible to suppose that they also might share in a common civic identity – something that is in fact implied in Williams's account of the three beads that connect Aboriginal and non-Aboriginal Canadians.

Citizenship as Reasonableness

The three conceptions of citizenship examined so far all fail, I argue, to meet one of the two conditions mentioned at the beginning of the chapter. The model of citizenship as nationality and the model of citizenship as liberal virtues are both unable to meet the reasonable pluralism condition. That is, both are too demanding in terms of what they require citizens to share in common. Both conceptions of citizenship are too "thick" to be compatible with the reasonable level of cultural, religious, and ethical diversity that is an unalterable feature of modern life. The model of citizenship as shared fate, on the other hand, fails for the opposite reason: it is too normatively "thin" to be a workable model of citizenship and thus doesn't meet the civic priority condition.

I now want to argue that there is an alternative conception of citizenship that does successfully meet both the reasonable pluralism condition and the civic priority condition: a conception of citizenship as reasonableness. A shared commitment to reasonableness is, I believe, both the normative minimum and the maximum that we can expect from citizens and is the best available way of meeting our two conditions. In the rest of the chapter, I will define reasonableness, explain why it offers the most attractive conception of citizenship (given the two conditions), and defend it from several important objections. At this point, I should note the obvious. The conception of citizenship as reasonableness is drawn almost entirely from the work of Rawls, and I do not claim any originality in advancing it – I only aim to show that it successfully meets our two conditions, and so, if we accept those conditions as valid, it is preferable to the conceptions of citizenship examined so far.[27]

For citizens to be reasonable, they must accept the following two key points. First, they must recognize the fact of reasonable pluralism and understand that this diversity of views is, as Rawls says, "not a mere historical condition that may soon pass away; it is a permanent feature of the public culture of democracy."[28] The assumption of permanence is obviously crucial in motivating an agreement on political issues between citizens who hold differing comprehensive doctrines. If I do not understand moral disagreement to be a permanent feature of democratic life, but rather as something that will likely disappear with the passage of time once everyone comes to accept the truth of my own position, then there is no compelling moral reason for me to fashion a political agreement with those citizens whose views differ from my own, other than for reasons of security and self-interest. For citizens to be reasonable, they must accept this point about permanence. They must accept that people whose views differ from their own are not simply irrational or self-interested, that it is possible (indeed likely) that rational people will reach different conclusions on a wide range of moral and ethical questions. If they do not, then principled agreement on political issues will be unlikely, if not impossible.

Second, reasonable citizens accept that such pluralism is best managed through the public use of reason. Because reasonable people disagree about the good life, they will have to eschew any appeals to conceptions of the good in justifying their political preferences. Put another way, only *public reasons* – that is, reasons acceptable to all reasonable citizens – can legitimate the coercive use of state power over its citizens. Public reasons are thus claims that appeal to "freestanding" political values and abstain from claims about the good life or other comprehensive metaphysical positions. This is sometimes misunderstood to be a strictly empirical claim about actual agreement. That is, any ideas or values where there is widespread agreement at the level of the political community must be freestanding or political – but this is a serious misreading of the concept.[29] This interpretation fails to understand what it means for an idea or value to be freestanding. A value or doctrine, to be properly freestanding, must be derived independently from any particular comprehensive doctrine, regardless of whether there is actual agreement about it. Thus, as Samuel Freeman points out, the fact that there may be widespread agreement on the truth of the Koran in some Islamic countries doesn't mean that the Koran can be classified as a political or freestanding doctrine in those communities.[30] A doctrine, to be political and not comprehensive, must be grounded in premises and values that *all* reasonable persons *would* assent to – whether or not they are currently members of the given polity.

Public reason requires an ideal of reasonable consensus between similarly motivated persons because it accepts the fact of reasonable pluralism. In the face of such reasonable pluralism, there can be no Archimedean point "outside" reasonable deliberation that can help us to determine who is right and who is wrong. Reasonable citizens accept the fact of reasonable pluralism and, having accepted this fact, recognize that the only legitimate way to achieve political co-operation is through a shared commitment to public justification that prohibits claims about the good life over which reasonable people disagree.[31] Citizens, then, "should be ready to explain the basis of their [political] actions in terms each could reasonably expect that others might endorse as consistent with their freedom and equality."[32] An important corollary to this, and one that is sometimes overlooked by deliberative theorists, is that those *listening* to the political proposals of others must do so in the same spirit of reciprocity. Every participant in a deliberative democracy has a moral obligation not only to frame his or her own reasons in terms of public reason but also to listen to the reasoning of others with the aim of trying to understand their claims in terms of public reason. Reasonable citizens will make a genuine effort to understand the arguments made by others and to sincerely consider the strength of their claims. Public reasoning, then, is a two-way process: the giving and receiving of reasons with the aim of arriving at a public justification.

This brief sketch of citizenship as reasonableness is enough, I hope, to make its attractions obvious. It clearly meets the reasonable pluralism condition, since acceptance of this fact is built in to the definition of a reasonable citizen. It also meets, I think, the civic priority condition, since it requires citizens to support only those positions that are publicly justifiable and to avoid making claims that rely on their own religious or otherwise controversial conceptions of the good life. In the political sphere, citizens are required to give *priority* to a political conception of democratic discourse over their own more comprehensive beliefs about the world. This ideal of deliberative, public justification is, incidentally, also a notable part of all three other conceptions of citizenship, although it is seen as subsidiary in importance rather than as the primary requirement of citizenship. In Miller's argument, for example, nationality is partly valued because it alone "can provide the sense of solidarity that makes" public deliberation over the common good possible.[33] Galston also specifically mentions, under the heading of general political virtues, "the disposition, and the developed capacity, to engage in public discourse ... [which] includes the willingness to set forth one's own views intelligibly and candidly as the basis of political persuasion rather than manipulation or coercion."[34] Williams also favours some form of deliberative democracy, although she might take issue with the exact formulation of citizenship as reasonableness.[35] There are, of course, important differences between the type of public deliberation favoured by these authors and the conception of reasonableness outlined here (Galston in particular has been critical of the Rawlsian conception of public reason).[36] The most important difference, however, is that a commitment to public justification is the primary requirement of citizenship in the reasonableness model, whereas it takes a secondary place in the other conceptions.

To test the conception of citizenship as reasonableness, we ought to subject it to the same type of scrutiny as the other three models examined so far. Given our conditions for a workable model of citizenship, there are broadly two ways in which the concept of reasonableness might be problematic. First, the requirement that citizens be reasonable in the way that I've described might be criticized as not "thick" enough. That is, it might fail as a workable model of citizenship because it can't generate a liberal democratic regime that is fair, functional, and reasonably stable. The mere demand that citizens try to resolve their political disputes by appealing to public (as opposed to nonpublic or comprehensive) reasoning might appear unable to achieve the sorts of liberal objectives highlighted by both Miller and Galston. In particular, one might wonder whether reasonableness is enough to create the sort of civic loyalty and virtues that both Miller and Galston see as crucial in sustaining liberal democratic societies. The central contention, of course, of both Miller and Galston is that citizens must share a thick set of characteristics to ensure that our civic responsibilities are given the right sort of priority. Even if their conceptions seem to require too much, it may well be that citizenship as reasonableness does not demand enough of citizens.

This concern is ill founded, I think, when we consider what being a reasonable citizen actually entails. Reasonable citizens must be tolerant of many ways of life that they disagree with, or even find abhorrent, because they recognize the fact of reasonable pluralism. Reasonable citizens must be committed to re-evaluating their own beliefs in the face of contrary public reasons on a given issue. Even if reasonable citizens do not modify their comprehensive beliefs, they are required to ignore the demands of their religious or ethical doctrines when they conflict with the demands of public reason. Think of the reasonable religious citizen whose doctrines hold stem-cell research to be immoral but who (let us say) accepts that there are no public reasons that support this view, that, in fact, public reason seems to favour the use of stem-cell research. Reasonableness requires the religious citizen in this case to (politically) support stem-cell research despite her own deeply and sincerely held moral convictions. This is surely a demanding conception of citizenship and one that entails many of the civic virtues valued in both Miller's and Galston's models.

If citizenship as reasonableness does not suffer from being too thin – that is, if it can meet the civic priority condition – then is it vulnerable to the opposite critique? Does the conception of reasonableness demand too much from citizens? In his recent book *Religious Convictions in Liberal Politics*, Christopher J. Eberle argues that reasonableness is too demanding to be a fair conception of citizenship.[37] He argues that justificatory liberals (which for our purposes can be read as those who endorse citizenship as reasonableness) have conflated two distinct principles. The first principle, that of pursuit, says that respect for persons requires us to pursue public justifications for the laws that we support. Eberle believes the principle of pursuit to be correct and so agrees with political liberals and deliberative democrats on the importance of public reason in politics. The second principle is the doctrine of restraint, which requires that we *only* support laws for which we have a public justification. A moment's reflection reveals that this is a far more demanding requirement than the principle of pursuit. As Eberle explains, it's one thing to say that I ought to *try* to find a public justification for laws that I support and quite another to say that I must always *have* a public justification for my favoured policies. What happens, Eberle quite reasonably asks, when I try to find a public justification but fail?

Eberle is centrally concerned with the question of what religious citizens should do when they have pursued a public justification but can't find one. He argues that, having looked for public reasons, such citizens have discharged the moral obligations of citizenship, and thus they are free to support their favoured law on religious grounds alone. To ask any more than this, Eberle claims, would make citizenship too demanding. This might seem to be the general problem of what to do when public reason "runs out." The problem is that Eberle's scenario isn't about what happens when public reason runs out – it's what happens when *one citizen* can't find any public reasons for the position that he supports. Strangely, there are no other citizens in this story. Eberle always poses the problem as one that arises for an individual citizen who can't find public reasons for his favoured policy, but this scenario actually needs more explanation.

What if our religious citizen lacks a public justification for his position *but someone else has found a public justification for the alternative position*? It is impossible to consistently believe (1) that morality requires citizens to pursue public justification and (2) that morality permits citizens to ignore public justifications when they exist. Eberle, however, seems to have committed himself to this untenable position. His error lies in a misconstrual of (1). Throughout the book, he speaks of the moral obligation that each citizen has to "pursue public justification *for his favoured coercive law*."[38] This moral obligation, however, is drastically different from, and much weaker than, (1). On Eberle's version of the principle of pursuit, we have a moral obligation to see if we can convince our fellow citizens of our policy positions once we have determined what our positions are, but we are under no obligation whatsoever to accept public justifications that conflict with our pre-established convictions. This is a strangely one-sided view of reasonable political dialogue. If reasonableness requires that we try to find reasons that our fellow citizens can accept when justifying *our positions to them*, then surely the flip side of this coin would entail a moral obligation to listen to and accept public reasons when others are justifying *their positions to us*. If you enter into a moral dialogue with others only on the condition that you will never change your position, then it seems clear that you haven't really entered into a *dialogue* at all but rather some sort of intransigent monologue. The more general point here is that public reason is not too demanding of citizens in the way that Eberle claims. It is too demanding only from the perspective of citizens who reject the idea of reasonableness to begin with.

There is, however, a third and much more troubling criticism of the conception of citizenship as reasonableness, which we can call the possibility problem. That is, how is it *possible* for citizens with radically different conceptions of the good life to agree on the same conception of public reason? Rawls argues that there can be an overlapping consensus on certain core political principles between reasonable people, even though such people will disagree about the good life. Reasonable people, however, are defined by Rawls as those who "will think it unreasonable to use political power, should they possess it, to repress comprehensive views that are not unreasonable, though different than their own."[39] Rawls claims that the possibility problem can be solved because an overlapping consensus on core political values between reasonable comprehensive doctrines is possible, but it turns out to be possible because the adherents of such doctrines are defined by their commitment to giving public reason priority over all other claims. In other words, Rawls's answer to the possibility problem may be seen as circular in a deeply troubling way. Citizenship as reasonableness is possible because reasonable persons will give it priority, but reasonable persons are predefined as those who accept the priority of reasonableness. To avoid circularity, citizenship as reasonableness seems to need an independent account of why reasonableness should have priority over all other values that avoids taking a "metaphysical" stance on the truth or falsity of those values.

The question of whether such an account is possible, or whether it is even necessary, is of profound import, but it will have to be set aside for the purposes of this chapter.[40] I don't think that the possibility problem fatally undermines the conception of citizenship as reasonableness. It still stands as a superior alternative to all three other models presented here. We cannot demand that citizens be more or less than reasonable without violating either the civic priority condition or the reasonable pluralism condition. Being reasonable in the manner described here is a demanding civic virtue but a *necessary* one in liberal democratic regimes where reasonable disagreement exists about the good life. Addressing the question of whether this vision of citizenship is *possible* in the face of such disagreement is another, separate question – one that has yet to be answered in a satisfactory way.

Conclusion

I'd like to conclude by bringing the discussion back to the issue of political representation in a democratic society. If we do adopt the general conception of citizenship as reasonableness, then who deliberates, and where does the deliberation take place? The defining feature of citizenship as reasonableness is the focus that it puts on *reasons* within political debate, and this doesn't necessarily favour participatory democracy over a more representative model. The norms of public reason are intended as an ideal standard that citizens, legislators, and justices are meant to approximate as best they can when engaged in political debate. Institutionalizing this ideal poses serious challenges, and, without detailed contextual knowledge, there's no reason to suppose that one particular group (citizens, legislators, or justices) will be best able to realize the ideal.

However, there do seem to be a few ways by which current liberal democratic regimes could increase the reasonableness of democratic decision making and increase the participation of ordinary citizens. Citizen juries (or policy juries), for example, are comprised of randomly selected citizens paid to deliberate on various policy questions or candidates in an election and then deliver a recommendation to the public.[41] The random selection of jurors follows a standard quota system that accounts for demographic elements such as age, race, income, and gender, making the jury a representative microcosm of the larger community.

In a similar vein, James Fishkin has been one of the pioneers in developing what he calls "deliberative polling."[42] Fishkin sees deliberative polling as a means of renewing civic participation in the original Athenian sense of face-to-face deliberations between ordinary citizens. Like citizen juries, except on a much larger scale, deliberative polls gather together a cross-section of citizens to discuss political questions. The citizens are provided with experts, information, and moderators in order to help them deliberate on the issues. A deliberative opinion poll thus differs from a traditional opinion poll because it "models what the public would think, if it had a more adequate chance to think about the questions at issue."[43] Deliberative polls use the same sampling system as citizen juries, thus ensuring that various demographic groups will be fairly represented. I mention the ideas of deliberative polling and citizen juries not to deny the importance of deliberation by elected representatives but to point out that it can be complemented by deliberation between ordinary citizens.

Still, if one accepts the account of citizenship as reasonableness offered here, then one of the important things for democrats should be not only *who* deliberates in a democracy (or *where* they should do so) but also *how* democratic debate ought to be conducted.

Acknowledgments

I would like to thank David Laycock for his comments on an earlier draft of this chapter as well as two anonymous readers. I am also grateful to David Miller and Micah Schwartzman for helpful comments on specific sections as well as for general discussions on the topics addressed here.

Notes

1. Rawls (1996), 36-37.
2. For more on the burdens of judgment, see Rawls (1996), 54-58.
3. I take it as given that we want our liberal democratic regimes to be fair, functional, and reasonably stable. This assumption is, I hope, relatively uncontroversial. I know of no theorist who argues for the virtue of regimes that are unfair, dysfunctional, and unstable.
4. Justifying the selection of these two conditions over all others is simply beyond the scope of this chapter, although I do not believe that they are in any way controversial. They are accepted, in some form or another, by almost all political theorists who write on the subject of liberal democratic citizenship.
5. Miller (1995). Also see Miller (2000), especially ch. 5.
6. Miller (1995), 90.
7. Miller (1995), 93.
8. Miller (1995), 96.
9. Miller (1995), 98; emphasis added.
10. For other recent critiques of Miller on this issue, see Moore (2001), 81-85; and Abizadeh (2002), 495-509. Other critiques of Miller on this question as well as other aspects of his theory can be found in Bell and de-Shalit (2003).
11. Miller (1995), 96.
12. Miller (1995), 27.
13. Miller (1995), 26.
14. Miller (1995), 98.
15. Galston (1991). Also see Galston (2002).
16. Galston (1991), 18.
17. Galston (1991), 224-25.
18. Galston (1991), 226-27.
19. Galston (1991), 222.
20. Galston (1991), 223.
21. Galston (1991), 165.
22. Galston (1991), chs. 4-8. Also Galston (2002), ch. 4.
23. See page 104 in this volume.
24. For more on the idea of an overlapping consensus, see Rawls (1996), 133-72.
25. See page 104 in this volume.
26. See page 93 in this volume.
27. I should note two other authors who have recently advanced book-length arguments in favour of a "Rawlsian" conception of citizenship similar (although different in certain respects) to the one offered here. See Callan (1997); and Laden (2001).
28. Rawls (1996), 36.
29. Richard Rorty, for example, has misunderstood Rawls in this way. See Rorty (1991), 175-96.
30. Freeman (2003), 39.
31. For further explanation of the concept of reasonableness, see Rawls (1996), 48-54; and Scanlon (1998), ch. 5.
32. Rawls (1996), 218.
33. Miller (1995), 98.
34. Galston (1991), 227.
35. See Williams (1998).
36. See Galston (1991), ch. 5; and Galston (2002), ch. 4.
37. Eberle (2002).

38 Eberle (2002), 68.
39 Rawls (1996), 60.
40 Susan Mendus and Catriona McKinnon have each recently tried to provide such an account. See Mendus (2002); and McKinnon (2002). For a recent essay that suggests that Rawls's political liberalism may not need such an account, see Laden (2003).
41 See, for example, Crosby (1995), 157-74; and Smith and Wales (2002).
42 Fishkin (1991, 1995). For a discussion of how deliberative polling might be incorporated into the electoral process, see Ackerman and Fishkin (2002).
43 Fishkin (1991), 1.

Part 3
Pluralist, Deliberative, and Participatory Challenges to Representation

8
The New Constitutionalism and the Polarizing Performance of the Canadian Conversation
Gerald Kernerman

> Canada's failure to ratify a constitution after almost twenty years of debate illustrates, like no other constitutional impasse, what is at the heart of the new constitutionalism. What is noteworthy in the Canadian case is not that Canadians have failed to ratify their constitution; it is that they have continued to try.
>
> – Simone Chambers (2001b), 64-65

> The dream of home is dangerous, particularly in postcolonial settings, because it animates and exacerbates the inability of constituted subjects – or nations – to accept their own internal differences and divisions, and it engenders zealotry, the will to bring the dream of unitariness or home into being.
>
> – Bonnie Honig (1996), 270

The defining narrative of Canada is of an unwieldy political project, always in search of unity and forever attempting to constitute itself as a political community. Despite great efforts by so many, the positions of Quebec and Aboriginal peoples within the Canadian political community remain unresolved, as do the situations of groups defined by ethnicity, race, religion, gender, and sexuality. A consensus on a common conception of the whole and, in particular, the relationship between the parts and the whole seems always to elude Canadians. The result is a continued preoccupation with determining their common identity *as Canadians* and a fixation on the sources of cohesion that will, at minimum, hold them all together as members of a single political community. For Peter Russell, one of the great narrators of the Canadian story, the problem is that Canadians have failed to constitute themselves as a people.[1] So they keep trying. And the story continues.

This narrative is so familiar to Canadians that some scholars suggest that it is – in its very continuation – constitutive of the Canadian political community. Where Canadian constitutional politics is usually interpreted in the terms of crisis, impasse, and failure, these scholars argue that the deliberations themselves are constitutive of a Canadian "people." Jeremy Webber calls these constitutive deliberations the "Canadian conversation,"[2] an idea that has been taken up in a number of ways by scholars of the "Canadian School" of political philosophy,[3] such as Simone Chambers, James Tully, Will Kymlicka, and Charles Taylor.[4] Webber asks: "Are democratic nations really defined by what their citizens agree upon? Is national identity, even in those countries with the strongest sense of themselves, typified by adherence to a single set of values? The answer must be no ... It isn't so much what citizens agree upon as the ways in which they disagree that is important. It is the distinctive structure of their fundamental debates – the issues that preoccupy their public life, the ways in which those issues are posed, the kinds of solutions discussed – that give a society its distinctive cast."[5] Similarly, drawing on Habermas's democratic reworking of contract theory, Chambers argues that, even though Canadians have been unable to agree on many substantive issues, they nevertheless manage, through their efforts, to constitute an open, diverse, and democratic version of "we the people." The Canadian political community is continually constituted, and the Canadian version of the contract legitimized, as Canadians deliberate *together* in pursuit of unity, meaning that Canadians succeed even as they appear to fail. Moreover, Chambers holds up the Canadian conversation as a model for the "new constitutionalism" because, she argues, it accommodates and reflects diversity, in contrast to the unitary American constitutional model.[6]

By shifting the focus from the imperative to achieve an agreement on substantive issues to a concern with the process of deliberation itself, the Canadian conversation thesis offers a provocative twist in our understanding of Canadian politics. However, the thesis is open to challenge on at least two levels. First, the operating logic of the Canadian conversation breeds polarization; to the extent that the Canadian conversation succeeds in constituting a political community, it is one characterized by nationalist contestation. Second, the Canadian conversation is so "successful" that it proliferates, routing a wide range of political struggles into its polarizing logic, with troubling implications for those pursuing transformative political projects.

To make this case, I begin by outlining the common logic of the Canadian conversation, where the presence of diversity is, paradoxically, both a source of anxiety and a distinctive basis for the Canadian political identity. In the next part, I then illustrate the polarizing effects of the Canadian conversation and its imperative to unity, focusing on the perennial debate over Quebec's place in the Canadian federation; the Canadian conversation, I argue, is a breeding ground for mutually reinforcing nationalist and identity-based recognition struggles. In the third part of this chapter, I illustrate how the Canadian conversation steers a wide range of transformative struggles into its polarizing dynamics, focusing on the debates over multiculturalism policy and women's inclusion in the Canadian conversation itself. In the manner described by Bonnie Honig above, the Canadian conversation always fails in its dreams of returning home yet succeeds to the extent that it civilizes Canadians, especially those struggling for justice and equality, into dreaming of a Canadian home space, a central feature of the ideological site that I call multicultural nationalism.

Common Operating Assumptions of the Canadian Conversation
The Canadian conversation is, like most deliberative processes, driven by multiple disagreements. At the same time, it presupposes a common operating logic, to which participants implicitly agree simply by taking part. This common logic defines the broad objective of the conversation and sets down rules and limits on how that objective may be reached, what can, and cannot, be said, and so on.[7] Much of what follows in this section will seem to be obvious, which is precisely the point: in this overcoded field, it helps to begin by defamiliarizing the obvious.

Before outlining my reading of the Canadian conversation and its common logic, let me emphasize that it is not limited to formal constitutional negotiations but instead emerges in a range of high-profile political arenas. Furthermore, while the logic of the conversation approximates the preoccupations and anxieties of many Canadians, it is not synonymous with them in any aggregate sense; instead, it is driven primarily by majoritarian concerns (understood very fluidly[8]) and only becomes "common" as the participants, through their participation, embrace and/or accept the logic in their different ways. At the same time, some obviously challenge or reject the logic of the conversation (even though their presence may be crucial to it, such as Québécois separatists[9]); others are indifferent to its concerns; while still others are excluded from the conversation altogether. With these clarifications in mind, I present my reading of the common operating logic of the Canadian conversation, focusing on four overlapping features.

The Unity Imperative
To begin with, and most obvious of all, those engaged in the Canadian conversation know what the conversation is about, in a broad sense: unity. Unity requires some form of agreement on what constitutes the Canadian political community – agreement on what it means for Canadians to use the word *we*.

The Diversity Challenge
The Canadian conversation rarely strays far from the topic of diversity since diversity is what must be dealt with in order to achieve unity. The

question, then, is how can Canadians achieve and maintain unity *despite all their diversity*? While the language shifts considerably, the logic remains: diversity represents a challenge (or dilemma, problem, or threat, etc.) to the unity (or stability, harmony, peace, or existence, etc.) of the country (or nation, community, or people, etc.) because it always has the potential to produce division (or dissent, conflict, antagonism, or violence, etc.); for the Canadian conversation to succeed, it must deal with (or manage, attend to, neutralize, resolve, or reconcile, etc.) Canada's diversity challenge.[10]

The fact that the Canadian conversation approaches diversity as a challenge is hardly extraordinary in itself. Still, the diversity challenge occupies an especially central place in the Canadian conversation, given the prevailing sense that Canada's diversity is distinctively challenging in both its form (with large French and Aboriginal minorities) and its extent.

The Embrace of Diversity

If the Canadian conversation is premised on the challenge of diversity, as a distinctively Canadian challenge, then it also presumes a distinctively Canadian response, which involves some form of embrace of diversity rather than an attempt to assimilate it. This entails a rejection of demands for uniformity, a rejection of the assimilationist notion that in order to live together Canadians must all be the same.

The Canadian conversation often depicts the accommodation of diversity as having deep roots in Canadian history, such as with the choice of federalism. While it often acknowledges that Canadian history is marked by numerous episodes of racism and exclusion, it tends to view this history as a narrative of liberal progress, with the accommodation and recognition of diversity widening steadily.[11] The defining moments in this historical narrative are the rejections of the various assimilationist policy proposals, such as the 1840 Durham Report and the 1969 Indian White Paper. The explicitly anti-assimilationist character of the Canadian conversation seems to reflect a political culture of considerable liberal tolerance, but the conversation often embraces diversity in a self-consciously forward manner that moves beyond the detachment and reserve characteristic of liberal toleration; the recognition and the accommodation of diversity are *themselves* frequently celebrated.

Consider the language of the Calgary Declaration of 1997, the most recent quasi-constitutional proposal, agreed to by all of the English Canadian premiers (i.e., agreed to by all but Lucien Bouchard, premier of Quebec). According to the fourth clause of the declaration, "Canada's gift of diversity includes Aboriginal peoples and cultures, the vitality of the English and French languages and a multicultural citizenry drawn from all parts of the world."[12] One does not *tolerate* a gift. One celebrates it.

To be clear, this approach to dealing with diversity as a gift is necessarily a majoritarian discourse (in this case, English Canadian), even if it is often internalized and expressed by minorities themselves. Given its emphasis on unity, on keeping all of the parts together, the Canadian conversation must attempt to constitute the political community in *inclusive* terms – but the results are inevitably troubled, since the challenge of diversity is premised on a threatening other, no matter how this other is embraced and celebrated.

At the same time, even while it constructs minorities as threatening to the political community, the embrace of diversity entails the exclusion of explicitly racist, xenophobic, or other anti-diversity discourses from the Canadian conversation. Canadians may not yet know what it means to be "Canadian," but, as far as the Canadian conversation goes, to be anti-diversity is to be un-Canadian. Those wary of the diversity embrace must, at minimum, disguise their arguments in acceptable language or risk being marginalized from the conversation. For example, to remain an active participant in the conversation, the former Reform Party was, throughout its brief history, forced to distance itself from the apparently racist or bigoted remarks made by its MPs.[13]

Identity in Nonidentity

The embrace of diversity makes the attempt to construct a common national identity far more difficult since there can be no resort to a religiously or ethnically defined national identity. This is a familiar dilemma, as British theorist Bhikhu Parekh explains: "A shared sense of national identity is necessary but also potentially dangerous, a force for both unity and division, a condition for the community's cohesion and reproduction which can also alienate large sections of its citizens and become a cause of its fragmentation." Parekh argues that it is necessary to centre the national identity on the political structure while making sure that it is open to multiple identities and forms of belonging and that each member of the community is valued equally.[14] In much the same way, although those participating in the Canadian conversation are endlessly pre-occupied with metaquestions of national identity, their approach to them is, given their diversity, necessarily subject to limitations. The Canadian conversation, although typical in its concern with national identity and diversity, is distinctive (or at least often assumes as much) in pursuing the solution *in* the problem by grounding national identity in diversity itself. Who are "we" Canadians? "We" are diverse!

While this approach seems to resolve Parekh's problem, it merely perpetuates it. On the one hand, the Canadian political identity or culture must remain, at least in appearance,[15] empty of content – except for the embrace of diversity itself; as a result, the path of *not* creating – or, at least, not imposing – a singular overarching identity is the defining feature of the

Canadian political identity.[16] On the other hand, even if the Canadian political identity is limited to its nonidentity, this does not mean that Canadians are uninterested in giving, or trying to give, content to it in a manner that all can agree to. The Canadian conversation continuously seeks a national political identity even as it is forced to reject the basic identity premise of traditional nationalist ideologies. As a result, Canadians are a political community in process, failing necessarily to actualize their desire to be imagined – except insofar as they keep trying. And keep trying they do.

The Unity Imperative (Continued)
The quest for identity in nonidentity cultivates even greater anxiety over the basis of national cohesion. It is necessary to determine how the various parts relate to one another, and to the whole, and especially how these parts will be kept together in the form of a whole. Arthur Schlesinger Jr. depicts the problem as follows: "One reason why Canada, despite all of its advantages, is so vulnerable to schism is that, as Canadians freely admit, their country *lacks such a unique national identity*. Attracted variously to Britain, France, and the United States, inclined for generous reasons to a policy of official multiculturalism, Canadians have *never developed a strong sense of what it is to be a Canadian*."[17] This may not be entirely fair – this approach appears to be distinctive, given the international attention that it has received.[18] At the same time, the Canadian conversation is consumed by fears of fragmentation – over the very continuation of the Canadian political community. Diversity is at once the basis for the Canadian political identity as well as the pre-eminent threat to Canada as a single political community. This leads to a search for some form of cement strong enough to bind Canadians together, and thus guard against fragmentation, but not so strong that diversity itself is assimilated. Canadian history can be read, indeed it has often been read, as an ongoing search for the cement of the Canadian political community and, in particular, a series of struggles over what that cement should look like, how it should operate, and how powerful it should be.

This concern with cementing diversity together, while familiar to Canadians, has emerged as one of the major problematics of contemporary social and political theory. Consider Jürgen Habermas's formulation: "[The] notion of constitutional patriotism appears to many observers to represent too weak a bond to hold together complex societies. *The question then becomes even more urgent:* under what conditions can a liberal political culture provide a sufficient cushion to prevent a nation of citizens, which can no longer rely on ethnic associations, from dissolving into fragments?"[19] Reflecting Habermas's question, Chambers insists that, "In giving up a unitary vision, however, we should not give up the goal of unity.

Constitutional negotiations and dialogue is still about speaking as 'We the people.'"[20] It is worth investigating what this insistence on the goal of unity entails. Even if all those taking part in the Canadian conversation agree that Canada's diversity, along with the embrace of that diversity, is a defining feature of the Canadian political community, they are still driven to achieve unity, which entails agreeing on what that embrace of diversity actually means. It is here that the Canadian conversation reaches an impasse.

The Polarizing Tendencies of the Canadian Conversation
Thus far, I have described the logic *common* to the Canadian conversation. Its disagreements are varied, but there is an important cluster of contestation around the question "*How* are the various manifestations of diversity to be understood and recognized, in relation both to one another and to the Canadian political community?" Achieving an agreement on the configuration of the parts and the whole(s) – whether in the form of a constitutional text or otherwise – is the central test of unity and the perennial aim of the Canadian conversation. Not surprisingly, there are a number of possible configurations, each of which places greater emphasis on some parts more than others. Still, the problem is not simply that there are different visions, since this is to be expected, but also that these visions are so polarized. This polarizing dynamic defines the Canadian conversation.

To illustrate this dynamic, consider the case of Quebec and its place in the federation. The de facto differentiation of Quebec has existed in practice and in constitutional and institutional terms for much of Canadian history, and there has been periodic debate over the form and extent of the differentiation. However, as every student of Canadian history and politics knows, the most explosive debate takes place over the question of how all of those differences should be understood, their implications for Quebec's relationship to the Canadian political community. The familiar disagreement is between those who hold that Canada is a single federal nation and those who argue that it is composed of two (or more) nations within a federal framework. While the pan-Canadian proponents demand that federalism be defined by ten equal provinces, each with access to the same powers and responsibilities, the dualist proponents argue that federalism should be asymmetrical, with differential access to powers and responsibilities for Quebec. The debate polarizes over whether the Canadian political community will be defined in symmetrical (equal citizens and provinces) or asymmetrical (Quebec as distinct) terms, with the distribution of national recognition hanging in the balance. For so long, the Canadian conversation has focused on bridging, reconciling, or transcending this divide; as so many of its participants have pointed out, the demands of each side appear to be compatible, especially in institutional terms. Still, every new proposal favours, or is interpreted as favouring, one conception over the other.

Why, then, is it so difficult to displace this opposition once and for all? Charles Taylor has described the opposition in the terms of a liberal versus a communitarian divide (or, as he labels them, "procedural" and "substantive" liberalism), where Quebec's communitarian liberalism clashes with English Canada's procedural version.[21] Since these positions are philosophically irreconcilable, he argues, English Canada must simply be open to Quebec's distinct version of liberalism. However, most English Canadians demanding equal citizenship do not reject Quebec's ability to pursue collective goals. Instead, as demonstrated from the Meech Lake and Charlottetown Accords to the Calgary Declaration, they reject Quebec's *special* ability to pursue these goals beyond what is allowed in other collectivities (i.e., provinces) in Canada. What they really desire is symmetry of communal powers across Canada – a kind of procedural communitarianism. The equality of English Canada does have the purpose of containing Quebec, while preserving and even celebrating it, within a symmetrical layer of provinces.

In response, Québécois assert their difference, rejecting the symmetry of equal provinces in favour of differentiated citizenship and asymmetrical federalism: not one of ten provinces but one of two (or three) nations. Such reversals are understandable, but there is a continual failure to displace the opposition itself, where Quebec's difference would no longer be placed in opposition to equality. The Canadian conversation is left in a holding pattern. The two sets of recognition demands clash since the basis of the Canadian political community upon which each pursues recognition is antithetical to the other. As the Canadian conversation continues, the effects of its inability to displace this opposition become more troubling. Just as the English Canadian "equal provinces" position becomes ever more aggressive in attempting to contain the difference of Quebec, Quebec's difference is further sharpened and accentuated in response. The debates increasingly assume a dogmatic, fundamentalist tone, revolving around divergent understandings of the basic unit/ies that will constitute the Canadian political community. The attempt to constitute the whole further constitutes the parts.

To be sure, the scholars of the Canadian School who endorse the idea of the Canadian conversation are well aware of the polarized character of this debate. Still, their responses are rather telling. According to Webber, "It sometimes seems that we are caught between two poles: either all groups should get special consideration or none should. We may be tempted to follow the Reform Party's approach, avoiding the problem altogether by treating all identically."[22] While Webber points to the ways in which Canadians disagree as constitutive of the Canadian community, the polarized pattern that I have been describing is obviously not what he has in mind. However, while it may not please Webber, these polarizing oppositions are a dominant feature of the Canadian conversation, and therefore, by his own definition, they serve to constitute the Canadian political community. Furthermore, this is not some sort of coincidental result. It is *because* the Canadian conversation aims for *agreement* on the character of the Canadian political community that it has these fragmenting effects.

Much like Webber, Kenneth McRoberts accuses those who operate according to the equal citizens and equal provinces model, such as Trudeau and his followers, as "misconceiving" Canada.[23] This implies that there is a correct conception of the Canadian political community – whether rooted in Canadian history or otherwise "out there" – that need only be grasped. However, the real misconception lies in the operating logic of the Canadian conversation itself, with the premise that the Canadian political community must be conceived and, furthermore, that this must be done in a manner with which Canadians can agree. *Any* attempt to conceive of Canada, however inclusive of diversity, will generate counterconceptions.

Of all the scholars of the Canadian School, James Tully alone seems to have come to an understanding along these lines. He characterizes the impasse as a problem of "diversity blindness," in which everyone continues to look at, and judge, the various proposals only through his or her own "federation story," a kind of language game based on different "modes or ways of experiencing Canada, of being Canadian."[24] The problem is that Canadians negotiate from the perspective of these diverse federation stories, presenting them as normative, leading to their reinforcement as the negotiations proceed. Just as Canada is heterogeneous, Tully suggests, so too are the conceptions of Canada that people have, meaning that "the requirement of unity is an illusion."[25] Despite this, rather than disengage from the Canadian conversation, Tully remains concerned to locate the spaces of agreement or "middle ground," which he does in the criss-crossing and overlapping of the various competing conceptions over time, through the evolving assortment of stories expressed in the Canadian conversation.[26] For Tully, as for the others, the conversation must continue, and of course it does.

The problem with his approach is that he presents the alternative conceptions as if they are simply different understandings, which just happen to conflict at various points, and may even generate sharp recognition struggles when they do, but need not conflict if only the participants took more time to understand one another and thus overcome their "diversity blindness." Tully's prescription, then, is to call for greater intercultural understanding, which seems to be reasonable enough, except that it is difficult to believe that the participants in the Canadian conversation are unaware of the diversity of their alternative conceptions. Far from being "diversity blind," it is more plausible that the differences and especially the perceived hierarchies are all that they can "see," at least politically. Each side is acutely aware of the other since neither conception has meaning or force except in its opposition. Furthermore, as the Calgary Declaration demonstrates, the strategy of each side is to appropriate as much of the "middle ground" into its position as possible, all the while maintaining the mutually exclusive (hierarchical) relationship between its conception and that of the other side.

As the scholars of the Canadian School like to point out, English Canada's various equality-type discourses are driven by nationalist concerns. I too am troubled by these nationalist concerns. Still, I am speaking here of a nationalist *debate*. Whether it uses the word *nation, political community, culture, group,* or *identity* or whether it proposes civic nationalism, liberal nationalism, constitutional patriotism, or some other formulation, each side of the debate is pre-occupied with achieving some form of unity that, however open to diversity it may be, leads to a clash of nationalisms and identities. Even though these nationalisms are different in their orientation, it is pointless to try to choose between them, since any one formulation will inevitably feed another; nor does it make sense to seek out the "middle ground," to demonstrate with reasoned arguments how close the two sides really are, since the terrain is so ideologically charged.

The Proliferating Tendencies of the Canadian Conversation

For the scholars who favour the Canadian conversation, the main issue is less that unity be achieved, especially in a formal constitutional sense, than that, where it is not achieved, it be continually sought. They argue that Canadians are constituted by their pre-occupation with the "we" question, the procedures that they employ in their deliberations, and the manner in which they disagree over the answers. The central tension in this approach is that the logic of the Canadian conversation, in its very continuation, holds the parts together even while cultivating their division. It keeps Canadians dis/unified – together in disunity. I am doubtful that these scholars would view the resulting "we" (divided but held together) as a legitimate basis for political community, and that Canada has held together in this way is partly a matter of luck, given the extremely close result of the 1995 Quebec referendum. Still, my concerns lie elsewhere.

Not only does the Canadian conversation continue, but it also moves far beyond the realm of formal constitutional negotiations or questions concerning Quebec and its place in the federation. Many other sites of contestation – such as those related to First Nations, ethnicity, race, gender, and sexuality – are drawn into the logic of the conversation, often framed in similarly dichotomous language (individual/collective, liberal/communitarian, equality/difference, citizens equal/citizens "plus," impartial/partial, etc.). Because Canadians have not succeeded in constituting themselves as a single "people," but continue to try, all of their democratic deliberations, but especially those involving diversity or difference, have the *potential* to get caught up in the unity question, in which cases such deliberations are faced with the task of trying to answer it – a breeding ground for nationalist and identitarian contestation. This is not to suggest that the logic of the Canadian conversation dominates all or even most democratic deliberations, only that it has the *potential* to dominate any one arena of deliberation at any given moment. To illustrate some of the dilemmas involved in this proliferation, I turn now to examine the multiculturalism policy.

The Multiculturalism Policy
The Canadian multiculturalism policy has been debated to a degree disproportionate to its budget. The policy first emerged, along with bilingualism, in the late 1960s and early 1970s as one element of Trudeau's unity strategy. As McRoberts has argued, Trudeau feared that a bicultural understanding of Canada would encourage Québécois nationalism, so he pursued multiculturalism instead, attempting to reduce the sharpness of the French/English divide by accentuating Canadian diversity more generally. It is not surprising, then, that the policy has always been regarded with suspicion in Quebec.[27]

In English Canada, the multiculturalism policy (including the original 1971 version and the more recent Multiculturalism Act, 1988) has been criticized on several fronts, yet an especially common criticism is that it encourages division and fragmentation. Writers such as Reginald Bibby, Neil Bissoondath, and Richard Gwyn argue that multiculturalism "ghettoizes" groups of people, weakening the bonds that hold Canadians together. They worry that, instead of encouraging attachments to the Canadian political community, the policy encourages group membership in particularistic communities, resulting in the rise of a disruptive and divisive identity politics.[28] According to Bissoondath, "multiculturalism has done little more than lead an already divided country down the path to further social divisiveness."[29] As a policy aimed at combating Canadian dualism, it is ironic that it is now charged with divisiveness. However, supporters of the multiculturalism policy have met the criticism squarely. In particular, Will Kymlicka argues that the policy manages tensions and has an integrationist effect, thereby enhancing cohesion and unity.[30]

Whether or not the multiculturalism policy manages tensions as Kymlicka argues, debate over the policy, and related policies and practices, is often dichotomous. The trigger points – around some form of diversity or difference – route a variety of otherwise distinctive emancipatory concerns over race, ethnicity, culture, and religion into debates over the character of the Canadian political community. Should racial, ethnic, and cultural minorities receive distinct recognition and support to preserve and develop their diverse backgrounds? Should school curricula reflect diverse traditions and histories? Should there be flexibility in the uniforms and headgear of Mounties to allow for religious diversity? Are affirmative action and employment equity programs justified? As these questions over justice, equality, and diversity are incorporated into the Canadian conversation, they are approached as problems (or solutions) for the whole, leading the discussion to polarize: hyphenated versus unhyphenated citizenship, liberalism versus communitarianism, "difference-blind" versus difference liberalism, and so on.

The critics and supporters of the multiculturalism policy and related policies present diametrically opposed interpretations of their *effects* – although far more notable is their implicit agreement on the criterion of judgment: does it appropriately manage the challenge of diversity, and does it enhance or weaken Canadian unity? However much they may disagree on other aspects (over justice, equity, cost, etc.), both critics and supporters take it for granted that cohesion should be a central criterion of success or failure.

Kymlicka has even suggested that the emphasis on unity is now the common concern in what he calls the "new multiculturalism debates." He argues that the normative philosophical debate over liberal justice and minority rights is "drawing to a close" (with the theorists of differentiated citizenship victorious) and that the debate has instead shifted toward issues of unity and integration.[31] However, in the Canadian context, the debate over the multiculturalism policy has never left this unity problematic.

Struggles over Gender Representation at Charlottetown
I turn now to my second example, women's struggles for inclusion in the Canadian conversation, which relates to the process of deliberation itself. According to Chambers, "The push to accommodate diversity, including diversities that have yet to develop, turns the contract into an open-ended conversation into which new voices can enter at any time."[32] With this in mind, it is worth exploring the dynamics of such discussions over inclusion as they occur in the Canadian conversation. I undertake this exploration by analyzing transcripts of the televised discussions and debates that took place during the 1992 Charlottetown referendum campaign.[33] Charlottetown was a significant departure from the much-criticized elitism and exclusivity of the patriation and Meech Lake processes of the

1980s. While there was much discussion of questions of inclusivity and representation throughout the Charlottetown process, these procedural discussions were framed in much the same dichotomous terms as the substantive components.

Following an open and engaged public consultation process, and in contrast to the "eleven white men" process of the Meech Lake negotiations, the Charlottetown Accord was negotiated by the eleven first ministers (still all white men, each with a formal constitutional veto) as well as two territorial leaders and four Aboriginal leaders (one white man, one white woman, three Aboriginal men, and one Inuit woman, none of whom had a formal constitutional veto). While this is hardly a model of inclusivity, Joe Clark, then federal constitutional affairs minister, was moved to proclaim that the accord was "decided at the most inclusive negotiating table ever in Canadian history."[34] This seemed to capture the prevailing sentiment. The only sustained criticism of the negotiations themselves came from the Native Women's Action Committee, which protested the exclusion of Aboriginal women from the negotiation process by pursuing court action in an unsuccessful attempt to halt the referendum.

The referendum campaign itself marked a high point for the Canadian conversation: it was engaged, public, and generally inclusive of a diversity of voices. In fact, Judy Rebick, then president of the National Action Committee on the Status of Women (NAC), was the most frequently heard "no" spokesperson on the television news (more than Preston Manning of the Reform Party or even Pierre Trudeau). Leading up to the referendum campaign, NAC had gone through extensive consultations with its member groups (it is an umbrella organization made up of hundreds of women's organizations) to develop its wide-ranging critique of the accord. In addition, Rebick and other NAC participants were supported by a network of feminist scholars, intellectuals, and activists from across the country, allowing them to make well-informed contributions throughout the campaign.

During the referendum campaign, there was considerable debate over questions of gender inclusion and representation – and one would have expected this debate to centre on the gender parity provision in the accord, which would have allowed each province to ensure parity in its seat allotment in a revised Senate.[35] Four provincial governments expressed an initial desire to do this, but negative reaction to the provision led them to backtrack before the referendum campaign had really begun – and there was surprisingly little discussion of the provision after that. Remarkably, much of the debate over gender and representation centred on the representative legitimacy of NAC and the other women's groups active during the campaign. This debate generated a series of dilemmas for these participants.

Dilemma of Exclusion/Inclusion

These women were criticized as illegitimate because they were unelected, a criticism that is doubly ironic considering that they were themselves attempting to challenge the legitimacy of an electoral system that results in their extreme under-representation. Furthermore, a referendum is a time for public deliberation, so it does not seem to make sense to challenge a speaker's participation based on rules governing the election of parliamentary representatives.

Dilemma of Im/Partiality

Despite the referendum setting and its orientation to public deliberation, assumptions of representative democracy prevailed insofar as elected representatives (especially federal and provincial) spoke frequently in the media in their *representative voices*. Certainly, beyond the politicians, there were also many writers, academics, commentators, and popular "citizen on a street corner"-type voices. The voices most often questioned, however, were those, such as NAC's, that emerged out of new social movement or interest group processes, the "special interests." In response, some women (especially feminist activists and politicians) pointed to their under-representation and questioned the traditional premise of impartial representation altogether, arguing that men could not possibly speak to their issues, needs, and experiences as women.

This type of strategic reversal is crucial, to be sure, but the dilemma is that women (and other traditionally under-represented and marginalized actors) are further categorized and grouped in the very process of gaining and justifying inclusion, all of which produces a tangle of static either/or frames of analysis. As the referendum continued, the media began giving more attention to other women (mainly conservative politicians and commentators), who emphasized their impartiality by insisting aggressively upon the irrelevance of their gender (or ethnicity, race, etc.) in their roles as politicians or in their decisions as citizens and voters. For many of these women, the common refrain was "NAC doesn't speak for me!" Such criticism was not limited to conservative women. For example, June Callwood, novelist and co-chair of the "Yes" Committee, commented, "I'm somewhat uneasy about all this pressure for gender equality, which deals only with genitalia and not with content. I've known some anti-feminist women, lots of them, and I've known some really fine pro-feminist men. There's something simplistic about thinking that one's gender defines character."[36]

As Callwood's unease suggests, it is as if women were presented with the choice of situating their voices in either a disembodied (impartial) manner or an essentialized (partial) manner. Of course, whatever path they "chose," their voices were marked as "women's voices" by virtue of their being faced with the choice. In contrast, speakers from traditionally over-represented groups were largely immune to such questioning and thus free to express themselves in a fluid manner, emphasizing their partiality on some issues (speaking, say, as "westerners" or "rural farmers") while assuming an impartial voice (as "Canadian") on others. While expression of provincial, regional, and language partiality garnered little attention, women participants were, as a whole, constructed as selfishly focused on issues of concern only to them.

Dilemma of Dis/Unity
One of the reasons that it was so difficult for NAC and other feminist or minority actors to displace the impartial/partial opposition was that, in their presence as differentiated voices seeking inclusion, and in having to justify their inclusion, they were continually criticized (given their resulting "partial" voices) for having a fragmenting effect on the Canadian political community. In a typical example, Joe Clark, then federal constitutional affairs minister, stated, "The problem with an interest group is that it focuses so narrowly on its narrow interests that it can lose sight of the country. In my view, that is what NAC has done here."[37] Many others put similar interpretations forward during and after the referendum campaign.

Linda Trimble has responded to these criticisms by demonstrating that women participants in the referendum campaign were – despite all of the efforts to construct them as hyper-particularistic – actually "good citizens" who made productive contributions in their own distinctive ways.[38] In making this case, Trimble displaces the impartiality/partiality dichotomy by arguing that women were other regarding and concerned for the whole. Unfortunately, she does this by displacing this opposition onto another when she adopts a "good citizen" (looking out for the whole) framing, which implies a contrast with a "bad citizen" (challenging the whole?). But why operate within this opposition?

Trimble's response illustrates further the sorts of dilemmas that the Canadian conversation generates for those struggling for inclusion. In questioning their under-representation, women are themselves questioned as illegitimate and unrepresentative. In the process, they are further grouped as "different," as driven by a partial perspective, as undermining the attempts of the Canadian conversation to constitute a people, and so on. In response, Trimble rejects the criticism, arguing that women were in fact acting as "good citizens," directed at strengthening the political community in their own distinctive ways. I have no disagreement with Trimble on this point, but what I find remarkable about her argument is that she feels moved to make it in the first place.

Is it possible that this type of response by those struggling for inclusion is what Chambers means when she speaks of the potential civilizing effects of the Canadian conversation? In participating in this terrain, women and other traditionally under-represented participants are conditioned to engage in these "civilizing processes," which orient them toward diffusing the threat that their own participation may represent for the constitution of the political community. Even so, Rebick and NAC are not easily "civilized," to be sure. In fact, Rebick was the Charlottetown referendum's prototypical "bad" citizen in her sustained pursuit of a transformative politics, which moved well beyond questions of under-representation to challenge the gender order itself. It is no wonder that other participants in the Canadian conversation constructed NAC as threatening. It *was*.

For those wishing to pursue a transformative politics, "bad" citizenship remains the preferred option, yet who would want to choose between these dichotomous options in the first place? As many Canadians now struggle for gender parity, with electoral reform increasingly on the agenda, it makes sense to steer clear of the Canadian conversation, in which questions of gender justice are so quickly supplanted by depoliticizing concerns over unity and stability.

Conclusion

The Canadian conversation operates on the ideologically charged terrain of multicultural nationalism, a space that manages a wide range of liberal contradictions over justice, equality, and diversity. Multicultural nationalism funnels political contestation over these contradictions into polarizing forms of deliberation over the most appropriate relationship between the political community and its parts. The drive to guard against fragmentation, to ensure unity, amounts at a certain level to a defence of these liberal contradictions – but it cannot dream the antagonisms away.

To return to Bonnie Honig's insight, discussed at the outset, since a Canadian home space is never constituted in a final sense, the Canadian conversation remains pre-occupied with cohesion and stability in the face of diversity. Participation in the Canadian conversation may involve rejecting the totalizing unity of Rousseau, but it still involves depoliticizing dreams of politics as home. There is an alternative, however. Those pursuing a transformative politics can refuse the invitation to participate in the endless quest for a Canadian home space. In rejecting the unity-driven logic of the Canadian conversation, they will be far better positioned to pursue creative political conversations instead.

Acknowledgments
Some of the ideas presented in this chapter are explored further in my forthcoming book, to be published by UBC Press in 2005. A version of this chapter was presented at the New School University, spring 2003, as part of the Sawyer Seminar series. I am grateful

to Courtney Jung, Abdollah Payrow Shabani, and the other members of the seminar for their helpful feedback. In addition, for their comments on earlier drafts, I would like to thank Idil Boran, Joe Carens, Simone Chambers, Rachel Kernerman, David Laycock, Ken McRoberts, Leah Vosko, and Reg Whitaker. Finally, I would like to acknowledge the generous assistance of a SSHRCC research grant (Federalism and Federations Program).

Notes
1 Russell (1992).
2 Webber (1994).
3 Beiner and Norman discuss the emergence of the Canadian School in their introduction to Beiner and Norman (2001); also see Ignatieff (2000), 11.
4 Chambers (2001b); Tully (1994, 1995); Kymlicka (1998), ch. 13; Taylor (1993); see also Blattberg (2003).
5 Webber (1994), 185-86.
6 Chambers (2001), 69-70.
7 What follows should be distinguished from the rules governing Habermasian discourse theory.
8 The fluid majoritarianism driving the Canadian conversation is implied through a range of majority/minority framings; at minimum, this majoritarianism is "English Canadian," although it is often far broader.
9 This is far from straightforward. The presence of René Lévesque during the patriation negotiations and the question of whether he was "on the same page" as the other first ministers is central to the continuing disagreement over the "night of the long knives" and whether Quebec's decision not to sign the Constitution Act, 1982, was a result of this betrayal or merely a logical consequence of Lévesque's separatist politics.
10 For a far more extensive discussion of the "problem of diversity," see Day (2000).
11 For a recent illustration of this narrative of liberal progress, see McLachlin (2003). Day (2000) provides an excellent examination of the history of Canadian state discourses concerning diversity.
12 "Premiers' Framework" (1997).
13 For examples of media coverage, see Harpur (1999); "Manning Panders" (1997); and Thompson (1997).
14 Parekh (2000), 231-32.
15 Appearance is key here – I am not suggesting that the Canadian political identity is actually neutral or empty, only that it is put forward as if it were.
16 As Moodley (1983), 329, argues, "In a country with a vague identity, in a society rich in geography and short of history, multiculturalism is propagated as the lowest common denominator on which all segments may agree." In addition, see Smith (1970), 272.
17 Schlesinger (1998), 17.
18 Michael Ignatieff (2000), ch. 1, discusses this attention.
19 Habermas (1998), 118.
20 Chambers (2001b), 69.
21 Taylor (1993, 1994). See also Cook (1966), 146; and Ignatieff (2000).
22 Webber (1994), 26.
23 McRoberts (1997).
24 Tully (1994), 161.
25 Tully (1994), 165.
26 Tully (1994), 161-62.
27 McRoberts (1997), ch. 5; Bloc Québécois MP Christiane Gagnon discusses this in Gagnon (1997), 42-45.
28 Bibby (1990); Bissoondath (1994); Gwyn (1995).
29 Bissoondath (1994), 89-90.
30 Kymlicka (1998).
31 Kymlicka (2001), 169. Presumably, Brian Barry (1999) would disagree with Kymlicka that the "old" multiculturalism debate is over.

32 Chambers (2001b), 64.
33 These transcripts include news stories, editorial essays, documentaries, interviews, debates, and "town hall meetings" derived from the CBC news programs *The National*, *The Journal*, and *Sunday Report* as well as from *The CTV News* between 3 September and 25 October 1992.
34 *The Journal*, 3 September 1992, Placement 1.
35 Section 23 (2) of the Charlottetown Accord (Draft Legal Text, 9 October 1992) states: "Subject to this Act, the legislature of any province or the legislative authority of any territory may provide for (b) any special measures to provide for equal representation of male and female persons."
36 *The CTV News*, 27 September 1992, Placement 7.
37 *The CTV News*, 15 September 1992, Placement 5.
38 Trimble (1998), 131-56.

9
Demanding Deliberative Democracy and Representation
Greg Pyrcz

Much recent work in Anglo-American political theory has considered the potential of deliberative democracy as a method for political and ethical determination.[1] Some of this literature has attended to political practice, either in the form of experiments in public deliberation or in identifying the discursive features of ongoing democratic processes.[2] The rest has been devoted to employing discursive constraints of a variety of competing conceptions of deliberative democracy as regulative ideals, speculating as to what might be concluded by citizens under the force of such constraints on issues that typically divide them, and determining how institutional arrangements and political practice might be governed by attention to these hypothetical considerations.

The discussion that follows identifies a demanding set of deliberative constraints, as epistemic devices for the deep identification of public choice.[3] These constraints can be found (and may be extended) in current democratic practice, and they otherwise serve as a regulative ideal, here with respect to the role of the democratic representative.

Demanding Deliberative Democracy

Demanding deliberative democracy[4] is a set of perfectionist proceduralist constraints upon deliberative processes grounded in humanist, epistemic ideals, wherein the insight of citizens, as autonomous, authentic, and free human beings,[5] is the basis upon which to discern together how it is best for us to live in community. It stipulates that discourse establishing or justifying fundamental conventions, norms, principles, and practices be regulated by three deliberative constraints: (1) the absence of power, defined widely to include psychological power; (2) an orientation to achieve unanimity of judgment; and (3) the assumption of high stakes (where those party to such deliberation are understood to have assumed that no patterns or projects of social/political/economic co-operation are available upon which to fall back, failing agreement).

Typically, these constraints are to be reserved for foundational discourse, where the determination of principles and practices that define and articulate the basic features of social, political, and economic life are set and renegotiated. They may also appear in seemingly narrower issues of ethics and politics, such as in the issue of a woman's right to choose, or in issues relating to punishment, where foundational regemic agreement is raised indirectly. Contemporary liberal democracy begs off these demanding conditions of political process, and its achievements accordingly are only accidentally productive in generating the deep resolution or respect of difference that more demanding deliberative democracy seeks. Indeed, liberal democracy can be seen as degenerative of the conditions of demanding discourse, by avoiding (or finessing) discussion where stakes are considered high and by remaining more or less open to the force of psychological power.[6]

I distinguish the proceduralist constraints in this account from seemingly less demanding or from otherwise idealized conditions of deliberation such as those found in Habermas and Rawls, although demanding democracy shares a family resemblance and is plainly indebted to both. It borrows from Habermas the idea that democratic discursive engagement may serve to transform and transcend, particularly, unjustifiably power-rich human relations, though it follows Mark Warren's critique of Habermas's insufficiently persistent attention to psychological conditions in the processes of securing democratic outcomes.[7] This critique could easily be extended to Rawls.

Demanding deliberative democracy borrows several ideas from the early Rawls. One is that proceduralist principles allow us to identify (and to legitimate) just regemic relations. Another is that seeking to achieve foundational terms of social co-operation, while relying on current foundations of advantage as a fail-safe, is both unproductive and morally if not logically incoherent. In this latter respect, my approach, rather than adopting Rawls's putative Kantianism, follows Hobbes on the force of an assumed "state of nature" in the transformation of civic relations. My approach also draws on Rousseau concerning the epistemological and justificatory force of constrained deliberative practice.[8] For both Hobbes and Rousseau (though in different ways), the act of social union was transformative of human beings, and much of this transformative force was to have issued from the realization of the intolerable conditions of human life characterized by its absence.

Another way of identifying demanding democratic deliberation is to contrast its underlying assumptions more broadly with the literature on deliberative, discursive, or mediative democracy of the past twenty years. Most of this literature advances two processes asserted to generate and secure new patterns of social co-operation. The first is the philosopher's assertion that sincere, open, and empirically grounded talk between persons employing the power of reason leads effectively to political development.[9] The second assertion is sociological, that discursive relations shared by persons constrained to behave in a certain way engender new consensus simply as a heuristic outcome of participants' social adaptation to common values discerned in the process. Transformative power is found in the practice of normatively oriented discourse itself. The more we speak together in respect of one another, it is held, the more we are prone to find (or produce) an identity-rich community of norms.[10]

Demanding democracy holds that neither the processes of reasoning nor those outcomes from merely speaking together realize the sort of human insight and accordingly the democratic development that a more demanding engagement of citizens would allow. It holds to a sharply constrained constructivism based on a belief that the best sort of human insight, and accordingly the best form of democratic development, is realized by more demanding discursive engagement. In this engagement, the regulative goal is to realize the truth of our human condition as the basis for democratic life. It contends, against some postmodern epistemology, that there are indeed discernible truths about our lives as human beings – our human condition, as it were. However, demanding democracy asserts that these truths are unknowable a priori; instead, they are discovered in speaking the truth of our common and differentiated lives when freed from untoward constraints, by the force of counterbalancing discursive constraints.[11] It contends further that such truths about us, requisite to the realization of the best form of democracy, require the engagement of folks from all walks of life. Those often dismissed as marginal have, when freed somewhat from domination and other debilitating features of their conditions, and asked alert and probing questions, provided access to insight too often overlooked.

In *Democracy, Rights, and Well-Being*, I apply such demanding epistemic constraints in consideration of issues of gender justice, democratic participation, punishment (as an account of sentencing), the democratic performance of the mass media, and the force of political obligation. In each, I try to show how ethical deliberation may be lodged – rather than in utilitarian calculation, rights language, abstract principles, or normative association – in a perfectionist procedure as a perspective for both judgment and transformative reconciliation. I argue that, where the employment of ambitious epistemic constraints is not productive of transformational realization closer to our deepest insights, using our common and diverse humanity as its subject, a better-realized pluralism is the outcome, as it were, reserving the force of our human insights for further reconciliation. The idea of democratic pluralism more fully realized in demanding deliberative democracy is taken up, in that work, in a treatment of the issue of gender justice.

In this treatment, I concede that demanding deliberative democracy may not, in the current context, lead to a new governing realization of the nature of and prospects for gender in human relations, a new demanding consensus, that is, beyond competing accounts and the diversity of lives. However, demanding deliberative democracy, as a set of conditions governing especially foundation discourse, does not lead back to prior monistic architecture and practice, governed by patriarchal or indeed any such prior "consensus," since it stipulates no fall-back position failing demanding democratic consensus. (If the purpose of discursive practice of this sort is to justify conventions, then presuming a fall-back position is a subtle way to beg the question.) Instead, in practice, such failure to forge a new demanding consensus on gender leads to a deeper and more fully appreciated sense of the significance and epistemic force of difference. Where the stakes are high, where no fall-back position is provided, and where discourse "fails," participants are driven to accept, and in the process more deeply to understand, the pluralism of sorts of lives, understandings, and values in respect of gender.

The simplest but admittedly imperfect metaphor for the process of demanding deliberative democracy is the democratic jury. Here high stakes are associated with judgment and sentencing, for the life of the convicted and for the integrity, self-respect, conscience, and reputation of the juror. In contrast, the metaphor for the rationalist discursive practice favoured by Habermas might be the seminar, where power is assumed not significantly to be in play and where the stakes are assumed to be more "academic." A competing metaphor for the sociological account regarding discursive practice, noted above, might be the currently popular practice of quasi-judicial mediation, where social peace rather than human insight or justice appears to be the principal goal. Here the outcome of discursive practice is open to a wide diversity of consensus as participants are encouraged to think of their own values as having no strong epistemic force, as claims not about truth and justice but simply of competing perspective and emotion.

The exclusion of psychological power from the process of deliberative democracy is meant to provide the fullest conditions of freedom in foundational and in subsequent democratic practice. It seeks, as much as possible, to secure the positive freedom of deliberating citizens. Unlike the treatment that this concept receives elsewhere, where it is thought to protect a backdrop of moral and social integrity and identity in fundamental choice making, "positive freedom" relates here to eradicating implicit and especially psychological constraints to self and social determination. The attention in demanding democracy to the possibility that identity is, at least for some, a matter of their victimization in relations of psychological power provides a compelling reason for favouring a more radical reading of positive freedom, as a psychological and existential achievement rather than as a moral one, as it is in Taylor.[12]

The strong orientation toward unanimity in demanding deliberative democratic decision making is not simply a means of securing consent and generating legitimacy for the regime, as it might be seen to do in liberal democracy.[13] It is also meant to protect discussion from collapsing into subtler forms of power or illicit consensus not grounded in positive freedom. Here the deliberative constraints of the democratic jury are again illustrative. The force of a veto in a jury's decision making is not to ensure that consent is complete. It is to militate against an easy bandwagon effect, achieved by jurors' dependency upon others for their sense of confidence or by rhetorical or easy psychological force. Unanimity, in this purpose, is not perfect, since it is possible for even the sturdiest juror to fall prey to psychological dependence and misplaced language. But it is the best that we can do in democratic deliberations and perhaps in human affairs more generally.

The unanimity orientation in demanding deliberative decision making is also central to its epistemic humanism. A unanimity rule most effectively secures that all possible sorts of human insight are engaged in the definition of foundational principles. Finally, this epistemological requirement (advanced by Mill in *On Liberty*) is especially compelling when combined with the high-stakes caveat of demanding deliberative democracy. When deciding with others how one's social life is to be conducted, where it is assumed that there is no justified social practice upon which to fall back if deliberations fail, citizens can afford no insight left hidden. The "high-stakes/no-fall-back" condition of demanding democracy also serves the democratic humanist epistemic mandate of demanding democracy. It seeks to energize the cognitive and social development of parties to democratic experience. Demanding democracy here draws on existentialist psychological assumptions, especially in asserting that crisis-like discursive conditions are more likely to have transformative force than are other conversations of even the most erudite, rational, and mannerly sort.[14] Demanding deliberative democracy aims not simply to find accommodation between parties but also to transform them, if only partially, to develop and, where necessary, to recover their common humanity in political community. This is its ambition, again, even where difference is left unresolved in a deeper, more fully realized, pluralism.

The conditions postulated here are similar to those imposed in the early Rawls. Persons in the original position (POPs) are to understand themselves as constituting, through their common decisions, the regemic foundation of their lives, of gaining through such deliberation a (public) sense of justice. In demanding democracy, parties must assume that a failure to agree to foundational principles will most likely not leave them where they were before: that is, within a society in which they profit or suffer from current conventions and practices of social co-operation. Instead, they are to assume that they will find themselves without conventions or secure patterns of co-operation and sociability upon which to depend for their happiness and personal integrity. This sense of the high stakes involved in foundational democratic communication is muted in Habermas, even as his ambitions too are foundational and transformational. The energy that such urgency provides, demanding democracy asserts, is necessary if foundational or refoundational work is really to develop/transform the cognitive, associative features of the citizen and enable deeper democratic realization.[15]

Democratic Representatives and Demanding Deliberation

I wish to turn now to how one might treat demanding deliberative democracy as a regulative ideal informing the conduct of democratic representatives, though plainly some of this work is done by the logic of conception itself. Representatives in demanding democracy are not those charged with merely amplifying and integrating the expression of public opinion. Nor do they merely stand in for and enact the subjective, the objective, or even the best interests of citizens. Nor are they to serve simply as regulators of social division, though aspects of these roles are woven into their work. Instead, these representatives are to employ the regulative ideal so as more deeply to engage the citizenry in processes of public deliberation, judgment, and autonomy.

Two processes would be central to representation in demanding democracy. The first would have the representative speculatively answer the following question: what, as citizens, would we favour in public policy were we not suffering those democratic deficiencies revealed in light of the regulative ideal?[16] Demanding democracy engages the representative in an epistemic, discursive relationship with citizens, setting the agenda of such engagement in initially speculative policy insights. Such speculation is predicated on discursive engagement with citizens, real and imagined, in light of the stipulated conditions of the deliberative ideal and especially by discounting in current public discourse the likely impacts of untoward psychological influences. Such discursive engagement is also to be predicated upon the assumption that the greatest social and economic impediments to deeply realized authentic voice have effectively been ameliorated.[17] A representative so governed by the perfectionist ambition of demanding democracy would need quickly and persistently to see the possibility that his or her speculative answers might be mistaken, premature, or in need of greater development. These are all ways in which the speculator may fail adequately to identify the reality or condition of his or her constituents or indeed of his or her life. Plainly, many who believe themselves to be most deserving of political authority might be less skilled than they would need to be in respect to this epistemic role. Others, who are now a great distance from political and intellectual authority, may indeed be quite a bit closer to the requirements of the ideal than is supposed. They enjoy an epistemic advantage, namely productive access to the truth of their own lives, and often easier access to the authenticity of others not currently holding conventionally established power or hobbled by the vainglory and surplus repression that can attend it.[18]

The second process would require our demanding representatives, singularly or in concert with others, to contribute to the formulation of public policy so realized, retesting it in the express judgment of citizens, again ensuring that their deliberations and expressed will were as well governed by the regulative ideal as was reasonably possible and guaranteeing that the expressed judgments and will of citizens indeed came to inform public policy.[19] This role might involve exciting citizens' sense of the stakes of deliberation and would include supporting policies that have as their goal upgrading the educational or otherwise debilitating social and economic conditions of citizens and speaking out against domination of public opinion by the mass media, by subpolity groups, or by the agencies of state.

These are epistemic roles, and, though they require somewhat different skills, both require a close, critical attention to the actual lives of human beings and a respect for their experience and deepest reflection. This aspect of demanding democratic representation resembles humanist pedagogic excellence, bringing out the expression of the truth of human lives by constraining contingencies that undermine their expression and inducing recognition of the value of their authentic experience and deeply considered insight as the means to the realization of the best form of human society.

It might be useful to contrast this account with the regemic role of the representative presumed in liberal democracy. When construed coherently and most powerfully in political argument, liberal democracy is strictly founded upon the autonomy of the individual, where autonomy is related to negative liberty. The role of the state is to convert (some of) the autonomy of individuals into a public autonomy, where such conversion is warranted by the consent of the citizen. The central example of such consent is that which authorizes the right of the state to punish those who transgress one's autonomy, expressed either as life or property. The various further rights of the citizen, to political speech, to assembly, to the information provided by a free press, and the like, are rights derived from and limited to the principle of negative liberty, as injunctions against nonconsensual, coercive interference.

In some accounts, of course, liberal democracy entails legal rights beyond those necessary to ensure the negative liberty of liberal autonomy, and these, typically stretching the coherence of the account, are formally recognized, sometimes as human rights. In strict, minimalist, de-ontological liberalism, however, when they are not otherwise entailed by negative liberty (as the right to life and property occasionally are), these other rights are made coherent by taking them as the outcome of consent rather than as ontological foundation.[20] In this regemic definition, the institutions and practices of democracy are treated as means for the expression of consent to public autonomy, and they are construed as having a heuristic, legitimation value. Most challenging here is the heterogeneity of citizens' preferences in public policy, a heterogeneity that modern liberal democracy finesses by sophisticated readings of rational choice and majority rule.[21]

Under the minimalist regulatory ideal of liberal democracy, the role of the representative is rather straightforward in theory, even where it too is difficult to realize in practice. She or he is to protect the inherent value of the regime, the autonomy of the citizen, construed as a form of negative liberty, by enacting only those policies grounded in the consent of the people, to serve as an effective conduit for the expression of this consent or as an agent for recognizing implicit consent. Comparative analysis indicates that this regulatory ideal is seldom realized fully or strictly in practice. The processes and institutional arrangements made for its realization differ across nations and indeed within nations. But the formal goal of the representative remains constant.

In a contrasting reading of liberal democracy, one less persuaded by the possibility of free will, the role of the representative is to ensure that citizens' subjective interests are effectively advanced in the composition and administration of public policy. The regulatory ideal here is the maximization of interest satisfaction consistent with the recognition of minority interests. And the corresponding representational skills are those of identifying and standing in for the expression and accommodation of competing interests.

It is perhaps not surprising, then, that the sorts of people whom we find drawn to the work of representation in liberal democracy, when committed to the integrity of the regime, are those with legal training. In either account of liberal democracy sketched above, the lawyer becomes a defining and astute metaphor for the liberal democratic representative.

The role of the representative envisaged in demanding deliberative democracy is, as we have seen, also determined by the competing ideal, though it pays much closer attention to the democratic conditions of the population to be represented. Representatives' work is to realize, in the formation of public policy options, the expression of deliberative voices that meet or nearly meet the procedural conditions prescribed by the ideal. They are to serve the recognition and the development of capacities associated with these conditions and enable ever-greater expression of freedom and insight in public autonomy. Where a citizen's contribution to the identification of the public good is absent or poorly conditioned, representatives seek to redress its conditions, and induce its expression, engaging the citizen with countervailing and often dialectically set considerations that might free them from democratically untoward conditions of deliberation. Often this simply requires saying to citizens that their expressed view might be more an outcome of their understandable desire not to appear at odds with their fellow and sister citizens than of their own authentic sense of the issue at hand, that they are suffering from an untoward bandwagon effect. It might simply involve stating third and fourth alternative accounts in a context where discourse seems to be governed by a false dichotomy. It might involve inviting people to consider critically the effect upon them of their consumption of the mass media. Or it might involve drawing attention to the more manipulative efforts of others who wish to condition public debate while remaining on higher ground themselves.

In demanding deliberative democracy, a representative exercises the following inescapably idealized, regime-revealing, and regime-favouring knowledge, skills, and abilities. She or he understands that adequate expressions of public autonomy entail a foundational will, a nearly unanimous commitment to the basic terms of co-operation, which must be open to revisitation every generation and occasionally within generations. This foundational project, governed by the conditions of demanding deliberative democracy and procedures coherent with them, is necessary if something less than unanimity is to be the basis of deciding less foundational questions of social co-operation and other issues of public choice. Setting tax policy or determining the scope of public health policies presumes, in this way, a more foundational and expansive will to engage in a form of social co-operation within a particular polity. Accordingly, foundational revisitations are ongoing epistemic requirements for the full development of the *demos* even if they consist only in the well-conditioned conjecturing proposed for the demanding deliberative representative, as discussed above.

To serve the ideal of demanding deliberative democracy, a representative would be able to engage the citizenry effectively and deeply. Without overdetermination by her or his own insights, she or he must discern what it is that we do indeed hold to be true of and good generally for us, when power is as well constrained as possible and when the stakes for our decisions are understood to be high. The representative's capacity presumes knowing, and respecting as parts of others' knowledge, a good deal about our common philosophic anthropology, the nature and logic of our needs and well-being, the terms of our self-respect, our human equality, our diversity, our capacity to care about the suffering of others, the value of private reflection, and the like. This capacity, moreover, extends to the ability to move others from conventional opinion to considered judgment, freeing us from (at least some of the) untoward forces constraining it.[22]

Such a representative would possess the ability to respect the expression of citizens' lives not out of any moral sense or political advantage but as a necessary epistemic means to identifying deeply found public autonomy and thereby as the means to securing a legitimate form of society with them. Moreover, to serve as a demanding interlocutor for the community, she or he would persistently be able and willing to interrogate and redress his or her own epistemic/humanist credentials and integrity, paying close attention to the impact of hubris and other psychological impediments in his or her own deliberative discursive effectiveness. A degree of modesty and openness is implied by the need to ensure that what one speculates and then comes to recognize as the truth known in the lives of others is not simply a reification of one's own (partial) insight. Where such self-disciplined modesty is absent, it might be generated as an outcome of adversarial relations in democratic bodies (and here we find a third role for the representative, similar to that played in contemporary parliamentary practice but identified by a different teleology). This sort of discipline is occasionally found in the adversarial relations between parties in the Canadian legislative process. It creates alertness to charges that one's hubris is not commensurate with one's democratic performance.

This idealized representative would persistently display the sort of modelling that enables citizens to champion human conduct consistent with the epistemic challenge of democracy, of seeking and standing for the truth, of resisting untoward deliberative compromises, and of being uncynically committed to the project of discerning at least as much of the truth of our human condition as collectively we can know of it. While the code of conduct associated with liberal democratic leadership (non-corruption and the like) would be necessary, it would not be sufficient for the sort of demeanour expected of a representative in demanding deliberative democracy. For instance, she or he would need the courage always to reveal and speak up against manipulation or the marginalization of truths and wills, even when her or his personal standing may be harmed by doing so.

Finally, the representative would need to moderate his or her required drive for epistemic engagement with a degree of patience. Political development ought not to be rushed more than the lives and reflection of its subjects allow. Moreover, while politics may be ubiquitous, the taste for it, even or perhaps mostly in its richest form, is more occasional. How often the transformational power of deliberative democracy may effectively be used to develop particular democracies is plainly an empirical question yet to be tested. While the representative must be ever ready to employ its devices in realizing the best of democracy, she or he might also be employed valuably in other, less demanding tasks, associated with other representational mandates, of standing in for and carrying to public choice the features and apparent interests of the citizenry. (It is plain that the sort of account proffered here, if closed to the idea of a mixed representational regime, would rightly appear too ambitious.) The sort of discretionary power that this provision of patience entails, knowing when to press for deeper engagement and when not to, is checked by the ideal's recognition of the people's ability to know. An effective representative, in this account, would be quick to read the public's meaning, including when democratic will has been overexercised. Representatives who failed to read such signs, of course, would pay for their misreading in electoral defeat.

As a further illustration of demanding deliberative democratic processes of representation, consider how such representation might work on the issue of capital punishment. Thinner epistemological accounts of representative democracy, such as minimalist liberal democracy, require that the representative reads polling figures that he or she is obligated to see are conducted accurately, where accurate empirical information and the views of others are available for citizens wishing to consult them. In addition, she or he needs to ensure that other viable means for citizens' expression of their consent to one or another policy, perhaps through an election campaign, are available and respected. Representatives would need to ensure that the scope of policy options is defined as widely as possible, that the subjective interests of all are effectively articulated, and that coercive manipulation of public choice by explicit threats is effectively prohibited.

In demanding democracy, the representative would be obligated to go well beyond the requirements of the liberal democratic paradigm. One must invite, occasionally even provoke, citizens to explore and articulate their deepest insights. One must ask them to consider that they may be affected by untoward forces such as the quality of crime reporting and crime-based narratives in popular culture, by the common desire to act as they anticipate others will, by the seemingly righteous contempt, even hatred, they feel for those who commit especially nasty crimes, by the sort of superficial evidence presented on both sides of such debates, and by a general sense of the powerlessness and social and self-loathing endemic in popular culture. One might invite citizens to imagine themselves as "pulling the switch" or as citizens on a capital crime jury, remind them that anyone might be subject to false accusation, or use other such thought experiments. Plainly, considerations such as these could cut either way, since one might alternatively assert, for instance, that modern sociology has blinded us to the real evil of murderers.

Setting questions as free as possible from current ideological/theoretical closedness or competing ideological overdetermination would be part of what conjecturing about and engaging the best thinking of citizens would require. Such engagement would need to be worked through in a context where the social and economic conditions of life would previously have been sufficiently ameliorated by legislative means to prevent the anger associated with those suffering economic or social injustice from informing their views on retributive justice. This much more demanding attention might well produce one of a variety of public judgments regarding use of the death penalty, since the conditions of demanding deliberative democracy, even with the sort of speculative features noted above, are not predictive. But they suggest the sort of work that the representative must do if he or she is genuinely interested in the best insights of citizens in informing public policy. In this respect, the representative would embrace the outcomes of proceduralist perfectionism of demanding deliberative democracy, on the belief, to paraphrase Rousseau, that the people, when properly consulted, never err.

The example of capital punishment, while direct, is not paradigmatic of the sort of institutional arrangements that occasion public decisions in democratic societies. The proceduralism of this account is ideal regulated, never or seldom perfectly or fully realized. Accordingly, what a representative would need to do in the circumstances of a more complex institutional setting, with party discipline, presidential or cabinet government, solidarity, and the like, is not fully given by the example of capital punishment, an issue typically associated with a more free-vote-oriented legislative process.[23] Nonetheless, decision making in more complex settings may entail the sorts of considerations upon which demanding deliberative democracy rests. Something of the sort was at work in the decision of the Canadian government's recent, apparently successful, attempts to shape the deliberative process of provincial sovereignty decisions, limiting discursive deliberative practice by means of the interpretive rules of the Canadian Clarity Act. Occasionally, election campaigns carry some of this quality, and it may be found in the adversarial relations between parties and between levels of government more regularly as political competition and party appeal.

In more complex settings, the role of the representative is to align himself or herself with and to serve those projects that feature the procedural objective that demanding deliberative democracy provides. It is further to support those policies that tend to ameliorate the conditions debilitating democratic development, and it is to engage one's constituents with a genuine interest in hearing the expression of their deepest insights.

There is no denying the high epistemic ambitions of the engagement that demanding deliberative discursive democracy entails, that its process operates from an ideal, or that "DDD" appears to be more statist and elitist than is currently favoured in liberal democracy. Notwithstanding these concerns, it is important to remember that, in demanding deliberative democracy, even the poorly conditioned wills of citizens must be respected as trumping the speculation of representatives as described here. This should be so even if the force of very poorly conditioned wills, such as the tyrannical personality, is mitigated by majority rule. Demanding deliberative democracy stops short of "forcing people to be free," since it holds the freedom of persons to be epistemically central to the full realization of human insight.

A Risk Assessment

All readings of representation presume something like a regulative ideal, and all practices of representation run risks of non- or poor performance. Any serious theory of representative democracy implicitly assumes a set of assumptions and expectations about representation that may or may not always be fully met in practice and a role for representatives that might not be perfectly played.

In the consent-based, strictly de-ontological account of minimalist liberalism, the central risk is found in determining what constitutes free (and especially implicit) consent. In rational choice theorists' interest-oriented, subjectivist reading of democracy, the representative serves as a conduit for expressing (the intensity of) subjective preferences or interests. This sort of representative mandate is also troublesome, since it invites and may even privilege the worst sort of epistemic weaknesses of unreflexive political consumerism. Here too the role of the representative is idealized and accordingly runs risks. How is one to be sure what subjective preferences or interests are, since they are reactive and transient, vary in intensity over time, and are often expressed in a time frame distinct from that of public decision? What is the impact of the mass media in psychological domination or in manufacturing or laundering preferences?[24] Whose subjective interests are they? How does agenda setting orchestrate the scope of possible political choice? What is to count as a certain test of the intensity of preferences or the actual ranking of interests, and how are considerations of intensity to be weighed against the plurality of subjective preferences? How do we know that folks are telling the truth when they cite their subjective preferences? As critics are quick to point out, in the poverty of our current horizons, getting these considerations wrong runs the risk of achieving the most troubling accomplishments in the name of democracy.

Other accounts of democratic representation carry thicker regulative ideals and are less subjectivist. Consider two variants here. The first calls on representatives to stand in, both descriptively and substantially, not for the intensity of express subjective preferences or interests but for the hierarchically ordered objective interests of those whom they represent. There are a variety of techniques and abilities associated with this account, and these relate the process of representation to an independent theory of the true and good. The risks associated with this complex idealization are also epistemic, getting the interests right, while they raise the spectre of limiting the autonomy and respect for persons otherwise rightly associated with the democratic imperative. Mill limits these risks both by idealizing a diversity of descriptive features of representatives in a pluralist society and by tying "the progressive interests" of humankind to the respect of individual autonomy. Marx does so by what he took to be the certainty of the science of historical, dialectical materialism. The success of both strategies requires a pedagogic effort and the laundering of some subjective preferences.

A second variant of a thick democratic account of representation takes the problem of democracy primarily as one of the character of the representative. Here the concept of interests and their adequate representation is replaced by a working conception of virtue, typically treated as the capacities and insights of a certain sort of person (wise, prudent, publicly minded, and strongly willed in support of these integrities). This account is found in Burke's infamous letter, in readings of Rousseau's republicanism (not my own) in which sturdy male citizens exercise the autonomy of all, and in Lenin's vanguard of the proletariat. Echoing the nonironic reading of the Socratic Philosopher Queen/King, the regulative ideal of such an account of representation requires that the central issue of representation in democracy is to ensure that the right sorts of people rule. Those democratically ruled in this fashion have, as their primary civic work, that of identifying, from a well-conditioned list, those citizens who possess and can be trusted to exercise the sort of human integrity that the regulative ideal champions.

In the first of these nonsubjectivist, thicker accounts, the regulative ideal attends to underlying (objective) features of the citizen; in the second, it attends to the personal qualities of the representative. In both, subjectively expressed interests are in play but not definitive of democratic outcomes. Here the risks run by the accounts of democratic representation are properly construed as unacceptably high, and they are considerably higher than those either of the various liberal readings or, I would contend, of my reading of a demanding democratic ideal.

Competing philosophical and sociological accounts of deliberative discourse noted earlier in the chapter also imply roles for representatives defined by their respective regulatory ideal. The risks that they run, in getting the right sort of reason to prevail (of ensuring, for instance, that right reason is not just the reason of those in power) or, in the sociological account, of finding a sort of social peace that isn't simply the deeper sublimation of injustice or inauthenticity, are not less troubling, to my mind, than those that demanding democracy runs.

The role for representatives in demanding democratic politics is, nonetheless, ambitious, since it requires the deepest respect for the truth of the lives of others as the epistemic requirements of democracy. And though its epistemic ambition does indeed run risks, it is not alone in running them. The risks that it runs are perhaps not as great as they first appear to be and are arguably worth taking nonetheless.

To summarize, the role of the representative envisaged in demanding deliberative democracy is determined by entailment of the regulative ideal and in respect of the conditions of the population to be represented. In the formation of public policy options, representatives are to realize the expression of deliberative voices that meet or nearly meet the conditions prescribed by the ideal. And they are to facilitate the development of citizens' capacities associated with the realization of these conditions, to enable ever-deeper realization and expression of public autonomy. While this account of democratic representation is admittedly controversial, it competes well with what even thoughtful representatives appear to understand of their role in democratic politics when they take the time to contemplate it fully. And this account of deliberative representation competes well, in the degree of idealization, with other accounts of representation.

Conclusion: Three Lines of (Friendly) Criticism

What might be said in criticism of such an account of democratic representation? Probably a fair bit more than I would like, though I turn here briefly only to three lines of possible vulnerability. The first can simply be conceded: demanding deliberative democracy requires idealized skills and commitments not widely exercised by those who currently hold public office. These skills and commitments may be difficult to recruit or engender, though most readers know of representatives who have worked at least partly in light of this sort of ideal.

A second vulnerability of my role identification for democratic representation is that the representative's role is implicitly therapeutic. This concern is also properly registered with competing, more participatory accounts of democratic engagement.[25] I concede that an analytic therapeutic is laced into the work of the representative given in demanding deliberative democracy and is especially evident in its existentialist psychological assumptions. Most prominent among these is the therapeutic self-interrogation, or adversarial interrogation, that I suggest representatives should undergo.

Still, current representative democratic politics does some of this sort of therapeutic work, regularly drawing the attention of the vainglorious or otherwise foolish political actors, the self-serving or closed-minded, to their democratic weaknesses. Moreover, in contrast to more participatory theories of democracy, demanding deliberative democracy does not require thick, psychologically oriented political engagement of democratic citizens with one another.[26] Much can be accomplished by setting the questions of public choice well, in light of the regulative ideal. Thick discursive relations between citizens may be valuable in the process of identifying the general will and may indeed have a further, democratic normative potential. But they are not strictly required in the version of deliberative discursive democracy that I am advancing.

This partial defence of demanding democracy has, I acknowledge, what looks like a serious democratic shortcoming: an even greater apparent elitism, in which only the most able among us are required to engage others in ways that might transcend the psychological dimensions of their political culture. But given our current practice of handing political culture over to the media industries, and our heavy reliance on leadership politics, the elitism of demanding democracy may still be defended on comparative grounds.

A third line of vulnerability would draw attention to the degree of abstraction and ambition of demanding deliberative democracy. Once again, I simply concede the idealized tenor of this sort of project but note that other variants of the proceduralist sort require a commensurate idealization. Indeed, as I have argued, all forms of democratic regime definition carry the burden of some ambitious assumptions that implicate the performance of representatives. We just become used to the ones that we are given to employ. The degree of idealization required in demanding deliberative democracy as a regulative ideal is arguably less than that of the proponents of participatory democracy, such as Benjamin Barber's "strong democracy" and no more idealized than the Habermasian ideal speaker or Rawls's POPs. I believe that my deliberative model, when carefully assessed, looks more inclusive, and more attentive to real citizens, than either of these models. Notwithstanding the risks that it runs, it remains a more appealing account of democratic citizenship, at least on foundational questions of social co-operation, than is provided by consumerist-styled liberal democracy, for which the best of citizens' insight appears as simply more of the same. And, unlike the prevailing model of democratic representative practice, demanding deliberative democracy has ennobling potential for both citizens and their representatives.

Acknowledgments

I wish to thank the two anonymous referees of this book for their generous and useful comments. Part of this chapter was presented to the annual meeting of the Atlantic Provinces Political Science Association in Saint John, October 2001. I am grateful for the comments offered at that time. Since much of my work emanates from earlier discussions with Tom Pocklington and Don Carmichael, I also wish to acknowledge the continuing value of their criticism. This chapter has as part of its lineage a discussion between David Laycock and me on the question of Rousseau and populism in Carmichael, Pocklington, and Pyrcz (2000).

Notes

1 This literature is well represented in two collections: Bohman and Rehg (1997); and Elster (1998).
2 See Uhr (1998). I have argued in an unpublished essay that the regulative ideals captured by the concept "demanding deliberative democracy" are at work in the Clarity Act in Canada (2000), which set a clearly put question and greater than majority expressions of public autonomy as conditions requisite to Canada's willingness to accept the terms of a sovereignty vote in Quebec or other provinces.
3 These particular constraints may be found at work in a number of my contributions to Carmichael, Pocklington, and Pyrcz (2000).
4 I refer to this conception variously as demanding deliberative democracy, demanding deliberative discursive democracy, demanding discursive democracy, or simply demanding democracy.
5 In Rousseauian terms, this is to be construed as not suffering from *"amour propre."* The reader will find throughout this chapter an account of democratic politics that serves as a reading of the connection between Rousseau's *Discourse on the Origins of Inequality* and *The Social Contract*.
6 The two paragraphs above follow closely my wording in Carmichael, Pocklington, and Pyrcz (2000), 21.
7 Habermas (1996) moves even further from his Frankfurtean roots in *Between Facts and Norms*. See Warren (1992).
8 I argue for this reading of Rousseau in Pyrcz (n.d.). This analysis is indebted to, though it parts company on the question of the centrality of interests with, the work of Joshua Cohen.
9 In its simplest rendering, this is Habermas's approach.
10 An example of this approach, again with some of the sophistication of the analysis removed, is found in Bellamy (1995).
11 Note that the process of demanding deliberative democracy is not one defined by reference to the language of interests, however progressively these are construed. In my view, the language of interests is a form of mediating political discourse that more often than not undoes the processes of deliberation for which it is meant to provide. Here I part company with Joshua Cohen's reading of Rousseau that places too much emphasis on the language of interests in Rousseau. Note also that the account is here indebted, in different ways, to the work of Nancy Rosenblum, Seyla Benhabib, and Bonnie Honig. As well, it should be plain that this account provides a reading of the processes requisite to the realization of the General Will in Rousseau's *The Social Contract*.
12 In "What's Wrong with Positive Freedom," *The Malaise of Modernity*, and *Sources of the Self*, Taylor is intent on expelling existential claims to radical freedom, primarily, I contend, as a way of protecting the ontological primacy of horizons of meaning.
13 See the brief discussion of consent theory as the heart of liberal democracy in comments below regarding the role of the representative in such a regime.
14 This is one way of reading Hobbes's state of nature argument in *Leviathan*.
15 Although "the sky is falling" strategy of false crises is easily made unproductive, the actual force of foundational decisions is often sufficient to engage the citizen in such processes so defined.

16 Something of this sort is at work in Rawls (1971), treated by him as a discussion with his reader. And it plainly is found in the work of the Legislator in Rousseau and arguably in the role of the magistrate.
17 While it is admittedly difficult to see how this is achieved in larger-scale contexts, the process has greater plausibility and history in smaller-scale deliberative contexts. The argument that I advance under "demanding deliberative democracy" suggests that understanding how this process can work in smaller scale provides a regulative ideal that enables us to identify strategies and outcomes in large scale that mimic the more ideal-friendly contexts of *some* small-scale democratic practice.
18 The epistemological perspective is implied in Rawls's (1971) perspective of the worst off in *A Theory of Justice*. Furthermore, one need not read much of Rousseau's *Second Discourse* to see that the representatives of the people in a poorly established social contract setting had many of the vices and few of the virtues of the proper founder or magistrate proffered in *The Social Contract*.
19 There are here again resonances of one reading of Rousseau's General Will, the role of the Legislator, and the role of magistrates in *The Social Contract*.
20 This reading of liberal democracy has most in common with the treatment given it by Macpherson (1977) and in this work's connection to his other work on "possessive individualism."
21 The role of testing the principle of majority consent as the means of resolving contested expressions of consent, by reference to turnout and the absence of resistance, is discussed in my "Democracy and Political Participation" in Carmichael, Pocklington, and Pyrcz (2000), 21-34.
22 Central here, of course, would be the realization that the domestication and inequality in the treatment of women is indeed an artifice that serves as an obstacle to the identification of both the truth about us as human beings and indeed any legitimate public autonomy founded on such truth.
23 Here I am indebted to one of the anonymous referees of this chapter for having drawn my attention to the need to address more problematic legislative contexts. What I have to say in this light is limited here and remains one of the subprojects of the work in which I am currently involved.
24 For a splendid discussion of laundering preferences, see Goodin (1996).
25 Benjamin Barber's work comes to mind here, as does Mark Warren's "The Self in Discursive Democracy" (1995).
26 Such a view is advanced by Barber (1984).

10
What Can Democratic Participation Mean Today?
Mark E. Warren

As we look back over the political landscape of the twentieth century at the beginning of this new millennium, two features stand out in relief. First, it was a bloody century, with Nazi, fascist, and Communist regimes alone costing over 150 million lives. The second feature, materializing mostly in the past fifty years, was a dramatic increase in the number of democratic countries. If, following Freedom House, we define democracies as "political systems whose leaders are elected in competitive multi-party and multi-candidate processes in which opposition parties have a legitimate chance of attaining power or participating in power," and which have a universal franchise, then there were no democracies in 1900. Only 22 of the 154 countries existing in 1950 were democracies, encompassing 31 percent of the world's population. Today 119 of the 192 existing countries count as democracies, encompassing 58.2 percent of the world's population. Eighty-five of these 119 also rank highly enough in protecting basic human rights and respecting the rule of law to count as liberal democracies.[1]

Democrats should have every reason to look back on the past fifty years with satisfaction. While the Freedom House threshold for democracy is not high, the gains are immensely important when measured in terms of threats to basic human welfare. Although democracies are quite capable of atrocities against their own populations, they have not carried out the large-scale atrocities engineered by nondemocratic countries in the past century, nor do they experience famines.[2] Moreover, democracies tend not to fight wars with one another, removing one of the most pervasive threats to human welfare. It is hard to overstate the importance of these developments, which we can appreciate only when placed in the context of the many tens of millions who died in the past century at the hands of nondemocratic regimes.

Without in any way diminishing the importance of these democratic trends for basic human welfare, however, we should also ask about the prospects for more robust democracy within the established liberal democracies. Here we should note a third significant feature of the twentieth-century political landscape. As democracy has spread, democratic expectations have diminished – from the view that democracy means equal chances to influence collective judgments to the rather sparse Freedom House definition of democracy as a universal franchise with institutionalized opposition.

The long-established norm of democracy is that a political system should maximize rule by and for the people. Within the tradition of liberal democracy, "the people" are understood as individuals, each of whom ought to benefit from collective self-rule. From this norm is derived that of political equality: every individual potentially affected by a decision should have an equal opportunity to affect the decision.

Major strains of liberal democratic thought and culture have held that political equality requires that individuals participate in the processes of collective decision making, if not as a moral requirement and developmental opportunity, then as a strategic necessity. But this view of democracy – variously conceived by Rousseau, Jefferson, Emerson, John Stuart Mill, John Dewey, and still espoused today by progressive democratic theorists – seems harder than ever to sustain given the constraints imposed by today's large-scale, complex, and pluralistic societies. To be sure, the very success of democracy should mean that the abstract expectations of democratic ideologies should have to adjust to more complex realities as they are put into practice. But as progressive democrats have long pointed out, the participatory ideals of democracy were pushed to the margins of mainstream liberal democratic theory and ideology following the rise of fascism and Stalinism and solidified by the Cold War.[3] Articulated most clearly by realist and elite theorists of democracy, such as Joseph Schumpeter, and reflected in Freedom House definitions, democracy became identified with the de facto existence of competitive elections. Niklas Luhmann, perhaps perversely, does Freedom House one better by defining democracy simply as "the bifurcation of the top of the differentiated political system by the distinction of government and opposition."[4] But even less sparse conceptions of democracy – those of American pluralism, for example – accept the major premise that political participation by most people most of the time will, of necessity, be limited to the act of voting.[5]

Although the hegemony of realist approaches to democracy is no longer supported by the Cold War, it still benefits from the apparent limitations imposed by scale, complexity, differentiation, and pluralism. I argue in the first two sections of this chapter, however, that the political landscape is now more favourable to participatory ideals than in the recent past. But to capitalize on the emerging realities in the post–Cold War world, progressive democrats will need to rethink what democratic participation can mean today within a political landscape beset by democratic paradoxes. In the final section, I suggest eight guidelines for a progressive democratic theory that would rise to the challenges.

The Problem of Diminished Democratic Expectations

Why should we worry about this third feature – this trend toward diminished expectations of democracy? Why should we not simply celebrate the enormously important impact that voting and opposition have had in stemming the most basic threats to human well-being? The easy answer is that the consolidation of these democratic institutions does not make the ideal of equal participation in collective self-governance any less valuable or desirable – expressing as it does the most basic human aspirations of freedom and self-determination. We should, therefore, retain such ideals as markers against which we can see the distance we have yet to go.

This is a perfectly good answer, but it doesn't illuminate very much. It fails to address the question of whether, in fact, the democratic ideals of equal participation in self-government have become so unrealistic in contemporary societies as to be irrelevant. Consider Norberto Bobbio's list of the promises of democracy that have been broken, even as democratic electoral institutions have taken hold.[6]

- The ideal of popular sovereignty, based on a contract among sovereign individuals, has proven to be modelled on the unified sovereignty of the prince. In modern pluralist societies, the people do not constitute an agent in the manner of a sovereign. Instead, rule is an effect of conflict and co-operation among groups. In short, popular sovereignty is an incoherent concept.
- Representation has turned out to reflect the interests and opinions not of individuals collectively but of organized group interests. "Democracy" has come to mean procedures that enable agreements among large organizations, in effect cutting the link between individuals and democratic self-government.
- Democracies have failed to eliminate oligarchic power. The only difference between an aristocracy and a democracy is that in the former "elites *impose* themselves" and in the latter "elites *propose* themselves."[7]
- Democracies have failed to expand the spaces within which decisions are made democratically, especially within the "two great blocs of power in developed societies" – big business and bureaucracy.[8]
- Democracies have not eliminated those "invisible powers" within bureaucracies, cabinets, security forces, and private organizations that escape public accountability.

- Democracies promised to educate individuals for citizenship. Today's democracies, however, are populated by citizens who are apathetic about politics and institutions that provide few if any opportunities for education through participation.

Although these failures were based on promises that could never have been met, Bobbio argues, contemporary realities make them less possible than ever before. In particular, democratic promises have been undermined by three trends.[9]

- The increasing role of technology and its requirements for expertise make it less likely that citizens can have the knowledge to participate in collective decisions.
- Democracies establish bureaucracies to deliver demanded services, but the growth of bureaucratic machinery limits the scope of democracy.
- More democracy means more demands, but more demands tend to generate ungovernable situations, especially when encumbered by inefficient democratic procedures.

Bobbio's realist assessments clearly have force: if we measure even the most advanced liberal democracies against the view that democracy involves equal participation in collective decision making, then they fall spectacularly short of the goal. Moreover, Bobbio's conclusions cut powerfully against the more archaic of participatory democratic ideals – those that imagine that modern societies can be reconfigured as self-governing associations in which collective decisions are made by all citizens, enabled on larger scales, if necessary, through delegates.[10]

But Bobbio's assessments fail to account for two emerging realities – those that together suggest that participatory democratic ideals may actually fare better in the future than they have in the recent past. First, although realists may counsel that democratic expectations should be lowered, and although they may argue that participatory expectations are increasingly irrelevant to the complex, large-scale societies, the people who inhabit these societies are not heeding their counsel. To the contrary, indications are that democratic expectations are growing. At first glance, this claim seems to be all wrong. Is there not widespread "apathy" about politics in the developed liberal democracies? In the United States, for example, rates of voting are low and stagnant, and most citizens remain relatively uninformed about and detached from political processes. And, although the United States may represent an extreme, other democracies have not been exempt from this malaise.[11]

Yet this celebrated apathy of citizens may be more complicated than it seems and may harbour shifts in democratic expectations. Indeed, the concept of "apathy" is not an entirely accurate description. Rather, over the past several decades, people in the developed democracies have become *disaffected* from their political institutions. They are now less likely to trust their governments and more likely to judge them incompetent, untrustworthy, and even corrupt. While the causes and meanings of these trends have been subject to considerable study and debate, it seems that disaffection reflects not apathy but increasingly critical evaluations of government.[12] The pattern is quite general: summarizing the findings of several large cross-national projects, Pippa Norris concludes that there "is a growing tension between ideals and reality. This may have produced the emergence of more 'critical citizens' or perhaps 'disenchanted democrats.'"[13]

The growing tension between ideal and reality could signify that governments are performing worse and are less democratic than they were several decades ago. Evidence suggests, however, that the gap has more to do with changing expectations. Campaign money, for example, has long held sway over the US Congress, but citizens are increasingly aware of its corrupting influence. As a result, they now judge Congress as more corrupt than in the past, in spite of increasingly strict ethical standards within the institution itself.[14] Support for democratic values remains strong, and citizens are increasingly levelling these expectations at their governments. They now expect more responsiveness, better performance, more accountability, and less incompetence and corruption. Moreover, citizens are now less deferential and have less respect for traditional forms of authority. Summarizing findings from the World Values Surveys, Ron Inglehart notes that "authority figures and hierarchical institutions are subject to more searching scrutiny than they once were." This trend is good for democracy: "the same publics that are becoming increasingly critical of hierarchical authority are also becoming increasingly resistant to authoritarian government, more interested in political life, and more apt to play an active role in politics. Although hierarchical political parties are losing control over their electorates, and elite-directed forms of participation such as voting are stagnant or declining, elite-challenging forms of participation are becoming more widespread."[15] These trends, suggests Pippa Norris, "may prove a more positive development which will ultimately strengthen democratic government if this signifies the growth of more critical citizens who are dissatisfied with established authorities and traditional hierarchical institutions, who feel that existing channels for participation fall short of democratic ideals, and who want to improve and reform the institutional mechanisms of representative democracy."[16]

If we were to view these trends through the realist model of democracy, then the apparent danger would be that identified by the "demand overload" thesis formulated by the influential collection *The Crisis of*

Democracy in the mid-1970s. Because the institutions of government cannot handle an upsurge in democratic expectations, the authors predicted crises of governability in the developed democracies.[17] But on average these crises have not developed. Rather, increasing disaffection from formal political institutions seems to be paralleled by increasing attention toward other ways and means of getting collective things done. Certainly part of the reason that individuals are "apathetic" about politics is that they conceive "politics" as equivalent to the state. If the state becomes less significant as a site of collective action, then individuals will judge "democracy" to be a less important part of their lives, which are likely to be organized around work, family and friends, school, clubs, recreation, and other kinds of association.[18] To be sure, the trends here are often ambiguous and enormously complex, as indicated by the debates surrounding Robert Putnam's thesis that in the United States social capital – the capacities for collective action built through association – has been in decline over the past several decades.[19] However, competing research suggests that new forms of political activity have emerged in the past two decades, especially at the local level. Everett Carll Ladd notes that, although traditional associations such as fraternal organizations are in decline, volunteerism has increased, small groups have proliferated, and bowling leagues have given way to kids' soccer clubs.[20] Moreover, the new communications technologies appear to be facilitating networks of small associations.[21] And consistent with Inglehart's thesis, Verba, Schlozman, and Brady found that nonelectoral participation oriented toward community problems and issues significantly increased during the period 1967-87.[22]

The second emerging reality is structural and tracks these changes in values and activities. Venues of collective action are increasingly pluralized and increasingly unlikely to be organized directly by the state.[23] The most dramatic developments over the past couple of decades include the rise in power of nongovernmental organizations (NGOs) in the international arena and the dramatic increase in associations devoted to problems of collective action that replace, displace, or work in concert with state powers.[24] Moreover, bureaucratic models of management are proving in many sectors – in government and business alike – to be less efficient and often less governable than flatter, looser, more democratic forms of organization. These trends are highly complex and ambiguous in their implications. But they do suggest that the realist model of democracy is outdated, not least because it focuses almost entirely on the possibilities for self-governance through the state while missing almost entirely the new venues of politics that correspond to the diminishing scope of the state as an agent of collective action.

If this picture of increasing democratic expectations combined with increasing opportunities for democratic participation is correct, then it portrays a new terrain for participatory democratic theory. Democrats who still believe that democracy means participation in collective self-governance would turn out to be more realistic about the emerging social and political landscape than the so-called realists. The problem is that reality is, once again, ahead of democratic theory, so we don't yet have the conceptual tools we need to assess these developments.[25] The increasing irrelevance of realist assumptions about the limits of democracy does not by any means make the case for democrats who hold participatory ideals, particularly since they too have often been guilty of the early modern republican imaginings of the sort that Bobbio indicts.

The New Landscape of Democracy

To assess opportunities for democratic participation, then, we must survey developments within the social and political landscape that provide the occasions for politics. While it would be possible to identify any number of developments, four seem to be especially significant for participatory ideals.[26] In mentioning these developments, I intend to make the impression, at least in the first instance, that the political landscape is so complex and ambiguous that highly general assessments to the effect that democracy is stuck, as it were, in its thin stage of development are virtually meaningless. On the other hand, abstract judgments about participatory possibilities are equally meaningless and will depend instead on the messy business of cataloguing the possibilities.

Globalization

It is now a cliché – albeit an important one – that numerous forces are pushing toward global interdependencies. These forces include the development of global markets in finances, capital investment, labour, manufacturing, and services. In addition, there is an absolute increase in the numbers of immigrants and refugees flowing across borders. Environmental degradation likewise pushes across borders, in many cases producing global effects. Global security alliances such as NATO are in flux as they seek to re-establish their missions in the aftermath of the Cold War. At the same time, new forms of communication are enabling new and effective global publics, especially in the areas of human rights and environmental issues. Given that they lack state-like capacities, these global publics have been remarkably successful in transforming international law into a global force. Some of these developments open new global venues of democracy while weakening the powers of predatory states. But the same developments lessen the significance of the state as a unitary collective actor and thus reduce the scope of what might be achieved through democratizing the state. Political integration of nations may, as in the European Union, enable progressive policies to be established at higher levels in ways that force the hands of member states on matters as diverse as food safety, labour standards, and the corporal punishment of children. But political integration also causes the centres of decision making to become that much more remote, open mostly to political elites. That is, the significance of even the minimal kind of democracy measured by Freedom House is lessened by these developments and precisely in those countries where democracy is most entrenched. It is not, then, simply that democratic promises have not been kept but also that the importance of those that might have been kept may be eroding, while politics is flowing into new channels.

Differentiation

Developed societies reproduce themselves through differentiated systems and sectors, each with its own distinct logics, purposes, criteria, and inertia. At the highest level of abstraction, states are differentiated from markets, with states attending to matters of social order through law and administration, while markets organize production and consumption via the medium of money. States and markets are in turn differentiated from systems of social reproduction located in families, schools, religious institutions, and other social groups. Developed societies likewise involve specialized systems for the reproduction of knowledge and culture located in universities, research programs, and institutions devoted to arts and culture. Differentiation tends to segment domains of collective action, not only owing to the efficiencies gained by specialization, but also because distinct sectors develop their own norms and criteria. Markets respond to effective demand, art responds to aesthetic criteria, states work within the domain of law with its procedural criteria, science responds to factual claims, families cultivate intimacy, and so on.

At the same time, differentiation fuels co-ordination difficulties between sectors, in part because the criteria embedded within sectors are often incommensurable. For example, social norms of solidarity often conflict with demands of the market; aesthetic judgments conflict with moral judgments; market-driven demands for technology conflict with pure science; and ethics of duty cultivated by religious and secular moral codes conflict with cost-benefit analyses and reasons of state. In differentiated societies, co-ordination difficulties also stem from the dispersion of the powers and capacities to organize collective actions across sectors. Under these circumstances, the state is no longer "head"; rather, it functions as the most visible point of negotiation among sectors, since it does not control the resources upon which it depends to organize collective actions. Indeed, it has been said that a measure of the success of liberal democratic constitutionalism is the extent to which capacities for collective action migrate into society.²⁷ So while the state's control over coercive resources makes it a key player – maybe even the *ultimate* player – it increasingly lacks capacities to contain and control political conflict, let alone engage in global planning. In short, differentiation increases sectoral capacities for collective action while also increasing the zones of political conflict and undermining political responsibility.²⁸

Complexity

While differentiation increases the capacity for collective actions, it also increases their complexity. As Ulrich Beck has argued, the era in which collective actions could be conceived on the *modern* model – as the application of rational plans overseen by social engineers – is over.²⁹ Even the most rational of large-scale collective actions produce unintended consequences, which in turn politicize their environments. Owing to the unanticipated side effects of engineering-based models of social change (e.g., the costs of monoculture, pesticides, and now genetic engineering in food production, dysfunctional neighbourhoods resulting from planned urban renewal, birth defects caused by new medicines, stockpiled nuclear wastes, etc.), there is broad public skepticism about large-scale planning – what in a similar spirit James Scott has referred to as the unmasked pretensions of "high modernity."³⁰ As Claus Offe puts it, "the larger the horizon of 'actually' possible options becomes, the more difficult grows the problem of establishing reflexive countertendencies which would make reasonably sure that one's own action remains compatible with the 'essential' premises of the other affected spheres of action."³¹ The "absence of concern for consequences" induces crisis and erodes tolerance for modernization processes.³² We have, in Beck's terms, entered into an era marked by the politics of risk avoidance. In a "risk society," collective actions include political calculations that distribute risk according to the constituencies mobilized by plans for action. Risk consciousness tends to focus on complexity and contingency, increasing the potential political opposition to any given collective action. As "various groups and levels of decision-making ... mobilize the legal means of the state against one another" in response to perceived risks, political institutions become subject to an "involuntary deceleration" of their capacities for governance.³³

Pluralization and Reflexivity

These developments are intertwined with changing patterns of individuation. Owing to their differentiation, complexity, and fluidity, modern societies array multiple biographical choices before individuals. As with other developments, this one is paradoxical as well. On the one hand, individuals are subject to the late-modern condition of choice. Choice cannot, as it were, be refused. On the other hand, the very complexity and fluidity of society that make choice necessary also make it difficult to foresee consequences, combining increasing responsibility for choices with increasingly uncertain horizons.[34] Add to this the fact that both choices and risks are unequally distributed, and we can see how protean, postmodern personalities can co-exist with closed, fundamentalist personalities, produced by different locations and experiences within the same kind of society.[35] Identity politics is, in part, the result of the kind of society that raises – indeed forces – the question "Who am I?" The process induces individuals to discover and think about how their social locations interact with their race, ethnicity, gender, age, religion, profession, regional attachment, and lifestyle. Insofar as this pluralism of identities is not merely a matter of interesting difference, it is the result of raised consciousness of differential distributions of risks – injustices, if you will.[36] The political consequences are ambiguous. On the one hand, the increased reflexivity provoked by these circumstances provides the space for ethical growth in politics.[37] Only reflexively conscious individuals can ask the political questions, as Max Weber put them,[38] "What should we do?" and "How should we live?" In this sense, politics permeates individuation as never before, as feminists noted two decades ago with the slogan "The personal is political." On the other hand, the presence of choice can also increase the temptations of countermodern reaction, as suggested by the rise of religious fundamentalism in the United States and elsewhere as well as the resurgence of right-wing nationalisms in Europe.

Eight Guidelines for Progressive Democratic Theory

From the perspective of democracy, then, the emerging landscape is paradoxical: many of these developments offer new opportunities to cultivate capacities for self-rule and generate multiple spaces within which self-rule can develop. Yet the same developments tend to undermine formal democratic institutions. As Offe notes in commenting on the changing fortunes of parties, legislatures, and other familiar political actors, "What turns out to be surprisingly and essentially contested is the answer to the question 'who is in charge?'"[39]

A democratic theory for the twenty-first century that retains participatory ideals should find its opportunities here: as Offe's question attests, where no one is in charge, new forms of governance become possible. But identifying these emerging possibilities will depend upon a theory of democracy attuned to these developments. Here are eight guidelines for a strategy of attunement.

1. Democracy ought to follow politics, not political institutions.

One result of these developments is that potentials for politics are now pervasive: they exist throughout society. Wherever there is political conflict, democratic responses are possible. Just as it is now common to refer to the politics of the workplace, the marketplace, the church, the school, the neighbourhood, and the family, so too it is appropriate to refer to *democratic* workplaces, markets, churches, schools, neighbourhoods, and families – although, of course, the meanings and mechanisms of democracy will differ within these different venues.

By "politics," I mean not all social relations but those where there is a need for collective action, under circumstances in which (a) there is disagreement about what to do and (b) one or more of the parties has the power to force the issue.[40] Democracy ought to be conceived as a response to politics generally rather than as a way of organizing the state specifically.[41] State-centred political institutions remain vitally important, but they capture increasingly fewer of the sites of politics and thus a relatively smaller domain in which democracy is important and participation is possible. No wonder people in the United States often say that they are interested in "issues" but not "politics" (by which they mean formal politics) or that they are interested in "making a difference" and will volunteer their time to civic or issue-oriented activities but have little confidence in their ability to make a difference through formal political institutions. The meaning of "democracy" should keep pace with the arenas of decision within which it is important – namely, where there is politics. Democracy matters where there is power in the face of conflict: individuals need equal power and voice where there are disagreements about what should be done when something must be done.

In arguing that democracy ought to follow politics, I am not suggesting that all collective decisions should be made through the mechanisms of democracy. Democracy is desirable where there is politics, but not all decisions are equally political and thus not equally deserving of the time- and attention-consuming mechanisms of democracy. Most of the collective decisions throughout our very complex societies are routine. Indeed, the vast majority of acts of legislatures – which are specifically designed for political conflict – pass unanimously and without contest. If we generalize this fact, then we can already see that complexity and scale *in themselves* are no argument against democratic participation, since participation matters most in those relatively few decisions in which there are conflicts of interest in the face of necessities for collective action. What is important is that institutions and organizations are designed so that they can revert to democracy as needed, on an issue-by-issue basis.[42] Then most decisions can be made by trusted authorities, attended to by interested parties, or simply work through routine agreements, rules, habits, traditions, markets, or market-like mechanisms, without harm to democracy. Far from being less relevant today, then, the radically democratic idea that democracy should inhere in society and economy is more relevant now than ever before. Democracy cannot be encompassing, as envisaged in those older theories of democracy that build on unitary notions of popular sovereignty, but it can be pervasive, existing as one mode of decision making among others, to be called upon when decisions are politicized.

2. **Opportunities for democratic participation in formal political institutions may be limited, but opportunities in society and economy are not.**

Opportunities for participating in formal political institutions will remain limited by factors inherent in today's liberal democratic societies. Most of these are familiar: the size and scale of states dictate that democracy will be representative in nature, with the occasional initiative or referendum.[43] For most decisions, most of the time, citizen participation will be limited to voting for representatives, petitioning, influencing public opinion, participating in public hearings, and protesting. Even these indirect modes of influence are limited, however, to the fact that today's liberal democratic states are embedded in capitalist market economies and are likely to continue to be for the foreseeable future.[44] Because the state functions as an economic manager of a system of production that is mostly in private hands, it cannot risk policies that limit profitability. Smaller and more local units of government are more vulnerable to limits imposed by those who control local or regional industries, with the ironic effect that, as constraints imposed by size and scale diminish, the limits imposed by economic vulnerabilities increase. Smaller is not always better with regard to democracy.[45]

But venues not directly organized by the state are not subject to the same kinds of limitation. While each kind of venue will be subject to its own kinds of constraint, they are often different from those that plague the state. Associations, for example, can sometimes effectively accomplish what states cannot.[46] For example, associations are becoming increasingly effective at altering market externalities such as environmental damage. Numerous associations are developing programs to certify products – wood products, for example – in effect allowing consumers to vote with their purchases for public goods such as ecologically sustainable forestry. These tactics are proving so effective that many firms involved in the exploitation of natural resources now seek to have their practices assessed and certified in order to retain and expand their markets. Such an example shows that associations, working under the protection but not direction of states, can address high-level structural forces such as global markets in ways that can be more effective than state action. Corporations often find ways to influence the state and can use their vast resources to pursue their interests through lobbying, contributing to campaigns, capturing regulatory agencies, or threatening to disinvest. But they have a harder time dictating the purchasing decisions of millions of consumers associated through their normative commitments. Although corporations can go public, associations of citizens are often viewed as more credible, which gives them a greater normative influence.[47]

3. Political association based on territory limits the scope of participation; association based on issues does not.

When places were less connected than they are today, territorially organized politics could encompass most of the issues relevant to the people living in the territory. Today many issues do not correspond to the territorial units through which state-based democracy is organized – problems relating to migration, labour, environment, terrorism, information systems, and markets, for example. Most of these emerging issues have been met with new ad hoc arrangements: NGOs, treaties and trade pacts, and networks of associations. The opportunities for citizens to exercise influence across borders, through publicity, political pressure, market pressure, direct action, and the like, have never been greater. Indeed, many predatory states that once ruled over their populations with impunity now find that they can no longer control information and that they must answer to NGOs for their abuses. Global corporations can find their practices under such scrutiny that they feel compelled to change for fear of losing their markets. By publicizing labour conditions in overseas factories, for example, a relatively small number of students at American universities forced several makers of shoes and clothing to commit to improved pay and work conditions in their overseas factories. Had these students sought to gain import controls through the US government to achieve the same objective, it is unlikely that they would have succeeded.

4. Issue- and sector-based devolution provide targets of opportunity for democratic participation.

One of the many ways in which states have been seeking to increase governability within politicized environments is to devolve functions to lower levels of government, to enter into so-called public-private partnerships, and to involve associations in governance. Devolutions are doubled-edged swords from a democratic perspective. They cut against democracy when centralized accountability is weakened without being replaced by other forms of accountability. Government programs can be captured by powerful interests. But the same developments can cut in democratic directions, especially when devolution opens spaces for participatory opportunities. Within the area of administrative lawmaking, for example, there has been a significant movement away from top-down imposition of rules and toward deliberative processes that involve the affected parties. In the

United States, devolution has also become the norm in social services, education, and some regulatory arenas, generating an explosion in associational activities devoted to these functions. These developments deserve the close attention of progressive democrats, not because devolution is necessarily democratic, but because democratic opportunities can accompany devolution.

5. Law can be used reflexively to structure democratic processes outside the state.

States will remain key organizers of politics for the foreseeable future. Although their powers as collective actors have diminished, states still control most means of coercion and remain the sole agent capable of making and enforcing legitimate and binding laws. This is so despite the emergence of international security regimes, which typically are constituted as voluntary associations of member states. The state's ultimate role as a coercive actor means that the democratic legitimacy of law remains essential. Moreover, since democratic agreement is emerging as the key source of legitimacy within postconventional societies, it is clear that the state remains a key target for democrats.[48]

But the state's role in deepening democracy may very well be different than in the past. To see this, we should notice that states use their defining resource – law – in two distinct ways. States use law – usually in the form of administrative rule making built on statute law – as a means of developing and carrying out collective projects decided by legislatures. States also use law *reflexively* to establish the rules of decision making, both within the state (in legislatures, courts, and administrative agencies) and within the economy and society.[49] While the function of law in structuring state venues of decision making is quite familiar, its role in structuring venues outside the state deserves closer attention. Here the logic of using law to establish decision-making processes is far from exhausted in its democratic implications and is in fact evolving in new directions.

To be sure, constitutional liberal democracies have always used their powers to constitute spheres of public judgment within society. Guarantees of free speech and association, combined with the political rights of voting and petition, generate, as it were, spaces outside the state within which the normative force of public opinion can develop and register itself within the representative branches of government. One result is that, because it is protected, society is also enabled as a source of collective judgment.[50] But as society has become more politicized, states have sought ways of devolving *decision making* – not just public debate and judgment – into society and economy in order to sustain governability.

One model, exemplified in the policies of Thatcher and Reagan, is simply to privatize decisions – in this way leaving them to the strongest social and economic powers. But there are democratic models as well. Law and other state resources can be used to construct democratic processes by setting the rules and equalizing the powers of participants. The oldest example is collective bargaining: the state legally enables labour to organize, to negotiate as a collective agent, and to threaten to withhold labour, thus increasing the powers of labour with respect to management. One result is that the relationship between workers and management is democratized: decisions that would otherwise be made and imposed by authoritarian means must now be negotiated, justified, and voted upon. Other examples of reflexive law are emerging. In 1970, the US government gave citizens the right to sue water polluters in civil court, in effect empowering citizen associations to act as enforcers of clean water regulations. In another instance, the State of Oregon now requires businesses to organize worker safety committees and empowers these committees to work with managers to attain compliance with safety guidelines. The state does not dictate how compliance will be attained; rather, it empowers the workers to influence the decision process. In still another experiment involving distribution of health care, the Oregon state legislature structured state-wide deliberative arenas and then provided money to interested associations to hire their own medical experts – thus levelling the deliberative playing field in an area requiring expertise. These examples are not ideal, but they are indicative. They suggest that state strategies to maintain governability in the face of demand overload can involve devolving political arenas in ways that increase opportunities for participation by precisely those disadvantaged by distributions of money, power, and knowledge.

6. **Democratizing society democratizes the state.**
Whether or not devolved decision making increases democracy (as in the above examples) or decreases democracy (as with Reagan-/Thatcher-style privatization) depends upon who is empowered. This in turn depends upon the relative strengths of social forces. Civil society associations are centrally important in this respect: they can generate the social power that can check economic power and produce state responsiveness. This point, of course, reflects the widely popular view that a strong civil society "makes democracy work."[51] This almost certainly has to be right but needs to be disaggregated. On the one hand, many kinds and mixes of associations are not very good for democracy, such as business associations that use their money to buy access to the political process. On the other hand, there are many things that the associations of civil society can do for democracy. These include, for example, developing the political and civic capacities of citizens, forming and framing public debates and opinions, and providing voice within the representative channels of

the state. So whether the associational ecology of a society is, in aggregate, "democratic" depends upon *who* is involved in *what kinds* of associations and whether, in aggregate, the mix of associations is so constituted as to carry out these functions. Despite the current enthusiasm for civil society, we know very little about what kinds of mixes are optimal for democracy. What is likely, however, is that the wide variety of democratic functions of associations also produces a very large number of opportunities for democratic participation. Clearly, progressive democrats should pay close attention to the associational terrain of liberal democracies.[52]

7. Even progressive democracy is subject to the division of political labour.

Because individuals cannot attend to all the collective decisions that affect their lives, it follows that they must rely on the representations and judgments of others and do so with most issues most of the time. The ideal circumstance for individuals would be a society that empowers and equips them to spend their participatory resources (their time, attention, interest, and knowledge) on the issues most salient to them. But with most issues at any given point in time, individuals must trust others to participate on their behalf. This need not be undemocratic: trust, when warranted, can enable an epistemic division of political labour that multiplies the effects of participation.[53] If I share interests with an association focused on environmental issues, then it will make sense for me to trust it to follow these issues and to pressure on my behalf. It is very likely that I will trust the association to represent me more than I trust my official political representatives. When I can trust others to participate on my behalf, I can reduce my engagement to passive and sporadic monitoring, enabling me to focus my time and resources on other issues. In aggregate, in a democratic society with high levels of participation, everyone will be participating in some kind of venue, but most people will trust others to attend to most issues that affect them.

8. Democratic equality is complex equality.

Participation is *democratic* when every individual potentially affected by a decision has an equal opportunity to affect the decision. It should be clear from the points above, however, that, whatever models of participation progressive democracy comes to involve, they will not be simple. Participation is likely to be issue based, segmented by sector, distributed among many different kinds of venues, and have different meanings and impacts within different venues. But if democracy looks like this, then it is difficult to conceptualize what equality could mean as it relates to participation.

With regard to equality, the attractions of the simpler model of participation – the model that stems from the early modern view that the state is the unified collective agent of people – are self-evident. This model enables us to establish a baseline meaning for political equality, describe its content, and then measure the amount of democracy according to these markers. Robert Dahl's criteria of democracy, for example, remain dependent upon simple equality.[54] In Dahl's well-known formulation, democracy requires

- equal and effective participation in making views known;
- voting equality;
- equal opportunity to gain enlightened understanding;
- equal chances to control the agenda; and
- inclusion of all adults.

The meaning of these criteria is clear when there is one highly significant target: namely, a bounded political unit controlled by a state – even if the constraints on achieving equality in each dimension are considerable, as Dahl rightly emphasizes.

But what if these markers of equality are eroding in their meaning as a consequence of the changes in the social and political landscape of democracy? Ironically, the same forces that multiply the opportunities for participation also make the standards of simple equality more difficult to conceive.

Here are just a few of the challenges. If some of the more significant venues of politics are nonterritorial, then the democratic standard of inclusion of all affected by collective decision making becomes even more difficult to achieve than within territorial units of decision making. Let us say that the people of the United States decided democratically not to deal with global warming, even though they produce more CO_2 emissions than any other country. If their decision contributes to the changing patterns of floods, storms, and droughts, then it will affect countless individuals in other nations. The fact that there are now nonterritorial ways of participating means that individuals in these affected countries can, as it were, include themselves – by working with global NGOs, addressing global publics, making common cause with environmental organizations within the United States, and so on. Yet, short of a formal global government, it is difficult to see how democratic rules of inclusion, equal voting, and equal control over the agenda could apply, since political units tend to form in ad hoc ways, drawing participants from those who push themselves forward for inclusion.

Similarly, the erosion of the state as a collective actor has been accompanied by a multiplication of political venues. Ideally, the rules of simple democratic equality would apply to each of these venues, at least insofar as they have an impact on individuals' lives. Yet the costs of simple equality in terms of time, knowledge, cumbersome decision making, and trade-offs against other goods multiply quickly with each new venue.

Likewise, because of complexity and differentiation, there are numerous spheres in which groups of individuals might organize themselves democratically (in scientific communities, workplaces, neighbourhoods, universities, social movements, churches, etc.) in ways that reflect the five markers of democratic equality for that particular organization. But each democratic organization may engage in collective actions that affect non-members. Even the most democratic of industrial collectives will have incentives to externalize costs onto the public, and scientists at the most democratic of universities will have scientific interests in experiments that may present public dangers. So, on the criteria of simple equality, the units of inclusion would have to extend to everyone who might be affected. Somehow we must conceive of democracy in ways that enable those affected by collective actions to hold the actors accountable. At the same time, however, the standards of democratic equality must allow individuals to maintain appropriate associations for distinctive purposes – and thus maintain the considerable advantages of complex, differentiated, and pluralistic societies.[55] If democratic equality is conceived in ways that fail to take into account those realities and their advantages, it will be irrelevant to modern societies.

These are only a few of the challenges; more could be added. But they are sufficient to make the case that democrats ought to rethink what democratic equality might mean in today's societies. Although I cannot develop a new conception of democratic equality here, it seems to me that any conception would build on the following strategies.

Individual political capacities   Although it is impossible to imagine that individuals could participate equally in the collective decisions that affect their lives, it is not impossible that individuals would have the capacities and opportunities to influence those decisions in which they choose to participate. This formulation allows for the fact that different issues are important to different people at different times and places in their lives. It allows for the possibility that all individuals might participate in collective self-governance but that they would do so in ways that are the most salient to their sense of self-governance, as they interpret self-governance. There are no formulas that will predict how individuals choose to optimize their political resources; what is important is that individuals have the capacity and opportunity to do so. Thus, consistent with many liberal conceptions of equality of opportunity, individuals ought to benefit from those achievable, baseline equalities that underwrite political capacities and opportunities. These include equality under the law, equal political rights, equal rights to personal security and some measure of privacy, basic economic security, and rights to education and information. The rights do not guarantee that individuals will choose to participate, but they enable individuals to participate when they choose.

Equality in voluntary associations   When individuals choose to participate, they need institutional venues that have points of access that enable participation. Ideally, individuals should have equal access to the full range of organizations and institutions that affect their lives. But how this equality manifests itself will depend upon the kind of venue. In general, the more resources controlled by an association or organization, the more important is equality of access. In the case of voluntary associations of a social nature – that is, where the resources are those of identity and solidarity rather than economic or coercive in nature – equality of access is not very important. Indeed, any state-imposed equality of access would destroy the voluntary nature of social associations, the pluralism of their types, and the presence of choices among types for individuals. Moreover, the representative functions of associations within a democracy require that associations discriminate in order to represent a coherent set of interests, purposes, values, and identities within public discourse. Rather, in such cases, participatory equality is achieved indirectly: (a) by the presence of multiple voluntary associations from which individuals can choose; (b) by the presence of associations that can represent an individual's interests, values, purposes, and identities; and (c) by the possibility of exit, which indirectly disciplines voluntary associations to attend to their memberships.

Equality in nonvoluntary associations   Equal access to decision making is more important for those kinds of associations that control resources such as coercive power, territory, economic means of livelihood, and information. These resources enable associations to impose effects on people – both on their own members and on others. It is because the state is a nonvoluntary association writ large, for example, that democrats typically see equality as more important here than, say, within a church. Within state-centred institutions, access to decision making can be equalized to some extent through familiar devices: public hearings, affirmative inclusion of those affected, freedom of information, and the like. Moreover, representative devices, especially those based on territory, can function in more egalitarian ways when they are complemented by representation through public-interest advocacy groups, since these groups capture interests and values not based on territory. Businesses also have nonvoluntary qualities, since they have capacities to impose effects on employees, stockholders, communities, and governments. Participatory equality can be increased here as well through some familiar devices, such as union and community representation on boards, and some novel ones, such as state-mandated worker safety committees.

Internalizing externalities through democratic resistance These "positive" means of increasing political equality, however, are necessarily limited. Market-oriented businesses answer in the first instance to profitability, limiting their responsiveness to those whom they affect. There are more general limitations inherent in complex, differentiated societies as well. Owing to sectoral differentiation, specialized learning and languages, and capacities to limit information, organizations that have high capacities to do things also have high capacities to exclude. And, when they exclude, they will also tend to produce externalities for which they are not accountable – costs such as pollution, risks and dangers of new technologies, congestion of transportation systems, degraded urban aesthetics, unemployment, risks to socializing children, and so on. It is thus important for influence to be equalized *negatively*, as it were, through contest.[56] Individuals affected by decisions should have the rights, protections, and capacities to call upon organizations to justify their decisions and resist imposed costs. The equal power to demand accountability and resist costs depends, in effect, on individuals having more or less equal capacities for obstruction. That is, participatory equality may not involve access to all points of decision making. But it should involve the kind of equality necessary to force closed organizations to limit or justify the costs that they impose on others.[57] Many of these powers already exist in one form or another and could be extended. These include standing to sue for civil damages, class action suits, protests, public criticism, boycotts, public hearings, and stakeholder representation. All such devices involve the support of states through rights, courts, and regulatory processes, but they enable direct oppositional participation by those affected. These devices function to increase participatory equality by negative means, empowering citizens to act as their own "boundary patrols."[58]

Limiting the convertibility of resources In pluralistic societies, part of the meaning of self-governance is that individuals can make choices, there are a variety of choices to be made, and lives are not measured on a single register. This means, of course, that criteria of excellence will differ, not just among individuals, but also within individuals constituted by multiple activities and attachments. Inequalities will emerge because individuals will pursue differing life plans, and each life plan will have different opportunity costs that cannot be later recovered. Moreover, some kinds of inequalities are inherent in the divisions of labour that come with complex, differentiated societies: some become better than others at surgery, airline security, negotiating political conflicts, making music, or any number of other pursuits.

As long as these inequalities are the result of choice rather than fate, they benefit individuals (because lives can be chosen and unique potentialities can be realized) as well as society (since we all benefit from the excellence of others). Their danger to participatory equality is not that they exist but that pre-eminence in one domain can often convert into pre-eminence in other domains. Capitalist societies, of course, favour those who are good at making money: those who are successful in the market can convert the proceeds into political power, friendship, and – as Gramsci and Veblen noticed – even cultural prestige. But ideally a society with multiple kinds and spheres of goods would limit convertibility so that, when inequalities are summed together, they produce what Michael Walzer calls *complex equality*. Economic gain should not be convertible into political power; wealth should not buy love or friendship; status should not convey wealth. In particular, in a democracy, neither power nor wealth should substitute for arguing and voting.[59] Complex equality develops when inequalities are sphere specific, in ways that produce a pluralism of spheres, engaging individuals differentially according to their identities, interests, capacities, and skills.[60]

There is no general formula as to what counts as a justified inequality, since this is itself a matter for democratic judgment. Walzer's view that the standards of each sphere will depend on the shared interpretations of participants makes sense if, as Walzer surely intends, voice is sufficiently well distributed that criteria follow from considered, revisable, serial judgments. The most we can say is that inequalities are suspect when the voices of those affected are absent. But where individuals are empowered to serve as boundary patrols between spheres, justifications of inequalities would be continually challenged and reworked.

These combined strategies do not meet the standards of simple equality, but it is unclear what these standards can mean in today's societies. Still, together they add up to an important kind of equality that retains the radical meaning of democracy: individuals would be able to expand their domains of self-governance into those arenas of collective decision making that they find important and salient to their lives.

There is nothing neat about the pluralistic and decentred future of progressive democracy that I have sketched here, nor, by its very nature, can any such sketch be definitive. What I hope to suggest, however, is that democracy beyond its minimalist definition is conceivable, possible, and indeed emerging in limited but important ways in the established liberal democracies. The case is counterintuitive: the very characteristics of today's societies often deemed to make the participatory ideals of progressive democracy irrelevant have changed the political landscape in ways that make participatory ideals important and even vital. On pain of making the charge of irrelevance come true, however, progressive democratic theorists need to rethink what democratic participation can mean in today's societies.

Acknowledgments

An earlier version of this chapter was delivered to the Europa Mundi/UNESCO conference, The Construction of Europe, Democracy, and Globalization, in Santiago de Compostella, Spain, March 2000. Thanks to Fernando Vallespín, Jane Mansbridge, and two anonymous reviewers for their comments and criticisms. This chapter was originally published in *Political Theory* 30, 5 (2002): 677-701. It is republished with permission from Sage Publications.

Notes

1. Freedom House (2000), 2.
2. Sen (1984); Dahl (1998).
3. Macpherson (1977); Barber (1984).
4. Luhmann (1990), 232.
5. Dahl and Tufte (1973).
6. Bobbio (1987), 27-36.
7. Bobbio (1987), 31.
8. Bobbio (1987), 32.
9. Bobbio (1987), 37-39. Cf. Zolo (1992).
10. Macpherson (1977), ch. 5; Arendt (1963), ch. 6.
11. Pharr and Putnam (2000); Norris (1999).
12. Orren (1997); Dalton (1999).
13. Norris (1999), 27.
14. Thompson (1995), 4-6.
15. Inglehart (1999), 236. Cf. Inglehart (1997), ch. 10; and Berry (1999).
16. Norris (1999), 27.
17. Crozier, Huntington, and Watanuki (1975).
18. van Deth (2000); cf. Mansbridge (1997).
19. Putnam (2000); cf. Skocpol and Fiorina (1999).
20. Ladd (1999).
21. Lin (2001), chs. 11-12.
22. Verba, Schlozman, and Brady (1995), 72.
23. Dryzek (1996); Van Til (2000).
24. Held (1995); Linklater (1999).
25. However, several democratic theorists have applied themselves to developing new theory attentive to emerging realities, including Dryzek (1996); Young (2000); Beck (1997); and Offe (1996).
26. The following four paragraphs are adapted from Warren (2001).
27. Preuss (1995).
28. Offe (1996), ch. 1.
29. Beck (1992).
30. Scott (1998).
31. Offe (1996), 9.
32. Offe (1996), 8.
33. Beck (1997), 107.
34. Giddens (1991).
35. Cf. the analyses in Connolly (1991); Lifton (1993); and Beck (1992), ch. 2.
36. Young (2000), ch. 3.
37. This development is analyzed by Jürgen Habermas (1990).
38. Weber (1946), 143.

39 Offe (1996), viii.
40 For elaboration, see Warren (1999b).
41 Dryzek (1996).
42 I make this argument in detail in Warren (1996, 1999a).
43 Dahl (1998), chs. 8-9.
44 Dahl (1998), ch. 14; Dryzek (1996).
45 Dahl (1998), 111-13; Young (2000), ch. 6.
46 Cohen and Rogers (1995); Hirst (1994).
47 Berry's research (1999) suggests that this is a key factor in explaining the successes of citizen groups as compared to special interest groups.
48 The most powerful account to date of the link between democracy and law is Habermas (1996).
49 These trends were first noticed and theorized by Teubner (1983). The term "reflexive law" is Teubner's.
50 Habermas (1996), chs. 6-8.
51 Putnam (1993); and Putnam (2000), ch. 21.
52 I provide a theoretical approach to these questions in Warren (2001). Cf. Cohen and Rogers (1995); and Hirst (1994).
53 Warren (1999a); cf. Bohman (1999).
54 Dahl (1998), 37-38.
55 Cf. Rosenblum (1998); and Young (2000), ch. 6.
56 Cf. Young (2001).
57 This argument is developed by Offe (1996), ch. 2, as the "utopia of the zero-option."
58 The term is from Walzer (1983), ch. 12.
59 Walzer (1983), ch. 1.
60 Cf. Rosenblum (1998).

11
Representing Pluralism: A Comment on Pyrcz, Warren, and Kernerman
Simone Chambers

The concept of representation stands at the centre of modern mass democracies. Not all citizens can be present in the actual process of governing, but the interests and concerns of all citizens need to be present if decisions are to be democratic. This is what Hanna Pitkin calls the paradox of representation: "making present *in some sense* of something which is nevertheless *not* present literally or in fact."[1] The possibility of authentic representation is further complicated by the growing concern for and sensitivity to pluralism. As pluralism grows, the number of points of view that need to be represented grows until we are back to the original problem. It is no more plausible to represent each and every point of view than it is to have each and every citizen present in governing. A workable representative democracy depends on the existence of common interests and shared goals, which are transmitted to representatives fairly and with minimum distortion and then pursued in public policy.

Several of the authors in this volume are interested in this process of transmission. Three chapters in particular challenge the viability of liberal models of transmission. For Greg Pyrcz in Chapter 9, the problem has to do with "raw" or undeliberated opinions. Representatives should not think of themselves as passive conduits for citizens' opinions. They have a pedagogical obligation to shape citizens' opinions and, when that proves to be too difficult, a moral obligation to pursue policies that citizens would choose if they were not suffering from psychological distortion. For a variety of reasons having to do with the complexity of social, economic, and political systems, Mark Warren doubts that elected representatives can pursue our goals and interests in a meaningful way. His decentred view of democracy in Chapter 10 downplays traditional representative institutions and stresses the role of grassroots activists as effective agents of citizens' interests and concerns. Gerald Kernerman's skepticism centres on the ability of elites to represent a political community in speech. He worries in Chapter 8 that any attempt to articulate a shared conception of the political community, to which all citizens could subscribe, distorts and does damage to the underlying pluralism.

In this chapter, I assess and compare the misgivings voiced by Pyrcz, Warren, and Kernerman. I argue that, although all three bring valuable insights to their topics, each presents a view of politics with unsatisfying implications for a theory of democratic representation. I then briefly explore what it could mean to think of democratic representation in a way that addresses these implications while still valuing the democratic objectives pursued by the three authors. Constitutional politics serves as my case. Here, it seems to me, is the classic dilemma of representing pluralism: on the one hand, constitutions, as well as the elites who write them, must articulate overarching shared principles; on the other, they must gain the support of a citizen body characterized by diversity. Constitutional politics raises questions for each of these authors that their individual perspectives are unable to answer. But if we take the three views together, the resulting mix moves us toward a better appreciation of the nature and demands of pluralistic representation.

Creating a Deliberative Vanguard

Greg Pyrcz is not very happy with liberal or pluralist accounts of democracy. In particular, he finds the view that representatives should in some sense be governed by raw public opinion to be highly problematic. Instead, representatives should base their policy judgments on discursively mediated opinion. This involves a transformative "engagement with citizens." The regulative ideal that stands behind this process is what Pyrcz calls demanding deliberative democracy. Authentic deliberation involves a power-free conversation in which the stakes are high and the goal is unanimity. Representatives thus engage citizens by asking "what, as citizens, would we favour in public policy were we not suffering those democratic deficiencies that are revealed in light of the regulative ideal." By this, I understand Pyrcz to mean that a representative should be able to engage in a counterfactual thought experiment such that he or she can arrive at what citizens would choose under ideal conditions and then use this outcome as the independent standard against which to check the empirical opinions of citizens and guide conversation and debate. Hence, "This aspect of demanding democratic representation resembles humanist pedagogic excellence, bringing out the expression of the truth of human lives by constraining contingencies that undermine their expression and inducing recognition of the value of their authentic experience and deeply considered insight as the means to the realization of the best form of human society."

Why do citizens need to be educated? Sometimes they don't, says Pyrcz, but often deliberation falls far short of demanding deliberation. Citizens in mass democracies, generally speaking, are suffering under conditions that distort deliberation and make authentic pursuit of shared principles difficult if not impossible. This distortion is primarily psychological and arises when individuals are overly swayed by others or indeed under the "psychological power" of others. It is not entirely clear what Pyrcz has in mind here, but one hint is that he appeals to Rousseau's idea of *"amour propre"* as the psychological state that we must try to overcome. The appeal to *amour propre* implies that the problem is deeply seated in society. Although we should do all that we can to improve the conditions under which citizens deliberate so as to mitigate *amour propre*, we are caught in a classic circle: as long as citizens are fettered by psychological distortion, they will not pursue correct policies, but citizens will be unable to free themselves from these fetters until the correct policies are in place. Enter the representative. Using a deliberative thought experiment, he or she will be able to bring the correct policy to the citizens in an effort to break this vicious circle.

I must admit to having serious reservations about this model. The asymmetrical relationship between citizen and representative is troubling. Conceiving of representatives as pedagogues or humanist educators places a paternalistic burden on them. Not many real-world representatives have the self-limiting capacity to carry the burden and still respect democracy. How will we find these pedagogues? Who will elect them – the psychologically fettered citizens? Even if there were such people, and they were elected, there is a larger problem. Deliberation – even demanding deliberation – is not a precise enough device to determine what is in the common interest. Even representatives of goodwill and superior intellect will not be able to figure out what citizens would choose if they were not suffering under psychological fetters. Pyrcz has not made the case that there would be any clear or determinate outcomes of the thought experiment. Therefore, he has not made the case that representatives could have the knowledge to perform their pedagogical function.

All participants in democratic deliberation should engage in thought experiments. These experiments are important sources of both arguments and self-limitation. We should ask ourselves questions such as the following. Who is likely to agree or disagree with this proposal? What would so-and-so say about the claim? How would such-and-such group be likely to react to this demand? How do my stated interests appear to others with other interests? Thinking through these questions honestly and reasonably is an essential part of democratic deliberation. But the tentative answers that we come up with have only limited reliability without the test of real interaction. One of the reasons why thought experiments have limited value is that it is impossible to do justice to the fact of pluralism in a thought experiment. Even if one could do justice to the existing diversity of opinion, which is very unlikely, one cannot predict which new voices will emerge. Pluralism itself is an ever-changing landscape of difference. This leads me to a second misgiving about this model.

Pyrcz sees the role of the representative as mediator of public opinion. The representative is supposed to encourage and foster debate that seeks near unanimity in judgment. Even if it were possible to figure out what citizens, as a whole, might agree to, there cannot be many such points of agreement. Surely, given the fact of pluralism, we must be suspicious of thought experiments that claim to arrive at many such unanimous outcomes. The vast majority of decisions that representatives must make will concern issues over which disagreement is not only likely but also eminently reasonable. Notwithstanding the regulative ideal of demanding deliberative democracy, the thought experiment conducted by Pyrcz's representatives allows, and probably even requires, his deliberative democracy to rise above the fact of pluralism entirely. This is problematic for a workable and just theory of democracy, and, more specifically for our purposes here, it creates major problems of legitimacy and accountability with regard to representatives. Pyrcz ignores pluralism on two counts: by relying too heavily on virtual rather than real deliberation, and by focusing deliberation on the goal of unanimity.

This is not to say that such thought experiments have no relevance. Those that result in unanimity have a limited yet important role to play in democracies, but they do not add up to a full theory of representation. Instead, I will argue that they have a special place within constitutional politics: that is, in those special moments when citizens are asked to articulate shared values, common goals, and principles of justice to which they can all adhere. Furthermore, although elites will often have the opportunity to guide debate, and are thus under a special obligation to think in terms of "what could all agree to," every citizen should be encouraged to take up this perspective when a certain type of question is on the agenda. Unlike Rousseau and Pyrcz, I do not think that citizens are so corrupted in their habits of thought that they are unable to rise to this task. And, anyway, even if they cannot fully rise to a level that we would like, this does not give us licence to form a deliberative vanguard.

Decentred Democracy

In Mark Warren's wide-ranging and rich analysis of democratic participation, the potential for meaningful influence on decisions is found outside the formal and traditional halls of power. Warren offers a marvellous description and analysis of the new landscape for democratic activity, the principal dynamics of which are all premised on the diminished scope of the state's role in modern political life. The forces of globalization, differentiation, complexity, and pluralization conspire to "offer new opportunities to cultivate capacities for self-rule and generate multiple spaces within which self-rule can develop. Yet the same developments tend to undermine formal democratic institutions." More and more spaces and dimensions are emerging in which the answer to the question "Who is in charge?" is unclear, and, "where no one is in charge, new forms of governance become possible." From here, Warren elaborates a number of ways in which democratic participation can be enhanced and made efficacious. In many instances, the problem of representation is bypassed in favour of direct action and participation. But even within this decentred and highly participatory model of democracy, representation has its place.

In Warren's decentred model of democracy, the most important form of representation is not legislative representation. The most important representatives are the ones who represent particular interests, values, and concerns in what has become known as the weak public: that is, civil society and the public sphere.[2] Warren notes that we live busy lives with many demands on our time. We cannot all be activists. Even robust democracy needs to understand the limits of a modern way of life. Democracy must rely on a division of labour and the delegation of tasks. As citizens, we often must trust "others to participate on [our] behalf." The relationship between citizen and representative is here built on trust – a trust that fellow members of a group will pursue the stated interests of the group. This trust is more likely to develop within issue-oriented associations of civil society than between citizens and legislatures: "I will trust the association to represent me more than I trust my official political representatives." When we join Greenpeace, NOW, or Citizens Against Leash Laws, we assume that the activists share and indeed represent our interests in the public sphere.

Warren's view of representation is the mirror image of the one put forward by Pyrcz. For Pyrcz, the representative should employ a deliberative thought experiment to seek out overarching and universal principles that all citizens, if sufficiently autonomous, would accept. As we saw, one of the problems with this view is that it fails to address the pluralism and the particularity of citizens and their concerns. Warren, in contrast, sees representatives – at least those to whom we should now transfer most of our democratic participatory and policy-oriented hopes – as entirely concerned with the particular and the plural. Here there is very little room for the overarching and universal side to politics. For the representative as activist, the ability to think noninstrumentally about the political community as a whole is not usually part of the job description. Whereas for Pyrcz there is a huge gap between the actual and particular interests of citizens, on the one hand, and the hypothetically derived principles that the representative pursues in the public sphere, on the other, for Warren there is a tight fit between interests and the goals pursued by representatives.

But what Warren appears to forgo is the possibility that citizens might also have interests and goals that are overarching and universal. The picture of politics that Warren leaves us with has little room for citizens to pursue large normative agendas at the national level. Whether this is because he believes that "system complexity" now undermines the pursuit of such agendas, or, more pessimistically, that such complexity virtually rules out the formulation of such agendas by citizens and their representatives, he has not offered us clues regarding the institutional foundations of either the creation or the "transmission" of such normative agendas.

Warren has both expanded the potential for meaningful political participation and limited its scope. While it is true that new forms of democratic governance are emerging in the spaces opened up by globalization, complexity, and differentiation, it is also true, as Warren himself admits, that the state is still the ultimate player: "States will remain key organizers of politics for the foreseeable future. Although their powers as collective actors have diminished, states still control most means of coercion and remain the sole agent capable of making and enforcing legitimate and binding laws." Citizens have limited opportunities for meaningful influence on decisions at this level. The reason is not simply that formal representative institutions in large, complex states are unresponsive. At a more fundamental and structural level, the state's representative institutions are, like the rest of the modern state, embedded in a capitalist economy: "Because the state functions as an economic manager of a system of production that is mostly in private hands, it cannot risk policies that limit profitability."

Thus, we are left with a question: although the new landscape might open up new places to participate and new ways to take some control over our lives, does all this activity add up to anything? Could it possibly add up to, say, some sort of transformation of our political and social world? Such transformative possibilities appear to be foreclosed. Democracy can no longer be the vehicle for transformation or even the pursuit of common goals. Decentred democracy is unco-ordinated democracy. There is no *demos*, just actions and associations, movements and issues.

This picture seems to rule out meaningful constitutional politics. If citizens cannot really affect institutions at the national level, why should they bother getting involved? Why should they even care or think about the big questions of foundational principles or basic justice? This seems to be a great loss in democratic politics. Not only does this picture drastically scale back the transformative potential of democratic politics, but it also risks reducing democracy to competitive pluralism – perhaps a *participatory* pluralism but a pluralism nonetheless. If citizens do not place their particular local pursuits and participation in some minimum context of overarching values and norms, then this is the risk. They are not likely to see their participation within that larger context unless they also participate in collective, *demos*-level politics. The decentred view of politics risks falling into a type of pluralism that sees politics as a competitive arena bound by external rules of engagement.

Pluralism Redux
At first sight, it would appear that Gerald Kernerman is interested in pursuing a line of argument that offers a way of bringing particular identities and overarching norms together. Although his topic is not representatives per se, or the expansion of democratic participation, he nevertheless touches on many of the same issues that I have raised in relation to Pyrcz's and Warren's arguments. Kernerman is concerned with the way that elites symbolically represent the interests, values, and identities of a political community. Like Pyrcz and Warren, he is worried about a slippage or lack of connection between citizens, on the one hand, and the policies and goals pursued in their name, on the other.

Kernerman's case is Canada. Kernerman notes that, at first glance, Canadians appear to share a common understanding of the nature of the Canadian political community: Canada is a multicultural community. As soon as we begin to specify what that might mean, however, the unanimity quickly disappears. In one camp are those who understand multiculturalism through the lens of equality, while in the other camp are those who understand multiculturalism as difference. The equality camp stresses elements such as the equality of all provinces and strong endorsement of individual rights as the best safeguards of multiculturalism. The difference advocates endorse asymmetrical federalism and differential treatments of Aboriginal groups, among other things.

The object of articulating an overarching vision of who we are as Canadians is to integrate the diverse identities into some shared normative bond. Thus, both camps adhere to the view that, despite multiculturalism, or perhaps especially because of it, Canadians need to recognize a unity within their diversity. This recognition is then to ensure that Canada holds together for strong cultural reasons rather than weak instrumental ones. But Kernerman argues that, as long as the dichotomy between equality and difference characterizes the debate, the goal of integration will fail. These two alternatives can be thought of as false universals. The multiplicity of identities as well as the complexity of and variation among the different issue areas cannot be reduced to one or the other conception of multiculturalism. To say that Quebec-English Canada relations, Aboriginal-non-Aboriginal relations, and ethnic and race relations could all be understood along either an equality-based or a difference-based conception of Canada fails to see the real differences between these cases.

According to Kernerman, the problem here runs very deep. It is not just that people trying to represent and articulate the nature of Canadian multiculturalism get it wrong. He seems to be saying that any attempt to articulate and symbolically represent Canadian multiculturalism will do injustice to particular identities. Attempts to represent a national identity will always end in attempts to contain and suppress identity. Struggles are flattened and scripted when redescribed within frameworks of equality or difference.

Although Kernerman begins with the promise of reconciliation, in the end there is no reconciliation. He rejects the possibility of an adequate or authentic representation at the most general level. If we are unable to articulate an overarching identity, then what are we left with? Like Warren's view, this view appears to end in pluralism. We let the differences play themselves out on a relatively fair playing field. We reach one modus vivendi after another but refuse to be drawn into the game of nation building. The bonds of "nationhood" are instrumental and not normative because, according to this view, we cannot all share a common set of values. Any attempt at articulating a normative unity denies multiplicity and fluidity.

Kernerman implies that we should not be seeking overarching statements of the common good or shared values or universal norms. Although there is an implicit normative endorsement of pluralism, we must resist trying to characterize that pluralism or embracing overarching principles for dealing with it. While his warning against false universals is well taken (this was the same worry I had with Pyrcz), his next step, that all universals must be false given radical difference, appears to lead us down a road already rejected. What is left looks a lot like what Robert Dahl described in 1956 in *A Preface to Democratic Theory*.[3] Here we have "interest group politics" with the only difference being that the groups are now primarily identity based. Democratic politics can be summed up by the series of compromises reached between groups.

What is wrong with this view of politics? Many criticisms have been levelled at pluralist theories of democracy, ranging from questioning the empirical claims to worrying about the normative implications.[4] For now, I will mention only one weakness in this view: marginalized and historically oppressed groups do not usually fare very well in the arena of competitive pluralisms. Without resources or numbers, groups such as Aboriginals have very little clout. While it is true that Aboriginal groups occasionally are in an advantageous bargaining position (as in the Meech Lake round of constitutional negotiations in 1989-90), this happens rarely and cannot account for the growing voice of Native Canadians within Canadian democracy. What can account for it is a changing conception of what justice requires.

While Canadians still cannot articulate a shared substantive identity, the national constitutional debate has yielded a collective rethinking of our obligations to Native peoples. Despite pockets of backsliding, the flare-up of hot spots, and a lack of agreement on the details, public opinion surveys as well as scholarly commentary indicate an observable shift by Canadians toward conceptions of Aboriginal self-government.[5] It is not so much that Canadians agree on a solution to the Aboriginal question; it is that they agree that Native Canadians should be sitting at the table, that they should be allowed to speak in their own voice, that they deserve to be heard.

This might not seem like much, but I would suggest that it signals a deep shift in Canadians' ideas of who the partners are in our collective conversation. Neither Kernerman's nor Dahl's model can account for this shift. It is the result of national-level debate in which *shared* conceptions of justice and the structure of the Canadian political community and membership evolve under the influence of new voices being really heard for the first time. Nor can this shift be captured in what Kernerman contends is the equality/difference divide that characterizes our debates. He is talking about what we argue about, while I am talking about whom we argue with. The explosion of interest (to be sure, some of it has been to find counterarguments) in what could be called the "indigenous point of view" over the past fifteen years suggests that the overarching normativity emerging in Canada concerns the articulation of fair and acceptable procedures of negotiation and not a substantive identity.

Constitutional Moments

The general issue raised by these three chapters has to do with the relationship between particular interests and identities and the possibility that multiplicity can coalesce into a democratic will or be represented in an overarching normative conception. Pyrcz, on the one hand, defends a strong conception of overarching normativity but at a great distance from the actual voices and interests of citizens. In the end, I think that allowing this distance leaves the democratic credentials of his demanding deliberative democracy looking rather suspect. Warren, on the other hand, focuses on real citizen participation. He takes seriously the real lives and concrete interests of citizens, but they appear to be denied the opportunity or at least the realistic incentive to democratically pursue a shared normative vision. For Kernerman, any pursuit of an overarching normative vision is confining.

I suppose that I not only want my cake but also want to eat it. I favour a view that attempts to steer a middle course in which the ideal democratic theory would contain elements from each of these three chapters: overarching normativity from Pyrcz, citizens speaking in their own voice from Warren, and recognition of difference from Kernerman. I can't develop this intermediate and integrated democratic theory here. But perhaps some exploration of one of the major challenges to any democratic polity, that of constitutional reform, can shed light on how the concerns of Pyrcz, Warren, and Kernerman can be addressed in ways that are mutually reinforcing and do not undermine some of the major legitimizing aspects of democratic representation.

For example, as I mentioned in my discussion of Pyrcz, constitutional politics can achieve many of the purposes that he values without violating democratic legitimacy. In particular, it can be pedagogical and universalistic yet maintain a real connection to the people. One example that comes to mind is the extraordinary case of South Africa. Here constitutional politics had much to overcome in the troubled and violent past of apartheid South Africa. Not only did the process need to bring together a population that had been literally killing each other, but it also had to introduce constitutional ideas, indeed the very idea of a constitution, to certain segments of the population for the first time. Here is a situation where it would appear that the Pyrcz "humanist educator" is exactly what is called for. And, to be sure, elites played a significant role in guiding the conversation. But constitutional success could not have been achieved without extensive and widespread citizen participation. Furthermore, the special role of participation could never have been replaced by a counterfactual thought experiment.

Early on in constitutional debates, elites insisted that wide popular consultation and participation were absolutely necessary for the legitimacy and stability of the Constitution.[6] In a speech to the Constitutional Assembly in January 1995, Cyril Ramaphosa said, "It is therefore important as we put our vision to the country, we should do so directly, knowing that people out there want to be part of the process and will be responding, because in the end the drafting of the constitution must not be the preserve of the 490 members of this Assembly. It must be a constitution ... [that] they feel they own, a constitution that they know and feel belongs to them. We must, therefore, draft a constitution that will be fully legitimate, a constitution that will represent the aspirations of our people."[7] The scale and ambition of the participatory project undertaken by South Africa is simply astounding and by all accounts unprecedented not simply in Africa but also anywhere. "The challenge was to find ways to enter into effective dialogue and consultation with a population of more than 40 million people. South Africa had a rural population, most of whom were illiterate and did not have access to print or electronic media. Moreover, South Africa has never had a culture of constitutionalism, or human rights, for that matter, which accordingly made it difficult to enter into consultation with communities that did not recognize the importance of a constitution."[8]

In talking about the establishment of constitutional democracy in South Africa, the legal activist Albie Sachs wrote that "the perspective that needs at least to be considered is that of constitution-making as a process rather than an event." If this is done, he continued, it is possible to involve "the people directly in the shaping and formulation of the rights of which they are to be holders."[9] Not only did citizens generate a sense of ownership in the Constitution, but broad participation also generated a rights culture with deep roots. The citizen participation program brought people together in a process governed by the very principles that South Africans were attempting to enshrine. That is, the process treated citizens (many of them for the first time) as equal, free, and deserving of respect. It did so by adhering to high standards of publicity, accountability, and dialogue. This type of constitutional politics is not possible to achieve through thought experiments. The point of this type of constitutional politics is not simply arriving at the right answer; rather, the point is the instantiation and entrenchment of principles by way of the process of participation itself. Here we see that representatives deliberating on behalf of citizens can never achieve full success.

Constitutional politics can also serve as a counterexample to Warren's view regarding the efficacy of citizen participation in national-level politics. While it might be true that on a day-to-day level citizen participation appears to have more meaningful impact if it is decentred and focused on nontraditional areas of civic engagement, it is also true that constitutional politics often represents a break with both the pettiness and the gratuitously exaggerated divisiveness over minor matters that easily characterize day-to-day politics in liberal democratic polities. Here we might think of generalizing from Bruce Ackerman's dualist approach to the American constitutional tradition. Constitutional politics has two gears according to Ackerman. Most of the time, the Constitution is a relatively stable set of principles that judges apply but do not radically alter. These principles form the backdrop to "normal politics." In this gear, citizens have little to do with the Constitution, and court decisions stay within a given interpretive paradigm.

But every once in a while, constitutional politics changes gears. During these "constitutional moments," citizens engage in higher lawmaking. These are often times of crisis or great change when nations are galvanized by issues and debate spreads and intensifies. In these moments, elites call on and listen to the "people." A collective re-assessment of values and principles results in a constitutional paradigm shift. These moments represent a popular constitutional amendment process outside the formal institutional channels of amendment. Ackerman identifies three such moments within the American tradition: "The Founding, Reconstruction, and the New Deal were all acts of constituent authority."[10]

Jürgen Habermas also sometimes hints that the efficacy of political participation at a state level must be understood episodically and tied to special moments. He notes, for example, that many factors might lead one to "be rather cautious in estimating the chances of civil society having an influence on the political system. To be sure, this estimate pertains only to a public sphere at rest. In periods of mobilization, the structures that actually support the authority of a critically engaged public begin to vibrate. The balance of power between civil society and the political system then shifts."[11] Warren's picture of democracy fails to take into account these special moments when participation can be raised to *demos*-level politics. The potential for a *demos*-level participatory politics is especially present in founding moments such as the South African case, but it can also arise at times of renewal or when a crisis calls for transformation. Some potential constitutional moments, however, fail to produce visible constitutional change. This was the case for Canada in the 1990s. Continuing a theme that I introduced in the previous section, I want to suggest, however, that, despite having no new Constitution, Canada has seen change as a result of its constitutional moment.

During the Charlottetown round of constitutional debate, one saw, as in the South African case, a new endorsement of participation and the central role that participation needs to play if Canadians are to forge a workable constitutional compromise. Concern for citizen engagement led to a relatively healthy and wide process of debate and consultation early on.[12] However, the opportunity for significant renewal, or even resolution of the most important issues, floundered in the final stages of the 1992 referendum campaign. That campaign was divisive and plagued by distrust, and the Charlottetown proposal went down to defeat.[13] Despite this divisiveness and distrust, and the failure to agree on a document, I would nevertheless maintain that Canadians have gained shared values through participation in the larger process of constitutional renewal.

There is a democratic paradox here relevant to my attempt to reconcile the concerns of Pyrcz, Warren, and Kernerman. While it appears that Canadians are further away than ever from a solution to the thorniest issues of constitutional reform, this might be because Canadians are closer than ever to a shared view of what the process of constitutional renewal ought to look like. This has been called "the paradox of participation."[14] As Canadians have a more democratic view of who should participate and which voices should be heard in constitutional politics, the possibility of coming to a *demos*-level agreement appears to recede on the horizon. Although constitutional agreement has always been difficult to reach in Canada, the criticism of an "eleven men in suits" approach to constitutional renewal sparked by the closed doors of Meech Lake negotiations has made that task even more daunting. For better or for worse, we now live in a world where citizens expect transparency and accountability by elites as well as some say in the process. Once again I want to suggest that, if we take a process-based rather than an outcome-based approach, the picture does not look so bleak.

The processes through which Canadians have tried and are still trying to resolve their deep differences are far more representative than they once were. They are more representative in the sense that more points of view are present and because more groups are speaking in their own voices. Today Canadian constitutional politics lives on in what could be called sidebars to "mega-constitutional" politics.[15] Rather than grand overarching debates that involve the nation as a whole, issues are being resolved on a case-by-case basis, often in bilateral or trilateral agreements.

This is particularly evident in the series of treaty negotiations going on around the country with regard to Aboriginal claims. These negotiations are parasitic on a deep shift in our shared attitude toward indigenous peoples as partners in an ongoing enterprise called Canada. While Canada has always had treaty relations with indigenous peoples, their "bargaining position" has significantly shifted. I place "bargaining position" in scare quotes because power cannot account for this shift. This shift has more to do with new normative expectations and conceptions of procedural legitimacy than with traditional power manoeuvring. In other words, the very possibility of moving forward bi- or trilaterally was opened up by larger *demos*-level shifts in what could be called procedural principles regarding whom we are obliged to listen to and deal with.

It is also the case that some constitutional issues, such as giving constitutional expression to Quebec distinctiveness, have simply been sidelined for the moment. The abeyance of mega-constitutional politics here is also part of the dualist account of constitutional politics. Mega-constitutional politics cannot be sustained over long periods of time. Citizens making or transforming fundamental law is, as I noted, episodic and tied to special and especially intense political moments. But if mega-constitutional politics is in abeyance, this does not mean that it is gone forever. We need to see when the next opportunity shows itself.

What does all this mean for my argument with regard to the three authors? In constitutional politics, valuable insights of Pyrcz, Warren, and Kernerman can be integrated, despite their broader disagreements. Constitutional politics involves working out overarching principles based on what all would agree to. Such politics can and ought to be participatory politics, in which citizens get a sense that their voices count for something and that they have some say in how their lives are organized. And, finally, constitutional politics often achieves this overarching normativity not simply in determinate outcomes to disputes but also in the adherence to and acceptance of the rules of the process itself. By taking a process approach to overarching normativity, we can maintain a maximum flexibility toward the ever-shifting identities and interests that make up modern pluralism. Representing pluralism at the constitutional level places an obligation on representatives to support and maintain fair and reciprocal procedures of participation and to engage in fair and reciprocal conversations with citizens in all their diversity.

Acknowledgment
I want to thank David Laycock for invaluable help in revising this chapter.

Notes
1 Pitkin (1967), 8-9.
2 Strong publics contain representative and parliamentary institutions in which authoritative decisions are taken. Weak publics contain informal institutions of civil society in which opinions are formed but no authoritative decisions are taken. See Fraser (1993), 109-42.
3 I would like to thank Melissa Williams for reminding me of the origins of democratic pluralism.
4 For the first, see Bachrach and Baratz (1962). For the latter, see Manin (1987).
5 See, for example, Cairns (2000).
6 Political negotiations in 1993 resulted in the agreement on thirty-four basic principles as the framework for a national constitution. Democratic elections in 1994 indicated popular support for the constitutional project. The 490 members of the National Assembly formed a committee of the whole house, which was the Constitutional Assembly. The Constitution was then framed by the Constitutional Assembly in consultation with the public but also using closed-door sessions of intense negotiation. The resulting document was reviewed by a Constitutional Court, which also took submissions from the public (the court sent it back for more work), and was passed into law by the National Assembly on 10 December 1996. For a more detailed history, see Gloppen (1997). The negotiations leading up to the 1993 agreement at Kempton Park were "widely criticized for being undemocratic, restricted to a narrow elite, and lacking transparency"; see Gloppen (1997), 256. This was one of the impetuses behind broadening citizen participation in the second phase.
7 Cited in Ebrahim (1998), 240. See also Sachs (1990), who had been advocating citizens' participation in the creation of a Bill of Rights for some time.
8 Ebrahim (1998), 241.
9 Sachs (1990), 17.
10 Ackerman (1998), 11.
11 Habermas (1998), 379.
12 For an evaluation of the role of citizen deliberation in the Charlottetown round, see Chambers (1998).
13 There were many reasons for the failure of the Charlottetown Accord.
14 Pal and Seidle (1993).
15 This is Peter Russell's term. See Russell (1993).

Conclusion
David Laycock

The preceding chapters have offered diverse contributions to a broader appreciation of connections between the conceptual foundations, social and institutional contexts, civil societal preconditions, and mechanisms of representation. Collectively, the authors have shown that the reach of representation within normative democratic theory is considerably greater than it might seem were we to think of representation simply in terms of political parties, legislative elections, and the relationships between citizens and the territorially defined victors in competitive struggles for the people's vote. In this Conclusion, I highlight shared themes from these chapters that help to advance this appreciation.

> **Contested citizenship and complicated constructions of political identities are often translated, in both theory and practice, into problems of representation.**

Several of the contributors illustrate that, when citizenship or identities become politically contested and problematic, adjustments to representative practices are one of the common ways of dealing with the political consequences. Melissa Williams shows how different experiences and conceptions of citizenship for Native peoples in Canada can be taken to imply different, but in some ways overlapping and complementary, representational structures and practices. In doing so, she builds on her earlier efforts to show that "The project of addressing the ways in which difference matters is one that depends crucially on institutions of political representation," and how it is "only through institutions of representation that marginalized groups may offer their distinctive perspectives on public matters in a manner that gives full credit to the agency of group members themselves," while denying "the option of members of privileged groups to allow them a voice or not."[1]

Susan Henders shows how "unbounded communities" in which European and Asian minorities participate can open doors to forms of self-government that transcend traditional and restrictive political identities. In doing so, she suggests, these unbounded communities also simultaneously lead to innovative construction of, and political work independent of, representative institutions and practices rooted in the nation-states that have been antagonistic to these minorities' citizenship.

Catherine Frost raises the prospect of deliberative solutions to the problems of "representational failure" in multicultural settings where citizenship is conceived in dramatically different ways by minorities and majorities. Greg Pyrcz argues that the transformation of citizens within a "demanding deliberative democracy" can significantly reduce the risk of illegitimate and community-harming decision making by representatives, even if it occasionally gives representatives an independence from their stated preferences that would worry many citizens of current liberal democracies.

On the ground of recent Canadian efforts at constitutional change, Gerald Kernerman points to a realm of rather sweeping representational failure. He argues that, over the past generation, attempts by political elites to construct Canadian identity in response to the tensions generated by multicultural nationalism have led to self-defeating efforts to represent either these internal national identities or undifferentiated citizens ("the people") in a public conversation about the Canadian community. By contrast, Simone Chambers contends that recent constitutional reform efforts have shown that inclusive representation in such "*demos*-level" political deliberation need not produce concrete constitutional reform to contribute valuable elements of "overarching normativity" in the shared and increasingly inclusive Canadian civic identity.

Shifting boundaries of citizenship remain complicated challenges to political representation, especially because these boundaries are increasingly nonterritorial.

This is an extension of the first theme across national and regional/provincial boundaries. In the case of representation for Native peoples in Canada, Williams argues that various proposals to make special provision for Aboriginal representation within existing Canadian legislatures can be complemented by both new federal representative institutions exclusive to Native peoples and a range of distinctively designed and territorially based structures of Native self-government. Her case for building complementary forms of Aboriginal representation rests on a conception of "citizenship as shared fate," which she believes reflects and is normatively sensitive to Native peoples' distinctive position in a modern multicultural community.

Mark Warren discusses the increasingly supranational range of citizen opportunities for responding to the effects of globalization, especially those opportunities arising from the "diminishing scope of the state as an agent of collective action." As state capacity in this sense diminishes, democratic participation should "follow politics, not political institutions," which often means looking for national boundary-crossing opportunities in economic and social issue-focused activity. Warren also contends that issue-based political association, within and beyond national boundaries, presents a wider range of opportunities for participation in creative and focused democratic activity than does territorially based political association. He contends that this will be true even as issue-based political associations create accountability challenges for those affected by their actions.

Susan Henders confronts another aspect of the nonterritorial extension of democratic citizenship in her discussion of self-governance in unbounded communities. This extension relies on a variety of existing or emerging international human rights regimes, on "multi-realmed citizenship" in the European Community, and even on "flexible citizenship" for Hong Kong entrepreneurs. These extensions may be loosely tied to conventional forms of representation. But minority group representation in European parliamentary and other decision-making bodies, and relationships with UN human rights agencies, do provide elements of "self-governance" that extend the citizenship rights and practices of minorities in the cases discussed by Henders.

Several contributors explore the boundaries imposed by language on citizenship and hence representation. Peter Ives deals with an overlapping set of challenges posed by decision making within the multilingual forums of the European Community. How are languages and their associated cultures valued within this community, and how is this reflected in linguistic accommodation within the community's representative and policy-making structures? How can one characterize or conceive of democratic deliberation over the use of multiple languages to engage in democratic deliberation about formally nonlinguistic issues? Will approaches to this question be powerfully shaped by the cultural perspectives that feature specific languages as ineliminable and intrinsic elements?

Gerald Kernerman suggests that a different type of language barrier has doomed the Canadian constitutional conversation to perpetual polarization and largely futile interaction among regional, linguistic, ethnic, and other groups. The language barrier is not one of language difference, as in the EU case, but one, ironically, of a language similarity: Canadians have almost all fallen into the practice of speaking the language of "national unity."

Finally, Louise Chappell shows that, for women's movement organizations representing their constituencies on a variety of issues, there is a challenging combination of territorially structured institutions within the federal state and supraregional concerns within the women's movement.

In Australia, women's interests and identities are configured by ethnicity, class, and gender; in Canada, representing women's multilayered citizenship is complicated further by key linguistic and regional/national minority factors. Chappell applies historical institutionalist analysis to show how important institutions are in channelling social movement attempts at nonparty representation.

> **While much contemporary democratic theory values "deliberation" over competitive and/or majoritarian decision making, most of this literature is silent on how deliberation is to relate to the forms of political representation that modern publics see as minimum conditions of democratic accountability and legitimacy. How can we understand connections between deliberation and political representation in ways that take issues of legitimacy and accountability seriously?**

Mark Warren's account of the transformation of conditions and opportunities for democratic participation doesn't directly address the challenges that this new scene presents to democratic representation. Still, his remarks are broadly suggestive in this regard.[2] His portrait touches on the proliferation of new venues for democratic action outside the state, quantum changes in levels of social complexity and differentiation since conventional representative institutions were designed, the way that modern "risk consciousness" expands political opposition to most collective actions, and the democratic "division of labour" that unavoidably attends the expansion of associational civil society. These prominent dimensions of the contemporary political scene, and many others covered in his broad-ranging discussion, all point to major changes in the social and political foundations of any specific set of deliberative and representational practices. Warren's chapter thus charts some of the key parameters and dynamics of new representational regimes in Western democratic polities.

Warren's discussion also points to the difficulties that citizens will have enforcing political accountability not just through conventional election-mediated representational channels but also in the new spaces of democratic action. Warren contends that new opportunities for self-rule will undermine hierarchical lines of authority and accountability, generate dispersed rather than converging patterns of decision making, deepen citizen doubts about the legitimacy of conventional governance structures, and generally reveal that we lack the proper conceptual tools to make sense of new experiments in self-government.

Melissa Williams employs a distinctive conception of citizenship to build a case for Aboriginal representation that she believes will withstand the democratic legitimacy challenge. It will do so because the multilevel, partly integrated, and partly separated structures of representation grounded in "citizenship as shared fate" can facilitate deliberation within Native communities and deliberation among Native and non-Native representatives. These complementary deliberative practices can produce decisions that Aboriginal peoples can justify on their own terms and with reference to the fate that they share with non-Native peoples in Canada. And they can be facilitated by a blend of Aboriginal group representation within Canadian legislatures, and Aboriginal decision making within institutions of self-government, in ways that do not require Native peoples to choose one or the other to salvage legitimacy for their new political institutions. Like all political representatives, future Aboriginal representatives will have to find ways to speak to and for a diverse constituency, in what Williams refers to as a "two-level game" in both the legislature and the constituency. Practising arts of deliberation and negotiation in each location, they will face the problem of legitimacy and accountability in the eyes of their constituents no less than their legislative colleagues, whether these colleagues are in fully Aboriginal or "shared fate" assemblies.[3]

Greg Pyrcz's "demanding deliberative democracy" puts a premium on deliberation under conditions of high stakes, community consensus, and epistemic clarity. Pyrcz argues that these conditions grant fundamental democratic decisions more legitimacy than conventional liberal democratic procedures can. Deliberative decisions made under such conditions will respect intracommunity difference, and citizen representatives can assist and sometimes guide public will formation in ways that amplify rather than undermine the community's genuine will, its "public autonomy." Pyrcz's demanding deliberative democracy does not require "thick political engagement of democratic citizens with one another" and leaves the responsibility for representative accountability to citizens largely to representatives and primarily on "foundational questions."[4] Nonetheless, his approach to democratic deliberation accords accountability as much theoretical attention as many deliberative democratic theorists do. It is worth noting that Robert Goodin's recent contribution to deliberative democratic theory takes a similar "thought experimental" approach to deliberation by both representatives and engaged citizens. Goodin advances "deliberative democracy within" as a way to formulate fair and legitimate policy decisions affecting future human generations and non-human environmental interests.[5]

Catherine Frost has concerns about Pyrcz's "ideal representative," his "deliberator by proxy." She sees no alternative but to transform citizens through "thick" public participation and, in so deliberating, have citizens genuinely codiscover and endorse solutions to problems of multicultural justice. She recommends focusing on innovative approaches to public participation and citizen ratification of contested policies that bridge rather than deepen cultural divides. This will take pressure off representatives, hence reducing the accountability problem, while expanding citizens' experience with dialogue about what justice requires of them and others in multicultural communities. Neither this experience nor its insights can be "represented," according to Frost, so the foundational democratic work of multicultural communities must be undertaken primarily by citizens, not representatives. This means that, if direct democratic devices come into vogue, we must find ways of adapting them to our need for foundational democratic dialogue, to make them work for, and not against, transformation of citizen preferences in directions congenial to multicultural social reality.

Simone Chambers also sees accountability and related will-transmission problems in Pyrcz's account of the way in which representatives engage in "thought experiments" rather than "thick political engagement of democratic citizens with one another." She contends that it is exactly such "thick political engagement" in recent constitutional reform processes that has transformed Canadian and South African citizenship in more inclusive and culturally sensitive directions. On her account, representatives by themselves can neither do the work required to transform citizenship in these positive ways, nor be reasonably held accountable for their shortcomings as supporters of "public autonomy," in the absence of such "thick political engagement."

From a more empirical angle, Louise Chappell discusses the role that the Canadian women's movement played in public constitutional deliberations in the early 1980s and early 1990s. She shows that participation in such deliberations by organized women's groups with supraregional concerns can make a key contribution to their outcomes and (as Chambers suggests in Chapter 11) to their political legacies. By contrast, Australian feminists between the 1970s and the mid-1990s chose largely "femocratic" means of shaping policy processes and state programs, having encountered considerable frustration pursuing their agendas through the conventional media of party politics and legislative representation. This is not to say that Canadian feminists have found prevailing federal or (in most cases) provincial parties and cabinets congenial to their policy preferences. Chappell points out that, since the mid-1980s, Anglo-Canadian feminists have responded to such frustrations with a major push to use the Supreme Court's interpretation of equality provisions in the Charter of Rights and Freedoms to offset the slow progress experienced through parties and legislatures and, in so doing, have moved much of their symbolic representational strength to the federal level of Canadian politics.

Contemporary enthusiasts of direct democracy often suggest that referendums are remedies for unaccountable decision making by elected representatives. Are there ways of squaring such direct expressions of popular will with both representation and deliberation? Or do referendums, conventional representation, and deliberation simply possess irreconcilable logics of democracy?

Avigail Eisenberg analyzes an instance of direct democratic decision making in British Columbia against the backdrop of other efforts to use referendums to render definitive public decisions on matters of minority community or group rights. In doing so, she shows the potential normative complexity of public responses to the most institutionalized and broadly popular alternative to "representational failure" in conventional North American politics. Eisenberg begins by acknowledging that referendums' advocates defend them as solutions to the illegitimacy and unaccountability of legislative representatives' decisions in particular policy areas. She cautions that multicultural democracies must handle such referendums with care. Legislatures have good reasons, based on considerations of justice for national minorities, to carefully regulate the use of referendums when majorities seek to strengthen the standing of formal equality rights within their local political cultures and legislative domains.

Such regulation should both encourage deliberation and compromise between majority and minorities and acknowledge the important practical force of a distinction between formal equality-seeking minorities, on the one hand, and distinct rights-seeking minorities, on the other. Eisenberg suggests that, if a multicultural community fails to take such a distinction among equality rights into account, then it will risk producing policy that reflects a dangerous tension between the logics of representative and direct democracy. Taking the distinction seriously, on the other hand, can create more space within which positive interactions between representation, referendums, and deliberation may occur.

Catherine Frost contends that the problem of squaring deliberation, referendums, and representation in the face of minority group calls for "complex equality" is thornier than this. However much representatives and elites might find Eisenberg's distinction between equality rights compelling, ordinary citizens typically believe that "referendums have legitimacy in spades." This is true, at least in Canada, as evidenced by behavioural research over the past fifteen years.[6] So, rather than put our energy into designing regulations for referendums that prevent the most egregious forms of voter manipulation and distortion of public dialogue, Frost suggests that we look at the historical, legal institutional, and political cultural foundations of citizen support for multicultural fairness. Are there resources in these domains that can augment processes of multicultural compromise while supporting the relatively rigorous legitimacy tests posed by average citizens?

Frost believes so and suggests that these resources will all ultimately be enhanced through experiments with deliberative democracy, in which citizens' reflective and considered judgments rather than representatives' guidance set the democratic agenda and facilitate multicultural compromise. She comes at the problem of reconciling logics of representation, deliberation, and referendums from a different angle than Eisenberg does. Still, Frost shares Eisenberg's conviction that, while it is difficult to reconcile these approaches to democratic decision making in practice, it can be done, with increased odds for success, if we emphasize innovation in deliberative dialogue.

At some level, however, the job of framing and facilitating venues and practices of deliberation seems to fall in the lap of representatives, even if their role in this regard goes some distance beyond regulation of referendum processes. Can this occasionally extend legitimately to representatives' decisions trumping citizens' conclusions about their shared political will, as Pyrcz contends? This raises the question of how much independence representatives should have from the combination of "imperative mandates" (instructed delegation) and "permanent revocability" (open-ended threat of recall proceedings). Bernard Manin argues that no modern representative democracy has systematically constrained the independence of representatives with mechanisms embodying either of these contrarepresentative principles.[7] But, as Eisenberg demonstrates, representatives will occasionally be invited by governments, or required by citizens, to accept constraints on their decision-making powers through initiatives or referendums. When this occurs, reconciling public deliberation by citizens and among representatives with regulative ideals grounded in conceptions of justice and equality is a major challenge.[8]

The increased social complexity and division of civic labour in Western polities brings a greater diversity in forms of participation and representation. This has been accompanied, and is in some cases driven, by a more demanding diversity in understandings of citizenship, equality, and rights.

Mark Warren's reconnaissance of the new terrain of democratic participation in Chapter 10 provides an excellent basis for appreciation of reconfigurations in modern relationships between deepening social complexity, on the one hand, and challenges to democratic will formation and representation, on the other. Warren contends that, while "state-centred institutions ... capture increasingly fewer of the sites of politics," this decline has opened up many new opportunities and spaces for the development of citizens' self-ruling capacities while tending to undermine parties, legislatures, and other "formal democratic institutions" that we have associated with democratic representation. Devolution of the democratic division of labour away from centralized state control presents many potential opportunities for activist citizens, but Warren maintains that we still lack the conceptual tools required to assess these developments.

Other contributors to this volume show, however, that these conceptual tools are being developed, often on the basis of careful examinations of particular types of new political activity both inside and outside the conventional channels of political representation. Melissa Williams, for example, proposes the notion of "citizenship as shared fate," discussed above, as a contribution to theorizing the requirements of citizenship, representation, and complex equality associated with the political needs of Canada's Native peoples. Jonathan Quong proposes an alternative and largely Rawlsian conception of "citizenship as reasonableness" that can meet what he calls the two key conditions of democratic citizenship. First, citizens must prioritize over their other commitments, and accept the "public use of reason" as the means of defending, those civic obligations that are foundational to a fair and stable liberal democratic regime. Second, citizens need to recognize the deep social diversity and a corresponding normative commitment to a "reasonable pluralism." Quong is more concerned with establishing these as the standards of democratic deliberation than specifying whether and how, in institutional terms, citizens, legislators, judges, and administrators might so deliberate. He appears to assume, however, that there can ultimately be the full range of authoritative decisions following democratic deliberation that Warren's account of "decentred democracy" casts doubt on.

Peter Ives provides a fascinating case study in how democratic will formation and policy deliberation have been made almost head-spinningly complex within the multilingual environment of the European Union. In his account, the civic division of labour within the Union has developed both within and alongside its many agencies and programs dealing with language use and education in its member countries. In doing so, they have followed two potentially incompatible paths in rationalizing particular kinds of language rights within the European Union's legislative and administrative domains, which can be theorized in terms of instrumental and expressive understandings of the value of language. Ives sees the Union's experiments in blending democratic deliberation, multilingual representation, and complex policy administration as revealing test cases for democratic representation within, and to, other multilateral or suprastate institutions, such as the World Trade Organization and the United Nations. His discussion reveals how valuable the specifics of institutions and policies are to our appreciation of the complex environment within which potentially antagonistic forms of citizenship and understandings of rights are developing, and why such specifics must inform our efforts to adapt democratic representation.

Social movement activity, and the notions of citizenship, rights, and equality that such activity expresses, are bound to be affected by the institutional complications presented by a federal state structure. Louise Chappell shows us how basic institutional factors such as electoral systems and divided jurisdictions within federalism have shaped feminist approaches to citizenship in Australia and how Quebec's distinctiveness within Canada, and post-1985 judicial interpretation of Canada's Charter of Rights and Freedoms, have decisive impacts on the particular meanings and policy expressions attached to citizenship, equality, and rights in English Canada and French Canada. The Canadian experience since 1982, in particular, shows how constitutional development processes and interpretation can shift not just the directions and targets of women's movement activity but also their understanding of equality and rights, in ways that cannot be accounted for simply with reference to changing theorization of these key public ideas by academic feminists.

Numerous alternative and emerging forms of political participation seem now to be "working around" the state or at least outside the most direct avenues of state discipline. In such situations, minority group representation is often, of necessity, largely strategic and/ or symbolic. How do or could such forms of representation relate to more traditional modes of representation within the state, and on what is their democratic legitimacy based?

Answers to these questions are only hinted at in this volume, but contributors have helped to frame them more effectively. For example, Mark Warren suggests that, because the political, economic, and social institutional context of democratic participation has shifted so dramatically over the past generation, and because the constraints posed by an international capitalist political economy on national democratic sovereignty are so substantial, we are still a long way from working out the ways in which "decentred" and often single-issue political activism can mesh with traditional forms of representation. He also suggests that, while accountability of such new democratic exercises to the broad public is problematic, it isn't obviously more so than that of elected legislators and state administrators to the same citizens. Social complexity necessarily deepens the difficulties that political institutions and processes have in vindicating their democratic legitimacy, but he believes that it is unproductive and democratically stifling to place a larger burden of self-legitimation on the work of citizens in new "democratic spaces" than on the work of citizens and representatives in more familiar political spaces. It may be difficult to specify general criteria of democratic legitimacy for organizations and practices that are neither formally authorized by nor accountable to those for whom they claim to speak. Nonetheless, such formalistic requirements would be unreasonable in light of how unaccommodating existing representative structures often are to nondominant social and economic voices.

Melissa Williams is also inclined to give the benefit of the doubt on questions of democratic legitimacy to innovative democratic representation and participation. In her discussion of the "two-level game" that Aboriginal Canadians must engage in to discharge their civic obligations of shared fate within the Canadian polity, she contends that we should not reject innovative experiments in political representation on the ground that their accountability must meet standards that our existing representative institutions do not. Doing so would lead us to undermine the progress that justice requires in the relations between Aboriginal and non-Aboriginal Canadians. The same plea for experimentation with new representative mechanisms can be found in Susan Henders's exploration of tentative steps taken in the direction of "emancipatory minority autonomy" in China and Europe, steps that are in many ways not dependent on a solid national institutional home or validation by "host" regimes.

The other authors also offer helpful elements of an answer to this question. Peter Ives shows the potential for experimentation in the case of the European Union's language policies, while Greg Pyrcz raises the possibility that representatives' accountability to a regulative ideal can promote democratic autonomy for citizens in ways that their direct control of representatives may not always manage. Avigail Eisenberg proposes a set of guidelines for the use of referendums in situations where the tendency to understand equality as undifferentiated treatment dramatically increases the chance that legitimate minority rights will be abridged. Simone Chambers argues that overarching political legitimacy was enhanced in Canada due to both official and unofficial decisions to expand the range of groups speaking in their own voices in recent constitutional dialogues. Catherine Frost contends that, while citizens now invest referendums with great legitimacy, participatory deliberation will produce a fuller engagement of their considered judgments of what justice requires. Such democratic processes will possess a more lasting legitimacy in lesser tension with the requirements of social justice.

In her comparative study of feminist political action in Canada and Australia, Louise Chappell shows that a good deal of women's movement activity works around (or in spite of) what women see as a patriarchal state. However, the strategies chosen by feminist activists to affect public policies are highly sensitive to the particular characteristics of federal state structures in Canada and Australia. And, given the importance of the Charter of Rights and Freedoms to their equality agenda, Canadian women's groups are content to ground legitimacy for their contributions to public life at least partly in the more supportive normative home of Charter rights. They do so rather than seek legitimacy exclusively in the often antagonistic or indifferent environments of provincial and federal legislatures, where majority preferences within mainstream parties consistently trump feminists' rights preferences.

With all of this diversity in modes of citizenship, forms of participation, and minority rights challenges to majoritarian decision making, does our normative defence and practical co-ordination of representative practices still require some shared understandings about citizenship and democratic political community? Or does the search for too much common ground of shared citizenship simply extend the powers of majorities and/or elites against minorities and/or disadvantaged citizens?
Among the contributors to this volume, Jonathan Quong, Melissa Williams, Greg Pyrcz, and Simone Chambers most directly engage the question of whether defensible new approaches to representation rest on foundations of a demanding common citizenship. Quong and Williams lay out specific conditions and commitments of this citizenship, with Williams more inclined to justify a differentiated, additional dimension of citizenship for Aboriginal Canadians than Quong feels comfortable with. It is notable, however, that Williams still looks for a common footing for Aboriginal and non-Aboriginal citizenship in Canada: "citizenship as shared fate." Pyrcz blends his account of the citizen's commitments with a set of requirements for legislators, which crucially includes engagement in thought experiments about citizens' real preferences. In principle, "demanding deliberative democracy" finds a common civic footing for citizens and representatives alike in the "regulative ideal" that prescribes key procedural constraints on, and educational enhancements for, deliberation by both citizens and representatives. Chambers devotes most of her attention not to conditions and commitments prior to deliberation but to the sense in which increasingly inclusive deliberation achieves a community-binding and normatively significant increase in broad public support for inclusiveness in basic national dialogues. Common citizenship grows in spite of, not because of, a consensus on particular policy or constitutional issues. This occurs because citizens discover that democratic inclusiveness is a necessary condition of legitimate political outcomes. Chambers's position is broadly compatible with that of Frost in Chapter 3. Frost places a heavy emphasis on the transformative

capacity of participation and deliberation, even in "multicultural unions" that offer much evidence of stubborn, culturally entrenched opposition to resolution of minority rights questions.

Louise Chappell makes no normative case for or against a common citizenship; instead, her account of feminist approaches to the political opportunity structures presented by the Australian and Canadian federal systems shows that the women's movement sees the practical necessity of working with shared understandings about citizenship and democratic political community while also insisting on distinctive understandings of citizenship to accommodate women's difference. The challenge lies in figuring out what combination of appeals and demands, based on what combination of common and distinctive conceptions of citizenship, will work – and are normatively defensible – in specific institutional settings.

Avigail Eisenberg, Gerald Kernerman, Susan Henders, and Mark Warren all have serious reservations about searching for a common citizenship. For Eisenberg, the risk of doing so in referendums is that minority groups who need specific rights to protect them from the majority inclination to "build undivided political community" will likely be denied them in unmediated majority rule decisions such as referendum votes. Eisenberg believes that many minorities, especially ethnic minorities, have good reasons to worry that referendums will "activate communal values" inconsistent with minority preferences or even ways of life. Kernerman also worries that, if recent Canadian constitutional reform experience is any guide, the search for a nation-binding equality is almost certain to ignore or misrepresent the preferences, interests, and identities of distinctive groups. This search is also likely to gloss over intragroup differences, as existed among women's movement organizations and leaders during the 1992 Charlottetown Accord referendum campaign.

Susan Henders offers reasons for suspicion about the willingness of most states to fairly acknowledge or facilitate the self-governing needs of national minorities. There is just too much historical and current evidence that most states stifle their minorities' aspirations for even modest degrees of institutionally grounded autonomy. Henders thus doubts whether national minorities should put considerable effort into finding common bases for citizenship with majorities prone to dominate them. She suggests that innovative expressions of self-governance through unbounded communities may be one part of the answer.

Finally, Mark Warren suggests that social complexity, powerful global economic forces, and a decentred civic division of labour have rendered the search for a common citizenship largely quixotic. We should not idealize citizenship or reify representation in democratic spaces that are either thoroughly compromised or simply no longer available to most of us. Warren articulates the vocation of democratic theory in terms that all contributors to this volume support in one way or another: democratic theory should discover and theoretically prepare new democratic spaces, guided by a dynamic conception of complex equality among differentially empowered citizens.

Many other themes and arguments in this volume will stimulate creative and critical reflection on democratic representation. In this Conclusion, I have only scratched the surface of the authors' contributions. On their behalf, I invite readers to join in the dialogues initiated here and to explore the ways in which representation and its discontents will remain central to the theory and practice of contemporary democracy.

Notes
1 Williams (1998), 239.
2 See Warren (2000) for a more complete account of the "democratic associational ecologies" that provide the context for such associational activity. His analysis is highly suggestive of the opportunities that a diverse associational life in civil society afford for representation of social interests and identities into the realm of policy development. This account also carefully indentifies the obstacles that skewed social resource distributions and associational structures themselves place in front of such democratization of policy development.
3 See Williams (2000) for a more general account of the potential relationship between deliberative and representative processes and institutions.
4 For a related approach to "democratic deliberation within," which parts company with Pyrcz on the question of the value of "thick" political engagement by citizens to deliberative processes, but shares his relatively low level of concern with accountability problems in deliberative democracy, see Goodin (2003). This book was published one year after Pyrcz's paper was initially presented.
5 See Goodin (2003).
6 See, for example, Blais and Gidengil (1991), chs. 2 and 3; Blais et al. (2002), 151-52; and Young (1999).
7 Manin (1997), ch. 5
8 The public debate over the terms of the Charlottetown Accord that preceded a national Canadian referendum on this constitutional reform package was arguably a reasonably successful reconciliation of deliberation, direct democracy, and representation. See Chambers (1998) and her chapter in this volume.

References

Abizadeh, Arash. 2002. "Does Liberal Democracy Presuppose a Cultural Nation? Four Arguments." *American Political Science Review* 96: 495-509.
Aboriginal Peoples' Commission, Liberal Party of Canada. 1995. "The Importance of the Aboriginal Vote." <http://www.liberal.ca/commissions/apc/whyvote/whyvote.asp> (15 December 2003).
Ackerman, Bruce. 1998. *We the People: Transformations*. Cambridge, MA: Harvard University Press.
Ackerman, Bruce, and James Fishkin. 2002. "Deliberation Day." *Journal of Political Philosophy* 10: 129-52.
Alakayak et al. v. State of Alaska.
Alfred, Taiaiake. 1999. *Peace, Power, Righteousness*. Toronto: Oxford University Press.
–. 2000. "Who You Calling Canadian?" *Windspeaker* (September). <http://www.ammsa.com/windspeaker/windguest2000.html#anchor3129870> (accessed 21 May 2002).
Amnesty International. 2001. *Amnesty International Report, 2001*. London: Amnesty International Publications.
Anderson, Alan, and James Frideres. 1981. *Ethnicity in Canada: Theoretical Perspectives*. Toronto: Butterworths.
Anthias, F., and N. Yuval Davis, eds. 1989. *Woman – Nation – State*. London: Macmillan.
Arendt, Hannah. 1963. *On Revolution*. New York: Viking Press.
Arieli-Horowitz, Dana. 2002. "Referenda in a Post-Consociational Democracy: The Case of Israel." *Israel Affairs* 8, 1/2: 146-62.
Arscott, Jane, Pauline L. Rankin, and Jill Vickers. N.d. "Canadian Experiments with State Feminism: Status of Women Machinery in a Federal State." Unpublished essay.
Bachrach, Peter, and Morton S. Baratz. 1962. "Two Faces of Power." *American Political Science Review* 56, 4: 947-52.
Bakvis, Herman, and William Chandler, eds. 1987. *Federalism and the Role of the State*. Toronto: University of Toronto Press.
Barber, Benjamin. 1984. *Strong Democracy: Participatory Politics for a New Age*. Berkeley: University of California Press.
Barbour, Stephen. 1996. "Language and National Identity in Europe: Theoretical and Practical Problems." In *Language, Culture, and Communications in Contemporary Europe*, ed. Charlotte Hoffmann, 28-45. Clevedon: Multilingual Matters.
Barker, Ernest. 1942. *Reflections on Government*. London: Oxford University Press.
Barnard, Frederick. 2001. *Democratic Legitimacy*. Montreal: McGill-Queen's University Press.
Barry, Brian. 1999. *Culture and Equality: An Egalitarian Critique of Multiculturalism*. Cambridge, MA: Harvard University Press.
"B.C. Liberals May Prove More Flexible than Thought: Post-Referendum Treaty Rhetoric Sounds Promising." 2002. *Vancouver Sun* 23 July: A14.

Beck, Ulrich. 1997. *The Reinvention of Politics: Rethinking Modernity in the Global Social Order*. Trans. M. Ritter. Cambridge, UK: Polity Press.
Beetham, David. 1991. *The Legitimation of Power*. Atlantic Highlands, NJ: Humanities Press International.
Bell, Daniel A., and Avner de-Shalit, eds. 2003. *Forms of Justice: Critical Perspectives on David Miller's Political Philosophy*. Oxford: Rowman and Littlefield.
Bell, David A. 1995. "Lingua Populi, Lingua Dei: Language, Religion, and the Origins of French Revolutionary Nationalism." *American Historical Review* 100: 1403-37.
Bell, Derrick A., Jr. 1978. "The Referendum: Democracy's Barrier to Racial Equality." *Washington Law Review* 54: 1-28.
Bellamy, Richard. 1999. *Liberalism and Pluralism: Towards a Politics of Compromise*. New York: Routledge.
Benhabib, Seyla, ed. 1996. *Democracy and Difference: Contesting the Boundaries of the Political*. Princeton: Princeton University Press.
Berlin, Isaiah. 1976. "Herder and the Enlightenment." In *Vico and Herder*, 143-216. London: Hogarth.
Berman, Antoine. 1992. *The Experience of the Foreign*. Trans. S. Heyvaert. Albany: State University of New York Press.
Bernard, F.M. 1965. *Herder's Social and Political Thought*. Oxford: Clarendon Press.
Berry, Jeffrey M. 1999. *The New Liberalism and the Rising Power of Citizen Groups*. Washington, DC: Brookings Institution Press.
Bibby, Reginald. 1990. *Mosaic Madness: The Poverty and Potential of Life in Canada*. Toronto: Stoddart Publishing.
Bissoondath, Neil. 1994. *Selling Illusions: The Cult of Multiculturalism in Canada*. Toronto: Penguin Books.
Bister-Broosen, Helga, and Roland Willenmyns. 1999. "Europe's Linguistic Diversity and the Language Policy of the European Union." In *Interdigitations*, ed. Gerald F. Can, Wayne Harbert, and Lihua Zhang, 713-22. New York: Peter Lang.
Black, Ian. 2002a. "EU Learns to Conduct Its Business with an English Accent." *Guardian Weekly* 4-10 April: 6.
–. 2002b. "European Parliament Minds Its Languages." *Guardian* 20 November: 15.
Blais, André, and Elisabeth Gidengil. 1991. *Making Representative Democracy Work: The Views of Canadians*. Research Studies 17, Royal Commission on Electoral Reform and Party Financing. Toronto: Dundurn Press.
Blais, André, Elisabeth Gidengil, Richard Nadeau, and Neil Nevitte. 2002. *Anatomy of a Liberal Victory: Making Sense of the Vote in the 2000 Canadian Election*. Peterborough: Broadview Press.
Blattberg, Charles. 2003. *Shall We Dance? A Patriotic Politics for Canada*. Montreal: McGill-Queen's University Press.
Blunden, Brian. 1998. "Culture, Commerce, and the Content Industries." Paper presented at European Telematics: Advancing the Information Society, Barcelona, 4-7 February.
Bob, Sam et al. v. British Columbia. 15 May 2002 BCSC 733. Docket L021077. Registry: Vancouver.
Bobbio, Norberto. 1987. *The Future of Democracy*. Trans. Roger Griffen. Minneapolis: University of Minnesota Press.
Bogdanor, Vernon. 1997. "Western Europe." In *Referendums around the World: The Growing Use of Direct Democracy*, ed. David Butler and Austin Ranney, 24-97. Washington, DC: American Enterprise Institute.
Bohman, James. 1999. "Democracy as Inquiry, Inquiry as Democratic: Pragmatism, Social Science, and the Cognitive Division of Labor." *American Journal of Political Science* 43: 590-607.
Bohman, John, and William Rehg. 1997. *Deliberative Democracy: Essays on Reason and Politics*. Cambridge, UK: Cambridge University Press.
Bolin, Brett, Sarah Croake, Maya Lagana, Brady Lay, Luke Mills, and Julia Williams. 2002. "Tracing the Regional Voice: Evaluating the Effectiveness of Routes for Multilevel Policy-Making," 31 May. <http://www.acad.carleton.edu/curricular/POSC/Maastric/reportCatalonia.pdf> (accessed 12 February 2003).

Borrows, John. 1992. "A Genealogy of Law: Inherent Sovereignty and First Nations Self-Government." *Osgoode Hall Law Journal* 30: 291-353.
–. 1997. "Wampum at Niagara: The Royal Proclamation, Canadian Legal History, and Self-Government." In *Aboriginal and Treaty Rights in Canada,* ed. Michael Asch, 155-72. Vancouver: UBC Press.
–. 2002. *Recovering Canada: The Resurgence of Indigenous Law.* Toronto: University of Toronto Press.
Bourdieu, Pierre. 1991. *Language and Symbolic Power.* Trans. Gino Raymond and Matthew Adamson. Cambridge, MA: Harvard University Press.
Boyer, Patrick. 1992. *Direct Democracy in Canada: The History and Future of Referendums.* Toronto: Dundurn Press.
Brady, Henry E., and Cynthia S. Kaplan. 1994. "Eastern Europe and the Former Soviet Union." In *Referendums around the World,* ed. David Butler and Austin Ranney, 174-217. Washington, DC: American Enterprise Institute.
Brennan, Deborah. 1994. *The Politics of Australian Childcare: From Philanthropy to Feminism.* Cambridge, UK: Cambridge University Press.
Burgen, Stephen. 2003. "Barcelona Faces a New Challenge of Diversity." *Times* 23 April: "Features," 5.
Busque, Ginette. 1991. "Why Women Should Care about Constitutional Reform." In *Conversations among Friends: Women and Constitutional Reform,* ed. David Schneiderman, 13-17. Edmonton: Centre for Constitutional Studies, University of Alberta.
Butler, David, and Austin Ranney, eds. 1994. *Referendums around the World: The Growing Use of Direct Democracy.* Washington, DC: American Enterprise Institute.
Cairns, Alan. 1995. "Reflections on the Political Purposes of the Charter." In *Reconfigurations: Canadian Citizenship and Constitutional Change: Selected Essays by Alan C. Cairns,* ed. Douglas Williams, 194-215. Toronto: McClelland and Stewart.
–. 2000. *Citizens Plus: Aboriginal People and the Canadian State.* Vancouver: UBC Press.
Callan, Eamonn. 1997. *Creating Citizens: Political Education and Liberal Democracy.* Oxford: Clarendon Press.
Campbell, David. 1998. *National Deconstruction: Violence, Identity, and Justice in Bosnia.* Minneapolis: University of Minnesota Press.
Carens, Joseph H. 2000. *Culture, Citizenship, and Community: A Contextual Exploration of Justice as Evenhandedness.* Oxford: Oxford University Press.
Carmichael, D.J.C., Tom Pocklington, and Greg Pyrcz, eds. 2000. *Democracy Rights and Well-Being in Canada.* 2nd ed. Toronto: Harcourt Brace.
Carson, Lorna. 2003. *Multilingualism in Europe: A Case Study.* Brussels: Peter Lang.
Chambers, Simone. 1998. "Contract or Conversation: Theoretical Lessons from the Canadian Constitutional Crisis." *Politics and Society* 26, 1: 143-72.
–. 2001a. "Constitutional Referendums and Democratic Deliberation." In *Referendum Democracy,* ed. Matthew Mendelsohn and Andrew Parkin, 231-55. London: Palgrave.
–. 2001b. "New Constitutionalism: Democracy, Habermas, and Canadian Exceptionalism." In *Canadian Political Philosophy: Contemporary Reflections,* ed. Ronald Beiner and Wayne Norman, 63-77. Toronto: Oxford University Press.
Chan, Kwok Bun. 1997. "A Family Affaire: Migration, Dispersal, and the Emergent Identity of the Chinese Cosmopolitan." *Diaspora* 6, 2: 195-213.
Chappell, Louise. 2001. "Federalism and Social Policy: The Case of Domestic Violence." *Australian Journal of Public Administration* 60, 1: 36-46.
–. 2002. *Gendering Government: Feminist Engagement with the State in Australia and Canada.* Vancouver: UBC Press.
Charlottetown Accord. 1991. "Consensus Report on the Constitution." <http://www.solon.org/Constitutions/Canada/English/Proposals/CharlottetownConsensus.html> (accessed 21 May 2002).
Charlottetown Accord. 1992. Draft Legal Text (9 October).
Chase, Bob. 1997. "Locke and Cultural Relativism." *Interpretation* 25, 1: 59-90.
Cheung, Jimmy, and Klaudia Lee. 2003. "Turnout Piles the Pressure on Tung Administration." *South China Morning Post* 2 July, <http://www.scmp.com>.
Cohen, Joshua. 1986. "An Epistemic Conception of Democracy." *Ethics* 97: 26-38.

–. 1995. "Reflections on Rousseau: Autonomy and Democracy." *Philosophy and Public Affairs* 15, 3: 275-97.

–. 1996. "Procedure and Substance in Deliberative Democracy." In *Democracy and Difference*, ed. Seyla Benhabib, 95-119. Princeton: Princeton University Press.

Cohen, Joshua, and Joel Rogers. 1995. "Secondary Associations and Democratic Governance." In *Associations and Democracy*, ed. Joshua Cohen and Joel Rogers, 7-98. New York: Verso.

Coleman, William D. 1987. "Federalism and Interest Group Organization." In *Federalism and the Role of the State*, ed. Herman Bakvis and William M. Chandler, 171-87. Toronto: University of Toronto Press.

Connolly, William. 1991. *Identity/Difference: Democratic Negotiations of Political Paradox*. Ithaca: Cornell University Press.

Corbett, David. 1990. "Australia's States and Canada's Provinces: The Pace and Patterns of Administrative Reform." In *Dynamics of Australian Public Management: Selected Essays*, ed. Alexander Kouzmin and Nicholas Scott, 294-310. Melbourne: Macmillan.

Coulmas, Florian, ed. 1991. *A Language Policy for the European Community*. Berlin: Mouton de Gruyter.

Coulombe, Pierre. 2000. "Citizenship and Official Bilingualism in Canada." In *Citizenship in Diverse Societies*, ed. Will Kymlicka and Wayne Norman, 273-93. Oxford: Oxford University Press.

"Council Decision of 21 November 1996 on the Adoption of a Multiannual Programme to Promote Linguistic Diversity of the Community in the Information Society." 1996. *Official Journal of the European Communities* L306 28 November: 40.

Cox, Eva. 1995. *A Truly Civil Society: 1995 Boyer Lectures*. Sydney: ABC Books.

Cox, Robert. 1981. "Social Forces, States, and World Orders: Beyond International Relations." *Millennium* 10, 2: 126-55.

Cronin, Thomas E. 1989. *Direct Democracy: The Politics of Initiative, Referendum, and Recall*. Cambridge: Harvard University Press.

Crosby, Ned. 1995. "Citizen Juries: One Solution for Difficult Environmental Questions." In *Fairness and Competence in Citizen Participation*, ed. Ortwin Renn, Thomas Webler, and Peter Wiedemann, 157-74. Boston: Kluwer Academic Publishers.

Crozier, Michael, Samuel Huntington, and Joji Watanuki, eds. 1975. *The Crisis of Democracy*. New York: New York University Press.

Cullen, Richard. 1992. "Constitutional Federalism and Natural Resources." In *Comparative Political Studies: Australia and Canada*, ed. Malcolm Alexander and Brian Galligan, 84-96. Melbourne: Pitman.

Dahl, Robert. 1998. *On Democracy*. New Haven: Yale University Press.

Dahl, Robert, and Edward R. Tufte. 1973. *Size and Democracy*. Stanford: Stanford University Press.

Dalai Lama. 1988. "Address to Members of the European Parliament, Strasbourg, 15 June." Dharamsala: Tibetan Government in Exile, <http://www.tibet.com/Proposal/strasbourg.html> (accessed 21 November 2003).

–. 1989a. "His Holiness the Dalai Lama's Nobel Prize Acceptance Speech, University Aula, Oslo," 10 December. Dharamsala: Tibetan Government in Exile, <http://www.tibet.com/DL/nobelaccept.html> (accessed 21 November 2003).

–. 1989b. "His Holiness the Dalai Lama's Nobel Lecture, University Aula, Oslo," 11 December. Dharamsala: Tibetan Government in Exile, <http://www.tibet.com/DL/nobellecture.html> (accessed 21 November 2003).

–. 1991. "Address to the Members of the United States Congress in the Rotunda of the Capital Hill in Washington, D.C.," 8 April. Dharamsala: Tibetan Government in Exile, <http://www.tibet.com/DL/rotunda.html> (accessed 21 November 2003).

–. 1992a. "His Holiness the Dalai Lama's Vision for a Free Tibet," 26 February. Dharamsala: Tibetan Government in Exile, <http://www.tibet.com/future.html> (accessed 21 November 2003).

–. 1997. "Speech of His Holiness the Dalai Lama at the 'Forum 2000' Conference, Prague, Czech Republic," 3-7 September. Dharamsala: Tibetan Government in Exile, <http://www.tibet.com/DL/forum-2000.html> (accessed 21 November 2003).

–. 1999. "Buddhism, Asian Values, and Democracy." *Journal of Democracy* 10, 1: 3-7.

Dalton, Russell. 1999. "Political Support in Advanced Industrial Democracies." In *Critical Citizens: Global Support for Democratic Governance*, ed. Pippa Norris, 57-77. Oxford: Oxford University Press.

Danese, G. 1998. "Transnational Collective Action in Europe: The Case of Migrants in Italy and Spain." *Journal of Ethnic and Migration Studies* 24, 4: 715-33.

Day, Richard J.F. 2000. *Multiculturalism and the History of Canadian Diversity*. Toronto: University of Toronto Press.

December 18. 2003. "Qui d'autre soutient cette campagne?" December 18. <http://december18.net/f-UNconvention.htm> (accessed 21 November 2003).

Delgado-Moreira, Juan. 2000. "Cohesion and Citizenship in EU Cultural Policy." *Journal of Common Market Studies* 38, 3: 449-70.

De Swaan, Abram. 1993. "The Evolving European Language System." *International Political Science Review* 14, 3: 241-56.

–. 1999. "The Constellation of Languages." In *Which Languages for Europe? Report of the Conference Held in Oegstgeest*, 13-24. Oegstgeest: European Cultural Foundation.

Dion, Stephan. 2001. "The Supreme Court's Reference on Unilateral Secession: A Turning Point in Canadian History." In *Canadian Political Philosophy*, ed. Ronald Beiner and Wayne Norman, 311-17. Toronto: Oxford University Press.

Dobrowolsky, Alexandra. 2000. *The Politics of Pragmatism: Women, Representation, and Constitutionalism in Canada*. Toronto: Oxford University Press.

Donovan, Todd, and Shaun Bowler. 1997. "Direct Democracy and Minority Rights: Opinions on Anti-Gay and Lesbian Ballot Initiatives." In *Anti-Gay Rights: Assessing Voter Initiatives*, ed. Stephanie L. Witt and Suzanne McCorkle, 107-26. Westport: Praeger.

–. 1998. "Direct Democracy and Minority Rights: An Extension." *American Journal of Political Science* 42: 1020-24.

Dowse, Sara. 1984. "The Bureaucrat as Usurer." In *Unfinished Business: Social Justice for Women in Australia*, ed. Dorothy Broom, 150-66. Sydney: George Allen and Unwin.

Dryzek, John. 1990. *Discursive Democracy*. Cambridge, UK: Cambridge University Press.

–. 1996. *Democracy in Capitalist Times: Ideals, Limits, and Struggles*. Oxford: Oxford University Press.

Dumont, Micheline. 1992. "Origins of the Women's Movement in Quebec." In *Challenging Times: The Women's Movement in Canada and the United States*, ed. Constance Backhouse and David Flaherty, 72-93. Kingston: McGill-Queen's University Press.

Eberle, Christopher J. 2002. *Religious Convictions in Liberal Politics*. Cambridge: Cambridge University Press.

Ebrahim, Hassan. 1998. *The Soul of a Nation: Constitution-Making in South Africa*. Cape Town: Oxford University Press.

Eco, Umberto. 1995. *The Search for the Perfect Language*. Trans. James Fentress. Oxford: Blackwell.

Eisenberg, Avigail. 1995. *Reconstructing Political Pluralism*. Albany: State University of New York Press.

–. 2001. "The Medium Is the Message: How Referendums Lead Us to Understand Equality." In *Referendum Democracy: Citizens, Elites, and Deliberation in Referendum Campaigns*, ed. Matthew Mendelsohn and Andrew Parkin, 147-68. New York: Palgrave.

Elections BC. 2002. *Report of the Chief Electoral Officer on the Treaty Negotiations Referendum*, 9 September. <http://www.elections.bc.ca/referendum/refreportfinal.pdf>.

Elster, Jon. 1986. "The Market and the Forum: Three Varieties of Political Theory." In *Foundations of Social Choice Theory*, ed. Jon Elster and Aanund Hylland, 103-32. Cambridge, UK: Cambridge University Press.

–, ed. 1998. *Deliberative Democracy*. Cambridge, UK: Cambridge University Press.

"English Still on the March." 2001. *Economist* 24 February: 50-51.

European Monitoring Centre on Racism and Xenophobia. 2001. *Diversity and Equality for Europe: Annual Report 2000*. Vienna: European Monitoring Centre on Racism and Xenophobia.

European Union Migrants' Forum. 1995. "Proposals for the Revision of the Treaty on European Union at the Intergovernmental Conference of 1996," May. <http://www.

europa.eu.int/en/agenda/igc-home/instdoc/ngo/migrant/htm> (accessed 21 November 2003).
Evans v. Romer, 854 P. 2d 1270 (Colo. 1993), p. 1.
"Executive Summary." 2001. *Eurobarometer Report 54: Europeans and Languages*, 1 (15 February). <http://europa.eu.int/comm/public_opinion/archives/special.htm> (accessed 21 November 2003).
Fanning, Ronan. 1983. *Independent Ireland*. Dublin: Helicon.
Farer, Tom J. 1993. "The UN and Human Rights: At the End of the Beginning." In *United Nations, Divided World: The UN's Roles in International Relations*, ed. Adam Roberts and Benedict Kingsbury, 240-96. Oxford: Clarendon.
Feinberg, Walter. 1998. *Common Schools/Uncommon Identities: National Unity and Cultural Difference*. New Haven: Yale University Press.
Ferguson, Ann. 1991. *Sexual Democracy*. Boulder: Westview.
Fishkin, James. 1991. *Democracy and Deliberation: New Directions for Democratic Reform*. New Haven: Yale University Press.
–. 1997. *The Voice of the People*. New Haven: Yale University Press.
Fishkin, James, and Robert Luskin. 2000. "The Quest for Deliberative Democracy." In *Democratic Innovation: Deliberation, Representation, and Association*, ed. Michael Saward, 17-28. New York: Routledge.
Fishman, Joshua. 1994. "On the Limits of Ethnolinguistic Democracy." In *Linguistic Human Rights*, ed. Tove Skutnabb-Kangas and Robert Phillipson, 49-61. Berlin: Mouton de Gruyter.
Fisk, Malcolm. 1996. "Recognising the Rights of Smaller Language Groups." *Planning Practice and Research* 11, 2: 177-90.
Flask, Carmel, and Betty Hounslow. N.d. "Government Intervention and Right-Wing Attacks on Feminist Services." *Scarlet Woman* 11: 11-21.
Føllesdal, Andreas. 1998. "Third Country Nationals as European Citizens: The Case Defended." Paper presented to the Workshop on Migrants, Minorities, and New Forms of Citizenship in the European Union. European University Institute, Florence, March.
Foster, R.F. 1988. *Modern Ireland 1600-1972*. London: Allen Lane.
Fraerman, Alicia. 2003. "Aznar Moves to Beef Up Immigration Law." *Inter Press Service* 19 May, <http://www.ipsnews.net> (accessed 21 November 2003).
Fraser, Nancy. 1993. "Rethinking the Public Sphere: A Contribution to the Critique of Actual Existing Democracy." In *Habermas and the Public Sphere*, ed. Craig Calhoun, 109-42. Cambridge, UK: Cambridge University Press.
Freedom House. 2000. *Democracy's Century: A Survey of Global Political Change in the 20th Century*. New York: Freedom House.
Freeman, Alan. 2002. "Dutch Voters Rally to Right in Ousting Government." *Globe and Mail* 16 May: A14.
Freeman, Samuel. 2003. "Introduction." In *The Cambridge Companion to Rawls*, ed. Samuel Freeman, 1-61. Cambridge, UK: Cambridge University Press.
Frey, Bruno S., and Lorenz Goette. 1998. "Does the Popular Vote Destroy Civil Rights?" *American Journal of Political Science* 42: 1342-48.
Frideres, James S., and René R. Gadazc. 2001. *Aboriginal Peoples in Canada*. Toronto: Pearson.
Friedlander, Robert A. 1981. "Autonomy and the Thirteen Colonies: Was the American Revolution Really Necessary." In *Models of Autonomy*, ed. Yoram Dinstein, 135-48. New Brunswick, NJ: Transaction Books; Faculty of Law, Tel Aviv University.
Frye, Timothy M. 1992. "Ethnicity, Sovereignty, and Transitions from Non-Democratic Rule." *Rethinking Nationalism and Sovereignty* (Special issue), *Journal of International Affairs* 45, 2: 599-623.
Fundació CEREM. 1998. "Report: The Participation of Immigrants and Ethnic Minorities in the European Cities, LIA Partnership (Local Partnership Integration Action), Final Version, Fundació CEREM, Adjuntamet de Barcelona, November." <http://www.lia-partnership.org/ftp/partic_en.doc> (accessed 21 November 2003).
Fung, Archon, and Erik Olin Wright, eds. 2003. *Deepening Democracy: Innovations in Empowered Participatory Governance*. New York: Verso.

Gagnon, Alain-G. 1995. "The Political Uses of Federalism." In *New Trends in Canadian Federalism,* ed. François Rocher and Miriam Smith, 23-44. Peterborough: Broadview Press.

—. 2001. "The Moral Foundation of Asymmetrical Federalism: A Normative Exploration of the Case of Quebec and Canada." In *Multinational Democracies,* ed. Alain-G. Gagnon and James Tully, 319-37. Cambridge, UK: Cambridge University Press.

Gagnon, Christiane. 1997. "Bloc Québécois: Integration Rather than Multiculturalism." In *The Battle over Multiculturalism: Does It Help or Hinder Canadian Unity?* ed. Andrew Cordozo and Louis Musto, 42-45. Vol. 1. Ottawa: PSI Publishing.

Galligan, Brian. 1990. "The Distinctiveness of Australian Federalism." In *Dynamics in Australian Public Management: Selected Essays,* ed. Anander Kouzmin and Nicholas Scott, 17-28. Melbourne: Macmillan.

—. 1995. *A Federal Republic.* Cambridge, UK: Cambridge University Press.

Galston, William. 1991. *Liberal Purposes: Goods, Virtues, and Diversity in the Liberal State.* Cambridge, UK: Cambridge University Press.

—. 2002. *Liberal Pluralism: The Implications of Value Pluralism for Political Theory and Practice.* Cambridge, UK: Cambridge University Press.

Gamble, Barbara. 1997. "Putting Civil Rights to a Popular Vote." *American Journal of Political Science* 41: 245-69.

Garcia, Caterina. 2001. "Les Stratégies internationales de la Catalogne: Nationalisme politique et pragmatism économique." In *Les Nouvelles relations internationales,* ed. Robert Comeau, 99-109. Montréal: Comeau et Nadeau.

Geddes, Andrew. 2000. "Lobbying for Migrant Inclusion in the European Union: New Opportunities for Transnational Activism." *Journal of European Public Policy* 7, 4: 632-49.

Giddens, Anthony. 1991. *Modernity and Self-Identity: Self and Society in the Late Modern Age.* Stanford: Stanford University Press.

Gillespie, James A. 1995. "New Federalisms." In *Developments in Australian Politics,* ed. J. Brett, J. Gillespie, and M. Goot, 60-87. Melbourne: Macmillan.

Gloppen, Siri. 1997. *South Africa: The Battle over the Constitution.* Aldershot, UK: Ashgate.

Gómez, Rosa Aparicio, and Andrés Tornos. 2000. "'Immigration and Integration Policy': Towards an Analysis of Spanish Integration Policy for Immigrants and CIMs." EFF-NATIS Working Paper 32, Instituto Universitario de Estudios sobre Migraciones, Universidad Pontificia Comillas de Madrid, January (manuscript).

Goodin, Robert E. 1986. "Laundering Preferences." In *Foundations of Social Choice Theory,* ed. John Elster and Aanund Hylland, 75-101. Cambridge, UK: Cambridge University Press.

—. 2003. *Reflective Democracy.* Oxford: Oxford University Press.

Gramsci, Antonio. 1975. *Quaderni del Carcere.* Ed. Valentino Gerratana. Vol. 3. Turin: Einaudi.

—. 1985. *Selections from Cultural Writings.* Trans. William Boelhower. Ed. David Forgacs and Geoffrey Nowell-Smith. Cambridge, MA: Harvard University Press.

Grand Council of the Crees (Eeyou Estchee). 1998. Factum of the Intervenor, Grand Council of the Crees (Eeyou Estchee). *Reference Re: Secession of Quebec,* 1998 S.C.C.

Gray, Gwendolyn. 1995. *Federalism and Health Policy: The Development of Health Systems in Canada and Australia.* Toronto: University of Toronto Press.

—. 1998. "How Australia Came to Have a National Women's Health Policy." *International Journal of Health Services* 28, 1: 107-25.

Grimm, Dieter. 1997. "Does Europe Need a Constitution?" In *The Question of Europe,* ed. Peter Gowan and Perry Anderson, 239-58. London: Verso.

Gubbins, Paul. 1996. "Sense and Pence: An Alternative Language Policy for Europe." In *Language, Culture, and Communications in Contemporary Europe,* ed. Charlotte Hoffmann, 124-31. Clevedon: Multilingual Matters.

Guiral, Antoine, and Didier Hassoux. 2003. "La Parité: Nouveau Graal de l'UMP en Corse." *Libération* 10 July. <http://www.liberation.com>.

Gutmann, Amy, and Dennis Thompson. 1996. *Democracy and Disagreement.* Cambridge, MA: Harvard University Press.

—. 2000. "Why Deliberative Democracy Is Different." In *Democracy,* ed. Ellen Frankel Paul, Fred D. Miller, Jr., and Jeffrey Paul, 161-80. Cambridge, UK: Cambridge University Press.

Gwyn, Richard. 1995. *Nationalism without Walls: The Unbearable Lightness of Being Canadian.* Toronto: McClelland and Stewart.
Habermas, Jürgen. 1990. *Moral Consciousness and Communicative Action.* Trans. Christian Lenhardt and Shierry Weber Nicholsen. Cambridge, MA: MIT Press.
–. 1996. *Between Facts and Norms: Contributions to a Discourse Theory of Law and Democracy.* Cambridge, MA: MIT Press.
–. 1997. "Reply to Grimm." In *The Question of Europe,* ed. Peter Gowan and Perry Anderson, 259-64. London: Verso.
–. 1998. "The European Nation-State: On the Past and Future of Sovereignty and Citizenship." In *The Inclusion of the Other: Studies in Political Theory.* Cambridge, MA: MIT Press.
–. 2000. "Crossing Globalization's Valley of Tears." *New Perspective Quarterly* 17, 4: 51-58.
–. 2001a. *The Postnational Constellation.* Trans. Max Pensky. Cambridge, MA: MIT Press.
–. 2001b. "Why Europe Needs a Constitution." *New Left Review* 11: 5-26.
Hajnal, Zoltan, and Hugh Louch. 2001. *Are There Winners and Losers? Race, Ethnicity, and California's Initiative Process.* San Francisco: Public Policy Institute.
Harpur, Tim. 1999. "MP Sorry for 'Wisecrack': Reform Leader Won't Discipline Jay Hill over Racist Comment." *Toronto Star* 30 October: A16.
Harvey, David. 1989. *The Condition of Post-Modernity.* Oxford: Basil Blackwell.
Healy, Judith. 1991. "Community Service Programs." In *Intergovernmental Relations and Public Policy,* ed. Brian Galligan, Owen Hughes, and Cliff Walsh, 188-213. Sydney: George Allen and Unwin.
Heisler, Martin O. 1990. "Ethnicity and Ethnic Relations in the Modern West." In *Conflict and Peacemaking in Multiethnic Societies,* ed. Joseph V. Montville, 21-52. Lexington, MA: Lexington Books.
Held, David. 1995. *Democracy and the Global Order: From the Modern State to Cosmopolitan Governance.* Stanford: Stanford University Press.
Helfer, Martha. 1990. "Herder, Fichte, and Humboldt's 'Thinking and Speaking.'" In *Herder Today,* ed. Kurt Mueller-Vollmer, 367-81. Berlin: de Gruyter.
Henders, Susan J. 1997. "Cantonisation: Historical Paths to Territorial Autonomy for Regional Cultural Communities." *Nations and Nationalism* 3, 4: 521-40.
–. 1999. "Special Status Regions: The Territorial Accommodation of Cultural Difference." DPhil diss., Oxford University.
–. 2000. "Region-States and the World: China Pushes the Envelope." *Policy Options* 21, 1: 88-89.
–. 2001. "So What if It's Not a Gamble? Post-Westphalian Politics in Macau." *Pacific Affairs* 74, 3: 342-60.
–. Forthcoming. "Ecological Self-Government: Beyond Individualistic Paths to Indigenous and Minority Autonomy." *Journal of Human Rights.*
Hirst, Paul Q. 1989. *The Pluralist Theory of the State: Selected Writings of G.D.H. Cole, J.N. Figgis, and H.J. Laski.* London: Routledge.
–. 1994. *Associative Democracy: New Forms of Economic and Social Governance.* Amherst: University of Massachusetts Press.
Hirst, Paul Q., and Veit-Michael Bader, eds. 2001. *Associative Democracy: The Real Third Way.* London: Frank Cass.
Holmes, Stephen. 1993. "Gag Rules or the Politics of Omission." In *Constitutionalism and Democracy,* ed. Jon Elster and Rune Slagstad, 19-58. Cambridge, UK: Cambridge University Press.
Hong Kong Special Administrative Region (HKSAR). 2003. "Treaties that Are in Force and Are Applicable to the HKSAR." Hong Kong: Hong Kong SAR Government, <http://www.info.gov.hk/info/exaffa.htm#annex2> (accessed 21 November 2003).
Honig, Bonnie. 1996. "Difference, Dilemmas, and the Politics of Home." In *Democracy and Difference: Contesting the Boundaries of the Political,* ed. Seyla Benhabib, 257-77. Princeton: Princeton University Press.
Horowitz, Asher. 1987. *Rousseau, Nature, and History.* Toronto: University of Toronto Press.
"How to Undermine Any Treaty Talks." 2002. *Globe and Mail* 5 July: A1.

Hurley, James Ross. 1997. "Executive Federalism." In *Public Administration and Public Management in Canada,* ed. Jacques Bourgault, Maurice Demers, and Cynthia Williams, 113-41. Sainte-Foy, PQ: Les Publications du Québec.
Ibbitson, John. 2001. "Get Set for BC Referendum Ride." *Globe and Mail* 18 May: A16.
Ignatieff, Michael. 2000. *The Rights Revolution.* Toronto: Anansi.
Inglehart, Ronald. 1997. *Modernization and Postmodernization: Cultural, Economic, and Political Change in 43 Societies.* Princeton: Princeton University Press.
–. 1999. "Postmodernism Erodes Respect for Authority, but Increases Support for Democracy." In *Critical Citizens: Global Support for Democratic Governance,* ed. Pippa Norris, 236-56. Oxford: Oxford University Press.
International Convention on the Protection of the Rights of All Migrant Workers and Members of Their Families. 2003. <http://www.december18.net/Unconvention.htm> (accessed 1 August 2003).
Ip, Regina. 2001. "How Security Helps Business." Speech by the Hong Kong SAR Secretary of Security to the Hong Kong Institute of Surveyors, 8 June. Hong Kong: Hong Kong SAR Government, <http://www.info.gov.hk/gia/general/200106/08/0608203.htm> (accessed 2 November 2002).
Irving, Helen. 1994. "A Gendered Constitution? Women, Federation, and Heads of Power." *Western Australia Law Review* 24: 186-98.
Ives, Peter. 1997. "The Grammar of Hegemony." *Left History* 5, 1: 85-104. Reprinted in *Antonio Gramsci: Critical Assessments,* vol. 2, ed. James Martin, 319-36. London: Routledge, 2001.
–. 1998. "Translating Political Situations: Gramsci's Linguistic Metaphors as Political Analysis." Paper presented at the Pacific North West Political Science Association, Victoria, 23 October.
–. 1999. "Competing Visions of Language and Community in a Unified Europe." Paper presented at the Annual Meetings of the Canadian Political Science Association, Sherbrooke, 7 June.
–. 2000. "Translating Revolution: Gramsci's Linguistic Metaphors." *Counter-Hegemony* 3: 36-45.
–. 2001. "A Grammatical Introduction to Gramsci's Political Theory." *Rethinking Marxism* 10, 1 (1998): 30-47. Reprinted in *Antonio Gramsci: Critical Assessments,* vol. 3, ed. James Martin, 212-30. London: Routledge.
–. 2003. *Gramsci's Politics of Language: Engaging the Bakhtin Circle and the Frankfurt School.* Toronto: University of Toronto Press.
Jenkins, Richard, and Matthew Mendelsohn. 2000. "The News Media and Referendums." In *Referendum Democracy,* ed. Matthew Mendelsohn and Andrew Parkin, 211-30. London: Palgrave.
Johnston, Darlene. 1995. "Native Rights as Collective Rights: A Question of Group Self-Preservation." In *The Rights of Minority Cultures,* ed. Will Kymlicka, 179-201. Oxford: Oxford University Press.
Johnston, Richard, et al. 1996. *The Challenge of Direct Democracy: The 1992 Canadian Referendum.* Montreal: McGill-Queen's University Press.
Johnston, Richard, and Stuart Soroka. 2001. "Social Capital in Multicultural Societies: The Case of Canada." In *Social Capital and Participation in Everyday Life,* ed. Paul Dekker and Eric M. Uslander, 30-44. London: Routledge.
Jones, Carol. 1999. "Politics Postponed, Law as a Substitute for Politics: Hong Kong and China." In *Law, Capitalism, and Power in Asia: The Rule of Law and Legal Institutions,* ed. Kanishka Jayasuriya, 45-68. London: Routledge.
Julios, Christina. 2002. "Towards a European Language Policy." In *European Integration in the 21st Century: Unity in Diversity?* ed. Mary Farrell, Stefano Fella, and Michael Newman, 84-201. London: Sage.
Kandiyoti, Deniz. 1996. "Women, Ethnicity, and Nationalism." In *Ethnicity,* ed. John Hutchinson and Anthony D. Smith, 311-16. Oxford: Oxford University Press.
Kastoryano, Riva. 2002. *Negotiating Identities: States and Immigrants in France and Germany.* Princeton: Princeton University Press.
Keating, Michael. 1999. "Asymmetrical Government: Multinational States in an Integrating Europe." *Publius* 29, 1: 71 ff.

Keck, Margaret E., and Kathryn Sikkink. 1998. *Activists beyond Borders: Advocacy Networks in International Politics*. Ithaca: Cornell University Press.

Ke-kin-is-uks et al. v. British Columbia. 28 March 2002, BCCA 238. Docket: CA029584. Registry: Vancouver.

Kelly, David, and Anthony Reid, eds. 1998. *Asian Freedoms: The Idea of Freedom in East and Southeast Asia*. New York: Cambridge University Press.

King, Loren A. 2003. "Deliberation, Legitimacy, and Multilateral Democracy." *Governance* 16, 1: 23-50.

Knight, Trevor. 2001. "Electoral Justice for Aboriginal People in Canada." *McGill Law Journal* 46: 1063-1116.

Kraus, Peter. 2000. "Political Unity and Linguistic Diversity in Europe." *Archives européennes de sociologie* 41, 1: 138-63.

Kymlicka, Will. 1995. *Multicultural Citizenship: A Liberal Theory of Minority Rights*. Oxford: Oxford University Press.

–. 1998. *Finding Our Way: Rethinking Ethnocultural Relations in Canada*. Toronto: Oxford University Press.

–. 2001. "The New Debate over Minority Rights." In *Canadian Political Philosophy*, ed. Ronald Beiner and Wayne Norman, 159-76. Toronto: Oxford University Press.

Kymlicka, Will, and Wayne Norman, eds. 1995a. *The Rights of Minority Cultures*. Oxford: Oxford University Press.

–. 1995b. "The Return of the Citizen." In *Theorizing Citizenship*, ed. Ronald Beiner, 283-322. Albany: SUNY Press.

Laclau, Ernesto, and Chantal Mouffe. 2001. *Hegemony and Socialist Strategy: Towards a Radical Democratic Politics*. 2nd ed. London: Verso.

Ladd, Everett Carll. 1999. *The Ladd Report*. New York: Free Press.

Laden, Anthony Simon. 2001. *Reasonably Radical: Deliberative Liberalism and the Politics of Identity*. Ithaca: Cornell University Press.

–. 2003. "The House that Jack Built: Thirty Years of Reading Rawls." *Ethics* 113: 367-90.

Lakoff, George, and Mark Johnson. 1980. *Metaphors We Live By*. Chicago: University of Chicago Press.

Laponce, Jean. 1987. *Languages and Their Territories*. Trans. Anthony Martin-Sperry. Toronto: University of Toronto Press.

LaSelva, Samuel V. 1996. *The Moral Foundations of Canadian Federalism*. Kingston: McGill-Queen's University Press.

Lau, Siu-kai. 2001. "The Hong Kong Special Administrative Region Government in the New Political Environment." In *Hong Kong Reintegrating with China: Political, Cultural, and Social Dimensions*, ed. Lee Pui-tak, 59-78. Hong Kong: Hong Kong University Press.

La Vopa, Anthony. 1995. "Herder's *Publikum*: Language, Print, and Sociability in Eighteenth-Century Germany." *Eighteenth-Century Studies* 29, 1: 5-24.

Laycock, David. 2000. "Populist Democracy." In *Democracy, Rights, and Well-Being in Canada*, ed. Don Carmichael et al., 36-55. 2nd ed. Toronto: Harcourt Brace.

–. 2001. *The New Right and Democracy in Canada*. Toronto: Oxford University Press.

Lee, J.J. 1989. *Ireland 1912-1985: Politics and Society*. New York: Cambridge University Press.

Lefevre, Marianne. 2000. *Géopolitique de la Corse: Le Modèle républicain en question*. Paris: l'Harmattan.

Lifton, Robert Jay. 1993. *The Protean Self*. New York: Basic Books.

Lin, Nan. 2001. *Social Capital: A Theory of Social Structure and Action*. Cambridge, UK: Cambridge University Press.

Linklater, Andrew. 1990. *Beyond Realism and Marxism: Critical Theory and International Relations*. London: Macmillan.

–. 1998. *The Transformation of Political Community: Ethical Foundations of the Post-Westphalian Era*. Columbia: University of South Carolina Press.

Locke, John. 1995. *An Essay Concerning Human Understanding*. Amherst, NY: Prometheus.

Loh, Christine. 1999. "Human Rights in the First Year – Genuine Restraint, or Buying Time?" In *The Other Hong Kong Report 1998*, ed. Larry Chuen-ho Chow and Yiu-kwan Fan, 49-72. Hong Kong: Chinese University Press.

Loos, Eugène. 2000. "Language Choice, Linguistic Capital, and Symbolic Domination in the European Union." *Language Problems and Language Planning* 24, 1: 37-53.
Luhmann, Niklas. 1990. *Political Theory in the Welfare State*. Trans. John Bednarz, Jr. New York: Walter de Gruyter.
Mackenzie, Catriona, and Natalie Stoljar, eds. 2000. *Relational Autonomy: Feminist Perspectives on Autonomy, Agency, and the Social Self*. Oxford: Oxford University Press.
Macklem, Patrick. 1995. "Normative Dimensions of the Right of Aboriginal Self-Government." In *Aboriginal Self-Government: Legal and Constitutional Issues*, ed. Royal Commission on Aboriginal Peoples, 4-54. Ottawa: Minister of Supply and Services Canada.
–. 2001. *Indigenous Difference and the Constitution of Canada*. Toronto: University of Toronto Press.
Macpherson, C.B. 1953. *Democracy in Alberta: The Theory and Practice of a Quasi-Party System*. Toronto: University of Toronto Press.
–. 1973. *Democratic Theory: Essays in Retrieval*. Oxford: Clarendon Press.
–. 1977. *The Life and Times of Liberal Democracy*. Oxford: Oxford University Press.
Macy, Joanna. 1992. *Mutual Causality in Buddhism and General Systems Theory: The Dharma of Natural Systems*. Albany: State University of New York Press.
Magleby, David B. 1984. *Direct Legislation: Voting on Ballot Propositions in the United States*. Baltimore: Johns Hopkins University Press.
Mamadouh, Virginie. 1999. "Institutional Multilingualism." In *Which Languages for Europe? Report of the Conference Held in Oegstgeest*, 119-25. Oegstgeest: European Cultural Foundation.
Mandell, Louise. 2002. "Recommended Referendum Ballot: A Legal Analysis," 25 February. <http://www.ubcic.bc.ca/docs/MP_referendum_analysis_022503.pdf> (accessed 20 November 2003).
Manifeste pour la vie. 1996. "Les Femmes du Manifeste pour la vie en appellent à la conscience et à l'engagement de tous." Reprinted in *Géopolitique de la Corse: Le Modèle républicain en question*, by Marianne Lefevre, 88. Paris: l'Harmattan, 2000.
Manin, Bernard. 1987. "On Legitimacy and Political Deliberation." *Political Theory* 15, 2: 338-68.
–. 1997. *The Principles of Representative Government*. New York: Cambridge University Press.
Manning, Elizabeth. 1998. "Interpretation Differs on English-Only Bid." *Anchorage Daily News*, 4 November.
"Manning Panders to Prejudice" [editorial]. 1997. *Toronto Star* 22 May: A32.
Mansbridge, Jane. 1991. "Feminism and Democratic Community." In *Democratic Community, NOMOS 35*, ed. John W. Chapman and Ian Shapiro, 339-95. New York: New York University Press.
–. 1992. "A Deliberative Theory of Interest Representation." In *The Politics of Interest Groups Transformed*, ed. Mark Petracca, 32-57. Boulder: Westview Press.
–. 1995. "A Deliberative Perspective on Neo-Corporatism." In *Associations and Democracy*, ed. Joshua Cohen and Joel Rogers, 133-47. New York: Verso.
–. 1997. "Social and Cultural Causes of Dissatisfaction with U.S. Government." In *Why the People Don't Trust Government*, ed. Joseph S. Nye, Jr., Philip D. Zelikow, and David C. King, 133-53. Cambridge, MA: Harvard University Press.
–. 1999. "Should Blacks Represent Blacks and Women Represent Women? A Contingent 'Yes.'" *Journal of Politics* 61, 3: 628-57.
–. 2000. "What Does a Representative Do? Descriptive Representation in Communicative Settings of Distrust, Uncrystallized Interests, and Historically Denigrated Status." In *Citizenship in Diverse Societies*, ed. Will Kymlicka and Wayne Norman, 99-123. New York: Oxford University Press.
Mariani, Marie-Thé. 1996. "Femmes contre la violence en Corse." L'annuaire au féminin: Le Guide des femmes interactives, <http://www.annuaire-au-feminin.tm.fr/98-02.html> (accessed 25 March 2002).
–. 2001. "Manifeste pour la vie." Pénélopes, <http://www.penelopes.org/pages/docu/paix/corse.htm> (accessed 25 March 2002).

Maslove, Allan M. 1992. "Reconstructing Fiscal Federalism." In *How Ottawa Spends: The Politics of Competitiveness 1992-93*, ed. Frances Abele, 57-77. Ottawa: Carleton University Press.
McFerren, Ludo. 1990. "Interpretation of a Frontline State: Australian Women's Refuges and the State." In *Playing the State: Australian Feminist Interventions in the State*, ed. Sophie Watson, 191-206. Sydney: George Allen and Unwin.
McIver, D.N. 1995. "The Crisis of Canadian Federalism." *Round Table* 334: 219-40.
McKinnon, Catriona. 2002. *Liberalism and the Defence of Political Constructivism*. Houndmills, UK: Palgrave-Macmillan.
McLachlin, Beverley. 2003. "The Civilization of Difference." Fourth Annual Lafontaine-Baldwin Lecture, 7 March, Halifax, NS.
McMillan, Alan D. 1995. *Native Peoples and Cultures of Canada*. Vancouver: Douglas and McIntyre.
McRoberts, Kenneth. 1997. *Misconceiving Canada: The Struggle for National Unity*. Toronto: Oxford University Press.
–. 2001. *Catalonia: Nation Building without a State*. Toronto: Oxford University Press.
Meehan, Johanna A., ed. 1995. *Feminists Read Habermas*. New York: Routledge.
Mendelsohn, Matthew, and Andrew Parkin. 2001a. "Introducing Direct Democracy in Canada." *Choices* 7, 5: 3-35.
–, eds. 2001b. *Referendum Democracy*. London: Palgrave.
Mendus, Susan. 2002. *Impartiality in Moral and Political Philosophy*. Oxford: Oxford University Press.
Mercredi, Ovide, and Mary Ellen Turpel. 1993. *In the Rapids: Navigating the Future of First Nations*. Toronto: Viking-Penguin.
Mill, John Stuart. 1963 [1861]. *Considerations on Representative Government*. Vol. 19 of *Collected Works*, ed. J.M. Robson. Toronto: University of Toronto Press.
Miller, David. 1995. *On Nationality*. Oxford: Clarendon Press.
–. 2000. *Citizenship and National Identity*. Cambridge, UK: Polity Press.
Monynihan, Maurice, ed. 1980. *Speeches and Statements by Eamon de Valera 1917-73*. Dublin: Gill and Macmillan.
–. 2000. *Citizenship and National Identity*. Cambridge, UK: Polity Press.
Moodley, Kogila. 1983. "Canadian Multiculturalism as Ideology." *Ethnic and Racial Studies* 6, 3: 320-31.
Moore, Margaret. 2001. *The Ethics of Nationalism*. Oxford: Oxford University Press.
Mouffe, Chantal. 1992. "Democratic Citizenship and the Political Community." In *Dimensions of Radical Democracy: Pluralism, Citizenship, and Community*, ed. Chantal Mouffe, 225-39. London: Verso.
–. 2000. *The Democratic Paradox*. New York: Verso.
Nathan, Richard P. 1992. "Defining Modern Federalism." In *North American and Comparative Federalism: Essays for the 1990s*, ed. Harry R. Scheiber, 32-46. Berkeley: University of California Institute for Governmental Studies Press.
National Action Committee on the Status of Women. 1987. *Action Now* 2, 7.
–. 1988. *Feminist Action* 3, 2.
–. 1992. *Action Now* 2, 4 and 7.
–. 1995a. *Action Now* 5, 1.
–. 1995b. *A Very Political Budget* [NAC press release].
Norris, Pippa, ed. 1999. *Critical Citizens: Global Support for Democratic Governance*. Oxford: Oxford University Press.
Nye, Joseph S., Philip D. Zelikow, and David C. King, eds. 1997. *Why People Don't Trust Government*. Cambridge, MA: Harvard University Press.
Offe, Claus. 1996. *Modernity and the State: East, West*. Cambridge, MA: MIT Press.
Ong, Aihwa. 1999. *Flexible Citizenship: The Cultural Logics of Transnationality*. Durham: Duke University Press.
Ó Raigáin, Pádraig. 1997. *Language Policy and Reproduction: Ireland 1893-1993*. Oxford: Clarendon Press.

Orren, Gary. 1997. "Fall from Grace: The Public's Loss of Faith in Government." In *Why the People Don't Trust Government*, ed. Joseph S. Nye, Jr., Philip D. Zelikow, and David C. King, 77-107. Cambridge, MA: Harvard University Press.
Painter, Martin. 1996. "Federal Theory and Modern Australian Executive Federalism." In *Public Administration under Scrutiny*, ed. John Halligan, 77-96. Canberra: Centre for Research in Public Sector Management, University of Canberra, Institute of Public Administration Australia.
–. 1997. "Federalism." In *Politics in Australia*, ed. Rodney Smith, 3rd ed., 194-215. Sydney: Allen and Unwin.
Pal, Leslie A. 1993. *Interests of State*. Montreal: McGill-Queen's University Press.
Pal, Leslie A., and F. Leslie Seidle. 1993. "Constitutional Politics 1990-2: The Paradox of Participation." In *How Ottawa Spends, 1993-1994: A More Democratic Canada*, ed. Susan D. Phillips, 143-202. Ottawa: Carleton University Press.
Parekh, Bhikhu. 2000. *Rethinking Multiculturalism: Cultural Diversity and Political Theory*. Cambridge, MA: Harvard University Press.
Pateman, Carole. 1970. *Participation and Democratic Theory*. Cambridge, UK: Cambridge University Press.
Patten, Alan. 2001. "Political Theory and Language Policy." *Political Theory* 29, 5: 691-715.
Petrucciani, Stefano. 1998. "Costellazione Europa, La Terza Via di Habermas." *Il Manifesto* 13 June: 18.
Pharr, Susan J., and Robert D. Putnam, eds. 2000. *Disaffected Democracies: What's Troubling the Trilateral Countries?* Princeton: Princeton University Press.
Phillips, Anne. 1991. *Engendering Democracy*. Cambridge, UK: Polity Press.
–. 1995. *The Politics of Presence*. Oxford: Oxford University Press.
Phillips, Susan D. 1991. "How Ottawa Blends: Shifting Government Relationships with Interest Groups." In *How Ottawa Spends: The Politics of Fragmentation*, ed. Frances Abele, 183-227. Ottawa: Carleton University Press.
Phillipson, Robert. 2003. *English-Only Europe? Challenging Language Policy*. London: Routledge.
Pierson, Paul. 1995. "Fragmented Welfare States: Federal Institutions and the Development of Social Policy." *Governance* 8: 449-78.
Pitkin, Hanna. 1967. *The Concept of Representation*. Berkeley: University of California Press.
–, ed. 1969. *Representation*. New York: Atherton.
–. 1987. "Representation." In *The Blackwell Encyclopedia of Political Thought*, ed. David Miller, 432-33. Oxford: Basil Blackwell.
"Premier Should Avoid Divisive Referendum." 2001. *Vancouver Sun* 18 May: A18.
"Premiers' Framework for Discussion on Canadian Unity" [Calgary Declaration]. 1997. Calgary, 14 September.
Preuss, Ulrich. 1995. *Constitutional Revolution: The Link between Constitutionalism and Progress*. Trans. Deborah Lucas Schneider. Atlantic Highlands, NJ: Humanities Press.
Przeworski, Adam, Susan C. Stokes, and Bernard Manin, eds. 1999. *Democracy, Accountability, and Representation*. New York: Cambridge University Press.
Putnam, Robert D. 1988. "Diplomacy and Domestic Politics: The Logic of Two-Level Games." *International Organization* 42, 3: 427-60.
–. 1993. *Making Democracy Work: Civic Traditions in Modern Italy*. Princeton: Princeton University Press.
–. 2000. *Bowling Alone: The Collapse and Revival of American Community*. New York: Simon and Schuster.
Pyrcz, Greg. N.d. "Emergent Democratic Theory in Rousseau's Second Discourse: Search for a Method." Unpublished manuscript.
Rankin, Katharine, and Kanishka Goonewardena. 2003. "The Political Economy and Cultural Politics of Ethnic Conflict in Asia." In *Democratization and Identity: Regimes and Ethnicity in East and South-East Asia*, ed. Susan J. Henders, 95-114. Lanham: Lexington Books.
Rankin, L. Pauline, and Jill Vickers. 1998. "Locating Women's Politics." In *Women and Political Representation in Canada*, ed. Manon Tremblay and Caroline Andrew, 341-67. Ottawa: University of Ottawa Press.

Rawls, John. 1971. *A Theory of Justice*. Cambridge, MA: Harvard University Press.
–. 1996. *Political Liberalism*. New York: Columbia University Press.
Réaume, Denise G. 2000. "Official-Language Rights." In *Citizenship in Diverse Societies*, ed. Will Kymlicka and Wayne Norman, 245-72. Oxford: Oxford University Press.
Rebick, Judy. 1993. "The Charlottetown Accord: A Faulty Framework and a Wrong-Headed Compromise." In *The Charlottetown Accord, the Referendum, and the Future of Canada*, ed. Kenneth McRoberts and Patrick Monahan, 102-106. Toronto: University of Toronto Press.
Reddy, Michael. 1979. "The Conduit Metaphor." In *Metaphor and Thought*, ed. Andrew Ortony, 284-323. Cambridge, UK: Cambridge University Press.
Reference Re: Manitoba Language Rights 1985 1 SCR 721.
Reference Re: Secession of Quebec [1998] 2 SCR 217.
Rocher, François, and Miriam Smith. 1995. "Four Dimensions of the Canadian Constitutional Debate." In *New Trends in Canadian Federalism*, ed. François Rocher and Miriam Smith, 45-66. Peterborough: Broadview Press.
Rorty, Richard. 1991. *Objectivism, Relativism, and Truth*. New York: Cambridge University Press.
Rosenblum, Nancy. 1998. *Membership and Morals: The Personal Uses of Pluralism in America*. Princeton: Princeton University Press.
Rousseau, Jean-Jacques. 1913. *The Social Contract*. Trans. G.D.H. Cole. Chicago: Great Books Foundation.
–. 1968. *The Social Contract*. Trans. Maurice Cranston. New York: Penguin Books.
–. 1973. *The Social Contract and Discourses*. Trans. G.D.H. Cole. London: Dent.
Royal Commission on Aboriginal Peoples. 1996. *Final Report*. Ottawa: Minister of Supply and Services Canada.
Royal Commission on Electoral Reform and Party Financing. 1991. *Reforming Electoral Democracy*. Vol. 1. Ottawa: Minister of Supply and Services Canada.
Ruiz et al. v. Hull et al. 191 Ariz. 441, 957 P.2d 984 (1998).
Russell, Peter. 1993. *Constitutional Odyssey: Can Canadians Become a Sovereign People?* 2nd ed. Toronto: University of Toronto Press.
Sachs, Ariele. 1990. *Protecting Human Rights in a New South Africa*. Cape Town: Oxford University Press.
Safran, William. 2000. "Spatial and Functional Dimensions of Autonomy: Cross-National and Theoretical Perspectives." In *Identity and Territorial Autonomy in Plural Societies*, ed. William Safran and Ramón Maiz, 11-34. London: Frank Cass.
Sallembien-Vittori, Pauline. 1999. "Considération sur la place et le rôle de la femme dans l'espace politique insulaire." In *Autonomies insulaires: Vers une politique de la différence pour la Corse?* ed. Centre Européen des Questions de Minorités (CMI), 125-32. Ajaccio: Albania.
Saward, Michael, ed. 2000. *Democratic Innovation: Deliberation, Representation and Association*. New York: Routledge.
–. 2003. "Enacting Democracy." *Political Studies* 51, 1: 161-79.
Sawer, Marian. 1990. *Sisters in Suits: Women and Public Policy in Australia*. Sydney: Allen and Unwin.
Sawer, Marian, and Jill Vickers. 2001. "Women's Constitutional Activism in Australia and Canada." *Canadian Journal of Women and the Law* 13: 1-36.
Scanlon, T.M. 1998. *What We Owe to Each Other*. Cambridge, MA: Harvard University Press.
Schlesinger, Arthur, Jr. 1998. *The Disuniting of America: Reflections on a Multicultural Society*. Rev. ed. New York: W.W. Norton.
Schwartz, Nancy L. 1988. *The Blue Guitar: Political Representation and Community*. Chicago: University of Chicago Press.
Searle, John. 1975. *How to Do Things with Words*. 2nd ed. Oxford: Clarendon Press.
Self, Peter. 1989. "Federal Institutions and Processes: An Economic Perspective." In *Australian Federalism*, ed. Brian Galligan, 69-97. Melbourne: Longman Cheshire.
Sen, Amartya. 1984. *Poverty and Famines: An Essay on Entitlement and Deprivation*. Oxford: Oxford University Press.
Shachar, Ayelet. 2001. *Multicultural Jurisdictions: Cultural Differences and Women's Rights*. Cambridge, UK: Cambridge University Press.

Shain, Yossi. 1999. *Marketing the American Creed Abroad: Diasporas in the U.S. and Their Homelands*. Cambridge, UK: Cambridge University Press.
Shapiro, Ian. 1999. *Democratic Justice*. New Haven: Yale University Press.
—. 2003. *The State of Democratic Theory*. Princeton: Princeton University Press.
Sharrock, David. 2003. "Catalan Children Leave Their Native Tongue in Class." *The Times* (London) 17 June.
Shore, Cris. 1997. "Governing Europe: European Union Audiovisual Policy and the Politics of Identity." In *Anthropology of Policy*, ed. Cris Shore and Susan Wright, 165-92. London: Routledge.
Simeon, Richard. 1972. *Federal-Provincial Diplomacy: The Making of Recent Policy in Canada*. Toronto: University of Toronto Press.
—. 1988. "Meech Lake and the Shifting Conceptions of Canadian Federalism." *Canadian Public Policy* 14, 3: S7-S24.
Simms, Marian, and Diane Stone. 1990. "Women's Policy." In *Hawke and Australian Public Policy*, ed. Christine Jennett and Randall Stewart, 284-97. Melbourne: Macmillan.
Sirianni, Carmen, and Lewis Friedland. 2001. *Civic Innovation in America: Community Empowerment, Public Policy, and the Movement for Civic Renewal*. Berkeley: University of California Press.
Siu, Helen F. 1994. "Cultural Identity and the Politics of Difference in South China." In *China in Transformation*, ed. Tu Wei-ming, 19-43. Cambridge, MA: Harvard University Press.
Skocpol, Theda, and Morris P. Fiorina, eds. 1999. *Civic Engagement in American Democracy*. Washington, DC: Brookings Institution Press.
Skutnabb-Kangas, Tove, and Robert Phillipson, eds. 1994. *Linguistic Human Rights*. Berlin: Mouton de Gruyter.
Smith, Alan. 1970. "Metaphor and Nationality." *Canadian Historical Review* 51, 3: 247-75.
Smith, Anthony D. 1997. "National Identity and the Idea of European Unity." In *The Question of Europe*, ed. Peter Gowan and Perry Anderson, 318-42. London: Verso.
Smith, David E. 1990. "The Federal Cabinet in Canadian Politics." In *Canadian Politics in the 1990s*, 3rd ed., ed. Michael S. Whittington and Glen Williams, 359-79. Scarborough: Nelson Canada.
Smith, Graham, and Corine Wales. 2002. "Citizens, Juries, and Deliberative Democracy." In *Democracy as Public Deliberation: New Perspectives*, ed. Maurizio Passerin D'Entreves, 155-77. Manchester: Manchester University Press.
Smith, Warren W., Jr. 1996. *Tibetan Nation: A History of Tibetan Nationalism and Sino-Tibetan Relations*. Boulder: Westview.
Soysal, Yasemin. 1994. *Limits of Citizenship: Migrants and Postnational Membership in Europe*. Chicago: University of Chicago Press.
Strong, Tracy. 1994. *Jean Jacques Rousseau: The Politics of the Ordinary*. Thousand Oaks, CA: Sage.
Taylor, Charles. 1994. "Politics of Recognition." In *Multiculturalism: Examining the Politics of Recognition*, ed. Amy Gutmann, 25-73. Princeton: Princeton University Press.
—. 1995a. "The Importance of Herder." In *Philosophical Arguments*, 79-99. Cambridge, MA: Harvard University Press.
—. 1995b. "Liberal Politics and the Public Sphere." In *Philosophical Arguments*, 257-87. Cambridge, MA: Harvard University Press.
Teghtsoonian, Katherine. 2000. "Gendering Policy Analysis in the Government of British Columbia: Strategies, Possibilities, and Constraints." *Studies in Political Economy* 61: 105-27.
Teubner, Günther. 1983. "Substantive and Reflexive Elements in Modern Law." *Law and Society Review* 17: 239-85.
Thompson, Allan. 1997. "Manning Faces Demonstrators." *Toronto Star* 22 May: A1.
Thompson, Dennis F. 1976. *John Stuart Mill and Representative Government*. Princeton: Princeton University Press.
—. 1995. *Ethics in Congress: From Individual to Institutional Corruption*. Washington, DC: Brookings Institution Press.
Tilly, Charles. 1992. "Futures of European States." *Social Research* 59, 4: 705-18.
Tovey, Hilary, Damien Hannan, and Hal Abramson. 1989. *Why Irish? Language and Identity in Ireland Today*. Baile Átha Cliath [Dublin]: Bord na Gaeilge [Irish Language Board].

Townsend, Lynn. 1994. "Report to the WESNET Steering Committee: The Establishment of Women's Emergency Service Network (WESNET Inc.)." Unpublished report.
"Treaty Referendum a Futile Exercise: There's No Point in Voting on Negotiating Principles if First Nations Don't Accept Them." *Victoria Times-Colonist* 4 July: A10.
Tremblay, Manon. 1997. "Quebec Women in Politics: An Examination of the Research." In *In the Presence of Women: Representation in Canadian Governments*, ed. Jane Arscott and Linda Trimble, 228-51. Toronto: Harcourt Brace.
Trimble, Linda. 1998. "'Good Enough Citizens': Canadian Women and Representation in Constitutional Deliberations." *International Journal of Canadian Studies* 17: 131-56.
Truchot, Claude, David Skinner, and Rocco Tanzilli. 1999. "Report on Session 3." In *Which Languages for Europe? Report of the Conference Held in Oegstgeest*, 89-92. Oegstgeest: European Cultural Foundation.
Trudeau, Pierre Elliott. 1968. *Federalism and the French Canadians*. Toronto: Macmillan.
–. 1992. *Trudeau: "A Mess that Deserves a Big NO."* Toronto: Robert Davies Publishing.
Tully, James. 1994. "Diversity's Gambit Declined." In *Constitutional Predicament: Canada after the Referendum of 1992*, ed. Curtis Cook, 149-99. Montreal: McGill-Queen's University Press.
–. 1995. *Strange Multiplicity: Constitutionalism in an Age of Diversity*. Cambridge, UK: Cambridge University Press.
–. 2001a. "Introduction." In *Multinational Democracies*, ed. Alain-G. Gagnon and James Tully, 1-34. Cambridge, UK: Cambridge University Press.
–. 2001b. "Democracy and Globalization: A Defeasible Sketch." In *Canadian Political Philosophy: Contemporary Reflections*, ed. Ronald Beiner and Wayne Norman, 36-62. Toronto: Oxford University Press.
Tung Chee Hwa. 1997. "Building Hong Kong for a New Era: Policy Address 1997." Hong Kong: Hong Kong SAR Government, <http://www.policyaddress.gov.hk/pa97/english/patext.htm> (accessed 21 November 2003).
–. 2000. "Policy Address 2000." Hong Kong: Hong Kong SAR Government, <http://www.policyaddress.gov.hk/pa00/pa00_e.htm> (accessed 21 November 2003).
–. 2003. "Capitalizing on Our Advantages, Revitalizing Our Economy: Chief Executive's Policy Address 2003." Hong Kong: Hong Kong SAR Government, <http://www.policyaddress.gov.hk/pa03/eng/policy.htm> (accessed 21 November 2003).
Uhr, John. 1998. *Deliberative Democracy in Australia: The Changing Place of Parliament*. Cambridge, UK: Cambridge University Press.
Urbinati, Nadia. 2000. "Representation as Advocacy." *Political Theory* 28, 6: 758-86.
US Department of State. 2000. "Hong Kong Country Report on Human Rights Practices for 1999." Washington, DC: State Department, Bureau of Democracy, Human Rights, and Labor, February, <http://www.usis.usemb.se/human/human1999/hongkong.html> (accessed 21 November 2003).
Valadez, Jorge M. 2001. *Deliberative Democracy, Political Legitimacy, and Self-Determination in Multicultural Societies*. Boulder: Westview Press.
van Deth, Jan. 2000. "Interesting but Irrelevant: Social Capital and the Saliency of Politics in Western Europe." *European Journal of Political Research* 37: 115-47.
Van Til, Jon. 2000. *Growing Civil Society: From Nonprofit Sector to Third Space*. Bloomington: Indiana University Press.
Verba, Sidney, Kay Lehman Schlozman, and Henry E. Brady. 1995. *Voice and Equality: Civic Volunteerism in American Politics*. Cambridge, MA: Harvard University Press.
Vickers, Jill. 1990. "Why Should Women Care about Constitutional Reform?" In *Among Friends: Women and Constitutional Reform*, ed. David Schneiderman, 18-24. Edmonton: Centre for Constitutional Studies, University of Alberta.
–. 1993. "The Canadian Women's Movement and a Changing Constitutional Order." *International Journal of Canadian Studies* 7-8: 261-84.
–. 1994. "Why Should Women Care about Federalism?" In *Canada: The State of the Federation*, ed. Janet Hiebert, 153-78. Kingston: Queen's School of Public Policy.
Walzer, Michael. 1983. *Spheres of Justice: A Defense of Pluralism and Equality*. New York: Basic Books.
–. 1998. "Disunited." *New Republic* 219, 3-4: 10-11.

Warren, Mark E. 1995. "The Self in Discursive Democracy." In *The Cambridge Companion to Habermas*, ed. Stephen White, 167-200. Cambridge: Cambridge University Press.
–. 1996. "Deliberative Democracy and Authority." *American Political Science Review* 90: 46-60.
–. 1999a. "Democratic Theory and Trust." In *Democracy and Trust*, ed. Mark E. Warren, 310-45. Cambridge, UK: Cambridge University Press.
–. 1999b. "What Is Political?" *Journal of Theoretical Politics* 11: 207-31.
–. 2001. *Democracy and Association*. Princeton: Princeton University Press.
–. 2002. "Deliberative Democracy." In *Democratic Theory Today: Challenges for the 21st Century*, ed. April Carter, 173-202. Cambridge, UK: Polity Press.
Watts, Ronald L. 1996. *Comparing Federal Systems in the 1990s*. Kingston: Institute of Intergovernmental Relations, Queen's University.
Webber, Jeremy. 1994. *Reimagining Canada*. Montreal: McGill-Queen's University Press.
Weber, Eugene. 1976. *Peasants into Frenchmen: The Modernization of Rural France 1870-1914*. Stanford: Stanford University Press.
Weber, Max. 1946. *From Max Weber: Essays in Sociology*, ed. H.H. Gerth and C. Wright Mills. New York: Oxford University Press.
Weiler, J.H.H. 1997. "Does Europe Need a Constitution? Reflections on Demos, Telos, and Ethos in the German Maastricht Decision." In *The Question of Europe*, ed. Peter Gowan and Perry Anderson, 265-94. London: Verso.
White, Graham. 1997. "Provinces and Territories: Characteristics, Roles, and Responsibilities." In *Public Administration and Public Management: Experiences in Canada*, ed. Jacques Bourgault, Maurice Demers, and Cynthia Williams, 167-76. Sainte-Foy: Les Publications du Québec.
White, Lynne T. III. 2001. "The Political Appeals of Conservatives and Reformers in Hong Kong." In *Hong Kong Reintegrating with China: Political, Cultural, and Social Dimensions*, ed. Lee Pui-tak, 3-38. Hong Kong: Hong Kong University Press.
Williams, Melissa. 1998. *Voice, Trust, and Memory: Marginalized Groups and the Failings of Liberal Representation*. Princeton: Princeton University Press.
–. 2000. "The Uneasy Alliance of Group Representation and Deliberative Democracy." In *Citizenship in Diverse Societies*, ed. Will Kymlicka and Wayne Norman, 124-54. Oxford: Oxford University Press.
–. 2003. "Citizenship as Identity, Citizenship as Shared Fate, and the Functions of Multicultural Education." In *Citizenship and Education in Liberal-Democratic Societies*, ed. Kevin McDonough and Walter Feinberg, 208-47. Oxford: Oxford University Press.
Wong, Lloyd L. 2002. "Transnationalism, Diasporic Communities, and Changing Identity: Implications for Canadian Citizenship." In *Street Protests and Fantasy Parks: Globalization, Culture, and the State*, ed. David R. Cameron and Janice Gross Stein, 49-87. Vancouver: UBC Press.
Wright, Erk Olin, ed. 1995. *Associations and Democracy*. New York: Verso.
Young, Iris Marion. 1989. "Polity and Group Difference: A Critique of the Ideal of Universal Citizenship." *Ethics* 99: 250-74.
–. 1997. "Deferring Group Representation." In *Ethnicity and Group Rights, NOMOS 39*, ed. Ian Shapiro and Will Kymlicka, 349-76. New York: New York University Press.
–. 2000. *Inclusion and Democracy*. Oxford: Oxford University Press.
–. 2001. "Activist Challenges to Deliberative Democracy." *Political Theory* 29, 3: 670-90.
Young, Lisa. 1999. "Value Clash: Parliament and Citizens after 150 Years of Responsible Government." In *Taking Stock of 150 Years of Responsible Government in Canada*, ed. F. Leslie Seidle and Louis Massicotte, 105-36. Ottawa: Canadian Study of Parliament Group.
Zacher, Mark W. 1992. "The Decaying Pillars of the Westphalian Temple: Implications for International Order and Governance." In *Governance without Government: Order and Change in World Politics*, ed. James N. Rosenau and Ernest-Otto Czempiel, 58-101. Cambridge, UK: Cambridge University Press.
Zimmerman, Joseph F. 1986. *Participatory Democracy: Populism Revived*. New York: Praeger.
Zolo, Danilo. 1992. *Democracy and Complexity: A Realist Approach*. University Park: Pennsylvania State University Press.
Zubyk, Brad. 2001. "No Ground to Be Gained with Liberal Referendum." *Victoria Times-Colonist* 13 March: A11.

Notes on Contributors

Simone Chambers is Associate Professor of Political Science at the University of Toronto. She is currently writing a book titled *Public Reason and Deliberation*, which investigates the deliberative turn taken by contemporary liberalism. Her primary areas of scholarship include political philosophy, ethics, critical theory, and constitutional theory. She is author of *Reasonable Democracy: Jürgen Habermas and the Politics of Discourse* and co-editor of *Deliberation, Democracy, and the Media* and *Alternative Conceptions of Civil Society*.

Louise Chappell is Senior Lecturer in the School of Economics and Political Science, University of Sydney, Australia. She has a BA from the University of New England and a PhD from the University of Sydney. Her areas of research include gender and politics, comparative politics, and human rights. She is the author of *Gendering Government: Feminist Engagement with the State in Australia and Canada*, which was awarded the 2003 APSA Victoria Schuck Award for Best Book in Women and Politics.

Avigail Eisenberg is Associate Professor of Political Science at the University of Victoria. She writes and teaches in the areas of political theories of pluralism, minority rights, democracy, and Canadian constitutionalism. She is author of *Reconstructing Political Pluralism* and co-editor (with Jeff Spinner-Halev) of *Minorities within Minorities: Equality, Rights and Diversity*.

Catherine Frost is Assistant Professor of Political Science at McMaster University. She graduated with a PhD in political theory from the University of Toronto in 2000, and has held research fellowships at the Hebrew University of Jerusalem and McGill University. Her interests include nationalism and nationalist argument, identity, multiculturalism, and communications theory. Her work appears in *The Journal of Political Philosophy* and the *Canadian Journal of Communication*.

Susan J. Henders is Assistant Professor of Political Science at York University. Among her publications are *Democratization and Identity: Regimes and Ethnicity in East and South-East Asia* (editor and contributor) and articles on identity and self-government in *Nations and Nationalism*, *Pacific Affairs*, and the *Journal of Human Rights*.

Peter Ives is Assistant Professor in the Politics Department at the University of Winnipeg, where he teaches political theory. He received his PhD in social and political thought at York University, and is the author of *Gramsci's Politics of Language: Engaging the Bakhtin Circle and the Frankfurt School*, and *Language and Hegemony in Gramsci* (forthcoming).

Gerald Kernerman is Assistant Professor of Canadian Studies at Wilfred Laurier University, specializing in Canadian politics and contemporary social and political theory. He holds degrees in Political Science from the University of Toronto, the University of British Columbia, and York University and has been a Canada-US Fulbright Scholar at Rutgers University as well as a SSHRC Postdoctoral Fellow at the University of Toronto. His book on multicultural nationalism is forthcoming with UBC Press and he is co-editor (with Philip Resnick) of *Insiders and Outsiders: Alan Cairns and the Reshaping of Canadian Citizenship* (also forthcoming).

David Laycock is Professor of Political Science at Simon Fraser University, whose research is focused in the areas of Canadian and comparative political ideologies and contemporary democratic theory. He is the author of *Populism and Democratic Thought in the Canadian Prairies, 1910-45* and *The New Right and Democracy in Canada*, as well as various articles and chapters on populism, co-operatives, and party politics.

Greg Pyrcz is Professor of Political Science at Acadia University, where he has taught for twenty years. His interests are in democratic theory and in the work of Jean-Jacques Rousseau. He is co-editor, with D.J.C. Carmichael and Tom Pocklington, and contributor to *Democracy, Rights, and Well-Being* (2nd ed.).

Jonathan Quong is Lecturer in Political Philosophy in the Government Department at the University of Manchester. He has published several articles on the topics of cultural rights and public reason, and is currently doing further work on the defensibility of political liberalism.

Mark E. Warren is Professor of Government at Georgetown University, and specializes in democratic theory and continental political thought. Recent publications include *Democracy and Association* and *Democracy and Trust* (editor), "What Does Corruption Mean in a Democracy?" in *American Journal of Political Science*, "A Second Transformation of Democracy?" in *New Forms of Democracy? The Reform and Transformation of Democratic Institutions*, and "Deliberative Democracy," in *Democratic Theory Today*.

Melissa S. Williams teaches political theory at the University of Toronto. She is author of *Voice, Trust, and Memory: Marginalized Groups and the Failings of Liberal Representation* and co-editor (with Patrick Hanafin) of *Identity, Rights, and Constitutional Transformation*. She serves as the current editor of *NOMOS*, the Yearbook of the American Society for Political and Legal Philosophy, and has recently co-edited (with Stephen Macedo) *NOMOS XLVI: Political Exclusion and Domination*. Williams has written articles on issues in contemporary democratic theory and the history of political thought, ranging across the themes of citizenship, deliberative democracy, toleration, education, Aboriginal rights, feminist theory, representation, and affirmative action.

Index

Aboriginal, defined, 115n1
Aboriginal Canadians: assimilation, 94; autonomy for, 113-14; and BC referendum, 13; and Charter of Rights and Freedoms, 81; and citizenship, 101-2; citizenship of, xviii, 93-4, 103; "communities of interest," 96; in competitive pluralism, 227-8; constituencies for, 96, 97, 112, 113; differences across, 113; differential treatments of, 226; enhanced representation for, 114; and federal government, 109; and federalism, 85; group identity, 85; in House of Commons, 98, 99, 109; identity, and citizenship, 103; and legitimacy of political institutions, 99-100, 102; in Parliament, 100; political identity and, 97; representation of, xviii, 93, 147-8, 150, 238; residential schooling, 94; in Senate, 98, 99, 111-12; territorial base, 110; treaties, 97; treaty negotiations, 232; unresolved position of, 161; urban, 110; voting by, 13, 93, 96-7
Aboriginal Council of Elders, 98
Aboriginal peoples, and referendums, 12-13
Aboriginal self-government, 94-5, 147-8, 150, 228; accountability for, 238, 244; in BC referendum, 13; and Charlottetown Accord, 4; conflict of obligations and, 102; and Constitution, 98-9; and constitutional democracy, 108; criminal justice system and, 110; institutions for, 110, 112-13, 114, 235, 238; legitimacy and, 112, 238; and natural resource protection, 110; normative-legal spaces, 108; and Parliament, 93, 97; Quebec sovereigntists cf., 113-14; and representation, 95, 96, 99, 101-2, 109-10, 114, 234; on reserves, 110; and shared space with non-Aboriginals, 108; social services and, 110; structure of, 100
Aboriginal women, in constitutional debates, 72, 111, 173
accountability: for Aboriginal self-government, 238, 244; of collective action, 214, 243; demanding deliberative democracy and, 238; of elections, x; of representative institutions, 18; of representatives, x, viii, 223, 240-1
Ackerman, Bruce, 230
Ahimsa, 133
Ajaccio (Corsica), 135
Alaska, referendums in, 12, 16
Alberta, feminists in, 66, 72, 75
Alfred, Taiaiake, 94, 99, 101, 103, 104
alienation vs. transformation, 60
Amnesty International, 126
Amsterdam Treaty, 31, 127
Anglo-Canadian feminists: Australian feminists cf., 76; and Charter of Rights and Freedoms, 81, 82, 239, 245; and federal government, 82; and federal structures, 72-6, 82-3, 239, 244-5, 246; and government decentralization, 73, 76, 86; and intergovernmental institutions, 84; and levels of government, 72; and provincial governments, 75, 86; territorial representation in federalism and, 85-6
Arieli-Horowitz, Dana, 14
Arizona, referendums in, 12, 16

Arscott, Jane, 76
Assembly of First Nations, 111
assimilation, 94
associations, xv, 211-12; community and, 202; democracy and, 211-12; issue-based, 236; nonvoluntary, 215-16; states and, 208; voluntary, 215. *See also* groups
Australia: ALP governments, 86, 87n18, 89n94; child care in, 71, 88n62; Constitution, 77, 78; Council of Australian Governments (COAG), 83; division of powers in, 78; equalization funding, 77-9; equal pay legislation, 79; Fraser government, 70, 71, 79; Grants Commission, 77; Hawke government, 88n62; Howard government, 84; local government in, 77; National Women's Health Program, 88n62; Office of the Status of Women, 79; Partnerships against Domestic Violence, 84; public vs. private spheres in, 78; Sex Discrimination Act, 79; sexual discrimination legislature, 78; Special Premiers' Conference, 83; Specific Purpose Payments (SPP), 77; state governments, 77-9; Whitlam government, 70-1, 88n54; women in, 237 (*see also* Australian feminists; women); women's health movement in, 71
Australian Broadcasting Commission (ABC), 71
Australian federalism, 77-9; Canadian federalism cf., 68t; complexity of, 69-70; double democracy in, 72; "dual citizenship" in, 86; feminists and, 69-72, 78; state governments in, 85; territorial representation in, 85-6
Australian feminists: and ALP governments, 86; Canadian feminists cf., 76; and federalism, 69-72, 76, 239, 243, 244-5, 246; femocratic strategies, 239; and intergovernmental institutions, 84; movement between levels of government, 69-72, 76; reform strategies, 78
Australian Labor Party (ALP), 70, 86
Austria: language of, 31; referendums in, 3, 14
autonomy: for Aboriginal peoples, 113-14; of Corsica, 135; emancipatory minority, 244; of Hong Kong, 130-1; of individuals, 185, 192; liberal, 53; linear causality and, 133; minority, 121-2; public, 185, 186, 188, 193, 238, 239;

for Quebec, 73, 113-14; and unbounded "self," 120

Banaszak, Lee Ann, 66-7, 86
Barber, Benjamin, 8, 194
Barcelona (Catalonia), 128
Barrera, Heribert, 126
Bastia (Corsica), 135
Beck, Ulrich, 205
Beetham, David, 56
Belgium: redistributive policies in, 144; referendums in, 3, 14
Bell, Derrick, Jr., 15
Benhabib, Seyla, 25
Berman, Antoine, 30
bias, and construction of civic identity, 148
Bibby, Reginald, 171
bilingualism, 51
Bissoondath, Neil, 171
Bister-Broosen, Helga, 46n42
Blunden, Brian, 39
Bobbio, Norberto, 199-200, 203
Bogdanor, Vernon, 14
Borrows, John, 95, 107, 115n3
Bouchard, Lucien, 164
Bourdieu, Pierre, 37
Bowler, Shaun, 6, 7, 10
Boyer, Patrick, 9, 20n13, 20n18
Brady, Henry E., 202
British Columbia: feminists in, 73, 76; referendums in, 4, 13, 14, 53, 240
British North America Act, 109
Buddhism: and democracy, 134; and Five-Point Peace Plan, 132-3; and general systems theory, 140n52; and nonviolence, 120
bureaucracies, 199, 200, 202
Burke, Edmund, 56, 192
businesses. *See* corporations
Busque, Ginette, 74
Butler, David, 15

Cairns, Alan, 93, 99, 117n37, 117n50, 149
Calgary Declaration, 164, 168, 170
California: Proposition 187, 15; referendums in, 15
Callbeck, Catherine, 89n94
Callwood, June, 174
Campbell, Kim, 89n94
Canada: Charter of Rights and Freedoms (*see* Canadian Charter of Rights and Freedoms); Constitution, 4, 98-9, 100; constitutional politics, 161-2, 231-3; division of powers in, 80-1; interest

groups funding, 82; multiculturalism, 226 (*see also* multiculturalism); national identity, 165-6, 227 (*see also* national identity); overarching normative vision in, 226, 244; provinces, 80-1, 168, 169 (*see also* provincial governments); redistributive policies in, 144; referendums in, 3-4; relations with Quebec, 3, 16-17; social policy, 80; universal programs, 73; vulnerability to schism, 166; White Paper (1969), 94, 164; women in, 237 (*see also* Anglo-Canadian feminists; Quebec, feminists; women); Women's Program, 82-3

Canadian Charter of Rights and Freedoms, 243; feminists and, 72, 75, 76, 81, 82, 83, 85-6, 239; and individual vs. group rights, 56; notwithstanding clause, 89n79

Canadian conversation, 106, 162, 163-7; assimilation within, 164; Charlottetown Accord and, 172-6; diversity and, 162, 163-4, 167; fragmentation in, 166, 169; majoritarianism in, 163, 165; multicultural nationalism and, 176; national identity in, 165-6; polarization in, 162, 163, 167-70, 236; potential civilizing effects of, 176; Quebec's difference and, 168; unity in, 163, 166-7, 170, 236; "we" question in, 170; women in, 172-6

Canadian federalism, 80-3; Australian federalism cf., 68t; centrifugal forces in, 81, 86; as complex equality, 56; cost-sharing, 73; decentralization in, 80; ethnoregionalism in, 80, 85; feminists and, 72-6; group accommodation within, 56; provincial governments in, 73 (*see also* provincial governments), 85; Quebec feminists within, 73; and social services, 73; territorial representation in, 85-6

Canadian feminists. *See* Aboriginal women; Anglo-Canadian feminists; Quebec, feminists

Carens, Joseph, 56-7, 103
Carmichael, Don, 115n8
Catalan language, 125-6
Catalonia: Cities against Racism program, 128; Generalitat, 125, 128; history, 125; immigrants in, 125-6, 127-8, 138; Local Integration Partnership Action, 128; multi-realmed citizenship, 119-20, 124-8; Parliament, 128; self-government, 126
Chambers, Simone, 161, 162, 166-7, 172, 176, 235, 239, 244, 245

Chappell, Louise, 236-7, 239, 243, 244-5, 246
Charlottetown Accord: Aboriginal Canadians and, 95, 98-9, 101, 109, 111-12, 114; and Canadian conversation, 172-6; citizen engagement in, 231; feminists and, 72-3, 75; gender representation and, 172-6, 246; Quebec's status and, 168; referendum on, 4, 9, 16-17
Chase, Bob, 28
Chomsky, Noam, 29
citizen juries, 156
citizens: apathy of, 200-1, 202; asymmetrical relationship with representatives, 222; attitudes toward authority, 201; in constitutional politics, 225-6; critical evaluations of governments, 201; discursive engagement with, 184-5, 187-8; education of, 185, 221-2, 229; and formulation of policy, 185; ideal, 186-7, 192, 193; overarching interests and goals, 224, 225, 228, 244; participation (*see* participation); preferences of, 58; psychological distortion of, 220; reasonable, 153. *See also* individuals
citizenship: of Aboriginal peoples, 93-4, 101-2, 103; boundaries of, 235-7; and boundaries of political community, 104; civic priority condition, 142, 145, 149, 150, 152; common, 245-7; conflict of obligations in, 103; cultural marginalization and, 104, 149; differentiated, 168; and diversity, 103, 119; education for, 200; equality of, 169; EU, 124, 126-7; European, and linguistic diversity, 41; flexible, 131, 236; "good" vs. "bad," 175-6; identity and, 103, 108; of immigrants, 127-8, 138; as interdependence, 142; justice and, 141; liberal democratic conception of, 141; as liberal virtues, 142, 145-7, 150; meaning of, 95; moral bond of, 93, 149; in multicultural societies, xiii, 105; multi-leveled, 139n13; multi-realmed, 119-20, 124, 126-7, 138, 236; and national identity, 143; and nationalism, 103-4; as nationality, 142, 143-5, 150; and nation-states, 103-4, 119, 121, 137; as reasonableness, 142, 150-5, 156, 242; reasonable pluralism condition, 142, 144, 145, 152; shared, 103, 245; as shared fate, 95, 104-9, 114, 124, 142, 147-50, 235, 238, 242, 244, 245; shared identity in, 95, 148; and

shared nation, 114; state monopoly on, 124; supranational, 125; and TCNs, 126-7, 128; theory, xiii-xiv; transnational, 42, 125
civil society, 25, 43, 62, 231; and democracy, 211-12, 224
Clarity Act, 190
Clark, Joe, 173, 175
COAG. *See* Australia, Council of Australian Governments
Cohen, Joshua, xv, xviii, 64n24, 195n11
Cold War, 203
collective actions: accountability and, 214; complexity of, 205; differentiation and, 204; erosion of state in, 213; pluralization of, 202; politics and, 207
collective bargaining, 211
collective decision making: and democracy, 207; equal participation in, 200; individuals in, 198, 212, 214-15
Colorado: Amendment Two, 11-12; referendums in, 11-12
Committee of the Regions (COR), 26, 37, 40, 124, 128
communitarianism, xiii, 168
communities: of interest, 96; moral, 143; of shared fate, 104-5; unbounded, 124, 234-5, 236, 246. *See also* groups
community associations, 202
community groups, 202, 214
competitive pluralism, 225-6, 227
complex equality, 54, 55-7, 61, 62, 212-14, 217, 240
complexity: democracy and, 205, 223-4; participatory ideals and, 205
The Concept of Representation (Pitkin), xiii
Congress of Aboriginal Peoples, 111
Conseil du statut de la femme, 74
consensus: on Canadian identity, 161; in demanding deliberative democracy, 182, 238; on gender, 182; overlapping, 148; and public reason, 151
constitutionalism, new, 162
constitutional patriotism, 166
constitutional politics, 225-6; in Canada, 231-3; "constitutional moments" in, 230; and day-to-day politics, 230; overarching principles and, 232-3; in South Africa, 229-30, 239; thought experiments in, 223
Contemporary Political Philosophy (Kymlicka), xiv
Convention on the Rules for Admission of TCNs to the Member States of the European Union, 126-7
corporations: global, 209; participatory equality in, 215-16; states and, 208-9

Corsica: autonomy of, 135; clan politics, 135; France and, 135, 136, 137; July 2003 referendum, 137; machoistic ideology, 136; Matignon Law, 137; nationalism of, 135, 136; nonviolence in, 120, 135-7; societal insecurity in, 138; terrorism in, 135; vendettas in, 135; violence in, 135, 136
Coulombe, Pierre, 63n19
Council of Ministers (EU): and immigration, 127; languages and, 31, 35, 37, 39-40
Cox, Eva, 69
Cree, referendums by, 16
The Crisis of Democracy, 201-2

Dahl, Robert, 213; *A Preface to Democratic Theory*, 227
Dalai Lama, 132, 134; Five-Point Peace Plan, 132-3, 133-5; Strasbourg Proposal, 132, 134
decision making: competitive, vs. deliberation, 237; democracy and, 211-12; equality in, 198; equalization of, 215; law and, 210; legitimacy and, xii; privatization of, 210-11; shared fate and, 148; in state-centred institutions, 215
Delgado-Moreira, Juan, 42
deliberation(s): on Canadian identity, 162; competitive decision making vs., 237; constitutive, 162; constraints upon, 179-80; language and, 25-6, 236; majoritarianism vs., 237; philosophical viewpoint, 180-1, 192-3; and reasonableness, 152; referendums and, 3, 6, 240; representation and, xiii-xiv, 237; sociological viewpoint, 181, 182, 192-3
deliberative democracy, 25, 26, 143; and citizenship as reasonableness, 152; and division of labour, 59; and EU language issue, 43; and intuitive sense of justice, 57; literature on, xiv-xv; and multiculturalism, 49, 62, 241; preference formation, 58
deliberative polling, xv, 156
demanding deliberative democracy, 179-84, 235; absence of power in, 179; accountability and, 238; capital punishment in, 189-90; and common interest, 187-8, 222; consensus and, 182, 238; discursive engagement of citizens in, 181, 187-8; elitism in, 194; epistemic humanism of, 183; exclusion of psychological power, 182-3, 221, 222; high stakes in, 179, 182, 183, 184,

221, 238; juries and, 182, 183; liberal democracy cf., 189, 191; patterns of social co-operation and, 180-1; pedagogy and, 185; and POPs, 183-4; positive freedom in, 182-3; reasoning and, 181; as regulative ideal, 194, 245; representatives' roles in, 184-91, 193-4; risks in, 191-3, 237; thought experiments in, 222-3, 238; truths in, 181, 185, 193; unanimity in, 179, 183, 221, 223
democracy: aristocracy vs., 199; associations and, 211-12; associative, xviii-xix; broken promises of, 199-200; and Buddhist teachings, 134; and changing citizen attitudes toward authority, 201; and citizenship education, 200; civil society and, 211-12, 224; collective decisions and, 207; and common good, 143; competitive pluralism and, 225-6, 227; complexity and, 205, 223-4; criteria for, 213; decentred model of, 224; decision making and, 211-12; deficit, viii, xv, 27, 38, 39, 43, 184; defined, 197, 198; deliberative (*see* deliberative democracy); demanding deliberative democracy; differentiation and, 204-5, 223-4; direct, x, viii, 8, 15; as equal participation, 200; ethnolinguistic, 35; expectations of, 198, 199-203; globalization and, 203-4, 223-4; increase in number of states, 197; and "invisible powers," 199; language and, 27, 32, 43, 50; and multiculturalism, 48-9, 240; nation-state and, 23-4; oligarchy and, 199; paradox of multicultural, 49, 53; pluralist theories, 227; pluralization and, 223-4; politics and, 206-8; and power blocs, 199; representation and, x (*see also* representation; representatives); representative vs. participatory, 156; special status claims in, 11; suprastate, 34; transformation and, 58-9, 225. *See also* liberal democracy
democratic corporatism, xviii
democratic equality, 215-16; as complex equality, 212-14; and individual political capacities, 214-15; in nonvoluntary associations, 215-16; pre-eminence and, 217; in resistance, 216; in voluntary associations, 215
democratic government vs. representative government, x
democratic justice. *See* justice
democratic resistance, 216
democratization, xii

de Swaan, Abram, 24
de Valera, Eamon, 51
devolution, 209-11
Dewey, John, 198
differentiation, 204-5, 223-4
direct democracy, x, viii, 8, 15. *See also* referendums
diversity, 147, 241-3; blindness, 169; in Canadian conversation, 162, 163-4; and citizenship, 103, 119; as gift, 164-5; in liberal democracies, 146, 150-1; and national identity, 165, 166; and nationality, 144; and reasonable pluralism, 141-2; within ridings, 113; unity and, 163-4, 170; unity within, 226
divisions of labour, 61, 216-17, 224, 237, 241, 242, 246
Dobrowolsky, Alexandra, 66
Donovan, Todd, 6, 7, 10
Durham Report, 164

Eberle, Christopher J.: *Religious Convictions in Liberal Politics*, 153-5
Eco, Umberto: *The Search for the Perfect Language*, 30
eEurope program, 37, 40
Eisenberg, Avigail, xxin40, 48, 49, 53-4, 55, 60, 61, 62, 240, 241, 244, 246
elections: and accountability of representatives, x; legitimacy of, 145; representation and, x
Emerson, Ralph Waldo, 198
English language: as de facto lingua franca, 26, 27, 37-8, 42, 43, 50; in EC, 32; *Economist* on, 37-8; in Europe, 26; *Guardian* on, 38; multilingualism and, 26, 27; as second language, 24, 43; in UN, 32; use by Irish, 52; as working language of EU, 25, 43
equality: complex (*see* complex equality); in decision making, 198; differentiated vs. undifferentiated, 53-4; multiculturalism as, 226; nationalism and, 170; in nonvoluntary associations, 215-16; provincial equality/difference divide, 168, 228; referendums and, 5, 7-8, 11, 13, 16-17, 18, 53-4, 55; in voluntary associations, 215
Erasmus program, 34
Erignac, Claude, 136
An Essay Concerning Human Understanding (Locke), 28
Europe: accommodation of range of languages in, 52; multi-realmed citizenship in, 124-5, 236; referendums in, 14. *See also names of individual countries*

European Charter of Regional or Minority Languages, 124
European Commission, 24, 26; languages of, 32, 37
European Court of Human Rights, 124, 125
European Court of Justice, 124-5
European Parliament, 128; languages and, 26, 31, 32, 37, 40; multilingualism in, 32
European Union (EU): anti-discrimination rules, 127; citizenship, 124, 126-7; complex equality and, 61-2; and cultural approach to language, 30; cultural programs, 34; division of labour within, 242; educational programs, 34-6; English as working language in, 25; enlargement of, 23; immigrant-inclusive citizenship, 127; interpretation service, 33; languages in, 24, 27, 31-4, 36-7, 38, 50, 236, 242, 244; linguistic diversity, 35-6; multilingualism in, 31-3, 35, 37, 49-52; official languages of, 25, 36; progressive policies and, 204; subsidiarity in, 124; TCNs in, 126-7, 128; translation of languages in, 31
European Year of Languages, 37, 41

federalism, 84-5; arguments in favour, 67; Australia cf. with Canada, 68t; criticisms of, 67; double-democracy within, 67, 69; dual citizenship in, 67, 69, 86; executive, 83-4; features of, 67; feminists and, 66, 76 (*see also* feminists), 86; gender vs. territorial interests in, 85; political opportunity structures and, 68t; referendums in, 14; representation of women in political leadership positions, 83-4; symmetric vs. asymmetric, 167-8, 226; territorialism, 85-6; trailblazers in, 67. *See also* Australian federalism; Canadian federalism
feminism: nonviolence and, 120; transitions in, xvii
feminists: innovative strategies of, 65, 66; as political theorists, xvii-xviii. *See also* Australian feminists; Anglo-Canadian feminists; Quebec, feminists
femocrats, 70, 75-6, 84, 239
First Nations, 115n1
Fishkin, James, xv, 156
Fishman, Joshua, 35
Flask, Carmel, 69-70
Foucault, Michel, xiv
fragmentation, 166, 169, 176
France, official language of, 33
Freedom House, 197, 198, 204
Freeman, Samuel, 151
French language, 32
Frey, Bruno S., 15
Frost, Catherine, 235, 238-9, 240-1, 244, 245-6

Gagnon, Alain-G., 85
Galligan, Brian, 69, 86
Galston, William, 142, 145-7, 152, 153; *Liberal Pluralism*, 147
Gamble, Barbara, 6, 15-16
gay and lesbian rights: and community size, 10; public commitment to, 9; referendums on, 6, 11-12
Geddes, Andrew, 127
gender: and Charlottetown Accord, 172-6, 246; consensus and, 182; identities, 135; in institutions, 65, 66; pluralism and, 182; in Senate, 173; vs. territorial interests in federalism, 85
General Will, 8, 58, 59
German language, 31, 32
globalization: citizen influence and, 209, 246; language and, 42-3; and participatory ideals, 203-4, 223-4, 236
Goette, Lorenz, 15
Goodin, Robert, xv, 238
good life, 147, 151, 152, 155
Gramsci, Antonio, 217
Gray, Gwen, 66
groups: community, 202, 214; marginalized, 227; minority (*see* minority groups); participatory equality and, 214-15; representation of interests, 199; roles for, xviii-xix; women's (*see under* women). *See also* associations; communities
Gubbins, 46n48
Gutmann, Amy, 59, 61
Gwyn, Richard, 171

Habermas, Jürgen, xv; on constitutional patriotism, 166; contract theory, 162; democratic deficit and, 44n6; on discursive practices, 180, 182, 184; feminist critiques of, 44n12; on ideal speaker, 194; on language and communication, 24-5; on languages, 26, 43, 44n6; and special moments in political participation, 231
Helsinki Summit, 38
Henders, Susan, 234-5, 236, 244, 246
Herder, Johann Gottfried, 27, 28, 29, 30, 50, 51

Hirst, Paul, xviii
Hobbes, Thomas, 180
Hong Kong: antisubversion law, 129; Basic Law, 129, 130; demonstrations in, 129; external autonomy, 130-1; flexible citizenship in, 131, 236; human rights in, 130-1; as hypercapitalist, 129; Legislative Council, 129; multi-realmed citizenship, 119-20, 128-32, 138; NGOs in, 130-1; and PRC government, 124, 129, 130; self-rule, 130; Sino-British Joint Declaration, 130; social conditions, 129; transnational middle class in, 132
Honig, Bonnie, 161, 163, 176
Hounslow, Betty, 69-70
House of Commons (Canada): Aboriginal representation in, 98, 99, 109, 113; and third chamber voting, 100
House of First Peoples, 100, 111
Humboldt, Wilhelm von, 27, 29, 30

identity/-ies: of Aboriginal peoples, 103; and citizenship, 103, 108; collective, 121, 137; gender, 135; individualistic, 119, 121; multiplicity of, 226; national, 105, 143, 162, 165, 227; politics, 206; and psychological power, 182-3, 221; shared, 105
immigration: in Catalonia, 125-6, 127-8; citizenship and, 127-8, 138; Council of Ministers and, 127; and EU, 127
Indian Act, 94; 1960 amendments, 93, 94
Indians: defined, 115n1. *See also* Aboriginal Canadians
individualism, in liberal democracies, 146
individual(s): collective decisions and, 198, 212, 214-15; and collective self-rule, 198; democratic equality and, 214-15; education for citizenship, 200; and equality in decision making, 198; groups of, 214; participation in self-government, 214; as "the people," 198. *See also* citizens; "self"
individuation, 205-6
Inglehart, Ronald, 201, 202
institutions: for Aboriginal self-government, 110, 112-13, 114, 235; accountability of, 18; agitators in, 65; citizens' effect on, 225; complex equality in, 55-6; and democratic expectations, 202; embeddedness in representation, xix; gendered nature of, 65, 66; ideologies underpinning, 65; justice and, 57, 61; legitimacy of, 18;

participation in, 208-9; political cultures and, 65; state-centred, 202, 207, 215; suprastate, 26; transformative potential, 60
interdependence, 104; citizenship as, 142; global, 203-4; networks of, 105-6
International Convention on the Protection of the Rights of All Migrant Workers and Members of Their Families, 128
International Covenant on Civil and Political Rights (ICCPR), 130
International Covenant on Economic, Social, and Cultural Rights (ICESCR), 130
Inuit, 115n1; referendums, 16
Inuit Tapiriit Kanatami, 111
Irish language, 33, 34, 51-2
Iroquois confederacy, 106
Irving, Helen, 66, 78
Israel, referendums in, 3, 14
issues: and individual participation, 214, 243; politics vs., 207; and territorially organized politics, 209
Ives, Peter, 48, 49-51, 57, 61-2, 236, 242-3, 244

Jefferson, Thomas, 198
Johnson, Rita, 89n94
Johnston, Richard, et al., 9, 21n64
juries: citizen, 156; and demanding deliberative democracy, 182, 183; policy, 156
just community/society, 49, 60
justice, 61; citizenship and, 141; competence in, 60; differentiated vs. undifferentiated equality and, 54; distributive, 103, 144; as evenhandedness, 56; of group-differentiated rights, 55; history and, 55, 57; intuitive sense of, 56-7; and laws and institutions, 55-6, 57, 61; multicultural, 48-9, 55-7, 59, 60, 61, 238-9; participation and, 60, 61; preferences and, 61; redistributive, 144; shared, 228
justification(s): and doctrine of restraint, 154; for laws, 154; legitimacy and, 105, 148; morality and, 154; and principle of pursuit, 153-4; public, 152, 154; reasoning and, 153-5; reciprocal, 105, 148

Kant, Immanuel, 180
Kaswentha, 106-8
Kernerman, Gerald, 220-1, 226-7, 228, 229, 231, 232, 235, 236, 246

Kirner, Joan, 89n94
Kraus, Peter, 33, 36, 38-9
Kymlicka, Will, xiii-xiv, 20n24-5, 44n12, 53, 63n14, 102, 109, 111, 121, 162, 171, 172; *Contemporary Political Philosophy*, xiv

Laclau, Ernesto, xiv
Ladd, Everett Carll, 202
language(s), 42; attachment to, vs. use, 51; Babel and, 30; common, 24; competition among, 36; computer translation, 39, 41; conduit metaphor of, 28-9; culture and, 29, 30, 39, 41, 51, 52; deliberation and, 25-6, 236; and democracy, 27, 50; democratic representation and, 32, 39, 43; discrimination against minority, 35; educational policies and, 36; engineering, 39, 41; of EU institutions (*see under* European Union [EU]); *Eurobarometer* survey on, 37; and European integration, 38, 50; German Romantic view, 26-7, 30; globalization and, 42-3; hierarchy of, 50; instrumental value, 26, 28-9, 30, 41, 43, 48, 50, 51, 52; intrinsic value, 29, 48, 50, 51, 52; Lockean view, 26, 28-9, 30, 41, 43, 48, 50, 51, 52; multiculturalism and, 24, 25; national, 36-7, 42; in Netherlands, 35; official, 25, 31-2, 33, 36; politics of, 24, 27; referendums on, 3-4; representation and, 32, 34, 39, 43, 236; standardization of, 24; state, 33; theoretical interest vs. empirical questions, 24, 27; translations, 31, 52; UN and, 32, 43; working vs. official, 31-2. *See also* bilingualism; multilingualism; *and names of individual languages*
Lawrence, Carmen, 89n94
law(s): complex equality in, 154; public justifications for, 154; use by states, 210-11
LEAF (Women's Legal and Education Action Fund), 73
legitimacy, 95-6; and Aboriginal self-government, 112, 238; of central Canadian institutions, 114; of communities of shared fate, 104-5; of complex equality, 54, 55-7; concept of, 102, 105; democratic decision making and, xii; of elections, 145; of minority self-governments, 120; as morally compelling, 149; of political decisions, 148; of political institutions, 99-100, 102; reciprocal justification and, 105, 148; of referendums, 54, 60, 240, 244; of representative institutions, 18, 120; of representatives, viii, 223; social complexity and, 243-4, 246; of state, 149; of women's groups, 173-6
Lenin, Vladimir Ilich, 192
Leonardo program, 34
Letzeburgesh language. *See* Luxembourg, language of
Lévesque, René, 9
Leydet, Domique, 113
liberal autonomy, 53
liberal democracy/-ies, xi; capital punishment in, 189; citizens' subjective interests and, 186; demanding deliberation and, 180; diversity in, 146, 150-1; individualism in, 146; lawyers as representatives in, 186; legal rights in, 185-6; minority rights in, 7; public policy and, 186; reasonableness in, 155; referendums in, 3; regemic role of representative in, 185; regulatory ideal of, 186; role of representative in, 186; virtues necessary for, 145-6, 153
Liberal Pluralism (Galston), 147
Life and Times of Liberal Democracy (Macpherson), xxin42
Lingua program, 34
linguistic diversity: as barrier, 39-40, 43, 50; communication and, 29; and cultural diversity, 41; as curse, 30, 32, 41; in EU, 35-6; and European citizenship, 41
Linklater, Andrew, 124, 125, 126
Locke, John, 26, 41, 50; *An Essay Concerning Human Understanding*, 28
Loos, Eugène, 26, 36, 37, 38, 43
Luhmann, Niklas, 198
Luxembourg: colonialism and, 52; language of, 31, 33, 34, 51

Maastricht Treaty, 31, 32, 34, 124
Macedo, Stephen, 103
Mackenzie, Catriona, 122
Macpherson, C.B.: *Life and Times of Liberal Democracy*, xxin42
Macy, Joanna, 133
Madison, James, x
majoritarianism, 3, 8, 10, 15, 120, 237
Malta, language of, 31, 33
Manifeste pour la vie, 135, 136-7
Manin, Bernard, x, 241
Manitoba, referendums in, 3-4
Manning, Preston, 173
Mansbridge, Jane, xv, xvii

Mariani, Marie-Thé, 135-6
Marx, Karl, 192
McKinnon, Catriona, 158n40
McRoberts, Kenneth, 169, 171
Meech Lake Accord, 72-3, 75, 84, 168, 172, 173, 227, 231
Melbourne (Aust.): Halfway House, 71
Mendus, Susan, 158n40
Mercredi, Ovide, 107
Métis, 115n1
Métis National Council, 111
Mill, John Stuart, 59-60, 192, 198; *On Liberty*, 183
Miller, David, 142, 143-5, 152, 153
minority groups: emancipatory self-government for, 119, 124, 244, 246; self-government (*see* minority self-government); special status claims, 7-8, 10-11, 16; women in, 65
minority rights: community size and, 7, 9; and level playing field, 53-4; in liberal democracies, 7; nation building and, 103-4; referendums and, 5, 53, 240, 244, 246; referendums vs. legislative processes for, 5-6, 55
minority self-government, 119, 120-3, 236, 246; and collective identity, 119, 121, 137; culture and, 121, 122, 123; emancipatory, 119, 120, 122, 124, 244, 246; freedom and, 123; identity and, 121; and relational vs. individualistic "self," 121-2, 137; representation and, 120-1; and secession, 122; of unbounded communities, 124, 234-5, 236, 246. *See also* Aboriginal self-government
monolingualism, 27
Mouffe, Chantal, xiv
Mulroney, Brian, 83
multiculturalism, 166, 171-2; citizenship and, xiv, 105; deliberative democracy and, 241; democracy and, 48-9, 240; as difference, 226; as equality, 226; and justice, 48-9, 59, 60, 61, 238-9; language and, 24, 25; vulnerability paradox, 49
Multiculturalism Act (1988), 171
multicultural nationalism, 163, 176
Multilingual Information Society Program, 40
multilingualism, 25, 43; broad vs. full, 50; complete, 32, 33; and defacto use of English, 26, 27; in EU, 31-3, 35, 37, 39, 49-52; institutional, 31-2, 33
multinationalism, referendums and, 3, 5, 18

multi-realmed citizenship, 119-20, 124-32
multi-realmed governance, 125, 138

National Action Committee on the Status of Women (NAC), 73, 75, 76, 82, 84, 173, 174, 175, 176
national identity, 105, 143, 162, 165, 227
nationalism(s): citizenship and, 103-4; clash within, 170; of Corsica, 135; equality and, 170; language standardization and, 24; multicultural, 163; Quebec, 74; referendums and, 9
nationality: citizenship as, 142, 143-5; definition of, 144; diversity and, 144
nations, as states, 143
nation-state(s): citizenship in, 103-4, 119, 121, 137; collective "self" vs., 119; democracy and, 23-4; language and, 24, 38; and minority autonomy, 121, 123; representation within, 124
Native American Rights Fund, 16
Native Women's Action Committee, 173
Native Women's Association of Canada, 111
Navajo Indians, 16
Netherlands: languages in, 35; referendums in, 3, 14
Newfoundland, feminists in, 66, 72, 73, 75-6
New South Wales, 70; women's health services in, 79
New Zealand, Maori representation in, 117n53
Nice, Treaty of. *See* Treaty of Nice
Niland, Carmel, 71
nongovernmental organizations (NGOs), 202
nonstatus Indians, 115n1
nonviolence, 120, 124, 138
Norman, Wayne, xiii-xiv, 20 n25
Norris, Pippa, 201
Northern Territory, 70

Offe, Claus, 205, 206
Ong Aiwah, 131
On Liberty (Mill), 183
Ontario, feminists in, 66, 72, 76
Oregon, reflexive law in, 211

Painter, Martin, 77
Parekh, Bhikhu, 165
participation: citizen, 156, 208-9; in collective decision making, 200; competence and, 59-60; and democracy, 198, 200; democracy

and, 60, 156; democratic, 49, 198, 200, 209-10, 212; devolution and, 209-10; following politics, 206-8, 236; ideals of, 203-6, 223-4; in institutions, 208-9; justice and, 60, 61; nonterritorial ways of, 213; outside state, 243; paradox of, 231-2; representation vs., xix; rights, 59; in self-government, 199; in South Africa, 229-30, 239; "thick," 58, 59, 238-9; transformation and, 58-9, 60; voting as, 198
pataicca samuppāda, 133
Pateman, Carole, xvi, 64n27
Patten, Alan, 29, 44n4
Peckford government, 73
People's Republic of China (PRC), 124, 129, 130
persons in the original position (POPs), 183-4
Phillips, Anne, xvi, xvii, 118n55
Phillips, Susan D., 83
Phillipson, Robert, 44n13
Pierson, Paul, 67, 86
Pitkin, Hanna, 118n55, 220; *The Concept of Representation*, xiii
pluralism, 147; in collective action, 202; competitive, 225-6, 227; and constitutional politics, 233; and gender, 182; of identities, 206; lack of overarching identity and, 226; reasonable, 141, 144, 145, 147, 149, 150, 151, 153, 242; reason and, 151; thought experiments and, 223
Pocklington, Tom, 115n8
polarization, in Canadian conversation, 162, 163, 167-70, 236
policy juries, 156
political opportunity structure (POS), 66, 68t, 84
political representation: defined, x. *See also* representation
political theory: citizenship in, xiii-xiv; feminism and, xvii-xviii; representation in, xii-xiii, 234-47
political will formation, 24, 43
politics: defined, 207; democracy and, 206-8; issues vs., 207; nonterritorial venues of, 213; participation following, 206-8, 236; states and, 210, 225, 241; transformative, 176
popular sovereignty, and representation, x-xi
A Preface to Democratic Theory (Dahl), 227
preferences: formation, 58; justice and, 61; majority vs. minority, 120; transformation of, 59, 60

privatization, 210-11
Prodi, Romano, 38
proportional representation (PR), 112
provincial governments: Anglo-Canadian feminists and, 66, 73, 75; federal government vs., 80-1; feminists and, 72, 76, 86; fiscal capacity, 81; opting-out of federal programs, 73; policy jurisdiction, 80; Quebec feminists and, 74
public autonomy, 185, 186, 188, 193, 238, 239
public spheres, 25, 43, 214, 224
Pujol, Jordi, 125, 126
Putnam, Robert, 202
Pyrcz, Greg, 49, 57-9, 62, 64n33, 220, 221-3, 224, 226, 227, 228, 229, 231, 232, 235, 238, 239, 241, 244, 245; *Democracy, Rights, and Well-Being*, 181-2

Quebec: autonomy for, 73; Bill 101, 36; communitarian liberalism of, 168; difference of, 168; as distinct society, 4, 16-17, 232, 243; feminists, 72, 74; place within federation, 162, 167-8, 170; provincial government, 74-5; referendums in, 4, 9-10, 16, 170; relations with Canada, 3, 16-17; secession, 4, 9, 16; sovereigntists, 113-14; sovereignty claims, 80
Québécois, unresolved position of, 161
Queensland, 70, 71, 79; Goss government, 87n18
Quong, Jonathan, 117n37, 242, 245

Ramaphosa, Cyril, 229
Rankin, L. Pauline, 66, 72, 73, 74, 75-6, 84
Ranney, Austin, 15
Rawls, John, xv, 180, 183; on allegiance of citizens, 149; liberalism of, 146-7; on overlapping consensus, 148, 155; POPs of, 183, 194; on reasonable people, 155; reasonable pluralism and, 141, 142, 150; on sharing fate, 105; *A Theory of Justice*, xiii
RCAP. *See* Royal Commission on Aboriginal Peoples (RCAP)
RCERPF. *See* Royal Commission on Electoral Reform and Party Financing (RCERPF)
Reagan, Ronald, 210, 211
REAL women's organization, 83
reason, public, xv, xvi, 151, 152, 153-5, 156, 242
reasonableness: citizenship as, 142,

150-5, 156, 242; deliberation and, 152; in liberal democracies, 155; shared commitment to, 150, 152
reasonable pluralism, 141, 144, 145, 147, 149, 150, 151, 153, 242
Réaume, Denise, 29, 44n12
Rebick, Judy, 73, 173, 176
recognition, politics of, 122
Reddy, Michael, 28
referendums, 49; and Aboriginal-non-Aboriginal relations, 3, 4; Aboriginal peoples and, 12-13; in Alaska, 12, 16; in Arizona, 12, 16; in Austria, 3, 14; ballot dissemination in, 13; in Belgium, 3, 14; in British Columbia, 4, 13, 14, 53, 240; in California, 15; in Canada, 3-4; cases launched against, 4; on Charlottetown Accord, 9, 16-17; in Colorado, 11-12; and communal values, 9-10, 246; and compromise, 3; by Cree, 16; deliberation and, 3, 6, 240; demonstration effect, 54; distinctive status and, 16-17, 18; in divided societies, 14-17, 17-18; double/compound majorities in, 13-14; in Eastern Europe, 14; elites and, 9, 17; English-only, 4, 12, 15-16; equality as undifferentiated treatment in, 53-5; equality-seeking groups vs. national minorities and, 11; equality- vs. rights-seeking groups and, 13, 240; and ethnic divisions, 14, 15-16, 17; factors influencing outcomes, 6-7; in federal systems, 14; framing of, 11-14, 53; frequency of use, 3, 14; on gay and lesbian rights, 6; group rights in, 53-5; by Inuit, 16; in Israel, 3, 14; language of unity vs. difference in, 14; on language policies, 3-4; and legislative processes, 5-6, 55, 240; legitimacy of, 54, 60, 240, 244; in liberal democracies, 3; majorities vs. minorities in, 4, 5-8, 9-10, 246; in Manitoba, 3-4; minority rights and, 5, 6, 17, 18, 49, 53, 240, 244; multinationalism and, 3, 5, 18; in the Netherlands, 3, 14; and political equality, 5, 8-9, 18; privileging of majorities in, 5-6; Quebec and, 3, 4, 9-10, 16-17, 170; reforms of, 54-5, 60, 62; regulation of, 240, 241; and representative accountability, 240-1; self-interest in, 7, 10; and special status claims, 7-8, 10-11, 16; in Switzerland, 6, 14-15; tabulation process, 11, 13-14; in US, 3, 6, 10, 12, 15; wording of, 12-13; in Yugoslavia, 9, 14; in Zurich, 15

reflective disequilibrium, 57
Reform Party, 165, 168, 173
Religious Convictions in Liberal Politics (Eberle), 153-5
representation, vii; of Aboriginal peoples, xviii; Aboriginal self-government and, 95, 96, 99, 101-2, 109-10, 114, 147-8, 150; African-American, in US, 96; citizenship and, 141; communitarianism and, xiii; decentred activism and, 243; deliberation and, 237; democracy and, ix; democratic theory and, x-xx; elections and, x; gender, 173; group identity and, 85; and group interests, 199; impartial, 174-5; institutional embeddedness, xi, xix; language and, 32, 34, 39, 43, 236; linguistic, 25-6; and minority self-government, 120-1; within nation-state, 124; normative values and, xi-xii; participation vs., xix; in political theory, xii-xiii; politics of presence and, xvii; popular sovereignty and, x-xi; poststructuralism and, xii; power relations and, xiii; regimes of, xi, xii, xx, xix; single-issue activism and, 243; territorial, 85-6; trust and, 212, 224; as "two-level game," 113, 238, 244; in women's groups, 174-5; and women's issues, xvii-xviii
representational failures, x, viii, xiv, xv-xvii, 120, 235, 240
representatives: accountability of, x, viii, 223, 240; asymmetrical relationship with citizens, 222; character of, 192; citizens' preferences and, 58; as conduits, xiv, 191, 220; contribution to formulation of policy, 185-7; and demanding deliberative democracy, 186, 193-4; demanding deliberative democracy and, 184-91, 187-9, 193; discursive engagement with citizens, 184-5, 187-8; ideal, 57, 58, 188, 191, 238; identification of ideal citizens, 192, 193; lawyers as, 186; legitimacy of, vii, 223; in liberal democracy, 185, 186; as mediators of public opinion, 223; and particular/plural, 224; patience in, 188-9; pedagogical role, 185, 220, 222; roles of, 192-3; and theory of true and good, 192; therapeutic role, 193-4; thought experiments by, 221, 222-3
rights: hierarchy of, 72-3. *See also* minority rights
risks: avoidance of, 205; choices and, 205-6; in demanding deliberative democracy, 191-3, 237

Rogers, Joel, xviii
Rousseau, Jean-Jacques, x-xi, xix, 57-8, 61, 62, 180, 190, 192, 198; *amour propre*, 222; Legislator, 59
Royal Commission on Aboriginal Peoples (RCAP), 95, 99-101, 111
Royal Commission on Electoral Reform and Party Financing (RCERPF), 95, 96-8, 99, 101, 109, 111, 112, 114
Royal Commission on the Status of Women, 73
Russell, Peter, 161

Saami parliaments, 100
Sachs, Albie, 230
Sallembien-Vittori, Pauline, 137
Sapir, Edward, 29
Sawer, Marion, 66, 70
Schlesinger, Arthur, Jr., 166
Schlozman, Kay Lehman, 202
Schumpeter, Joseph, 198
Scott, James, 205
The Search for the Perfect Language (Eco), 30
"self": autonomy and, 120; collective, 119, 133; Corsican, 137; individualistic, 121-2, 133; individual understandings of, 138; and linear causality, 133; minority, 121-2; and "other," 120, 121, 133; relational vs. individualistic, 121-2; unbounded, 120
Self, Peter, 77-8
self-government: Aboriginal (*see* Aboriginal self-government); in Catalonia, 126; collective "self" and, 119; contestation over meaning of, 123; Dalai Lama's vision of, 133; equal participation in, 199; individual participation in, 214; linear causality and, 133; minority (*See* minority self-government); new opportunities for, 237; right to, 94-5; unjustness in, 122-3
Senate (Canada): Aboriginal representation in, 98, 99, 111-12; gender parity in, 173; triple-E, 98
Shachar, Ayelet, 49
Shapiro, Ian, xiii
shared fate: citizenship as, 95, 104-9, 114, 124, 142, 147-50, 148, 235, 238, 242, 244, 245; historical imagination and, 105-6
social services: and Aboriginal self-government, 110; and Canadian federalism, 73; women and, 73
Socrates program, 34, 35, 40
South Africa, constitutional politics, 229-30

South Australia, 70; women's health services in, 79
sovereignty, popular, 199
states: associations and, 208; as collective actors, 213, 225; corporations and, 208-9; critical evaluations by citizens, 201; globalization and, 203-4, 223-4, 236; and individual vs. public autonomy, 185; markets and, 204, 208; multiplication of political venues, 213-14; as nations, 143; participation outside of, 243; politics and, 210, 225, 241; public judgment and, 210; use of law, 210-11
status Indians, 115n1; franchise and, 93, 94
Stoljar, Natalie, 122
Strange Multiplicity (Tully), 106
subsidiarity, in EU, 37, 38, 124
supranational citizenship, 125
supranational political agencies, 24
suprastate institutions, 26
Supreme Court of Canada, 4, 239; Aboriginal contributions to, 98
Switzerland: redistributive policies in, 144; referendums in, 6, 14-15; suffrage movement in, 66, 67
Sydney (Aust.), women's refuges in, 71

Tasmania, 70, 79
Taylor, Charles, xiii, 162, 168, 183
Telematics program, 39, 40
Thatcher, Margaret, 210, 211
A Theory of Justice (Rawls), xiii
third-country nationals (TCNs), 126-7, 128
Thobani, Sunera, 76
Thompson, Dennis, 59, 61
thought experiments, 221, 222-3, 238, 239
Tibet: collective identities and, 138; democracy in, 134-5; nonviolence and, 120, 132-5; self-rule, 134-5; as Zone of *Ahimsa*, 133-4
Tilly, Charles, 36-7
Treaty of Amsterdam. *See* Amsterdam Treaty
Treaty of Maastricht. *See* Maastricht Treaty
Treaty of Nice, 26, 31
Treaty of Rome, 31
Trimble, Linda, 175
Trudeau, Pierre, 17, 81, 82, 169, 171, 173
Tully, James, xiv, 122-3, 162, 169-70; *Strange Multiplicity*, 106
Turpel, Mary Ellen, 107

two-row wampum belt, 95, 106-8, 124, 133, 148, 150

unanimity, 179, 183
unbounded communities, in minority self-government, 124, 234-5, 246
UN Human Rights Committee, 130-1
Union of New Brunswick Indians, 94
United Nations, 26, 242; Convention on Elimination of All Forms of Discrimination against Women, 88n61; languages and, 32, 43
United States: African-American representation in, 96; campaign money in, 201; devolution in, 209-10; majority-minority districting in, 96; referendums in, 3, 6, 10, 12, 15; suffrage movement in, 66-7
unity, and diversity, 163-4, 170, 226

values: freestanding, 151; shared, 148-50
Veblen, Thorstein, 217
Verba, Sidney, 202
Vickers, Jill, 66, 72, 73, 74, 75-6, 82, 84, 85
Victoria (Aust.), 70, 71
Voice, Trust, and Memory (Williams), xviii
voting: by Aboriginal peoples, 97; as democratic participation, 198; by third chamber, 100

Walzer, Michael, 44n6, 217
Warren, Mark, xv, xvi, xviii-xix, 180, 220, 223-5, 226, 228, 229, 231, 232, 235-6, 237, 241-2, 243-4, 246-7

Watts, Ronald L., 83, 84
Webber, Jeremy, 106, 162, 168-9
Weber, Max, 206
Western Australia, 70, 71
Whorf, Benjamin Lee, 29
Willenmyns, Roland, 46n42
Williams, Melissa, xv, xvi, 44n12, 124, 142, 147-8, 150, 152, 234, 235, 237-8, 242, 244, 245; *Voice, Trust, and Memory*, xviii
Williams, Robert A., Jr., 106-7
women: Aboriginal (*see* Aboriginal women); in Australia, 70-1, 237 (*see also* Australian feminists); in Canada, 172-6, 237 (*see also* Anglo-Canadian feminists; Quebec, feminists); difference of, xvii; as "good" vs. "bad" citizens, 175; legitimacy of groups, 173-6; from minority vs. majority groups, 65; organizations, 173-6, 236-7; in political leadership, 83-4; refuge movement in Australia, 70-1; representational processes and, xvii-xviii; social services and, 73; under-representation of, 174-6
World Trade Organization, 26, 43, 242
World Values Surveys, 201
Wran government, 71, 79

Young, Iris Marion, xii, xiv-xv, xvi, xvii, 53
Yugoslavia, referendums in, 9, 14

Zone of *Ahimsa*, 133-4
Zurich, referendums in, 15

Printed and bound in Canada by Friesens
Set in Stone by Brenda and Neil West, BN Typographics West
Copy editor: Dallas Harrison
Proofreader: Deborah Kerr
Indexer: Noeline Bridge